Other Books by David deSilva

Seeing Things John's Way

Sacramental Life

4 Maccabees: Introduction and Commentary

An Introduction to the New Testament

Perseverance in Gratitude

Paul and the Macedonians

Praying with John Wesley

New Testament Themes

The Hope of Glory

Despising Shame

HONOR, PATRONAGE, KINSHIP & PURITY

Unlocking
New Testament
Culture

DAVID A. deSILVA

IVP Academic

An imprint of InterVarsity Press
Downers Grove, Illinois

InterVarsity Press
P.O. Box 1400, Downers Grove, IL 60515-1426
World Wide Web: www.ivpress.com
Email: email@ivpress.com

InterVarsity Press® is the book-publishing division of Inter-Varsity Christian Fellowship/USA®, a movement of students and faculty active on campus at hundreds of universities, colleges and schools of nursing in the United States of America, and a member movement of the International Fellowship of Evangelical Students. For information about local and regional activities, write Public Relations Dept., InterVarsity Christian Fellowship/ USA, 6400 Schroeder Rd., P.O. Box 7895, Madison, WI 53707-7895, or visit the IVCF website at <www.intervarsity.org>.

Scripture quotations, unless otherwise noted, are adapted from the Revised Standard Version of the Bible, *copyright 1946, 1952, 1971 by the Division of Christian Education of the National Council of the Churches of Christ in the USA. and are used by permission.*

Chapters three and four were published previously as "Patronage and Reciprocity: The Context of Grace in the New Testament," Ashland Theological Journal 31 (1999): 32-84, *and are reprinted by permission.*

Cover illustration: Erich Lessing/Art Resource, N.Y.

ISBN-13: 978-0-8308-1572-2

Printed in the United States of America ∞

Library of Congress Cataloging-in-Publication Data

DeSilva, David Arthur.
   Honor, patronage, kinship & purity : unlocking New Testament culture / David A. deSilva.
     p.   cm.
   Includes bibliographical references and indexes.
   ISBN 0-8308-1572-4 (pbk. : alk. paper)
     1. Bible. N.T. — Socio-rhetorical criticism.   I. Title.

   BS2380 .D47 2000
   225.9'5 — dc21

                                                                                        00-057546

P	30	29	28	27	26	25	24	23	22	21	20	19	18	17	16	15	14	13	12
Y	31	30	29	28	27	26	25	24	23	22	21	20	19	18	17	16	15	14	13

*To the faculty and administration
of Ashland Theological Seminary,
men and women after God's own heart
whom I'm favored to call friends*

Contents

Abbreviations

Translations of the Bible

KJV	King James Version
NIV	New International Version
NRSV	New Revised Standard Version
RSV	Revised Standard Version

The Apocrypha and Septuagint

Add Esth	Additions to Esther
1-2 Esd	1-2 Esdras
Jdt	Judith
1-2-3-4 Macc	1-2-3-4 Maccabees
Sir	Wisdom of Ben Sira (Ecclesiasticus)
Tob	Tobit
Wis	Wisdom of Solomon

Babylonian Talmud

b. Sanh	Sanhedrin

Old and New Testament Pseudepigrapha

Acts Pet	Acts of Peter
Jub	Jubilees
T. Gad	Testament of Gad
T. Levi	Testament of Levi

Classical, Hellenistic, Early Christian Authors

Aristeas
   Let. Aris.   *Letter of Aristeas*

Aristotle
   Nic. Eth.   *Nicomachean Ethics*
   Pol.   *Politica*

Cicero
   De Offic.   *De Officiis*

Dio Chrysostom
   Or.   *Orationes*

Diodorus Siculus
   Bib. Hist.   *Bibliotheca Historica*

Dionysius of Halicarnassus
   Rom Ant.   *Roman Antiquities*

Epictetus
   Diss.   *Dissertationes*

Fronto
   Ad M. Caes.   *Epistulae ad Marcum Caesarem*

Homer
   Od.   *Odyssey*

Ignatius
   Smyrn.   *To the Smyrneans*

Isocrates
   Ad Dem.   *Ad Demonicus*

Josephus
   Ag. Ap.   *Against Apion*
   J.W.   *Jewish War*
   Life   *Life of Flavius Josephus*

Juvenal
  Sat.   *Satirae*
Lucian
  Peregr.   *On the Passing of Peregrinus*
Philo
  Decal.   *De Decalogo*
  Hypoth.   *Hypothetica*
  Joseph   *On the Life of Joseph*
  Spec. Laws   *On the Special Laws*
Plato
  Euthyphr.   *Euthyphro*
Pliny (the younger)
  Ep.   *Epistles*
Plutarch
  Con. Praec.   *Coniugalia Praecepta*
  Mor.   *Moralia*
  Plac. Philos.   *De Placita Philosophorum*
Seneca
  Ben.   *De Beneficiis*
  Ep. Mor.   *Epistulae Morales*
Sophocles
  Col.   *Oedipus at Colonus*
  Oed.   *Oedipus the King*
Tacitus
  Ann.   *Annales ab Excessu Divi Augusti*
  Hist.   *Historiae*
Thucydides
  Hist.   *History of the Peloponnesian War*
Xenophon
  Cyr.   *Cyropaedia*
  Oec.   *Oeconomicus*

Journals and Books
  AB   Anchor Bible

ABD	*Anchor Bible Dictionary*
AUSS	*Andrews University Seminary Studies*
BSac	*Bibliotheca Sacra*
BTB	*Biblical Theology Bulletin*
CBQ	*Catholic Biblical Quarterly*
CBQMS	Catholic Biblical Quarterly Monograph Series
HTR	*Harvard Theological Review*
JAAR	*Journal of the American Academy of Religion*
JBL	*Journal of Biblical Literature*
JETS	*Journal of the Evangelical Theological Society*
JSNT	*Journal for the Study of the New Testament*
JSNTSup	Journal for the Study of the New Testament Supplement Series
JSOT	*Journal for the Study of the Old Testament*
JSP	*Journal for the Study of the Pseudepigrapha*
JSQ	*Jewish Studies Quarterly*
JPS	Jewish Publication Society
LCL	Loeb Classical Library
NovT	*Novum Testamentum*
OTP	*The Old Testament Pseudepigrapha*
RelSRev	*Religious Studies Review*
RevQ	*Revue de Qumran*
RQ	*Restoration Quarterly*
SBLDS	Society of Biblical Literature Dissertation Series
SBLMS	Society of Biblical Literature Monograph Series

SEG	Supplementum Epigraphicum Graecum
TDNT	*Theological Dictionary of the New Testament*
TJ (n.s.)	*Trinity Journal* (new series)

Preface

I have found the study of the cultural context of the New Testament to shed new light on the sacred Scriptures and on the ways in which they would shape disciples and communities of faith. More important, many of my seminary students have discovered the same, sharing with me how such investigations have opened up the New Testament and their visions of ministry in new and exciting ways. I am grateful for the opportunity now to share these studies with a wider readership of those who are committed to their own faith formation and to the building up of strong Christian congregations. Thanks are especially due to Daniel G. Reid at InterVarsity Press for his support of this project from the beginning, his encouragement during the months of writing and his comments and suggestions. I remember with gratitude also the long hours spent by Steve Hawkins in copyediting and by the IVP staff otherwise involved in preparing this book for publication. I could not have produced this book were it not for the support I felt from many local sources as well. I would particularly name that part of the family of God at Ashland Theological Seminary, a community that has welcomed me, encouraged me and affirmed my ministry of writing by honoring the time that such a ministry demands. This community of faith has also helped keep me focused on the ultimate goal for all biblical scholarship, and I hope this book will serve to advance that higher goal. I would also name the ongoing love and encouragement of my wife, Donna Jean, my sons, James Adrian and John Austin, and my parents, J. Arthur and Dorothy deSilva, each in his or her own way making the task more pleasant.

Introduction: *Cultural Awareness & Reading Scripture*

"My words were taken out of context!" We frequently hear some prominent individual saying these words to object that a journalist has misrepresented his or her speech. Perhaps you have used this familiar expression to correct a false impression that has been created by a third party. This person may have used your exact words but removed them from the close connection with an event, a place or a series of other words that would have allowed them to convey your true meaning. Your words convey a very different meaning if a listener repeated them without also relating the social setting in which you said them or without explaining the events that evoked them. The potential for misunderstanding increases exponentially if that listener is communicating with someone from another culture, with different customs and even a different language. The reporter would need to explain what significations your words would have in your cultural context or else risk serious misunderstanding. If we would concern ourselves that our words not be taken out of context, or that we not report someone else's words out of context, we should be far more careful with the words of Jesus, Paul or James—or, as so many Christians take these words to be, the words of God.

Biblical scholars have grown increasingly aware of the importance of looking at texts not only in their historical or literary or social contexts but also in their cultural contexts.[1] "Culture" includes those values, ways of

---

[1]See, for example, Jerome H. Neyrey, ed., *The Social World of Luke-Acts: Models for Interpretation* (Peabody, Mass.: Hendrickson, 1991); Joseph H. Neyrey, *Honor and Shame in Matthew* (Louisville: Westminster John Knox, 1998); Bruce J. Malina, *The New Testament World*, 3d ed. (Louisville: Westminster John Knox, 1993); Bruce J. Malina and Richard Rohrbaugh, *Social-Science Commentary on the Synoptic Gospels* (Philadelphia: Fortress, 1992).

relating and ways of looking at the world that its members share and that provide the framework for all communication. The readers of the New Testament shared certain values, such as honor, and codes of forming and maintaining relationships, such as patronage and kinship, and ways of ordering the world, expressed frequently in terms of purity. If we are to hear the texts correctly, we must apply ourselves to understand the culture out of which and to which they spoke. We need to recognize the cultural cues the authors have woven into their strategies and instructions. This enterprise prevents potential misreading of the texts. Modern readers, too, are fully enculturated into a set of values, ways of relating and so forth. Without taking some care to recover the culture of the first-century Greco-Roman writers and addressees, we will simply read the texts from the perspective of our cultural norms and codes.[2] Negatively, then, this task is essential as a check against our impositions of our own cultural, theological and social contexts onto the text.

We should be concerned that we do not import into the text what is not there (and take those impositions as word of God!). But also we should take care not to miss what it is that the text does seek to convey and what effect and formative power it would wish to have on us and our communities of faith. To immerse ourselves in the cultural context of the New Testament authors and hearers is to open ourselves up to hear the New Testament with the fuller resonances it would have had for authors and addressees alike. We will enter more closely into the rhetorical strategies and impact of the texts, and see how the New Testament authors were working toward redefining honor, kinship and purity as well as creating a new patron-client relationship between God and Jesus' followers. We will begin to see how the New Testament texts use deep-rooted values and codes to uphold a faithful and obedient response to God, and to sustain the new community in its quest to be conformed to the image of Christ and no longer to the society from which it had separated itself.

If, then, we divorce the texts from the original cultural context—those basic values and scripts that shaped the world of the original authors and

---

[2]Russ Dudrey expresses this danger very well: "Unless we understand New Testament social history sympathetically within its cultural settings—which are ancient and alien to ours—we are predisposed to misinterpret the social realities reflected there. The result is that we will superimpose our modern questions and social agendas onto the ancient texts in order to receive the answers we expect back again clothed in biblical authority" (" 'Submit Yourselves to One Another': A Socio-Historical Look at the Household Code of Ephesians 5:15-6:9," *RQ* 41 [1999]: 27).

hearers—we will miss much of the instruction that the texts wish to give and add much that the texts do not wish to say. Seeking to understand the cultural context of the New Testament will, however, enhance the hearing of "those who have ears to hear." My goal in writing this book is to introduce the reader to another dimension of the context within which the New Testament texts were composed and within which they effected the purposes of God for their readers. I hope that it will assist the reader in arriving at a more authentic hearing of the New Testament on its own terms. This is, after all, the goal of all responsible exegesis (that is, biblical interpretation). Together with investigation of the historical context, the manners and customs assumed and explicated in the text, the interaction with oral and written traditions available to the author and audience woven into a text, and so forth,[3] investigation of the cultural context of the early Christian leaders and their congregations enables a more nuanced and dependable analysis of what it is that God sought to accomplish through these texts. From that point, we may discern more richly and reliably what God's word to believers in our cultural context might be.

This volume provides a concise guide to some of the more prominent and prevalent aspects of the culture that gave birth to the early church—honor, patronage, kinship and purity. In chapters one, three, five and seven, the reader will encounter a picture of each of these facets of the New Testament cultural environment painted from classical, Hellenistic and Roman-era sources, as well as from the Jewish Scriptures.[4] In this

---

[3]Readers interested in learning more about exegetical methods (tools for interpreting the New Testament) may wish to begin with Joel B. Green, ed., *Hearing the New Testament* (Grand Rapids, Mich.: Eerdmans, 1996).

[4]I must stress here the importance of both the Jewish and Greco-Roman environments for the shaping of early Christianity. When investigating the context of the early church, this can never be an either-or situation but always a both-and situation. The tendency still exists to turn a blind eye to the Greco-Roman environment (or to deny its influence on early Christianity), not as a result of careful investigation but rather as an ideological conviction that then shapes (and largely determines) the results of investigation. Judaism is seen as the only vehicle for divine revelation and thus becomes the only permissible influence on the early church (because any influence from the Greco-Roman world would be "pagan" and "polluting"). Paul himself articulates a different view in Romans 2:14-16: there is much that the "Gentile" understands of God's standards. There are a number of considerations that should also lead one to seek out the influences on the early Christian movement from both backgrounds:

1. The Hellenization of Judaism progresses quite quickly and pervasively during the third and second centuries B.C., such that the allegedly "pure" channel of revelation is already displaying the colors of Greek and Roman philosophy, ethics and culture before the time of the Maccabees, and is certainly at an advanced level by the time of Paul (see the "Jewish"

way, the world of the early Christians will be fleshed out by means of the
testimony of its inhabitants and from the texts that continued to exercise
an influence on those first-century people who read them.

From this immersion in the Jewish and Greco-Roman background, the
remaining chapters move forward to show how attention to these cultural values (e.g., honor and purity) and scripts (e.g., kinship and patronage) help us to enter into the New Testament writings themselves and
grasp the impact they sought to have on the communities to which they
were addressed. Chapters two, four, six and eight will therefore assemble a broad sampling of New Testament texts in order to display how
attention to hearing these words in their cultural contexts makes possible
rich contributions to theology (e.g., a richer understanding of grace and
the relationship of grace and works), to the social identity of the church
(as a kinship group, as a community called to purity and holiness, as
recipients of God's favor), and to the ethos of the church (the factors that
motivate radical discipleship, the guidelines for interactions with one
another in the church). The result will be a recovery of the ideology of
the early Christians as this is inscribed in the inspired texts themselves—

---

texts like 4 Macc and the works of Philo). Palestine is part of this Hellenization process and
by no means insulated against it (see the decisive work of Martin Hengel, *Judaism and Hellenism*, 2 vols. [Philadelphia: Fortress, 1977]). Jerusalem itself was remade into a Greek city
between 175 and 167 B.C. and, while the Torah was eventually restored as the law of the
land by the house of Judas Maccabaeus, the Greek institutions remained. There were large
and influential centers of Greek culture throughout Palestine by the death of Herod the
Great. The cultural context of Palestine is not entirely distinct from the cultural context of
Greek and Roman culture.

2. As we shall see, the level of "culture" at which this book is operating is a very basic one
throughout the Mediterranean "cultures." Both Jewish and Greco-Roman sources are
deeply concerned about honor and dishonor, construct and reflect patron-client and bene-
factor-beneficiary relationships and obligations, can interpret places, people and actions in
terms of purity and pollution language, and contemplate the meaning of kinship, the
proper roles of members of a household, and the ethos that should guide kin in their interaction with one another.

3. The context of the early Christian mission as it is represented in the New Testament is
predominantly Gentile, moving through Greek and Roman cities. To say that Paul's gospel
and ethics are shaped solely by Jewish backgrounds is to introduce cultural imperialism
into the mission of the very one who claimed that there was in Christ neither Jew nor
Greek.

The New Testament is therefore treated here as Mediterranean literature rather than
Semitic literature. It is written in Greek, reflecting not only Jewish but Greek forms of argumentation throughout, Greek philosophical and ethical topics, and interacting with specific
aspects of Greco-Roman culture throughout (whether positively, as in Acts 17, or negatively, as in Rev 13).

their vision for the community, their portrayal of relationship with God and each other (and the values that are to manifest themselves in those relationships), and the strategies of early Christian leaders for directing and enabling discipleship and the formation of vital communities of faith.

These two enterprises are undertaken with a view to integrating the ideology articulated in the New Testament into the life of the modern community of faith and the life of the individual believer. We are given a fresh opportunity to see how these facets of the texts can help us to shape our interactions with fellow believers so as to encourage discipleship more fully, integrate service and evangelism into our "faith response," examine and critique the boundaries that separate us from those God wishes to love, and recover the kind of intimacy and solidarity that is meant to characterize the shared life of all who call on the name of Jesus. In short, this volume seeks to equip readers to become better readers of Scripture so that they may become better shapers of disciples and faith communities. This volume seeks chiefly to contribute, therefore, not to investigation of the past (although I hope it will accomplish this), but to recovering the resources of the early church for strengthening commitment to Jesus, the way he taught, and the people he called together in the present, both within the local church and throughout the global church.

The discussions strive to be comprehensive, taking in as much of the New Testament as possible for the limited length of the book, without any desire to be exhaustive. I have sought to provide several solid examples of each facet of the four cultural contexts covered, enough for the reader to be able to recognize the employment of these topics elsewhere in the text. The volume will be *best* used if the reader keeps the New Testament open and refers to each passage that is discussed. Some of these passages will be rather fully discussed within the chapter, but it is important to read the text itself and not merely the discussions about it. Moreover, many texts are simply referred to in passing or in parenthetical references. These are included as opportunities for the reader to go to the Bible, read the passage or verse, and look for the connection with the specific aspect of the cultural context being treated in that paragraph. Following this procedure will mean a slower reading but will result in a much more complete training in reading the New Testament with sensitivity to its cultural environment and its contexts of meaning, preparing the reader far better for his or her own future forays into study of the Word.

One

HONOR & SHAME
Connecting Personhood to Group Values

T*he culture of the first-century world was built on the foundational social val*ues of honor and dishonor. Seneca, a first-century Roman statesman and philosopher, wrote: "The one firm conviction from which we move to the proof of other points is this: that which is honorable is held dear for no other reason than because it is honorable" (*De Ben.* 4.16.2). Seneca claims that his peers regard honor as desirable in and of itself, and dishonor as undesirable in and of itself. Moreover, he understands that the concept of "honor" is fundamental and foundational to his contemporaries' thinking. That is, he expects them to choose one course of action over another, or to approve one kind of person over another, and, in short, to organize their system of values, all on the basis of what is "honorable." From the wealth of literature left to us from the Greek and Roman periods, including the New Testament, it appears that Seneca's analysis of the people of his time was correct.[1]

In his book on ethics Aristotle lists two motives that people might have

---

[1]For a close investigation of honor language at work in several major Greek, Latin and Jewish authors, see David A. deSilva, *Despising Shame: Honor Discourse and Community Maintenance in the Epistle to the Hebrews*, SBLDS 152 (Atlanta: Scholars Press, 1995), chaps. 2 and 3; for discussion of honor in the world of Homeric and Classical Greece, see Arthur W. Adkins, *Merit and Responsibility: A Study in Greek Values* (Oxford: Clarendon, 1960) and the

for choosing some course of action: honor and pleasure (*Nic. Eth.* 3.1.11 [1110b11-12]). Honor, however, is viewed as the first and foremost consideration. Isocrates, an Athenian orator who was Aristotle's senior, advised his young pupil that, while honor with pleasure was a great good, pleasure without honor was the worst evil (*Ad Dem.* 17). Those who put pleasure ahead of honor were considered to be more animal-like than human, ruled by their passions and desires. He also placed the value of honor above one's personal safety (*Ad Dem.* 43), an evaluation that would persist through the centuries. In the first century B.C. a teacher of public speakers held up honor and security as the two primary considerations when trying to win an audience over to support the course of action the speaker promoted. He recognized, however, that one could never admit a course to be safe but dishonorable and still expect to win (*Rhetorica ad Herennium* 3.5.8-9). Quintilian, a teacher of rhetoric from the late first century A.D., holds up the "honorable" as the fundamental factor in persuading people to adopt or avoid a course of action (*Institutes* 3.8.1); from Aristotle to Quintilian, successful orators were the ones who could demonstrate that the course of action they advocated led to the greatest honor.

Honor and dishonor played a dominant part in moral instruction as well. In his collection of advice *To Demonicus* [*Ad Dem.*], Isocrates repeatedly uses the phrases "it is disgraceful" and "it is noble" (rather than "it is right" or "wrong," "profitable" or "unprofitable") as sanctions for behavior. Aversion to disgrace and defense of honor is to guide his student's conduct in friendships, in enmity, in private life and in public office. One can observe a similar phenomenon in the book of Proverbs (or in other Jewish wisdom literature, like the Wisdom of Ben Sira): the promise of honor and threat of disgrace are prominent goads to pursue a certain kind of life and to avoid many alternatives.[2] Thus the students

---

correction and refinement of his study in Bernard Williams, *Shame and Necessity* (Berkeley: University of California Press, 1993). The persistence of these values in Mediterranean culture is demonstrated by Julian Pitt-Rivers, "Honour and Social Status," in *Honour and Shame: The Values of Mediterranean Society*, ed. John G. Peristiany (London: Weidenfeld and Nicolson, 1965), pp. 21-77. An excellent overview of the work done in applying these insights to New Testament study between 1981 and 1993 can be found in Halvor Moxnes, "Honor and Shame: A Reader's Guide," *BTB* 23 (1993): 167-76.

[2]See also Aristotle *Rhetoric* 2.6.26 on the general power of shame for social control: "There are many things which they either do or do not do owing to the feeling of shame which these men [i.e., the public whose opinion matters to the doers] inspire."

of the Jewish sages are led to value giving alms and pursuing justice in one's dealings with other people, since these lead to honor (Prov 21:21), while they are led to fear adultery, oppression of the poor and disrespect toward parents as the road to disgrace (Prov 6:32-33; 19:26, respectively).

Honor is a dynamic and relational concept. On the one hand, an individual can think of himself or herself as honorable based on his or her conviction that he or she has embodied those actions and qualities that the group values as "honorable," as the marks of a valuable person. This aspect of honor is really "self-respect." On the other hand, honor is also the esteem in which a person is held by the group he or she regards as significant others—it is the recognition by the person's group that he or she is a valuable member of that group. In this regard, it is having the respect of others. It was a problematic experience when one's self-respect was not matched by corresponding respect from others, but strategies could be developed to cope with discrepancy here. While the powerful and the masses, the philosophers and the Jews, the pagans and the Christians all regarded honor and dishonor as their primary axis of value, each group would fill out the picture of what constituted honorable behavior or character in terms of its own distinctive set of beliefs and values, and would evaluate people both inside and outside that group accordingly.

The meaning of *shame* is somewhat more complicated. If honor signifies respect for being the kind of person and doing the kinds of things the group values, shame signifies, in the first instance, being seen as less than valuable because one has behaved in ways that run contrary to the values of the group. The person who puts personal safety above the city's well-being, fleeing from battle, loses the respect of society. His worth is impugned; he "loses face"; he is disgraced and viewed as a disgrace. In a second sense, however, shame can signify a positive character trait, namely a sensitivity to the opinion of the group such that one avoids those actions that bring disgrace. Out of shame of this kind, a woman refuses an adulterous invitation; a soldier refuses to flee from battle.

Those living or reared in Asiatic, Latin American, Mediterranean or Islamic countries have considerable advantage in their reading of the New Testament in this regard, since many of those cultures place a prominent emphasis on honor and shame. Readers living in the United States or Western Europe may recognize immediately that we live at some distance from the honor culture of the first-century Greco-Roman world (including the Semitic peoples in the East). In our culture the bottom line for decision-making is not always (indeed, perhaps rarely) identifying the honorable thing to do. In the corporate world, for example, the "profitable" frequently acts as the central value. Considerations of right and wrong are also prominent, but these are based on internalized values or norms rather than values enforced by overt approval or disapproval by the larger society. Typically we do not talk about honor and shame much (the one place where I've recently observed honor as an openly discussed, coordinating value was at a service honoring a newly inducted Eagle Scout), but we do wrestle with "worth," with "self-esteem," with the push and pull of "what other people will think." The vocabulary has greatly receded, but the dynamics are very much still present. We want to know that we are valuable, worthwhile people, and we want to give the impression of being such.[3]

Our move toward individualism (and the accompanying reluctance to communicate openly with others, especially those beyond our circle of acquaintances, friends and kin) has contributed greatly to tempering the dynamics of honor and shame in our culture. We are less likely to openly challenge others or to openly censure them where they transgress values we consider to be central to our group or to the society. Nevertheless, there are aspects of our experience and our culture that do come closer to the cultural environment of the first-century world and perhaps can help us get in touch with the social dynamics of that world.

We are aware, for example, of the effects of peer pressure, particularly on adolescents. Those who do not conform are ostracized, insulted and often the targets of physical violence (or at least the threat of violence). All of this is unofficial from the standpoint of the authority figures in the schools, but it is nevertheless a potent force in the lives of the students. Moreover, belonging in one group—conforming to its culture and finding affirmation there—often means conflict with another group. The intellec-

---

[3]It has been popular in recent literature to characterize the ancient Mediterranean world as an "honor culture" or a "shame culture" in contrast to a "guilt culture," a label often attached to the modern world. (America has also been described as a "rights" culture.) Such lines cannot, however, be drawn in a hard and fast way. The ancient world knew both the experience of shame and feelings of guilt as deterrents to behavior (see Eric R. Dodds, *The Greeks and the Irrational* [Berkeley: University of California, 1966]), just as the modern person can wrestle both with guilt and shame (see Robert Karen, "Shame," *The Atlantic Monthly*, February 1992, pp. 40-70).

tuals ("geeks") are a close-knit bunch, affirming one another in their group culture, but their worth as persons comes under the attack of the more physical crowd ("jocks"), and vice versa. There is also the artsy crowd, the social crowd, the rebel crowd, the drug crowd and so forth. Within each group, peer pressure enforces conformity and castigates difference. Those too deeply touched by the jeers of others may change their whole images to secure approval rather than ridicule. Additionally, those readers who have been exposed to the cultures of gangs, whether in urban or suburban environments, have encountered a culture in which "respect" is a primary value (a greater value than even human life) and "disrespecting" is a challenge that cannot go unanswered.

This is not to suggest that the world in which the early church developed was like an immense high school locker room, nor that Mediterranean culture was developmentally more primitive than modern culture (something that might be inferred from the adolescent model of peer pressure above). Far from it. That world was every bit as culturally and socially sophisticated as ours and, in some ways, far clearer and more articulate about the values that defined and guided each group. However, we do need to become sensitive to the social dynamics—to the power—of honor and shame in the lives of the first Christians and their contemporaries if we are to hear the texts of the New Testament with their full force. Placing a mental bookmark in our own memories of experiencing (and contributing to) peer pressure can begin to open up those parts of us that are still sensitive to honor and shame to the challenge and the gifts of the Christian Scriptures.

The Vocabulary of Honor

Before we look at the New Testament, we need to learn the language of honor and dishonor in the first-century Greco-Roman world (which includes the Jewish subculture, one of many native cultures that had been absorbed into first the Greek then the Roman empire).[4] Words like *glory*,

---

[4]For a fine survey of honor language in 1 Peter, see John H. Elliott, "Disgraced yet Graced: The Gospel According to 1 Peter in the Key of Honor and Shame," *BTB* 24 (1994): 166-78. Elliott's rigorous analysis of this letter, particularly his inventory of places where honor and shame language enters into the letter, provides a helpful model for readers to apply to other texts. His work is, in turn, deeply informed by Bruce J. Malina and Jerome H. Neyrey, "Honor and Shame in Luke-Acts: Pivotal Values of the Mediterranean World," in *The Social World of Luke-Acts: Models for Interpretation*, ed. Jerome H. Neyrey (Peabody, Mass.: Hendrickson, 1991), pp. 25-66.

reputation (doxa), honor (timē) and *praise (epainos),* together with verb and adjectival forms, are frequent. Their antonyms, *dishonor (aischunē), reproach (oneidos), scorn (kataphronēsis), slander (blasphēmia),* together with the adjectives and verbs derived from these roots, are also prominent. Such word searches provide a starting place for us to "hook into" the texts as first-century Christians would have, but they are starting places only. Many concepts and terms would also resonate directly with considerations of honor and dishonor for them, but to hear this we have to learn more about these resonances.

First, honor can be ascribed to a person on account of accidents of birth or grants bestowed by people of higher status and power. A person's parentage and lineage became, in many ways, a starting point for honor: "A person's honor comes from his father," wrote Ben Sira (Sir 3:11), a fact confirmed by the practice of the eulogy, which began celebrating the deceased person's honor by recalling the honor of his or her ancestors and immediate parents. Thus a person of the "house of David" begins with a higher honor in the Jewish culture than a member of the "house of Herschel," and thus insults (or assaults on a person's honor) often involve one's descent ("You spawn of snakes" [Mt 3:7, my translation]; "You are of your father, the devil" [Jn 8:44, my translation]). A person's race could also become a factor in the esteem or lack of esteem with which he or she was held. In Judea, *Samaritan* was a term of reproach; in Egypt, native Egyptians were regarded as less honorable than the Greeks who comprised the ruling class. Honor can also be ascribed later in life, whether through adoption into a more honorable family (as Octavian, later the Emperor Augustus, had been adopted by Julius Caesar as a son: Octavian's honor rating rose considerably by that grant), through grants of special citizenship status or through grants of office. All of these are, again, prominent in the New Testament, as Christians are said to be adopted by God, made citizens of heaven and given the honorable office of priesthood (see, for example, Gal 4:4-7; Phil 3:20; 1 Pet 2:9).

Second, honor can be achieved as well as ascribed. In the first instance, this occurs as one persists in being "virtuous" in one's dealings, building up a reputation—a name—for being honorable and embodying virtues prized by the group. Thus the soldier who displays above-ordinary courage is singled out for special honors, the generous benefactor is proclaimed at public festivities and commemorated in inscriptions, the loyal client or friend comes to be known as such and is welcomed by other patrons into the household on that basis, and the Torah-observant Jew is seen to be pious and held in high regard by fellow Jews. Again, the importance of such achieved honor is reflected in the incorporation into the funeral oration of accounts of the virtues of the deceased and the ways in which these virtues were enacted throughout life. In the second instance, honor can be won and lost in what has been called the social game of challenge and riposte.[5] It is this "game," still observable in the modern Mediterranean, that has caused cultural anthropologists to label the culture as "agonistic," from the Greek word for "contest" *(agōn)*.

The challenge-riposte is essentially an attempt to gain honor at someone else's expense by publicly posing a challenge that cannot be answered. When a challenge has been posed, the challenged must make some sort of response (and no response is also considered a response). It falls to the bystanders to decide whether or not the challenged person successfully defended his (and, indeed, usually "his") own honor. The Gospels are full of these exchanges,[6] mainly posed by Pharisees, Sadducees or other religious officials at Jesus, whom they regarded as an upstart threatening to steal their place in the esteem of the people. Consider, for example, Luke 13:10-17:

> Now he was teaching in one of the synagogues on the sabbath. And just then there appeared a woman with a spirit that had crippled her for eighteen years. . . . When Jesus saw her, he called her over and said, "Woman, you are set free from your ailment." When he laid his hands on her, immediately she stood up straight and began praising God. But the leader of the synagogue, indignant because Jesus had cured on the sabbath, kept saying to the crowd, "There are six days on which work ought to be done; come on those days and be cured, and not on the sabbath day." But the Lord answered him and said, "You hypocrites! Does not each of you on the sabbath untie his ox or his donkey from the manger, and lead it away to give it water? And ought not this woman, a daughter of Abraham whom Satan bound for eighteen long years, be set free from this bondage on the sabbath day?" When he said this, all his opponents were put to shame; and the entire crowd was rejoicing at all the wonderful things that he was doing.

---

[5]Pitt-Rivers, "Honour and Social Status," p. 27; Malina and Neyrey, "Honor and Shame," p. 30.

[6]See Jerome H. Neyrey, *Honor and Shame in the Gospel of Matthew* (Louisville: Westminster John Knox, 1998), pp. 44-52, for a fuller discussion of this phenomenon and its appearance throughout Matthew's Gospel.

Jesus' violation of the prohibition of work on the sabbath day suggests to the synagogue leader that Jesus claims to be "above the law" (specifically, Torah) on account of his power to heal. The synagogue leader does not cast doubt on Jesus' abilities in this regard; he assumes it. He does, however, challenge Jesus' right to perform a work, even a good work, on the sabbath. Even though his words are directed at the crowd, it is nevertheless a challenge directed at Jesus. Jesus offers a piercing response (riposte), pointing out that the synagogue leaders themselves will care for their animals on the sabbath, how much more ought he, then, care for "a daughter of Abraham" (notice the use of genealogy here to highlight the woman's value). The result, according to Luke, is that Jesus wins this exchange. His rivals lose face on account of their unsuccessful challenge (they are "put to shame"), while Jesus' honor in the crowd's eyes increases (they rejoice at his works).

A second and more complicated example appears in Mark 7:1-16. Jesus' disciples eat their food without performing a ritual purification of their hands (the Pharisees were not concerned with hygiene but with purity laws), so the Pharisees challenge Jesus' honor—what kind of teacher can he be if his disciples transgress the revered "tradition of the elders" (that was attaining a status equal to the written Torah)? Jesus responds, this time with a counterchallenge. He challenges the Pharisees' honor as followers of Torah, citing an instance where their tradition stands in contradiction to the written Torah (indeed, one of the Ten Commandments), allowing him even to apply a devastating quotation from Isaiah in his riposte. The reader is reminded of the public nature of this exchange as Jesus addresses his last comment to the crowd (Mk 7:16). Presumably, Jesus has successfully warded off the challenge and even caused his opponents to lose face with the counterchallenge. In telling these stories, moreover, the Gospel writers make the Christian readers into the public that witnesses the exchanges and gives its own verdict on who won and who lost. Their own positive estimation of Jesus (as an honorable person and as a reliable teacher of the way to please God) is confirmed as they read these challenge-riposte stories actively and appraisingly.

Such exchanges basically characterize Jesus' relationship with the religious leaders and groups with which he is, in essence, in competition.[7]

---

[7] In Luke's Gospel alone, see 4:1-13; 5:29-39; 6:1-5, 6-11; 7:1-10 (not hostile); 7:18-23 (not hostile); 7:39-50 (notice that the challenge does not even have to be articulated!); 10:25-28;

Even those scribes who appear to ask a polite and "innocent" question
are seen actually to be posing challenges, trying to trip up Jesus, to cause
him, at first, to lose face (and, with it, his following) and, later, to step into
a chargeable offense. An individual's honor can also be on the line, as it
were, when the individual receives a gift from a social equal—since failure to reciprocate will result in diminished honor, this is also a challenge-
riposte situation, although it is not a hostile one. Hence Isocrates advises
his student to "consider it equally disgraceful to be outdone by your enemies in doing injury and to be surpassed by your friends in doing kindness" (*Ad Dem.* 26), that is, to take pains to win when presented either
with negative or positive challenges, so that his honor will remain undi-
minished.

In addition to recognizing how a text or speaker weaves in references
to topics of ascribed honor or achieved honor, we need also to become
aware of how honor and dishonor are symbolized in the physical person,
as well as in the "name" or reputation of a person. The way a body is
treated is often a representation of honor or dishonor: thus the head of a
king is crowned or anointed, but the face of a prisoner is slapped and
beaten (e.g., Mk 15:16-20; Lk 22:63-65). Binding, mutilating and eventually killing are also part of the assault on (indeed, the erasure of) the deviant criminal's honor. The relative placement of bodies is also a
representation of honor. Thus a king is often seated on a level higher than
others, and subjects bow deeply to the ground before a ruler to acknowledge symbolically the difference in honor and the reverence due the sov-
ereign. Enemies once subjected are thrown at the feet of the victor, as a
representation of the new order and relationships established (see 1 Cor
15:24-28; Heb 1:13). Seating order at feasts or in synagogues is an important signal of the relative status of the guests or worshipers. Jesus' censure of those who vie for the "best seats" is a critique of the honor-seeking
customs of his day (Mt 23:6-7; Mk 10:35-37; Lk 14:7-11). Applying Psalm
110:1 to Jesus—"The LORD says to my Lord, 'Sit at my right hand' "—fixes

11:14-20; 11:37-54; 13:10-17; 14:1-6 (Jesus initiates here); 15:1-32 (the three parables are an
extensive riposte here to the Pharisees' challenge; the series end with the surly older
brother refusing to welcome his brother and join the party, a parting counterchallenge
aimed at the Pharisees and the scribes); 16:14-18; 19:39-40, 45-48 (Jesus initiates, and the
riposte comes at the end of the week!); 20:1-19 (the parable is part of Jesus' counterchal-
lenge/riposte); 20:20-26, 27-40. In Luke 20:41-47, Jesus closes that last series of exchanges
with renewed challenges of his own, which go unanswered until the crucifixion.

Jesus in the position of highest honor in the Jewish and Christian cosmos (Mk 12:35-36; Heb 1:13; 12:2). Clothing also is regularly used as a symbol of one's honor or status. Thus Esther can exchange her "robes of honor" for "mourning garments" (Add Esth 14:1-2; 15:1), and King Artaxerxes' honor is so magnificently displayed in visible signs (seating, garments, tokens of wealth like gold and jewels) that Esther faints upon seeing him (Add Esth 15:6, 11-14).[8]

In addition to paying close attention to the way bodies are treated, attired and arranged with regard to other bodies, we need to consider the way a person's name is treated. The name is another place where a person's honor is symbolized and toward which honor or dishonor can be directed. Praising or "sanctifying" God's name or making God's name "known" are expressions for giving God honor or spreading God's honor (Tob 3:11; 8:5; 11:14; 14:8-9; Mt 6:9; Jn 17:6, 26; Rom 9:17; 15:9). When God's name is "spoken ill of"[9] because God's people disobey God's commands or live immorally (Rom 2:24; 1 Tim 6:1), God's people are participating in the dishonoring of God; God's name is also "spoken ill of" by his enemies (Rev 13:6; 16:9), resulting in God's vindication of his honor through the punishment of those enemies. Doing something or asking for something "in the name" of Jesus invokes Jesus' honor: good works or service becomes a vehicle for increasing Jesus' fame, and answered prayers will result in the celebration and spread of Jesus' honor (i.e., through testimony). The Christians also each have a name, that is, a reputation: Jesus prepares them for the ruin of their "good name" among their neighbors on account of their commitment to Jesus but assures them that the loss of their "good name" here wins them eternal honor before God (Lk 6:22).[10]

---

[8]See Matthew 11:7-8, where Jesus begins to extol John for having greater honor and worth than anyone, including "those who wear soft robes" in their "royal palaces." John's clothing, while reminiscent of Elijah, also defined his status as someone who stood "outside" the social hierarchy of civilization (see also Heb 11:37-38). When the soldiers mock Jesus, part of their sport includes "dressing him up" as the king that, in their eyes, he falsely claimed to be (Mk 15:16-20); their mock coronation is their way of challenging (and negating) his claim to this honor.

[9]*Blaspheme* means, essentially, to hurt the reputation of someone.

[10]There are many instances, of course, where the New Testament authors merely mention that someone's name is so-and-so. In these places a name is just a name. Where a name represents a person, or the estimation of a person in the eyes of others, it is a cipher for the honor and worth of that person. The symbolizing of honor in name is ancient, as attested by the very frequent (and almost exclusive) use of *name* in this manner in the Psalms.

Finally, we should mention the ways in which gender roles impinge on conceptions of honorable behavior. In the ancient world, as in many traditional cultures today, women and men have different arenas for the preservation and acquisition of honor, and different standards for honorable activity. Men occupy the public spaces, while women are generally directed toward the private spaces of home and hearth. When they leave the home, they are careful to avoid conversation with other men. The places they go are frequented mainly by women (the village well, the market for food) and so become something of an extension of "private" space. In the fifth century B.C., Thucydides wrote that the most honorable woman is the one least talked about by men (*Hist.* 2.45.2). Six hundred years later Plutarch will say much the same thing: a woman should be seen when she is with her husband, but stay hidden at home when he is away ("Advice on Marriage" 9). Both her body and her words should not be "public property" but instead guarded from strangers. She should speak to her husband and through her husband ("Advice on Marriage" 31-32). In second-century B.C. Jerusalem, Ben Sira is expressing the same delineation of a woman's sphere and honor (Sir 26:13-18).[11]

The psalmists give God honor as they "bless his name," pray that the "name" of Israel or the "name" of the individual petitioner not "perish forever" (that is, pray that God will preserve the honor and the honorable memory of Israel or the individual), and ask God to obliterate the "name" of their enemies.

[11]There are some notable exceptions to this general rule. Judith, the heroine of the apocryphal book bearing her name, wins honor by lulling the general of the enemy troops besieging Israel into a drunken stupor in the expectation of sexual gratification and then beheading him as he slept on his bed. The author of 4 Maccabees depicts a mother urging her seven sons on to accept martyrdom for the sake of God and fidelity to God's Torah, praising her for being more "courageous" (the Greek word is more like "manly," being based on the word for a male person) than men. Plutarch dedicates a lengthy essay, "On the Bravery of Women," to stories in which women's courage ("manliness") exceeded that of the men around them and is held up as exemplary to men and women alike. Women are therefore certainly not excluded from seeking to embody courage, generosity or justice. Indeed, they are encouraged to be virtuous in these ways as well. Nevertheless, even the courageous heroines mentioned above know that their honor is inseparably linked to the virtue of sexual exclusivity and that damage there will undermine any achievement of honor in another arena. Judith therefore quickly points out that, although she used her charms on General Holofernes, he never actually had her (Jdt 13:6). The mother of the seven martyrs also acts to preserve her body from the defiling touch of the soldiers by throwing herself into a fire (4 Macc 17:1), and the author of 4 Maccabees closes his book with a speech by the mother in which she testifies to her chastity throughout life (4 Macc 18:6-9).

The reason for this relegation of women to private or nonmale areas is rooted in the ancient conception of a woman's place in the world. She is not seen as an independent entity or agent but as embedded in the identity and honor of some male (her father, if she is unmarried, her husband after she marries). If she fails to protect her honor, for example by engaging in extramarital intercourse or by displaying "looseness" by providing males outside her family with her company or her words, she actually brings shame upon her husband or father. A daughter or a wife was regarded as a point of vulnerability in the man's rearguard against disgrace. It is for this reason that Ben Sira considers the birth of a daughter a liability (Sir 42:9-14) and offers such strong words about the potential loss incurred through women (Sir 26:10-12).

Despite the progressiveness of the New Testament authors with regard to attacking the distinction between Jew and Gentile that was central to Jewish identity, and despite Paul's conviction that even the distinctions between male and female, slave and free, are valueless in Christ (Gal 3:28), we do find a good deal of space given over to promoting (or simply reflecting) the larger society's view of female honor within the pages of the New Testament. Thus 1 Corinthians 11:2-16, where Paul attempts to convince the Corinthian Christians that women must pray with their heads covered, also reflects the view that female honor is embedded in male honor in naming the husband as the "head" of the wife, who is incorporated conceptually into his "body." Two passages from the pastoral epistles (1 Tim 5:8-12; Tit 2:4-5) attempt to reinforce within Christian culture the values of sexual exclusivity (even for the widow after a first husband has died) and the delineation of the appropriate female sphere as the home. Two passages are repeatedly in the forefront of debate because they appear strongly to forbid female speech in public worship, which has obvious bearing on the issue of ordaining women:

> Women should be silent in the churches. For they are not permitted to speak, but should be subordinate, as the law also says. If there is anything they desire to know, let them ask their husbands at home. For it is shameful for a woman to speak in church. (1 Cor 14:34-35; see also 1 Tim 2:11-12)

These passages continue to be the topic of endless debate, but relevant for our concern here is the fact that they reflect the same conviction articulated by Plutarch, namely that a woman's words are for her husband's ears, not for the public ear.[12]

Honor and Group Values

The focus of ancient people on honor and dishonor or shame means that they were particularly oriented toward the approval and disapproval of others. This orientation meant that individuals were likely to strive to embody the qualities and to perform the behaviors that the group held to be honorable and to avoid those acts that brought reproach and caused a person's estimation in the eyes of others to drop. As a group discovered and defined those qualities that it needed its members to display in order for the group to survive, the desire to be honored would ensure that the members would all do their part to promote the health and survival of the group.

For this reason courage, for example, was held in extremely high regard. In the classical period the safety of a whole city depended on the willingness of its (male) citizens to embrace the dangers of armed conflict, to risk life and limb (quite literally). Both the fallen soldier and the living veteran were therefore honored by the group, while the deserter became a reproach. The desire to be honored and to avoid being disgraced kept most citizen soldiers in the thick of the battle, preferring death with honor to safety with disgrace. Because most public works and civic improvements depended on the initiative of wealthy citizens, generosity (benefaction) was also highly and visibly honored. The desire for honor made the

---

[12]There is a notable discrepancy between the conception of the congregation as public, as non-kin or outsiders before whom women are to be silent and withdrawn, and the conception of the church as family—related by the blood of Jesus, as it were—throughout the greater part of the New Testament. In 1 Corinthians 14, Paul's chief concern appears to be the impression that will be made on the visitor to the congregation—the one "outsider." I would consider it likely that the passages limiting women's public voice and presence are introduced as part of the early church leaders' attempts to show outsiders that the Christian movement is not subversive but inculcates the same "family values" (with regard to women, children and slaves in the household) as the dominant, non-Christian culture. The reason for this is first to diminish the slander against the Christian group (namely that it "turned the world upside down" and was a source of instability and trouble for "good" people), and second, to make the group more attractive to the people around it. Making a concession to ancient cultural values normative for the church in every age seems to me to be erroneous, particularly since it is done at the expense of so many passages that speak of the gifting of all believers—including the gift of prophesy being poured out on "sons and daughters," both slave and free men and women (Acts 2:17-18)—for the building up of the church.

wealthy willing to part with vast sums of money for the good of the city. The list could go on endlessly: the virtues and behaviors that preserved the order and stability of a culture, and made for its growth and improvement, were rewarded with honor. Those who did their part in both the private and public spheres were affirmed as valuable persons of worth. Those who violated those values, whether through adultery (attacking the stability of the family), through cowardice (undermining the security and the honor of the group), through failing to honor the gods or the rulers (risking the loss of their favors), through ingratitude (being unjust toward the generous and threatening to diminish their willingness to be generous) were held up to contempt. The group would exercise measures designed to shame the transgressor (whether through insult, reproach, physical abuse, confiscation of property—at worst, execution) so that the transgressor would be pressured into returning to the conduct the group approved (if correction were possible) and so that other group members would have their aversion to committing such transgressions themselves strongly reinforced. Honoring and shaming became the dominant means of enforcing all those values that were not actually legislated and of reinforcing those values that were covered by written laws.

When a particular group lives in relative isolation from other groups—that is, when all the people one is likely to meet in a given lifetime share the same values and bestow honor and dishonor accordingly—the process of keeping group members committed to the group values is relatively simple and consistent. Retaining the commitment of the next generation is also not a great challenge. They are nurtured in an environment in which there is little, if any, disagreement concerning what behaviors are honorable and what behaviors are disgraceful. They see the social sanctions of praise and shaming applied consistently, and they absorb the group values without question.

This, however, is not the situation of the first-century Mediterranean world,[13] particularly in its cities where there is a wide representation of the various cultures available in that world concentrated in a small space. In taking just a cross section of the situation at the time of Jesus or Paul, we find first a dominant culture, that of Hellenism, with its distinctively

---

[13]Nor is it the situation of much of the modern world, in which the complexity of maintaining a particular group culture is made all the more challenging by strong emphases on multiculturalism and pluralism.

Greek set of values. This is the dominant culture because all those in power share it, from the emperor in Rome to the local elites in Asia Minor, Syria and Egypt, even to Herod Agrippa in Palestine. It is also the majority culture, since Hellenism had by this time been penetrating local cultures in the Eastern Mediterranean from Macedonia through Egypt (including Palestine for three centuries). There were, however, many other groups living within this world, trying to preserve their distinctive values while adapting to the necessities of living in a world empire. Prominent among these minority cultures is the Jewish culture. Formerly a dominant culture in its own right, the Judean people had become a subcultural group within empires dominated by other people for six centuries.[14] In Palestine and especially among communities of Jews living in the Diaspora, negotiating commitment to Jewish values and making a life in the midst of a Gentile world were challenging tasks. There were also voluntary groups promoting their own set of values and their own distinctive culture. Among this category one would find the Greco-Roman philosophical schools like Stoicism, Epicureanism and Cynicism as well as the early Christian movement.

What made this multicultural environment challenging is the fact that each group defined honorable and dishonorable conduct according to its own distinctive set of values and beliefs. Sometimes these values would overlap (and the strategy of both Jewish and Christian apologists was often to stress the areas of overlap and commonality). Frequently, however, the values would clash. The same behavior that one group would hold up and reward as honorable, another group could censure and insult as disgraceful, and vice versa. It was difficult to remain committed to the law of Moses when doing so brought ridicule and barred one from being affirmed as honorable by the majority or dominant culture. It was difficult to keep the ideals of Stoicism foremost in one's mind when the majority of people paid little heed to those ideals, scoffed at philosophy and acclaimed those who were rich in external goods (like wealth or crowds of followers or positions of power) rather than in virtue. This made for keen social tension and pressure on the

---

[14]The century of "independence" under the Hasmonean house (the family of Judas Maccabaeus: see 1 Macc for the establishment of the dynasty) could be considered an exception, save for the fact that by that point already more Jews were living outside of Palestine than within. They were thus still, by and large, living as an ethnic subculture within a larger empire.

individual member of a particular group.

In order to make this scenario clearer, let us consider the specific example of the plight of Jews in the ancient world and the ways in which they might negotiate this tension. Within the Jewish culture, observance of God's law, the Torah, was a primary mark of the honorable man or woman. Ben Sira, for example, reaffirms this as the group's core value—the fundamental and foundational source of a person's worth:

> What race is worthy of honor? The human race. What race is worthy of honor? Those who fear the Lord. What race is unworthy of honor? The human race. What race is unworthy of honor? Those who transgress the commandments. Among brothers their leader is worthy of honor, and those who fear the Lord are worthy of honor in his eyes. The rich, and the eminent, and the poor—their glory is the fear of the Lord. It is not right to despise an intelligent poor man, nor is it proper to honor a sinful man. The nobleman, and the judge, and the ruler will be honored, but none of them is greater than the man who fears the Lord (Sir 10:19-24).

For Ben Sira, keeping God's covenant is the essential ingredient to establishing a person as honorable, while transgression of Torah leaves even the powerful and mighty without true honor.

Even while Ben Sira teaches this saying to his students, however, those students will experience the ridicule and censure of non-Jews precisely because they keep Torah. The law of Moses forbids any kind of dealings with idolatrous worship, and so the honorable Jew never frequents a Gentile temple. The rest of the world, however, regards the paying of proper respect to the gods (namely, the deities depicted by the idols loathed by Jews) as an essential characteristic of the honorable person—the pious and just person who gives the gods their due. Jews are, in the eyes of the majority, as good as atheists and every bit as dishonorable. Circumcision, the mark revered among Jews as a sign of being included in the covenant of Abraham and the covenant of Moses, was viewed as a barbaric mutilation of the human body by the Greek culture. Moreover, strict observance of Torah means keeping watch over what one eats and, as it came to be applied, with whom one eats. Between the prohibition of idols (which would be present and honored even at a private dinner party given by a Greek or Roman) and the dietary and purity laws of Torah, Jews were severely restricted in their interactions with non-Jews. The majority culture, however, placed a high value on civic unity and on participation in the life of the city in all its aspects (e.g., religious festivals, business guilds and the like), with the result that Jews appeared to them to keep strictly to themselves and to harbor barbaric suspicions of (or even hatred of) other races. This became another source of ridicule and insult directed against Jews, whose very way of life (the Torah) came to be despised as a body of xenophobic and retrogressive laws.[15]

The Jew is thus faced with a disturbing contradiction. If he lives by Torah, he will be honored and affirmed as a valuable member of the community by his Jewish peers, but he will also be regarded with contempt and even find his honor openly assaulted by the majority of the Greco-Roman population. In such a situation it cannot be taken for granted that a Jew will remain such. If he desires the approval and affirmation of the members of the Greco-Roman culture (and the opportunities for advancement, influence and wealth that networking in that direction can bring), he may well abandon his strict allegiance to Jewish values. This was the course chosen by many Jews during the Hellenistic period.[16] Most Jews, however, chose to remain faithful to their ancestral law and customs, and to preserve their culture and its values. To do so, they had to develop strategies for keeping themselves and their fellow Jews sensitive to Jewish definitions of the honorable and, at the same time, insulated from non-Jewish verdicts concerning honor and dishonor.

These strategies would be common to many minority cultures attempting to secure the allegiance of their members and to defuse the pressures those members might feel from people outside the group. They can be found at work in Jewish writings, in the writings of Gentile philosophers promoting their way of life, as well as in the early Christian texts called

---

[15]Prominent examples of ancient anti-Jewish sentiments can be found in Josephus *Ag. Ap.* 2.121, 258; Tacitus *Hist.* 5.1-5; Juvenal *Sat.* 14.100-104; and Diodorus of Sicily *Bib. Hist.* 34.1-4; 40.3.4.

[16]See, for example, the eagerness even of priestly families in Jerusalem itself to remove the mark of circumcision, to throw off the Mosaic restrictions on their dealings with a Gentile world, and to achieve status as a Greek city in the eyes of the Greek elite in Antioch (1 Macc 1:11-15; 2 Macc 4:7-15; especially noteworthy is 2 Macc 4:15, "disdaining the honors prized by their ancestors and putting the highest value upon Greek forms of prestige"). There are several stories of individuals who apostatized from their Jewish roots and became highly honored and influential in the "larger" arena of politics, for example, Tiberius Julius Alexander, the nephew of the devout Old Testament scholar Philo of Alexandria. Tiberius Alexander, having left behind Torah observance, went on to become prefect of Alexandria and, in A.D. 46-48, governor of the province of Judea.

the New Testament.[17] First, group members need to be very clear about who constitutes their "court of reputation," that body of significant others whose "opinion" about what is honorable and shameful, and whose evaluation of the individual, really matters. Their eyes need to be directed toward one another, toward their leaders, and, very frequently, toward beings beyond the visible sphere (for example, God or the honored members of the group who have moved to another realm after death) as they look for approval[18]—and thus directed away from those people who do not share the group's values and whose negative estimation of the group threatens to erode individual commitment. Connecting the opinion or approval of this potentially small body of visible "significant others" to the opinion and approval of a larger or more powerful body of significant others (God, the heavenly hosts, the saints throughout the ages, the church of God in every place) also helps to offset the "minority" status of its values. Adherents to a minority group (such as the church or synagogue) must believe that, even though the majority of people around them have a different and contrary set of values, the majority is really the deviant body since it doesn't live in line with the cosmic order. The group will then award honor to its members that adhere to the way of life promoted by that group, and use shame and censure to try to bring the wayward members back into line with group values. Members will be encouraged to interact more with, and invest themselves more in, other members of the group. The importance of these relationships must outweigh any advantages that might be perceived in exchanging this network of support and affirmation for the "friendship of the world."

A second critical strategy is, more or less, the mirror image of the first. Group members need to understand (and to articulate for one another) why the approval or disapproval of outsiders does not matter to the members of the group and why it is no reflection of the group members' true honor and worth. This often takes the form of stressing the ignorance

---

[17]A detailed analysis of these techniques at work in Plato, Seneca, Epictetus (three Greco-Roman philosophers), Jeshua Ben Sira, the Wisdom of Solomon, and 4 Maccabees (three Jewish works produced between 200 B.C. and A.D. 70) can be found in chapter three of my *Despising Shame*.

[18]The eyes are not always directed "outside" the individual. Epictetus, the Stoic philosopher, is often concerned with empowering moral autonomy—that is, stressing the importance of "self-respect" as the philosopher examines his or her own life, finds that he or she is indeed walking in the ideals of the philosophy and extending affirmation to himself or herself on the basis of living up to those internalized norms.

of outsiders who, because they do not know what the group members know about God and God's values, do not have all the facts necessary to make an informed evaluation about anyone's honor or lack thereof. It also involves reminding group members of the shameful conduct of outsiders whose persistence in sin against God and refusal to do what is right in God's eyes marks them as dishonorable people whose opinion can carry no weight (if the despicable despise you, what does that matter?).

When group members do experience insult, scorn and hostility at the hands of the members of the majority culture, they need to have ways of interpreting this experience positively from within the worldview of the group. For example, perseverance in the face of the shaming tactics of the larger society can become a "noble contest" (akin to an athletic competition) in which giving in is the greatest disgrace and remaining firm is an honorable victory. Rather than being felt as a demeaning, degrading experience, society's assaults on the group can become an opportunity to show courage or to demonstrate a person's loyalty to God or to have his or her moral faculty exercised and strengthened. In this way, group members will be insulated against the strong pull the experience of disgrace will have on them and will be protected from being pulled into the values of the majority culture (which is one of the aims of the shaming techniques).

Finally, the group will use considerations of honor and shame to reinforce for its members what behaviors and goals they ought to pursue, and to dissuade them from any activities or attitudes that will hinder the group's survival (or the solidarity of its members). In the literary remains of these groups (e.g., the works of Seneca, Ben Sira or Paul), we find the guiding voices of minority cultures motivating their audiences to pursue or leave off particular courses of action based on the affirmation or demonstration that such a course would result either in honor or disgrace. If the course of action promoted by the group leader does not seem to lead to honor as the broader culture defines it, that leader will frequently offer some defense or explanation for his claim that the course leads to honor where honor lasts forever or "really counts." In these texts we also find models for behavior being set forward. Some figures are held up as praiseworthy, with the expectation that hearers will be led to emulate that figure in the hope of being recognized themselves as praiseworthy; alternatively, some figures (whether living or past) will be singled out as disgraceful and censurable so that the hearers will be averted from imitating the kind of life he or she embodied.[19]

Honor and dishonor, then, are not only about the individual's sense of worth but also about the coordination and promotion of a group's defining and central values, about the strategies for the preservation of a group's culture in the midst of a complex web of competing cultures, and about the ways in which honor or dishonor are attained, displayed and enacted. As we keep the dynamics of this rather complex model in mind, however, we can begin to approach the New Testament writings with a much greater sensitivity to how these texts speak to honor-sensitive hearers, develop a distinctively Christian definition of what gives a person worth and value (i.e., makes one honorable), and sustain commitment and obedience to Jesus and his teachings in a largely unsupportive world.

---

[19]Analysis of these strategies takes us into the study of classical rhetoric. The handbooks on rhetoric written between the fourth century B.C. (Aristotle) and first century A.D. (Quintilian) give modern readers a great tool for understanding how an ancient argument was constructed and how it would affect its hearers—how it would appeal to their minds and their emotions as it sought to lead them to take a certain course of action. These handbooks were written to teach orators how to persuade their hearers to do what the orator wanted them to do. This is helpful because the New Testament texts are in fact all seeking to persuade the hearers to do something: Gospels seek to shape community life and individual behavior, just as epistles and visionary works like Revelation try to move the hearers toward or away from certain actions (or to reinforce certain values). While few New Testament authors are likely candidates for formal rhetorical training, all of them would have had the benefit of the informal training of hearing orators at work, of learning inductively the art of persuasion. Looking at how persuasion happened, and specifically at how orators would appeal to honor in the course of their attempts at persuasion, throws much light on how the New Testament texts would have been heard by, and would have made an impact on, their first-century hearers. For a starting point, please see David A. deSilva, *The Hope of Glory: Honor Discourse and New Testament Interpretation* (Collegeville, Minn.: Liturgical Press, 1999), pp. 14-26.

Two

HONOR & SHAME IN THE NEW TESTAMENT

T he early Christians proclaimed a message and stood for values that differed from, and indeed contradicted, core values within the dominant Greco-Roman culture as well as the Jewish subculture within which the church arose. Their non-Christian neighbors, therefore, subjected the early Christians to censure and other shaming techniques, designed to bring these deviant people back in line with the values and behaviors held dear by the surrounding culture (whether Jewish or Greco-Roman). The authors of the New Testament devote much of their attention, therefore, to insulating their congregations from the effects of these shaming techniques, calling the hearers to pursue lasting honor before that court of God whose verdict is eternal. These authors continue to use the language of honor and shame to articulate the value system of the Christian group, and to build up the church into a court of reputation that will reinforce commitment to those values through honoring those who distinguish themselves in acts of love, service and faithful witness and through censuring those who fail to embody those values.

Twenty-first century churches can learn much that is useful from the New Testament authors with regard to forming vital communities of disciples undaunted in their pursuit of complete obedience to Jesus by the world around them. The study of honor and shame language in the New Testament feeds directly into the building up of the church now, even as it did in the first century.

Assaults on the Honor of the Early Christians

Jesus gave his followers every indication that attachment to him would make them fall in the estimation of their neighbors:

> Blessed are you when people hate you, and when they exclude you, revile you, and defame you on account of the Son of Man. (Lk 6:22)

> A disciple is not above the teacher. . . . If they have called the master of the house Beelzebul, how much more will they malign those of his household! (Mt 10:24-25)

Similarly, John the evangelist recalls that even some prominent and high-placed Jewish leaders believed in Jesus but kept silent about their convictions because "they loved human glory more than the glory that comes from God" (Jn 12:43). And, indeed, being known as a "Christ-follower" did prove to be a source for dishonor and the manifestations of one's neighbors' lack of esteem (insult, abuse, assault).

Rarely in the first century were Christians killed (i.e., lynched). Far more rarely were they executed on official orders (Nero's brief persecution appears to be the only imperial act against Christians in the first century),[1] but very frequently they experienced the rest of the spectrum of society's strategies for "correcting" those who had deviated from honorable paths. In Jerusalem and Judea, particularly in the years immediately following the resurrection, the Christian movement was identified as a deviant group and suppressed. Its leaders were cajoled, threatened, whipped (their honor publicly assaulted) and even killed (Acts 4:1-3; 5:17-18, 40-41; 7:54—8:3; 12:1-4; 1 Thess 2:14). Throughout Asia Minor and Greece, Gentile Christians experienced the social pressure of their non-Christian neighbors:

> You endured a hard struggle with sufferings, sometimes being publicly exposed to abuse and persecution, and sometimes being partners with

---

[1] It is highly contested whether Domitian actually instigated or supported the persecution of Christians. See the penetrating critique of the commonly held view that Domitian was a "second Nero" to the church in Leonard L. Thompson, *The Book of Revelation: Apocalypse and Empire* (Oxford: Oxford University Press, 1990), pp. 96-132, 171-85; and Adela Y. Collins, *Crisis and Catharsis: The Power of the Apocalypse* (Philadelphia: Westminster Press, 1984), pp. 84-110.

those so treated. For you had compassion for those who were in prison, and
you cheerfully accepted the plundering of your possessions, knowing that
you yourselves possessed something better and more lasting. (Heb 10:32-
34)

Conduct yourselves honorably among the Gentiles, so that, though they
malign you as evildoers, they may see your honorable deeds and glorify
God when he comes to judge. . . . Keep your conscience clear, so that, when
you are maligned, those who abuse you for your good conduct in Christ
may be put to shame. . . . Beloved, do not be surprised at the fiery ordeal
that is taking place among you to test you, as though something strange
were happening to you. But rejoice insofar as you are sharing Christ's sufferings, so that you may also be glad and shout for joy when his glory is
revealed. If you are reviled for the name of Christ, you are blessed, because
the spirit of glory, which is the Spirit of God, is resting on you. But let none
of you suffer as a murderer, a thief, a criminal, or even as a mischief maker.
Yet if any of you suffers as a Christian, do not consider it a disgrace, but glorify God because you bear this name. (1 Pet 2:12; 3:16; 4:12-16)

The references to society's attempts to pressure the Christian "deviants" back into conformity with Greco-Roman or traditional Jewish values could be multiplied indefinitely.[2] It is noteworthy that maligning,
reproach, beatings, imprisonments and financial ruin are mentioned frequently and explicitly, but lynching or execution only rarely: their neighbors were trying to reclaim these wayward members of their society.

Why should such social pressure be brought to bear on this group?[3] To
the outsider, this Jesus movement appeared to undermine the sacred and
central values of the society, pulling formerly good and reliable people
into a subversive cult. First, the leader figure of the movement was executed in a manner suggestive of sedition: crucifixion was commonly associated with the punishment of political revolutionaries. Greeks and
Romans might view Jesus, then, as a rebel who sought to overturn the
peace. Jews regarded him as a "deceiver" (a false teacher), a "sorceror"
(his miraculous deeds went unquestioned; the source of the power, how-

---

[2]There are many examples in the New Testament of communities of Christians enduring
their neighbors' coercive measures (see Phil 1:27-30; 1 Thess 1:6; 2:13-14; 3:1-4; 2 Thess 1:4-5;
Rev 2:9-10, 13). Paul mentions his own endurance of these measures in nearly every letter
attributed to him.

[3]For a more detailed explanation of anti-Christian sentiment and its sources, as well as an
analysis of how this sentiment came to expression in one noteworthy manifestation of social
pressure (Heb 10:32-34), see my *Despising Shame: Honor Discourse and Community Maintenance
in the Epistle to the Hebrews*, SBLDS 152 (Atlanta: Scholars Press, 1995), pp. 146-64.

ever, was a matter of debate)[4] and a "blasphemer" (the charge that comes out in his trial before the Sanhedrin). Those who elected to follow such a subversive and disgraced man were immediately suspect in the eyes of both audiences.

With regard to Greco-Roman values, the message about this Christ was incompatible with the deeply rooted religious ideology of the Gentile world, as well as the more recent message propagated in Roman imperial ideology. Hints of the other side of the argument appear in statements made by New Testament authors. Central to the conflict is the fundamental religious shift made by converts to the Christian movement: "You turned to God from idols, to serve a living and true God" (1 Thess 1:9). Christians shared the Jewish conviction that there was in fact only one God and that all the gods of the Gentiles were empty nothings. To the pagan, however, these gods were the guardians of the stability of the world order, the generous patrons who provided all that was needed for sustaining life, as well as the granters of individual petitions. The presence of idols throughout and the incorporation of some act of reverence toward the gods into every public festival, every assembly (whether for the business of the city or the meeting of a trade guild), and every private dinner party was a constant reminder to the individual of the care and protection of the gods—as well as the necessity of giving the gods their due and maintaining their favor. Piety was indispensable to an individual's good reputation,[5] especially since reverence toward the gods was interwoven so deeply into the domestic, social, civic and political aspects of Greco-Roman life. Plutarch regarded piety toward the gods (and the belief in their rule) as the bedrock of government: "It would be easier to build a city without the ground it stands on than to establish or sustain a government without religion" ("Reply to Colotes" 31).[6] The rejection of

---

[4]These are labels associated with Jesus in the few rabbinic references to him (see b. Sanh. 43a; 107b). These labels have important connections with the materials preserved in the Gospels (see especially Mt 9:34; 10:25; 12:24-28 on the charge of sorcery and Mt 27:63-64; Lk 23:2, 5, 14 on the charge of deceiving the people), suggesting that they preserve accurately the "outsider's" view of Jesus. On labeling and social control, see Bruce J. Malina and Jerome H. Neyrey, "Conflict in Luke-Acts. Labelling and Deviance Theory," in *The Social World of Luke-Acts: Models for Interpretation*, ed. Jerome H. Neyrey (Peabody, Mass.: Hendrickson, 1991), pp. 97-124.

[5]Isocrates advises his student: "Revere the gods, both by performing sacrifices and keeping your vows. Honor the gods at all times, but all the more at public festivals. This will give you the reputation for being pious and law-abiding" (*Ad Dem.* 13, my translation).

[6]Plutarch *Moralia* 1125E, my translation. See the whole paragraph in *Mor.* 1125D-E.

the gods by the Christians made them "atheists" and colored them as a subversive element in the society, a potential cancer in the body politic.

Strict avoidance of participation in idolatrous worship meant that the Christians would need to remove themselves from much of the public life of their city.[7] As Ramsey MacMullen correctly observes: "There existed . . . no form of social life . . . that was entirely secular. Small wonder, then, that Jews and Christians, holding themselves aloof from anything the gods touched, suffered under the reputation of misanthropy."[8] First Peter 4:3-4 captures something of the response from the pagan side: "You have already spent enough time in doing what the Gentiles like to do, living in licentiousness, passions, drunkenness, revels, carousing, and lawless idolatry. They are surprised that you no longer join them in the same excesses of dissipation, and so they blaspheme." Of course, the author is painting Gentile conduct in the most negative of colors here, so as to reinforce the Christians' distaste for their own former lives and thus their aversion to returning to that life. Nevertheless, he still captures the essence of one important source of the unpopularity of Christians: their defection from the solidarity they formerly showed with their pagan neighbors at public worship, at public festivals, at social gatherings. Such a violation of that solidarity, and the feelings of rejection and even indignation it would arouse, is more than enough to motivate unofficial persecution. Seeing their neighbors and former friends defect from that way of life might, additionally, even threaten their own assurance that their own behavior and convictions about the world were ultimately "correct"—a questioning that can result in conversion, of course, but more frequently in hostility. By shaming the defectors they reaffirm the absolute veracity of their own way of life: if they succeed in winning back the "deviant," their own security is also reconfirmed.[9]

---

[7]The early Christians struggled to justify participation in idolatry so that they would not have to sever so many important connections with their networks of friends and patrons, their involvement in government and their good name. See, for example, the evidence for this attempt in the negative responses of Paul and John (1 Cor 8:1-13; 10:14-22; Rev 2:14-15, 20).

[8]Ramsey MacMullen, *Paganism in the Roman Empire* (New Haven, Conn.: Yale University Press, 1981), p. 40. Tacitus *(Ann.* 15.44) attributes Nero's ability to get away with scapegoating the Christians to the general unpopularity of the Christians for their "hatred of the human race."

[9]Pliny, governor of Bithynia and Pontus (Roman provinces located in the north and west of what is now Turkey) in A.D. 110-111, expresses a deep satisfaction when his prosecution of those charged with being Christians causes a revival of traditional Greek and Roman religion in his province (see Pliny *Ep.* 10.96).

To the rejection of their gods and rejection of their lifestyle, the Christians added rejection of their neighbors' very world order. The central conviction of this movement was a revolutionary premise: Jesus would return, put an end to the reign of the current world rulers and establish his own kingdom in their stead.[10] The gospel of Jesus was a warning about God ripping into the fabric of society, calling day-to-day life to an abrupt halt and judging all according to the standards of this minority group. It spoke of "wars and rumors of wars," of the self-destruction of the glorious empire, and of cosmic conflagration before a new order was established. The Christians' neighbors, however, placed their hope in the perpetual rule and enforced peace of Rome and her power; for them, the stability necessary to sustain their often precarious existence came from the emperor's careful rule and the protection afforded by legions of soldiers, able to rebuff any assault from without. The inhabitants of the Mediterranean knew all about the ravages of "wars and rumors of wars" and wanted no part of it: the "Roman peace" was their golden age. Thus apocalypse and empire, "kingdom of God" and "Eternal Rome," were incompatible ideals, and the group that proclaimed the end of the Roman peace made itself the enemy of the common good.

So much for Gentile anti-Christian sentiments. The non-Christian Jewish population also had strong reasons for attempting to dissolve through erosion of commitment the sect that had grown up in its midst. First, it had grave reservations about Jesus' way of keeping Torah and his assaults on central Jewish symbols like the sabbath and the temple.[11] When Jews became Christ-followers, their Jewish families might feel the social pressure to cut them off, so as to say to their neighbors, "We do not approve of what they do. Do not attach their shame to us."[12] Jesus clearly anticipated that many of his followers might face

---

[10]Thus to "turned to God from idols," Paul adds "and to wait for his Son from heaven" (1 Thess 1:10). The centrality of the return of Christ to take history into his own hands is, of course, everywhere attested in the New Testament (Mt 24:5-31 and parallels; Acts 3:19-21; Rom 13:11-14; 1 Cor 15:24-28; Phil 3:20; 1 Thess 2:12; 2 Thess 1:6-10; Heb 1:13; 9:28; 10:37-38; 12:26-29; 1 Pet 1:5; 4:5, 7; 2 Pet 3:7-13; Rev 11:15-19; chaps. 19-21).

[11]Disagreements about the temple's importance and the fulfilling of the Torah appear to have been the precipitating factors in the mob lynching of Stephen (Acts 6:13-14).

[12]Jerome H. Neyrey writes that those who lost property and possessions, who fell into poverty because of their attachment to Jesus, who were estranged from their families and basic support base "would not be the objects of compassion or sympathy. They got what they deserved, because they did not suffer 'misfortune'. They experience shame from family and kin for their rebellion against family tradition" (Neyrey, "Loss of Wealth, Loss of Fam-

bearing this cost (Mt 10:34-37; 19:29). Second, the non-Christian Jews took exception to the way in which Jewish Christians lowered the boundaries between themselves and the Gentiles. Thus Paul discerns the primary aim of Jewish persecution to be "hindering us from speaking to the Gentiles so that they may be saved" (1 Thess 2:16).

Separation from the Gentiles was a core value of Jewish culture from the beginning. When Jews desired to "become like the Gentiles" again, assimilating to Gentile culture and breaking down the boundaries, disaster overtook the people of Israel. This truism of history was deeply reinforced for the Jews by the events of 175-164 B.C., in which the Jewish leadership sought to make Jerusalem a fully Greek city and stamp out the customs (like circumcision, monolatry and dietary regulations) that separated Jews from the larger world in which they wanted to become players. When resistance grew, the Hellenistic overlord Antiochus IV took measures to enforce this policy, and a brutal period of oppression ensued: "Those whose ways of living they admired and wished to imitate completely became their enemies and punished them" (2 Macc 4:16). Only after many Jews suffered heroic martyrdom (rather than transgress Torah) and many others fought successfully alongside Judas Maccabaeus and his brothers was peace and Torah observance restored.

Those who wrote about this period used it to teach the lesson that neglect of Torah and the marks of the covenant for the sake of making it easier to relate to Gentiles only leads to national disaster.[13] When Paul, therefore, proclaims that circumcision is meaningless in God's sight, urges Jewish Christians to eat freely with Gentile Christians rather than to keep kosher (or force the Gentiles to keep kosher so that they can have table fellowship), and declares that the dividing wall of hostility has been broken (Eph 2:14), he is striking at the heart of what it means to be Jewish. To prevent this new outbreak of Torah neglect, non-Christian Jews act speedily to shower the leaders and their followers with disapproval and disgrace in the hope of cauterizing the open wound on the

---

ily and Loss of Honour: The Cultural Context of the Original Makarisms in Q," in Philip F. Esler, *Modelling Early Christianity: Social-Scientific Studies of the New Testament in Its Context* [London: Routledge, 1995], p. 156).

[13]See the full accounts, with their interpretation, in 2 Maccabees and 4 Maccabees; for an analysis of the latter text and its reinforcement of the basic Deuteronomic conviction that transgression of Torah leads to disaster, see David A. deSilva, *4 Maccabees*, Guides to the Apocrypha and Pseudepigrapha (Sheffield, U.K.: Sheffield Academic Press, 1998), pp. 134-41.

body of Israel. Because of this persecution, some Jewish Christians attempt to Judaize the Gentiles in their midst (Gal 5:11; 6:12) and put their non-Christian Jewish neighbors, friends and relations at rest.

For these and other reasons the Christians' neighbors sought to dissuade them by any means available from continuing in this deviant way of life and to return to being "decent" people who supported the values and stability of Greco-Roman society.[14] We find, therefore, the New Testament authors responding in varying degrees to two critical issues arising from this situation. First, since the values of the new community are, at many points, radically different from the values of the dominant culture (or Jewish ethnic subculture) in which the converts were first reared, the leaders of the group must be attentive to the persistence in the new community of those old definitions and models of what is honorable and how honor is attained, maintained and displayed. Thus, a fair portion of these texts is dedicated to reinforcing the group's definition of what makes a person honorable as opposed to what other cultures promote as honorable behavior. Second, the New Testament authors address the potentially erosive effects of the dominant culture's negative evaluation of the group members (expressed at the light end of the continuum by reproach, moving through abuse, disenfranchisement and the occasional lynching at the heavy end), while at the same time attempting to strengthen the "alternative court of reputation" so that members will continue to pursue honor in terms of the group's values.[15]

---

[14]Thus, John H. Elliott rightly says: "The nature and weapons of the attack on the Christians is a classic example of public shaming designed to demean and discredit the believers in the court of public opinion with the ultimate aim of forcing their conformity to prevailing norms and values ("Disgraced yet Graced: The Gospel According to 1 Peter in the Key of Honor and Shame," *BTB* 24 [1994]: 170).

[15]The following discussion will proceed thematically; readers interested in detailed analysis of honor discourse at work in a specific New Testament text should consult David A. deSilva, *The Hope of Glory: Honor Discourse and New Testament Interpretation* (Collegeville, Minn.: Liturgical Press, 1999), which contains exegetical essays on Matthew, John, 1 and 2 Thessalonians, 1 and 2 Corinthians, Hebrews, and Revelation. Elliott's article "Disgraced yet Graced" focuses on 1 Peter. Excellent discussions on Romans can be found in Halvor Moxnes, "Honor, Shame, and the Outside World in Paul's Letter to the Romans," in *The Social World of Formative Christianity and Judaism*, ed. Jacob Neusner et al. (Philadelphia: Fortress, 1988), pp. 207-18, and Halvor Moxnes, "Honour and Righteousness in Romans," *JSNT* 32 (1988): 61-77. Jerome H. Neyrey's commentary, *2 Peter, Jude*, AB 37C (New York: Doubleday, 1993), affords excellent insights into all the cultural backgrounds of those short texts. By far the most innovative and accessible study of honor and shame in Paul is Robert

The Case of Jesus

The very story at the center of the church's faith already forces a decision concerning the reliability of the world's estimation of honor and shame. Jesus suffered crucifixion, known as an intentionally degrading death, fixing the criminal's honor at the lowest end of the spectrum and serving as an effective deterrent to the observers, reminding them of the shameful end that awaits those who similarly deviate from the dominant culture's values.[16] Paul no doubt understated the case when he referred to the proclamation of this cross as the wisdom of God as a "stumbling block" to Jews and "folly" to Gentiles. No member of the Jewish community or the Greco-Roman society would have come to faith or joined the Christian movement without first accepting that God's perspective on what kind of behavior merits honor differs exceedingly from the perspective of human beings, since the message about Jesus is that both the Jewish and Gentile leaders of Jerusalem evaluated Jesus, his convictions and his deeds as meriting a shameful death, but God overturned their evaluation of Jesus by raising him from the dead and seating him at God's own right hand as Lord.

The evangelists had also, in many respects, provided resources to buttress the community against the outsiders' view of their leader. They present Jesus as an honorable figure whose opponents were in fact acting dishonorably in seeking his demise. Many of the features of the encomium, the funeral speech in praise of the deceased, are addressed by the Gospels:[17] those who were accustomed to hearing encomia would also

---

Jewett, *Saint Paul Returns to the Movies: Triumph over Shame* (Louisville: Westminster John Knox, 1998). Jewett interacts not only with Pauline texts and critical scholarship, but he uses the popular medium of film as a way of connecting Paul's message about honor with the concerns of twentieth-century Western culture.

[16]Martin Hengel provides a detailed description of the humiliation attached to this form of execution in his book, *Crucifixion in the Ancient World and the Folly of the Message of the Cross* (Philadelphia: Fortress, 1977); see also Jerome H. Neyrey, "Despising the Shame of the Cross," *Semeia* 68 (1996): 113-37.

[17]*Encomia* focused on the origins, nurture and advantages-by-birth of the individual, the virtues manifested by the subject in his or her deeds, and the kind of death the subject died. The chief sources for information on encomia are the rhetorical handbooks (*The Rhetorica ad Herennium* 3.6.10-3.8.15 contains a strikingly complete outline; see also the discussion of Theon of Alexandria's advice on giving funeral speeches in Henri I. Marrou, *A History of Education in Antiquity* [New York: Mentor, 1964], pp. 272-73); fuller discussions of the Gospels as encomiastic biography can be found in my *Hope of Glory*, chaps. 2 and 3; a fine, comprehensive survey of Matthew from this standpoint can be found in Jerome H. Neyrey, *Honor and Shame in the Gospel of Matthew* (Louisville: Westminster John Knox, 1998).

understand how the Gospels were constructing encomia in praise of the dead-yet-living leader of the Christian group. The birth stories in Matthew and Luke present Jesus as the descendent of the most noble stock in Israel (Mt 1:1-16; Lk 1:27, 32, 69) and at the same time reach to Jesus' divine parentage (Mt 1:18-20; Lk 1:35; Jn 1:1-18). These same infancy narratives affirm that he was set apart by God for a special and noble destiny, namely the deliverance of his people and of the world (Mt 1:21; Lk 1:32-33; 2:10-11; Jn 4:42). Angelic messages and astronomical omens (i.e., the star) enhance this impression. The Gospels are filled with accounts of Jesus' "deeds of virtue," chiefly his acts of healing and exorcism, which are acts of beneficence and result in the increase of his fame.[18] It is those who oppose Jesus who are shown at every turn to be dishonorable: they refuse to give God his due (Mt 21:33-44); instead of continuing to act openly against Jesus, like honest people, they retreat to acting secretly in their efforts to dispose of him (Mt 26:3-5, 14-16, 59-61); ultimately, their motives are attributed to "envy," a mark of dishonorable people (Mt 27:18).[19]

While the outside world might regard his crucifixion as a shameful death that signaled his opponents' defeat of their rival, the evangelists present Jesus' death in such a way that reader will clearly understand it as a noble death. Those who died to bring benefit to others or to save others from danger (such as soldiers on the battlefield, who die to preserve the people back home) were understood to have died honorably: they laid down their lives voluntarily to benefit their friends or fellow citizens, displaying their virtue in death more clearly than most display in life. The materials preserved by the evangelists explicitly address these topics. First, they emphasize the voluntariness of Jesus' death: "No one takes [my life] from me, but I lay it down of my own accord" (Jn 10:18). Jesus' foreknowledge of his death,[20] even of the very hour of his betrayal

---

[18]On Jesus' healings and on his death as acts of benefaction, see chapter four.

[19]See the discussion of the emotions of envy and emulation in Aristotle *Rhetoric* 2.10-11: Aristotle regards "emulation" (somewhat, but not exactly, akin to jealousy) as an emotion of the virtuous, since when these people observe others in possession of good things, they fit themselves to acquire the same (the result being, they better themselves), while "envy" is an emotion of the dishonorable, since they wish to deprive the virtuous of the fruits of their virtue.

[20]This is seen most prominently in the passion predictions (Mk 8:31; 9:30-31; 10:32-34 and parallels in Mt and Lk; Jn 3:14-15). The journey to Jerusalem is presented explicitly as a voluntary procession to the cross.

and arrest,[21] the prayer in Gethsemane (Mt 26:39, 42; Mk 14:36), and Jesus' power in the midst of arrest (Mt 26:52-53; Jn 18:3-11) all emphasize that Jesus laid down his life for others voluntarily. It was a gift, not a defeat. Second, the Gospels emphasize that Jesus accepted death specifically with a view to benefiting others: "The Son of Man came not to be served but to serve, and to give his life a ransom for many" (Mk 10:45). Jesus dies in order to bring about forgiveness of sins, a fact celebrated not only in the Gospel story but in the central ritual of the Christian group, namely the Eucharist (Mt 26:27-28; 1 Cor 11:23-26; see also Jn 1:29; Heb 10:1-10). Jesus' death "on behalf of [his] sheep" brings them eternal life (Jn 3:14-17; 10:10-11, my translation). The death of Jesus was in every respect, then, an honorable death, despite the vehicle by which it was effected. The failure on the part of the world to understand this fact speaks of their ignorance, not Jesus' degradation.

The New Testament defense, as it were, of Jesus' honor affects the early Christians in several important ways. God's affirmation of being "well pleased" with Jesus (God's only two direct communications in the Synoptic Gospels; see Mt 3:17; 17:5), an affirmation that is finalized in God's raising of Jesus from the dead (overturning human estimations of Jesus: Acts 2:32, 36; 3:14-15), assures those who hear him and follow his way that they are the people who truly please God, whose honor God will likewise vindicate on the last day. In the paradigm of the maligned group leader who, rejected by society, becomes God's right-hand regent, the Christians come to terms with their own relationship to society's approval. At the close of the parable of the wicked tenants, Jesus cites Psalm 118:22-23 as a scriptural warrant for this paradigm: "Have you not read this scripture: 'The stone that the builders rejected has become the cornerstone; this was the Lord's doing, and it is amazing in our eyes'?" (Mk 12:10-11). What human beings reject as worthless and dishonored by a marvel of divine intervention appears at the top of the honor scale.

Jesus' case becomes then the demonstration of the ignorance and upside-down mentality of the society, as well as the guarantee of the reversal and vindication that God will grant to all Jesus' followers. As such, it becomes a precedent that will be applied to the Christian group

---

[21]See Matthew 26:18, 21, 31-32, 45; in John, this is his knowledge of "the hour" (Jn 2:4; 7:6-8; 12:23; 13:1, 11, 18-30). In this last passage, Jesus even takes the lead in sending his betrayer out to do the job.

members as well. Particularly interesting is the application of Psalm 118:22-23 first to Jesus and then seamlessly to the situation of believers in 1 Peter 2:4-8:

> Come to him, a living stone, though rejected by mortals yet chosen and precious in God's sight, and like living stones, let yourselves be built into a spiritual house, to be a holy priesthood, to offer spiritual sacrifices acceptable to God through Jesus Christ. For it stands in scripture: "See, I am laying in Zion a stone, a cornerstone chosen and precious; and whoever believes in him will not be put to shame." Honor, then, is for you who believe;[22] but for those who do not believe, "The stone that the builders rejected has become the very head of the corner," and "A stone that makes them stumble, and a rock that makes them fall." They stumble because they disobey the word, as they were destined to do.

The author has described Jesus in 1 Peter 2:4 as a "stone . . . rejected by mortals yet chosen and precious in God's sight," a description combining echoes of Psalm 118:22-23 with Isaiah 28:16. This second passage, which is then explicitly quoted in 1 Peter 2:6, ends by promising that "whoever believes in him will not be put to shame." The addressees of 1 Peter, currently being intentionally shamed by their neighbors (see above), are thus told that their trust in Jesus will result in their future vindication. Verse 7 makes this conclusion even more explicit: "Honor, then, is for you who believe," just as honor came to the One who had been "rejected by mortals."

The author of Hebrews also appeals to the example of Jesus as a warrant for his audience to set aside their concern for society's negative evaluation of and response to them: just as Jesus "despised shame" (that is, understood the folly of society's attempts to shame him and divert him from his goal) and thus arrived at his seat at the right hand of God (Heb 12:2), so the Christians are not to "grow weary" as they struggle against

---

[22]I have replaced the "To you then who believe, he is precious" with "Honor, then, is for you who believe." Translators of this passage from the KJV on have been reading the adjective "precious" (*entimon*) from vv. 4 and 6 into v. 7, where, however, the author has shifted to the related noun "honor" (*timē*). Since two adjectives exist (*entimos, timios*) for "precious," and the author of 1 Peter has chosen to use neither of these in favor of employing the noun, I must conclude that we have here a fossilized translation error passed down through the generations of translators. First Peter has, instead, moved the discussion forward in v. 7 from the "preciousness" of Jesus to the "honor" that belongs to believers, and to the dishonor that will befall the unbelievers. This reading also preserves the parallelism between 2:7a and 2:7b: "to you . . . who believe . . . for those who do not believe . . ."

the pressures they face (Heb 12:3-4).[23] The fact that, after voluntarily humbling himself in obedience to God, Jesus was exalted to the place of greatest honor by God (Phil 2:5-11) becomes a warrant for believers also to humble themselves in the assurance that God will look after their honor and manifest it in the future (Phil 2:1-4). Here Paul appeals to Jesus' example specifically to curtail competition and rivalry over status within the Christian movement, showing that the precedent of Jesus was as useful for regulating relationships within the group as for strengthening the group against erosion from without.

Convening the Court of Reputation

Like the leaders of other minority cultures in the first century, New Testament authors were also careful continually to point the members of the Christian group away from the opinion that non-Christians might form of them toward the opinion of those who would reflect the values of the group and reinforce the individual's commitment to establish his or her honor and self-respect in terms of those group values. It is this latter group that must constitute the "court of reputation," the sole body of significant others whose approval or disapproval should be important to the individual.

Most prominent within this court of reputation is God, whose central place is assured because of God's power to enforce his estimation of who deserves honor and who merits censure. Jesus brings this powerfully to expression in the well-known saying: "Do not fear those who kill the body but cannot kill the soul; rather fear him who can destroy both soul and body in hell" (Mt 10:28). In executing the deviant, the society bestows the fullest measure of disgrace and disapproval, but Jesus considers society's "worst" as trivial compared to the punishment coming to those who merit God's verdict of "deviant" and "dishonorable." God's power to place the final stamp of approval or censure is brought into sharp focus by the conviction that God has appointed a day (see Acts 17:31)—the Day of Judgment—when he will hold the whole world accountable to his standards. On that day, God will award grants of honor to those who

---

[23]Hebrews 11 presents several examples of those heroes of faith who similarly embraced temporary disgrace in the world's eyes in order to remain faithful to God and receive the honors God had appointed for them. For a detailed analysis of this theme in Hebrews, see my *Despising Shame*, chap. 4.

have lived to please him and heap disgrace upon those who have lived contrary to his values. The belief in a Day of Judgment is foundational to the elevation of God's estimation of the individual as the opinion of first importance: "We make it our aim to please him. For all of us must appear before the judgment seat of Christ, so that each may receive recompense for what has been done in the body, whether good or evil" (2 Cor 5:9-10). At that time God will also bring all secret things to light and thus make a reliable assessment of nobility and lack of nobility, or worth, possible (1 Cor 4:3-5).

Commendation on that day is the only commendation that ultimately matters, so that Christians are throughout the New Testament urged to live so as to "be found blameless before our God and Father at the coming of our Lord Jesus with all his holy ones" (1 Thess 3:13, my translation),[24] and so as to hear the words "well done, good and faithful servant" pronounced by the mouth of the Master (Mt 25:14-30). Indeed, the more focused the individual believer is made to be on receiving that commendation on the day of visitation, and the more concerned he or she is made to be about not falling into the group at the "left hand" of the Judge (Mt 25:31-46)—the group that is rebuked as "wicked and lazy," "worthless" or "evildoers" (Mt 25:26, 30; 7:23)—the more firmly committed he or she will be to remaining loyal to the group and to embodying the behaviors and virtues it promotes so as to be "pleasing in his sight" (Heb 13:20-21). In this way they will be enabled to "have confidence and not be put to shame before him at his coming" (1 Jn 2:28).

In order to sharpen this focus on God's approval or disapproval, and thus to keep the believers' ambitions focused on securing their honor through pleasing God rather than by surrendering to society, New Testament authors frequently remind the churches that God's grants of honor or dishonor are of far greater significance than human affirmation or censure. Thus Paul carries out his ministry strictly with a view to pleasing God, not people—whether they are his potential converts or his Jewish-

---

[24]Note how Paul in this verse draws a picture of those who will witness the evaluation of the believer: God, Jesus and "all his holy ones." Whether these holy ones are construed as angelic beings, as is made explicit in Jesus' vision of this scene in Matthew 16:27 (angels were also called "holy ones" in early Jewish apocalypses like 1 Enoch), or as the human believers who had died or even who are gathered together from every place on that day (see Mk 13:26-27), the arena is filled with observers, making the possibility for honor—and for disgrace—on that day great indeed.

Christian colleagues with a stricter sense of Torah's application in the new community (Gal 1:10; 1 Thess 2:4-6). Similarly, believers are instructed to live for God's approval rather than human approval. They are to seek the circumcision of the heart that God values rather than circumcise their flesh so as to gain the approval of conservative Jewish Christians (Rom 2:29). They are to seek God's approval by their pious actions (whether prayer, fasting or almsgiving) rather than engage these actions for the sake of human approval (Mt 6:1-18).[25]

These authors repeatedly underscore the contrasting, indeed often contradictory, courses of action commended by God and one's society: "What is prized by human beings is an abomination in the sight of God" (Lk 16:15). Awareness of this difference continues to insulate believers against society's attempts to shame them, since the Christians know they pursue a more lasting and significant grant of honor. In John's Gospel, concern for the estimation of other people cripples discipleship: "How can you believe when you accept glory [honor, *doxa*] from one another and do not seek the glory [honor, *doxa*] that comes from the one who alone is God?" (Jn 5:44). Those among the Jewish leaders who "loved human glory more than the glory that comes from God" keep their belief in Jesus hidden from their colleagues so as not to lose face in the Jewish community (Jn 12:42-43). Such concern for reputation among humans, however, poses the greatest threat to one's reputation before God: "Everyone therefore who acknowledges me before others, I also will acknowledge before my Father in heaven; but whoever denies me before others, I also will deny before my Father in heaven" (Mt 10:32-33). Those who keep their eyes on honor at the last day will thus be emboldened to witness boldly to their association with Jesus and with the way of life he taught, so that they, in turn, will receive his testimony before the "court of reputation" whose verdict is eternal.

By focusing on God's approval, the Christian's desire will be to "live up to (walk in a manner worthy of) the gospel" or "the Lord" (see Eph 4:1; Phil 1:27; Col 1:10; 2 Thess 1:11-12) rather than living up to the expectations and standards of the cultures they left behind. The opinion of those

---

[25]The reason for this is not just purity of motive, although this is important. It is also crucial that the Christian not continue to seek the approval of his or her non-Christian neighbors on the basis of religious activity, since this would draw him or her back into the piety of the pre-Christian existence for the sake of pleasing the neighbor and recovering a good reputation.

who award honor and censure by standards alien to the Christian culture is bracketed as being of no real concern. Occasionally one finds in the New Testament that even some inside the new community still evaluate worth based on the world's values. When sisters or brothers judge "from a human point of view," their opinion of the worth of their fellow believer must be disregarded as well.

How can God's affirmation (or disapproval) be experienced by the believer? Certainly we should not overlook the possibility of the direct experience of this through prayer and through the practice of the presence of God. God's direct affirmation of Jesus, the Son "with whom I am well pleased," in Matthew 3:17 and 17:5, for example, encourages the possibility that the testimony of the believer's conscience can provide important reassurance of God's affirmation in the midst of the experience of unbelievers' censure (Rom 8:16-17; 1 Jn 3:21-22).

Another important channel of access to God's estimation is Scripture, which James insightfully likens to a mirror (Jas 1:22-25). As the Scripture is read, the individual believer sees his or her conduct and commitments reflected in what the oracles of God declare to be pleasing in God's sight, or perhaps sees his or her behavior and attachments reflected in what God censures in the record of divine revelation. Thus "gazing intently, looking into the perfect law of God" as if into a mirror shows the person a reflection of God's approval or disapproval of the individual's conduct. The person who acts in accordance with what he or she sees in the word of God "will be blessed in what he or she does," that is, enjoy God's approval and favor (Jas 1:22-25, my translation).

Perhaps the most prominent vehicle envisioned by the authors of the New Testament for the individual believer's awareness of when he or she stands in honor before God or merits divine censure is the community of faith. Paul models how the community of faith can reflect God's evaluation of the believer in the thanksgiving sections that begin most of his letters (see, for example, Rom 1:8; 1 Cor 1:4-9; Col 1:3-8; 1 Thess 1:2-10; 2:13-16). By thanking God for certain qualities exhibited by these congregations, or for certain activities that they have been engaging, he affirms that those qualities and activities are indeed pleasing in God's sight—indeed, a blossoming of virtue that is the very work of God's Spirit in their midst. Hearing their leaders' commendations and rebukes, couched as these are in terms of what is honorable or censurable in God's eyes, also brings the believers before the divine "court of reputation," as it were, identifying for them where they have a strong claim to honor and where their honor is threatened. For this reason it is important that the early churches esteem their leaders (see 1 Thess 5:13), particularly local leaders, not only because their service merits the honor of the group but because they have a primary responsibility for keeping the group members mindful of God's standards, calling back the wayward.

One's fellow believers will be the most visible and, in many senses, the most available reflection of God's estimation of the individual, and so the New Testament authors are deeply concerned with building up a strong community of faith that will reinforce individual commitment to the group.[26] John, for example, effectively reduces Jesus' commandments to one, namely, that the Christians "love one another as I have loved you" (Jn 15:12; 13:34; see also Paul's emphasis on this mutual love in 1 Thess 3:12; 4:9-10). The bonds between believers should be so strong—the affective ties so firm—that an individual believer would be willing to lay down his life for the sake of a sister or brother in the faith (Jn 15:12-13; 1 Jn 3:16). Such a lofty principle calls for directions for practical application, and John provides this:

> How does God's love abide in anyone who has the world's goods and sees a brother or sister in need and yet refuses help? Little children, let us love, not in word or speech, but in truth and action. (1 Jn 3:17-18)

The Christian group is called to share, to serve, to support one another as Jesus gave himself for them—unselfishly and without reservation. Writing to addressees who had known the full range of society's deviancy-control techniques (short of mob lynching or legal execution; Heb 12:4), the author of Hebrews captures even more completely the essence of the kind of community that enables its members to withstand social pressure:

> Let mutual love ["fraternal love," *philadelphia*] continue. Do not neglect to show hospitality to strangers, for by doing that some have entertained angels without knowing it. Remember those who are in prison, as though you were in prison with them; those who are being tortured, as though you yourselves were being tortured. (Heb 13:1-3)

The author invokes the ethos of kinship, specifically the love character-

---

[26]On the role of a community committed to the same worldview and ethos in sustaining the commitment of each individual member of the community to "see" the world the same way and internalize the same values, see Peter L. Berger, *The Sacred Canopy: Elements of a Sociology of a Religion* (New York: Doubleday, 1967), chaps. 1 and 2.

istic of siblings, which represented the pinnacle of friendship and the most enduring and intimate of relationships.[27] Adopting a kinship ethic meant mutual sharing of resources as any had need, as well as a firm commitment to one another. They were to be family, a call that was all the more essential given the networks of relationships that a believer could potentially lose in the ancient world. This kinship was to extend beyond the local group to the provision of hospitality to traveling sisters and brothers. Hospitality in the early church served to create strong bonds between local churches, facilitating communication and mission work between churches and allowing an itinerant leadership to keep linking local cells together. The love of sisters and brothers of Christ is most needed where the censure of society is most keenly felt. The author therefore urges the hearers to reach out to those most acutely targeted by the society for deviancy-control techniques, letting them know that the family they joined will not desert them, and letting each other know at the same time that their bond is stronger than society's hostility.

This kind of intense in-group reinforcement and mutual commitment makes the verdict of the group, not the verdict of society, the one of ultimate importance for the individual caught in-between. The strong affection and support within the group makes these relationships primary for each member—he or she would be more willing to sacrifice relationships with outsiders than lose face before the people the member really cares about, and whose commitment to each other is "to the death." Once the community of faith becomes the primary reference group for the individual believer, then mutual exhortation can have its full effect. Members can reinforce for one another and stimulate one another on to what constitutes honor in God's sight and in the sight of the group, dissuading one another from what would bring shame (see 1 Thess 5:11, 14; Heb 3:12-13; 10:24-25).

The local congregation, moreover, is part of a matrix of such cells empire-wide, and New Testament authors will frequently call the local church's attention to this fact. Frequently this happens simply through greetings being passed on from one church or group of churches to another (Rom 16:16; 1 Cor 16:19), or the mere mention of the activities happening in other churches (such as the endurance of hostility; 1 Thess

---

[27]Aristotle includes his discussion of fraternal love within his discussion of friendship (*Nic. Eth.* 8.12.1-8 [1161b11-1162a34]); see also Plutarch "On Fraternal Affection" (*Mor.* 478-490).

2:14-16) or in conjunction with other churches (such as the collection effort, which unites the churches of Macedonia and Achaia in a group relief effort; 2 Cor 8:18-24). Such mention keeps the local cell aware that it is part of a much larger movement and not an insignificant group. Authors may also call attention to this global network to remind a local congregation that its dedication to Christ and the group has won it fame abroad in these other cells (1 Thess 1:6-10; 2 Thess 1:3-4), so that the believers are compensated for the loss of esteem they suffer in their neighbors' eyes by the fame they win in the eyes of Christians empire-wide. Paul will even call a local congregation to take up a certain course of action out of concern for its honor in the eyes of the other congregations of believers (2 Cor 8:24; 9:1-5), and also to conform to the norms followed by the larger Christian culture (1 Cor 7:17; 11:16; 14:33).

Christians can remain committed to "walking as Jesus walked," to bearing witness to the author of their salvation, and to standing by the community of those called out by God as they set their hearts fully on being approved by God and seeking honor before God, Christ and the holy angels on that day when all shall be judged by God. Because the unbelievers will use the power of shaming to impose their values on the believers, and to call them back to a way of life that supports and perpetuates the values of the non-Christian culture, it is imperative that the believers' sense of worth be detached from the opinion of unbelievers. Rather, their engagements with one another, their mutual esteem and support, and their awareness of the many who affirm them in their Christian commitment (God, the angelic hosts, the church throughout the world, the people of faith throughout the ages)[28] will strengthen them for the journey.

Invalidating the Opinion of Outsiders
As the Christians are looking away to God's approval, New Testament

---

[28]John uses these topics to great advantage in Revelation. By describing at length in chapters 4 and 5 the celestial liturgy and the ranks of myriads of angelic beings who worship the one God and the Lamb, and by extending those circles to include all creatures in heaven and on earth and under the earth, he makes the idolatrous members of the majority culture look very much like the minority, cosmically speaking (for example, when they finally appear in Rev 9:20-21 as those who will not abandon their deviant way of life), who are powerless in the face of the God and the Lamb they affront (Rev 6:15-17). The Christians are thus emboldened to see themselves as the "normal" ones and the idolaters as the "deviants," and thus remain true to their convictions despite the hostility they encounter and losses they face. For a more detailed discussion, see deSilva, *Hope of Glory,* pp. 184-90.

authors also explain why the approval or disapproval of outsiders should not matter to the members of the group, or why it is no reflection of the group members' true honor and worth. Usually this takes the form of stressing the ignorance of outsiders or their shamelessness.

Those who do not have faith do not have all the facts necessary to make an informed evaluation concerning what is honorable and what is censurable. The non-Christians are therefore frequently said to be "in darkness" and even "of the darkness" (Jn 8:12; 12:46; Eph 4:17-20; 1 Thess 5:3-8) as opposed to being enlightened (2 Cor 4:1-6; Heb 6:4; 10:32) or "children of light" (1 Thess 5:5). This contrast stresses the fact that outsiders lack essential information—for example, the fact that God's judgment is soon coming (1 Thess 5:1-3) or God's standards of what is honorable conduct (1 Thess 4:1-5). The fact remains, however, that God's judgment is impending: when it arrives, those who now in ignorance oppose the Christian movement will be made aware of their error and their shame while the "children of light" enter into their honorable destiny. Christians make their choices and evaluations with the full benefit of this knowledge and so are in a better place to understand what is praiseworthy and to pursue and achieve it. This topic appears in the Gospels as well. As Jesus censures the Pharisees as "blind guides," for example, the disciples of Jesus can apply the critique to the disciples of the Pharisees and their descendants, the rabbis (Mt 23:16-17, 19, 24). Jesus' criticism of the Pharisees' "ignorance" of what God requires of those who would keep God's covenant assures the Christian readers that their way of keeping Torah—the way taught by Jesus, in whose resurrection by God one sees God's affirmation of his instruction—is in fact the way that pleases God, despite the assertions of their rivals to the contrary.

The ignorance of outsiders comes to expression in several other ways as well. New Testament authors may specifically target their inability to form reliable estimations of people. Both John and Paul, for example, contrast those who "judge by appearances" with God, who judges by the heart (Jn 7:24; 2 Cor 5:12). God had already spoken a definitive word in 1 Samuel 16:7 on this point that the heart, and not the outer person, provides the true criterion of assessment. The opinion of outsiders is thus based on flawed premises and is not a reliable guide for the believers to follow if they hope to be found truly honorable when God comes to judge. Their ignorance, moreover, is attributed both to delusion but also to purpose. Because they "refused to love the truth and so be saved" and "took pleasure in unrighteousness," God intensifies the delusion that holds them in darkness, with the result that God will ascribe dishonor to them on the Day of Judgment (2 Thess 2:10-12). The society's resistance to the Christian group is thus transformed completely from an experience of shaming that might weaken the believer's resolve, into a demonstration of the society's alienation from the truth and God's verdict of condemnation on the outsiders.[29]

The negative evaluation outsiders form of and enforce on Christians is offset not only by considering the ignorance of these unbelievers, such that they are unable to form a reliable evaluation of worth, but also their dishonorable conduct, indeed, their utter shamelessness in the light of God's revelation of God's standards.[30] To be shamed by the shameless is ultimately no shame at all.[31] In fact, contemplating the vice of their detractors almost transforms their experience of rejection into a sign of the believers' honor. Contrary to the dominant-cultural view of participation in idolatrous forms of worship as an honorable mark of piety, Paul declares idolatry to be the true source of dishonor (Rom 1:18-32). On account of its commitment to idolatry, the non-Christian Gentiles have become a debased, shameless crowd, handed over to the domination of the passions and every kind of vice. What is perhaps most poignant about this passage is that the pinnacle of their degradation is not merely their participation in such conduct: "They know God's decree, that those who practice such things deserve to die—yet they not only do them but even applaud others who practice them" (Rom 1:32). The unbelievers form

---

[29]The author of Hebrews also affirms that the world's rejection of the virtuous, faithful people of God is not a reflection on the believers' honor but rather shows the unbelievers' dishonor. Concerning those most pushed out to the margins and most pressured by a hostile world he says, "The world was not worthy of them" (Heb 11:38, my translation).

[30]Paul captures both reasons to disregard the unbelievers' estimation of one's conduct in Ephesians 4:17-20: "Now this I affirm and insist on in the Lord: you must no longer live as the Gentiles live, in the futility of their minds. They are darkened in their understanding, alienated from the life of God because of their ignorance and hardness of heart. They have lost all sensitivity and have abandoned themselves to licentiousness, greedy to practice every kind of impurity." An honorable person will not be concerned about the opinion that people of this sort may form of him or her since it will not be based on the criteria that truly distinguish between the noble and the base.

[31]The believers are also assured that the hostility of these unbelievers—the hostility with which they hope to pressure the Christians back into conformity with the dominant culture's way of life—is itself displeasing to God and incurs God's wrath (1 Thess 2:14-16). Knowing this will also help the believers endure rather than surrender to those measures that not only assail the Christians but bring down God's anger on the outsiders.

again an unreliable court of reputation, commending what is actually wicked and shameful (see Phil 3:18-19). Their very sense of honor and value is upside down, as their lives testify. Therefore, the Christian experiencing their pressure to "join them in the same excesses of dissipation" (1 Pet 4:4) should not be moved away from his or her honorable course of action.

Johannine literature also contributes to the Christians' impression that the censure (or honor, for that matter) that the outside world might offer the believers ought to be disregarded on account of the judges' own lack of honor. In Revelation, for example, those who cling to idolatrous worship are also presented as those who engage in all manner of wicked conduct and who have made a pact with the forces of chaos, Satan, the enemy of God (Rev 9:20-21; 12:1—13:8). They are committed to vice and to impiety, despite having been given many opportunities to repent (and no matter what God does in the future, they will still manifest this dishonorable character). In John's Gospel those who remain apart from the Christian group do so because of their commitment to wickedness:

> And this is the judgment, that the light has come into the world, and people loved darkness rather than light because their deeds were evil. For all who do evil hate the light and do not come to the light, so that their deeds may not be exposed. But those who do what is true come to the light, so that it may be clearly seen that their deeds have been done in God. (Jn 3:19-21)

All who stand outside the community of disciples show by that very fact that they prefer vice to virtue. They prefer dishonorable conduct to the light of God that first reveals the nature of that conduct but then empowers one to set it aside. All such statements in Scripture serve to insulate the community against the pressure of society's attempts to "rehabilitate" them. Christians will see the course of "rehabilitation" as the course back to darkness, back to vice, back to a disgraceful status in God's sight that would merit God's punishment at the Day of Judgment.

Two other strategies assist believers in setting aside the opinion of nonbelievers. First, the New Testament authors commend as honorable many who "despised shame" in order to remain steadfast in their quest for the honors God had prepared for them. The most prominent of these, of course, is Jesus, who endured the low point of society's ascription of disgrace en route to the high honor God had appointed for him (see Phil 2:5-11; Heb 12:2), but he is joined by many others from among the people of faith throughout the ages. Notable among these is Abraham, presented in Hebrews 11:8-16 as willing to leave behind an honorable existence in a homeland for the low-status life of a resident alien and foreigner for the sake of attaining citizenship in the "better" and "heavenly" homeland that God prepared. Moses, too, understood that solidarity with despised and abused slaves was of greater worth than remaining as heir to the crown of Egypt, since the latter afforded only "fleeting pleasures" while the former brought one eternal "reward" (Heb 11:24-26). Jesus, Abraham and Moses made the correct choices because they weighed honor and advantage through the eyes of faith—in the eyes of unbelievers, all three during their lifetimes would have been considered to have made foolish choices, incurring the loss of honor. Disregarding the opinion of outsiders (the world) is thus presented as a necessary step to achieving honor where it counts eternally.

Finally, the same visions of reversal and divine judgment that focus the believer on God's estimation as the evaluation of greatest importance also assist in insulating the believer from society's negative sanctions. The believers may endure the scorn and censure of their neighbors, knowing that the day is coming when the majority culture that scorns the group will be put to shame and the group will come into its own honor. On the Day of Judgment not only will God affirm the honor and virtue of those who have responded to him with trust and obedience, but he will also censure the disobedient and enforce the status degradation (e.g., through punishment) of those who now have the upper hand on the believers (see 2 Thess 1:6-10; 1 Pet 4:5).

When Dishonor Is No Dishonor
In addition to preventing the experience of insult, scorn and shame from having its intended effect on the Christians by pointing out the ignorance and shamelessness of the outsiders (that is to say, by explaining that the people censuring the believers are themselves incapable of rendering reliable judgments about the noble and the shameful), New Testament authors also seek to help the believers make sense of those experiences in ways that will not cause them to question their commitment to the group. They even go so far as to turn the very experiences of society's deviancy-control techniques into marks of honor within the group. The frequency with which these texts address the topic of shame from outside the group reveals the importance of insulating members from the strong

pull the experience of disgrace will have on them. The predictability or normalcy of the experiences, the commendation of perseverance as a means of demonstrating loyalty and courage, the interpretation of the hardships as God's training of the believers or as a noble contest or battle in which the Christians have the possibility of an honorable victory over their antagonists simply by persevering are topics intended by New Testament authors to inform and protect the group from being pulled back into the values of the majority culture.

The leaders of the Christian movement, beginning with Jesus himself (see Mt 10:17-18, 24-25; 24:9-10), prepared their followers for society's censure and rejection ahead of time. By stressing that it was to be expected, and indeed that it was predictable, these leaders hoped that it would not be disconfirming when it actually occurred. That is to say, it should not catch the Christians off guard; it should not surprise them and cause them to question their new commitments. Given what happened to Jesus, it is only natural that the world should act the same way toward his followers (Jn 15:18-21), but also given the honor that Jesus now enjoys after enduring the hostility of sinners (Heb 12:3), it is also endurable! Jesus' predictions of society's attempts to shame them into silence and surrender are specifically intended by him to arm them ahead of time to encounter it and persevere (Jn 16:1-4). Paul followed the same procedure in Thessalonica: "We sent Timothy . . . to strengthen and encourage you for the sake of your faith, so that no one would be shaken by these persecutions. Indeed, you yourselves know that this is what we are destined for. In fact, when we were with you, we told you beforehand that we were to suffer persecution; so it turned out, as you know" (1 Thess 3:2-4).

The experience of shaming was meant by outsiders to make the Christians feel abnormal and make them wish to retreat back into the safety of conformity. Paul, however, turns the experience of being shamed into something "normal" for the existence of believers in the world. The believers in Thessalonica find replicated in their own experience the well-established pattern of rejection known by Paul (1 Thess 2:2; 3:7; see also Phil 1:30) and by their sister churches in Judea (1 Thess 2:14).

Suffering for Jesus' sake is even transformed into a badge of honor before God. This strategy represents perhaps the strongest tool the minority group has for reversing the effects of society's attempts to reign the "deviants" back into line with dominant cultural values. The response of the twelve apostles to the Sanhedrin's marking them with the whip as deviants requiring correction becomes paradigmatic: "They rejoiced that they were considered worthy to suffer dishonor for the sake of the name" (Acts 5:41). The author of 1 Peter, writing to Christians throughout Asia Minor, seeks to inculcate a similar response among them to their experiences of their neighbors' insult and abuse:

> Rejoice insofar as you are sharing Christ's sufferings, so that you may also be glad and shout for joy when his glory is revealed. If you are reviled for the name of Christ, you are blessed, because the spirit of glory, which is the Spirit of God, is resting on you. But let none of you suffer as a murderer, a thief, a criminal, or even as a mischief maker. Yet if any of you suffers as a Christian, do not consider it a disgrace, but glorify God because you bear this name. (1 Pet 4:13-16; see also 3:14)

The pattern of Jesus is invoked as the first means of understanding the "blessedness" of suffering the world's hostility. Sharing the lot of Jesus for the sake of association with his name now will mean sharing in his lot in glory as well. Indeed, the believers should see society's negative response to them as a sign of the "spirit of glory"—the honor of being part of God's own family and sharing with his Son—resting on them. Pronouncing such a person "blessed" (*makarios*) essentially means pronouncing him or her "honorable,"[32] or perhaps in some contexts, "favored." *Happy* is too weak a synonym for this term, which is used more to affirm a person as occupying a noble or divinely favored status.[33]

A further rationale for the surprising estimation of those disgraced by the society as "blessed" appears in Jesus' beatitudes:

> Blessed are you when people hate you, and when they exclude you, revile you, and defame you on account of the Son of Man. Rejoice in that day and leap for joy, for surely your reward is great in heaven; for that is what their ancestors did to the prophets. (Lk 6:22-23)[34]

---

[32]See the rich discussion of the meaning of *blessed* by Kenneth C. Hanson, "How Honorable! How Shameful! A Cultural Analysis of Matthew's Makarisms and Reproaches," *Semeia* 68 (1996): 81-111.

[33]Revelation 20:6 and 22:14 also pronounce "blessed" or "honorable" those who have suffered the world's shaming most intensely (execution in Rev 20:6; those who "washed their robes" are those who endure the "great ordeal," which is not God's plagues but the beast's campaign against godliness [Rev 7:13-14]).

[34]See also the parallel saying at Matthew 5:11-12. Luke 6:26 goes on to turn praise and honor on the lips of the outside world into a sign of dishonor within the community of disciples by the same logic, namely, that the ignorant world spoke well of the false prophets.

The appeal to the historical precedent of the prophets of Israel, many of whom suffered severe degradation at the hands of the rulers of Israel and Judah,[35] provides proof that those people who were most honorable could also be most openly disgraced by their neighbors. The fact that Jews had for centuries revered the names of Jeremiah and Isaiah overturns any shame that their kings might have tried to impose upon them. The followers of Jesus can have the same confidence when they encounter impositions of dishonor from outside.

Paul states this same rationale in terms of a more general principle: "Indeed, all who want to live a godly life in Christ Jesus will be persecuted. But wicked people and impostors will go from bad to worse, deceiving others and being deceived" (2 Tim 3:12-13). Godliness—and those who pursue virtue—is simply persecuted by a dishonorable world. Because of this, the Christians should feel confirmed that they have chosen the honorable path when their unbelieving neighbors assail them and tear them down.

The early church leaders also used the metaphor of the athletic contest to turn endurance of hardships into an opportunity to manifest the virtues of courage and endurance,[36] recasting society's hostility as the antagonist over which the believer can win an honorable victory—and the crown of the victor—simply by persevering in his or her Christian commitments:

> Therefore, since we are surrounded by so great a cloud of witnesses, let us also lay aside every weight and the sin that clings so closely, and let us run with perseverance the race ("contest," *agōn*) that is set before us, looking to

---

[35]Although the deaths of the prophets are not mentioned in the books bearing their names, legends arose in Israel depicting the brutal martyrdoms of these men (see *The Lives of the Prophets* [J.H. Charlesworth, ed., *OTP,* 2:379-400]; the tales are collected and abridged in David A. deSilva and Victor H. Matthews, *Untold Stories of the Bible* [Lincolnwood, Ill.: Publications International, 1998], pp. 102-14).

[36]This image was commonly employed by Jewish authors, whose audiences often found themselves also the brunt of society's shaming (see 4 Macc 6:9-10; 16:16; 17:11-16; Philo "Every Good Person is Free" 26-27), as well as by Greco-Roman philosophical writers, for whom the great contests were not the Olympiads but wrestling with insults, with hardship and with the passions and weaknesses of the flesh that seek to subvert the person's reason and commitment to virtue (see Dio Chrysostom *Or.* 8.15-16; Epictetus *Diss.* 1.18.21; 1.24.1-2; 3.22.56). For further reading on this topic, see Victor C. Pfitzner, *Paul and the Agon Motif: Traditional Athletic Imagery in the Pauline Literature* (Leiden: Brill, 1967); Noah Clayton Croy, *Endurance in Suffering* (Cambridge: Cambridge University Press, 1998); deSilva, *4 Maccabees,* chap. 4.

Jesus the pioneer and perfecter of our faith, who for the sake of the joy that was set before him endured the cross, disregarding its shame, and has taken his seat at the right hand of the throne of God. Consider him who endured such hostility against himself from sinners, so that you may not grow weary or lose heart. In your struggle against [*antagōnizomenoi*] sin you have not yet resisted to the point of shedding your blood. (Heb 12:1-4; see also Heb 10:32)

The metaphor works because athletes needed the qualities of persever-ance and endurance, particularly in the face of pain but also in the face of the jeering of the crowd. Giving up in the face of such jeering or because the body hurt would mean defeat and dishonor, but the athlete who per-sisted despite the opposition of people, antagonists and personal weak-ness would be honored.

In this passage the author calls the Christians' attention to the specta-tors whose approval they are to court as they engage in the contest. It is the people of faith throughout the ages, with Jesus conspicuously at the center, who now watch how the Christians run the same gauntlet of soci-ety's antagonism. They compete not merely against their unbelieving neighbors but ultimately against the power of sin itself (making surren-der all the more disgraceful and impossible to contemplate). The meta-phor is a powerful resource indeed, as it turns the experience of being victimized by a hostile society into an opportunity for victory, empower-ing the victim to choose to follow his or her own convictions rather than succumb to coercion.

The author of Hebrews also ennobles the experience of reproach, ridi-cule and even physical violence at the hands of unbelievers as being God's training of his children for citizenship in the kingdom (Heb 12:5-11). This is explicitly not punitive discipline (not "chastisement" for sins committed by the believers)[37] but character-shaping exercise, building up their commitment to God and the strength of their trust and loyalty, sharpening their investment in the unshakable kingdom they are about to receive. As parental discipline, it becomes a proof of their being God's legitimate sons and daughters rather than illegitimate children for whom a parent does not take such care and forethought.[38] In addition to courage

---

[37]The interpretation of this passage as educative or formative discipline, rather than puni-tive discipline, has been definitively established by Croy, *Endurance in Suffering* (who also traces and ably explains the development of a "punitive" misreading of the passage).

[38]It is essential to recognize that the author of Hebrews is discussing in Hebrews 12:5-11 the very

and endurance, then, perseverance becomes an opportunity to demonstrate reverent submission to God (after Jesus' own example, Heb 5:8-9).

Endurance of the world's deviancy-control measures is also an opportunity to demonstrate one's fidelity to and trust in God (1 Pet 1:6-7) or one's sincerity and integrity. Paul uses his own experience of sufferings in the latter manner, offering his endurance of shame—both verbal and physical degradation (2 Cor 6:4-10; 11:23-25)—as proof that he does not use the gospel as a means of enjoying temporary gains or pleasures (like the Sophists, who peddle philosophies for a living), but for the highest of ideals. Modeling the confidence of one who has remained loyal to Jesus despite earthly adversity and disgrace, Paul believes that God will surely vindicate those who remained faithful: "No one who believes in him will be put to shame" (Rom 10:11; cf. 2 Tim 1:8, 12). Endurance now means incomparable honor eternally (2 Cor 4:17-18).[39]

The Christian Riposte to the Outsider's Challenge

The honorable person subjected to insult or to some other challenge to honor is culturally conditioned to retaliate, to offer a riposte (see discussion in chapter one) that will counter the challenge and preserve honor in the public eye intact. Christians confronted with such attacks on their honor as verbal challenges, reproachful speech and even physical affronts would be sorely tempted to respond in kind, playing out the challenge-riposte game before the onlookers. Beginning with Jesus, however, Christian leaders sought to cultivate a specifically Christian riposte— the believer is allowed to respond to the challenges made against his or her honor, but directed to do so in such a way as reflects to the out-

---

same kind and source of suffering he has been considering since 10:32-34 (the community's earlier experience of society's shaming techniques on account of their commitment to Jesus), the models of Abraham, Moses and the martyrs in chapter 11, and the example of Jesus (and the believers' own contest with society's pressures) in 12:1-4. That is to say, Hebrews 12:5-11 does not address all kinds of suffering, like disease or domestic abuse— only those hardships imposed on one by unbelievers (or false Christians) because one has stepped out in faith and allegiance to Jesus. To apply the principle of God's parental training too broadly risks theological disaster and the conjuring up of an abusive God.

[39]Assurance of God's vindication of the honor of the martyred and marginalized Christians is also a prominent topic in Revelation. See Revelation 11:3-13, in which God overturns the disgrace heaped on his witnesses (the ultimate disgrace in the ancient world, by the way— to be left unburied after death). The cry of the martyrs for vindication in Revelation 6:9-11 is explicitly answered in 11:18, and their disgrace turned to highest honors as co-regents with Christ in 20:4-6.

side world the virtues and values of the Christian group.

> You have heard that it was said, "An eye for an eye and a tooth for a tooth."
> But I say to you, Do not resist an evildoer. But if anyone strikes you on the
> right cheek, turn the other also; and if anyone wants to sue you and take
> your coat, give your cloak as well; and if anyone forces you to go one mile,
> go also the second mile. (Mt 5:38-41; see also Mt 5:44; Lk 6:28, 35)

Followers of Jesus overcome challenges to honor not through using the
same currency of insult or violence that the outside world throws at them,
but rather they meet hostility with generosity, violence with courageous
refusal to use violence, curse with blessing from God's inexhaustible
resources of goodness and kindness.

Paul expands on the teaching of Jesus by urging the Christian to "take
thought for what is noble in the sight of all" (Rom 12:17) rather than
repaying "evil for evil." One finds in Paul and 1 Peter a deep concern to
demonstrate to outsiders that being Christian is in fact honorable. On the
one hand, Christians are never allowed to choose their course of action
out of desire or need for the affirmation of the outside world. They are to
remain focused on God's approval and on the actions that lead them,
regardless of the world's response. On the other hand, however, there is
the explicit hope articulated in the New Testament that by pursuing the
course that God approves, the nobility of the Christian community will be
made apparent to those outside the church, who still have some ability to
recognize virtue even if they pursue vicious paths in the name of virtue
(like idolatry). Some concern for the group's reputation is also in keeping
with the conversionist emphasis of the Christian movement, since the
"multitude" only go by hearsay rather than investigating the facts.[40]

The Christian posture in regard to how it elects to respond to its attack-
ers is very similar to the course promoted by Plutarch in his treatise
"How to Profit by One's Enemies" (*Mor.* 86B-92F):[41] " 'How shall I defend
myself against my enemy?' 'By proving yourself good and honourable' "
("How to Profit" 4, *Mor.* 88B). It will distress the enemy more than being
insulted, Plutarch writes, to see you bear yourself with self-control, justice

---

[40]See Isocrates *Ad Dem.* 17; Luke gives the impression that the Christian group had a poor
reputation empire-wide: "With regard to this sect we know that everywhere it is spoken
against"(Acts 28:22).

[41]Elliott helpfully calls attention to this comparative text in his discussion of the response to
outsiders promoted in 1 Peter ("Disgraced yet Graced," p. 171).

and kindness toward those with whom you come in contact. The insulted person must use the insult as an occasion to examine his life and rid himself of any semblance of that vice ("How to Profit" 6, *Mor.* 89D-E). In the same way, the author of 1 Peter urges Christians throughout Asia Minor, "Conduct yourselves honorably among the Gentiles, so that, though they malign you as evildoers, they may see your honorable deeds and glorify God when he comes to judge" (1 Pet 2:12). "Keep your conscience clear, so that, when you are maligned, those who abuse you for your good conduct in Christ may be put to shame" (1 Pet 3:16). By means of honorable conduct, the author hopes to overturn the reproach that society attaches to the name of "Christian": "For it is God's will that by doing right you should silence the ignorance of the foolish" (1 Pet 2:15). At the very least, he adjures the believers to do nothing that might actually add to or justify the bad reputation of the group: "But let none of you suffer as a murderer, a thief, a criminal, or even as a mischief maker" (4:15).[42] Advice given to wives and slaves (1 Pet 3:1-7; 2:18-25; see also Tit 2:9-10), young men (Tit 2:6-8) and women (Tit 2:4-5), and to the group as a whole, can be seen as serving the goal of offering proof through noble conduct that the group is truly honorable (whether or not the outsiders ever actually come to admit this: at the last judgment they will be forced to do so).

At many other points one can find New Testament authors showing concern for living with integrity (see 2 Cor 1:12; 4:2; 6:3-4; 1 Tim 3:7), showing the congruence of the message of Jesus with the virtues implanted, as it were, in the hearts of Gentile and Jew alike (Rom 2:14-16). Thus Paul is careful to administer the collection for the sisters and brothers in Judea with regard for "what is noble not only in God's sight but in the sight of human beings" (2 Cor 8:21, my translation). Another notable arena in which the Christians are called to demonstrate their virtue is through beneficence not only within the community of faith (essential though this is to the maintenance of the group's commitment and solidarity) but also toward all (Mt 5:43-48; 1 Thess 3:12; 5:15). Benefaction is unmistakably recognizable in the ancient world as honorable in and of itself, reflecting also God's own character. If the outsiders do not respond nobly with gratitude but rather keep maligning the believers, that will be

---

[42]Second Peter 2:2 expresses an awareness that bad conduct by people calling themselves Christians only confirms the majority culture in its opinion of the group and is highly detrimental to the cause of Christ.

just another confirmation of the outsiders' debased character. The Christian group thus keeps walking the fine line between remaining independent of society's response (approval or censure), while also striving to enhance the honor of the group through embodying the highest ideals, overcoming evil by doing good (Rom 12:21).

The Christian's Honor

The early church leaders frequently reminded the believers that joining the Christian group did not merely bring them dishonor in the eyes of the world that refused the gospel. The believers have also gained incomparable honor because of their attachment to the group. The author of 1 Peter, sensitive to the fact that he writes to people whose self-respect has come under serious fire from without, dedicates the first two chapters of his epistle largely to affirming the honor that is theirs in Christ. The language of elevation to priesthood provides him with an important vehicle for conveying the honor that believers now enjoy as those fitted to approach God with confidence in holiness:

> Let yourselves be built into a spiritual house, to be a holy priesthood, to offer spiritual sacrifices acceptable to God through Jesus Christ. . . . You are a chosen race, a royal priesthood, a holy nation, God's own people, in order that you may proclaim the mighty acts of him who called you out of darkness into his marvelous light. Once you were not a people, but now you are God's people. (1 Pet 2:5, 9-10; see also Rev 1:5-6; 5:9)

The emphasis in these verses on God's selection of each of the believers to become part of God's own people also speaks to the honored and favored status conferred on the Christian.

Most impressively, becoming a disciple of Jesus brings with it adoption into God's family and a share in Christ's honor (Jn 1:12-13; Rom 8:14-17; Heb 2:10; 3:1-6, 14; 1 Pet 1:23). In this regard, God ascribes the honor of God's own household to the believer.[43] The exaltation of Jesus to the place of highest honor in the cosmos (Eph 1:20-22) is thus an honor in which all faithful believers now share (Eph 2:6). This honor, though possessed by the Christian, is yet fully to be enjoyed and yet to be manifested to the

---

[43]See Jewett, *Saint Paul Returns to the Movies*, p. 12: "To be 'set right' in the context of the 'righteousness of God' (3:21), and with reference to humans who have fallen short of the 'glory of God,' is to have such glory and honor *restored*. This is not an achievement but a gift of grace."

world. It remains their inheritance (1 Pet 1:4). Their full investment with, and indeed their full discovery of the magnitude of, the honor that God has conferred on them through adoption into his family will occur at the future appearing of Jesus. When the glorified Christ's own honor is revealed to the world, then the honor of his followers will be revealed as well (Col 3:4; 2 Thess 1:10-12; 2:14). The Christians look forward to receiving an unshakable kingdom (Heb 12:28), an enduring city (Heb 13:13-14) in which the believers will be invested with their full honor as God's children, where that honor will be manifested and not assaulted.

More immediately, the believers gain the esteem and respect of their sisters and brothers as Christ takes shape within them and as their actions show his love. Communities of faith are met with international fame across the web of churches empire-wide as they reach out in support of fellow-believers, endure bravely the opposition of unbelievers, or shine as examples of trust and firmness in their commitment to Jesus (see Rom 1:8; 1 Thess 1:7-9; 2 Thess 1:4).

Pressures to conform to the values of the Greco-Roman culture or Jewish subculture, and temptations to assess worth and honor in light of those alien values, do not come only from outside the Christian community. After all, every member of the church during the first generation of its existence in a given locale was first socialized into one or the other of those cultures. One finds, therefore, early Christian leaders combating the tendency to import what are now to be considered alien standards and values into the Christian group. The challenge here is to prevent the members' "primary socialization" from overriding or short-circuiting their full secondary socialization into the Christian worldview and ethos. The Christians needed to reinforce clearly and distinctly for one another the group's values as the path to honor. There was no room for acculturation of those values to the definitions of honorable behavior they "left behind" at their conversion.

Jesus, James, Paul and most New Testament voices take the time to clarify the true basis for honor and to correct intrusions of dominant-cultural (or Jewish ethnic subcultural) ways of attaining or asserting honor. The prevalence of these discussions suggests that one's primary, non-Christian socialization is surprisingly persistent, and Christian leaders need to show special vigilance in this regard. Jesus, for example, confronts head-on the manner in which the majority culture thinks of greatness in terms of power over others and precedence before others, a conception that manifests itself in the disciples' conversations at least twice on the road to Jerusalem (Mk 9:34-35; 10:35-45 and parallels). True honor consists rather in serving the sisters and brothers after the model of Jesus, the servant leader who "came not to be served but to serve" (Mk 10:45). The disciples, and the later readers of the Gospels as well, are jolted into realizing the vast difference between what counts as honorable or great in the world and what makes one great or honorable in God's sight: "The one who is least among you all is the one who is great" (Lk 9:48, my translation).

James and Paul both combat the tendency to honor the rich above the poor, thus replicating within the community the majority culture's conviction that a person's honor or worth is proportionate to his wealth (see 1 Cor 11:20-22; Jas 1:9-10; 2:1-9). Ethnicity can no longer be a cause for claiming honor above others (Rom 1—3; 11:19-20),[44] whether the Christian Jew would consider himself privileged beyond and more honorable than the Christian Gentile, or the Christian Greek would cling to the dominant culture's perception of the Greek as more honorable than the barbarian. In a world that valued visible signs of divine possession and proximity to God's power, God's gifts and endowments of the believers are not permitted to become a ground for competition for honor among believers (1 Cor 4:7). Similarly, spiritual knowledge does not create an enlightened elite within the church, where building up one another in love (rather than becoming puffed up) is the way to act honorably and be recognized as honorable (1 Cor 8:1-2).

An especially critical issue for Paul in the Corinthian correspondence is detaching the believers there from their tendency to evaluate a person's worth by appearances, that is to say, by charisma, observable strengths and polished performances (2 Cor 5:12).[45] The case of Jesus proves, Paul argues, the unreliability of these criteria in determining honor (whether evaluating one's own honor, the honor of a fellow believer or the honor of various leaders and teachers), since the "world in its wisdom," that is, acting and selecting according to its criteria of worth, failed to recognize God's wisdom (1 Cor 1:18-31). Only God's work in the believer, trans-

---

[44]So, rightly, Jewett, *Saint Paul Returns to the Movies,* p. 10: "Removal of 'boasting' undercuts the superiority claims of every system of gaining honor through performance or inherited status"; also, p. 13: "No one gains this honorable, righteous status by outperforming others or by privilege of birth or wealth."

[45]For a fuller discussion, see deSilva, *Hope of Glory,* chap. 5.

forming the mortal into the image of Christ, bringing the life of Christ to life in the frail human (and, in the face of death, even the strongest and most gifted human is frail), gives a person any claim to honor. Valuing oneself or others on the basis of the "outer person," that is, the endowments of our mortal person or our performance, is folly, since no strength of the outer person can avail in the face of death. Paul's decision not to try to hide his weaknesses or work to make his appearance "perfect" and semi-divine as a means of gaining respect and authority (which was the goal of most public speakers) reflects his firm conviction that such a way of valuing and trying to convey value was fundamentally opposed to God's values (again, revealed most clearly in the extreme case, the case of Jesus). Thus the only "boast," or "claim to honor," that Paul will allow is boasting "in the Lord" (1 Cor 1:31; 2 Cor 10:17) and "in one's weaknesses" (2 Cor 11:30; 12:5-10). Only where the character and person of Jesus becomes visible in the individual (which Paul found most where his human strengths ran out) does one find cause for self-respect, and the group needs to reinforce this as the central criterion for bestowing honor.

Another essential and pervasive aspect of this re-education of the Christians concerns the replacement of the basic competitive model of establishing one's honor with a cooperative model. The believers, as children of God, become what sociologists would call a fictive kinship group, that is, a collection of people who are not genealogically related but who nevertheless consider one another as family, attempting to relate at that higher level of intimacy, belonging and mutual commitment. As sisters and brothers, believers share honor within one household, working together toward the advancement of the honor of all members of this family rather than competing with one another for honor as if between unrelated individuals. Thus Jesus criticizes the scribes and the Pharisees for loving to be honored in ways that set them above and apart from their fellow Israelites, forbidding his own disciples to create or pursue such distinctions: "They love the head table at banquets and the first seats at the synagogue and greetings in the market place and to be called 'Rabbi' by people. But do not you be called 'Rabbi,' for One is your teacher and you are all sisters and brothers" (Mt 23:6-8, my translation). Honor is not truly gained by competing against one's own kin. Similarly, Paul urges his friends in Philippi to lay aside all rivalries over recognition in the church, choosing instead "in humility [to] regard others as better than yourselves" (Phil 2:3). Instead of clinging to claims of certain recognition, the Christians are simply to relinquish those claims (seedbeds of faction-alism that they are) and offer recognition and honor to the other members of the body.

Believers are summoned to honor one another and to affirm one another's value in God's sight and in the sight of the group (see Rom 12:10; Phil 1:17; 2:3-4; 1 Pet 5:5-6; 3 Jn 9-11). There is certainly no room for dishonoring or shaming fellow Christians for any reason other than their departure from the norms of the faith. The poor Christian is not to be treated shabbily and made to feel ashamed because he or she is poor (1 Cor 11:21-22; Jas 2:6-7); believers are not to disdain one another on the basis of indifferent matters of custom (Rom 14:3, 10)[46] or on the basis of promoting some spiritual gifts as more distinguished and distinguishing than others (1 Cor 12). Such would only push the shamed believers away from the group and back to the bosom of society to no good purpose. Shaming must be reserved only for the enforcing of vital group norms of honorable conduct (see 1 Cor 6:5; 15:34; 2 Thess 3:6, 14-15; 1 Tim 5:20, and discussion below).

Instead the interactions within the group must reflect the honor of each person in God's eyes and according to God's standards. This means tak-ing special care to bestow honor on the "less presentable" ones:

> Those members of the body that we think less honorable we clothe with greater honor, and our less respectable members are treated with greater respect; whereas our more respectable members do not need this. But God has so arranged the body, giving the greater honor to the inferior member, that there may be no dissension within the body, but the members may have the same care for one another. If one member suffers, all suffer together with it; if one member is honored, all rejoice together with it. (1 Cor 12:23-26)

---

[46]Jewett helpfully comments on Romans 14—15 as an attempt to remove the tendency to disparage fellow believers over matters that were indifferent to God: "In place of the ordi-nary Greco-Roman assumption that the strong should dominate the weak while holding them in contempt, Paul argues that 'we the powerful are obligated to bear the weaknesses of the powerless and not to please ourselves. Let each of us please the neighbor for the good, toward upbuilding. For also Christ did not please himself, but as it is written, "The reproaches of those who reproach you fell upon me" ' (Rom 15:1-3)" (*Saint Paul Returns to the Movies*, p. 15). This Psalm text may be read now as referring not to the reproaches of those who reproach God, but of those who reproach the neighbor—identifying with the weak sister or brother, the strong believer willingly takes on the reproach falling on that weak one.

Within this single paragraph, three related concerns are brought together. First, Paul uses the metaphor of the body as a means of helping the Christians in Corinth understand the importance and suitability of intentionally affirming the honor of those who have honor in God's sight but, by society's criteria (the criteria of the Christian's primary socialization, learned in the pre-Christian period of one's life) would be of no account. Second, the relationship between this kind of attitude toward one another and the maintenance of unity and concord within the church is made explicit. Third, Paul articulates a kinship ethos as far as both loss and honor are concerned. The advancement of the honor of one member of the family means advancement for all members of the family, such that it becomes only right to rejoice at one another's being honored and even to promote one another's honor (rather than promote one's own at the expense of others). The Christian community that nurtures this kind of ethos will see tremendous growth and be equipped to do acts of ministry worthy of God.

Honor and Shame Within the New Community

Once the distinctively Christian criteria for what constitutes honorable and dishonorable behavior have been established, and group members' focus has been taken wholly off the verdict of the unbelieving world and fixed on God's approval and the intimations of that approval reflected in one's fellow Christians and in the leaders of the group, then honor and shame can be used within the group to reinforce commitment to live out the group's values. Leaders can harness the hearers' natural desire for honor to promote the courses of action or attitudes necessary for sustaining the Christian movement as the path to honor before the court of reputation that matters and to dissuade them from any attitudes, behaviors and commitments that might prove detrimental to group solidarity or contrary to group values, labeling it as the path to dishonor before that body of significant others. Where the majority of this minority culture can agree, it can encourage individual members to embody shared values by bestowing honor on those who manifest them, and it can even use shaming techniques (although notably not the same techniques to which the outside world has subjected them!) to correct members who stray beyond the shared norms.

The promise of being honored in God's house reinforces the value of not yielding to the lusts of the body (2 Tim 2:20-22), of serving Jesus (Jn

12:26), of taking up the posture of servant to the Christian community (Mk 10:41-45), and of extending hospitality and material support to the sisters and brothers in need (2 Cor 8:1-7, 24; Philem 7; 3 Jn 5-8), to name but a few examples. "Dying in the Lord" is held up by John as an absolute good, an absolute claim to being deemed honorable: " 'Blessed are the dead who from now on die in the Lord.' 'Yes,' says the Spirit, 'they will rest from their labors, for their deeds follow them'" (Rev 14:13). John is redefining the criteria for a "good death," with loyalty to the Lamb and the group's core values (in his situation, monolatry and disentangling oneself from the sinful prosperity of the imperial system would be prominent) at the center. The makarism carries weight whether this death is violent or natural. The important point is that the hearers will associate perseverance "in the Lord," whatever that may entail, with a noble death, a good death.

The threat of disgrace before God sustains commitment to forgive one another (Mt 18:23-35); to tend the hungry, sick, destitute and imprisoned (Mt 25:31-46); and to remain loyal to the Lord who saved them rather than bring dishonor to his name through defection (Heb 6:4-8). Looking again to Revelation, John graphically depicts the public (indeed, cosmic) humiliation that awaits those who yield to the pressures to participate in idolatrous ritual and especially emperor cult—being physically degraded through punishment in the sight of an honorable audience, the holy angels and the Lamb (Rev 14:9-11). Those who yield are labeled "cowardly" and "faithless" (Rev 21:8) and are excluded from the honor and favors prepared by God for his people. As particular acts or general attitudes are linked in the believers' consciousness with honor or disgrace as the consequences, their own ambitions and aversions are being reprogrammed in terms of the distinctive ethos of the Christian culture.

Leaders will thus frequently remind the hearers of honorable and shameful behavior through words such as those above. Members will then reflect this information back to one another in their conversations and even in their nonverbal communication. Honor and shame do not work in the Christian culture only at the level of the internalization of values, however. Across the New Testament the early shepherds were themselves "activating" the church as a "court of reputation" as they held up certain believers to be honored, shamed others and encouraged the churches themselves to create a dynamic social environment in which honoring and shaming actively supported the group's values and reinforced individual commitment to embody those values. Leaders like Paul or the author of Hebrews openly praise (honor) believers who embody the group's values and whose energies or commitment have advanced the group's well-being (whether locally and translocally). For example, the Christians in Thessalonica are commended for their loyal work and loving labors in the Lord, and particularly for their steadfastness in the face of opposition, by means of which, they find out here, they have become a model for emulation throughout the regions of Macedonia and Achaia (1 Thess 1:3, 7). The author of the letter "to the Hebrews" indirectly praises the hearers for their past stance of courage and solidarity in the face of society's shaming strategies (Heb 10:32-35), an honorable course in which they now need to persevere. The seven oracles to the seven churches in Revelation 2 and 3 show a masterful and quite explicit combination of praise and censure, as Jesus affirms those who have manifested steadfastness, loyalty and love toward him and one another and censures those who have made far too much room for the dominant culture's values and prized pursuits. This praise and censure, being heard by the churches throughout the province, is very public and thus even more powerful an affirmation and deterrent as each local church's fame throughout the circle of churches is augmented or diminished as the Judge makes his appraisal known.

These same oracles display another important strategy being used throughout the New Testament: they intentionally direct the hearers and channel their ambitions for honor toward the honors bestowed by God or by the group for having embodied the group's values (see also 1 Thess 3:12-13; 2 Thess 1:11-12; 2:14). Whether their current behavior has merited praise, censure or a mixture of the two, each church is invited to pursue a specific course of action that Jesus will affirm, and each is invited more broadly to aspire to "conquer" and thus receive the honors and awards promised to "everyone who conquers" (Rev 2:7, 11, 17, 26-28; 3:5, 12, 21). This summons to conquer spurs the hearers on to orient themselves toward the society as if in a battle (in the context of Satan's war against God and its last desperate campaign in the power of Rome and the cult of the emperors, see Rev 12—13), and to embody endurance and courage as they resist the enemy's pressures to surrender.

Fear of shame before one's fellow Christians in the local assembly or concern about loss of honor in the eyes of the translocal Christian group now becomes a powerful motivation for investment of oneself in the activities and processes that sustain the minority culture. Paul, for example, uses this fear of being dishonored with a view to securing maximum participation in the relief efforts for the sisters and brothers in Judea:

> Openly before the churches, show them the proof of your love and of our reason for boasting about you . . . to the people of Macedonia, saying that Achaia has been ready since last year; and your zeal has stirred up most of them. But I am sending the brothers in order that our boasting about you may not prove to have been empty in this case, so that you may be ready, as I said you would be; otherwise, if some Macedonians come with me and find that you are not ready, we would be humiliated—to say nothing of you—in this undertaking. (2 Cor 8:24—9:4)

The Corinthians have already won a reputation for generosity among the churches (a desirable honor, to be sure) thanks to Paul's boasting about them, but this reputation is now on the line: the Corinthians must put their money where Paul's mouth is, as it were, if they are to confirm their honor in the sight of their Macedonian sisters and brothers. If they fail to support this relief effort generously, their reputation among the churches will suffer loss.[47]

Not just the leaders of the movement but the members themselves are called to exercise social control within the group. On the positive side the believers are called on to honor those who distinguish themselves in service to the church (1 Cor 16:15-18; Phil 2:29-30; 1 Tim 3:13; 3 Jn 12), the effect of which is to encourage even broader investment in these kinds of group-building and sustaining activities. Even Jesus, however, also prescribes the use of censure and public rebuke (shaming) within the Christian community for the brother or sister who persists in living contrary to the way of life taught by him (Mt 18:15-18). Notably, this process begins in private, for the first concern of kin is to protect rather than damage the honor and standing of their sisters and brothers. If a private meeting, and then a meeting with but two or three others, fails to correct the sister or brother, then the whole assembly has an opportunity to censure the behavior (now made public) and call for reformation. The final stage in the process is shunning. Loss of these important relationships is the final strategy that the church will employ, and in many cases this will finally bring about repentance (if the church has been functioning properly as the individual's primary reference group and primary network of support).

---

[47]Romans 15:25-27 suggests that Paul's stratagem met with success.

Paul likewise calls upon the local community to discern when an individual member has left the honorable paths and to "restore such a one in a spirit of gentleness" (Gal 6:1; see Heb 3:12-13)—censure is not to be sharp or demeaning, but the group's values are nevertheless to be upheld and the erring lovingly led back to the path that God honors. If the person persists, however, in flouting the group's values, shunning again becomes the last measure of social control (see 1 Cor 5:9-11).

> Now we command you, beloved, in the name of our Lord Jesus Christ, to keep away from brothers and sisters who are living in idleness and not according to the tradition that they received from us. . . . Have nothing to do with them, so that they may be ashamed. Do not regard them as enemies, but warn them as brothers and sisters. (2 Thess 3:6, 14-15)[48]

Other New Testament voices continue to cultivate an ethos of accountability within the group. John, for example, underscores Christians' responsibility for addressing deviance and pulling the wayward back to firm commitment to the uncompromised values of the group (Rev 2:14, 20). Toleration of deviance and transgression becomes a blot not merely on the honor of the transgressors but on the whole church, which is censured for not exercising its responsibility to help all its members remain true to God's standards. While the church cannot be held responsible for the transgression itself (thus only the idolaters within the church will actually experience the Lord's punishment (Rev 2:22-23), the lives of the transgressors are, to some extent, in the hands of their sisters and brothers who must make every effort to reclaim them for life: "My brothers and sisters, if anyone among you wanders from the truth and is brought back by another, you should know that whoever brings back a sinner from wandering will save the sinner's soul from death and will cover a multitude of sins" (Jas 5:19-20). Accountability within the Christian community is still not altogether popular in Western Christianity, being seen as the kind of "intrusion" into the private areas of one's life characteristic of groups labeled "cults." Nevertheless, the early Christians recognized it as an essential part of

---

[48]I replace here the NRSV "believers" with "brothers and sisters." "Believers" is the NRSV's attempt to avoid the gender-specific "brother," but kinship language in the New Testament is central to Christian identity and should not be replaced. While less stylistically pleasing, "brothers and sisters" both preserves the sense of the Greek *adelphos* and avoids the problem of a gender-specific reference.

maintaining the community of faith and expressing Christian love and pastoral care.

People in the Greco-Roman world were concerned not only with their own honor but also were careful to give honor to whom it was due. Isocrates had advised his student, "Fear the gods, honour your parents, respect your friends, obey the laws" (*Ad Dem.* 16), advice that is incorporated into the Christian culture as well (see Rom 13:7; 1 Pet 2:17). People were particularly careful to honor those who were more powerful and on whose goodwill one's well-being depended. For this reason, early Christians were guided as much by considerations of the honor due God as by consideration for their own honor—indeed, the two were inseparably linked. As Christians honor the one God as he merits, offering worship, fidelity and obedient service, they continue to share in the honor of being part of God's household and God's own people. As they guard God's honor in their actions, they have the assurance as well that God will preserve and vindicate their honor at the last day. Any course of action that would show dishonor toward God or bring the name of Christ into disrepute must be avoided at all costs since the Christian who affronts God would then become the target of God's anger and satisfaction of God's honor. This, and not conflict with the larger society, is the most dangerous threat to the believer's honor and the thing that can prevent their arrival at the "glory" reserved for them in the kingdom.

The author of Hebrews uses this topic extensively, since some of the addressees have begun to withdraw themselves from visible attachment to the community of Christians, presumably because they have lost their stomach for continuing to live as shamed people in the eyes of the majority. Such visible detachment from the group (which would surely be noticed and approved by the unbelieving neighbors) brings disgrace on the name of Christ, for those who defect (or simply try to blend back into society while maintaining a private and hidden faith) bear witness to the unbelievers that Jesus and his promises are not worth what they cost to keep (Heb 6:4-8; these passages will be analyzed more fully later in chapter four). The lack of trust in God's ability to make their loyalty worthwhile (Heb 3:7—4:11; 10:37-39) demonstrates the lack of value such people place on God's gifts and the sanctification that cost Jesus so dearly (Heb 10:29; 12:15-17). Such lack of respect for God provokes God's anger and will bring upon their heads the "fiery zeal that is about to consume God's adversaries" (Heb 10:27, my translation) when he comes to judge

(Heb 10:29-31). Fear of provoking God, once having been received into his favor, becomes a powerful resource for motivating perseverance in the group.

We close our survey of the ways in which New Testament texts address issues of honor and incorporate honor and shame into their strategies for group formation with this topic since it provides a focusing point for the vast amount of diverse material that has preceded. The believer who lives above all things for God's approval on the last day, considers how he or she can honor God in all places and endeavors, and assists the community of disciples to maintain this same focus will admirably fulfill the calling of a disciple and ably contribute to the building up of the church.

Rethinking Honor in the Church Today

The points of connection between the needs of the early church and the plight of the church in both the modern Western world and in non-Western countries are impressive. Latin, Islamic and Oriental cultures are strikingly close to the classical world in terms of focusing on "honor" and "shame" as concepts that motivate the individual to conform to the values of the dominant culture (or at least the majority culture). The application of the foregoing discussions to Christian communities in those environments will be entirely natural. It may be surprising to discover, however, how much we have in common with the social dynamics of the first-century Mediterranean in the modern Western world. The machines of conformity have become perhaps more subtle and more institutional, but their wheels turn nonetheless.

In North America and Western Europe we find ourselves struggling to "work out our salvation" in the midst of a majority culture defined by pluralism and materialism. A mid- to late-twentieth-century believer is socialized into the gospel on the one hand and on the other hand into a society that holds up position, wealth and ownership of prestige items as measures for self-respect. To say that Christians are persecuted would perhaps exaggerate the situation for the majority of believers in the West, but we nevertheless cannot fail to notice more subtle pressures being exerted on us to soften our commitment to "one faith, one Lord" in the name of toleration, pluralism and multiculturalism. Desire to make room at the table for everyone's beliefs, perspectives and cultural traditions has made it very unpopular to claim to have the Truth and to try to win others from their traditions to one's own. This pressure can be exerted in many ways. Religion can be declared out of place in public spaces like businesses and schools. Those who attempt to bring religion into those spaces are made to feel ashamed for not respecting boundaries.[49] In academia, of course, those who hold to a confessional or evangelical faith can be scorned by their more liberal and "free-thinking" colleagues as intellectual cowards or even as charlatans who use academic language to bolster premodern worldviews. The privatization of religion in the West—the widely shared conviction that an individual's religion is a private matter not to be discussed openly, much less challenged—contributes greatly to the social pressure that fosters pluralism and trammels evangelism.

While America would not be described as an "honor" culture, individual Americans still seek to find their self-respect in achieving those marks society sets forth as the definition of successful. These definitions are communicated by our families of origin, who were themselves perhaps only partially socialized into the Christian ethos; by our educators who motivated study by pointing to the promising, well-paying careers and potential for advancement it would bring; by the endless barrage of commercials telling us what we should aspire to possess and display; and by the role models our society selects and elevates through very public award ceremonies and other avenues of idolization. We still are raised to seek the approval of the group and to act so as to gain recognition. In some circles, people are taught to value themselves based in socioeconomic terms (position within the professional class, wealth and ownership of prestige items) and to show their approval or disapproval of others based on similar values. In other circles, people lay claim to honor within the group based on physical strength or sexual conquest.

These facts place the Christian community in the midst of a majority culture and a dominant culture that neither shares nor supports its primary values. All the work done by the New Testament writers to insulate believers from their own internalization of those alien values and from the approval or disapproval of those who live by them will still be relevant work for the leaders of the twenty-first-century church. Attention to how New Testament authors directed their congregations to construct

---

[19]This is the light end of the shaming techniques. Such intrusions of religion can also lead to litigation, to expulsion from the space (i.e., having one's employment terminated) and the like.

their honor will also help us in our quest for self-respect, our cultural confusion about how to value ourselves and one another. More to the point, it will help us discover how bodies of Christians (churches) can form strong communities that encourage pursuit of what God values in a life and that free individuals from seeking their sense of honor from the dry wells of the secular world.

Becoming more sensitive to the cultural context of honor as a core social value attunes us to hear more clearly what the New Testament has to tell us about where our own personal value—our self-respect, our validation—comes from, about what gives us our worth. (The same word in Greek, *timē*, meant "worth, price, value," as well as "honor.") Reading and meditating on the Scriptures with this focus will assist our liberation from trying endlessly to establish our worth and self-respect through the avenues the world lays open before us and incites us to pursue. In the United States, some of the more frequently traversed roads to worth are acquisition, upward mobility, competition, sexual conquest or affirmations of attractiveness, independence, insisting on our rights, affectations of superiority based on ascribed status like race, class, "birth" or "breeding" (including education, refinement and the like). The New Testament writings hang an unmistakable dead-end sign at the mouths of these avenues, summoning us to measure ourselves and one another by such yardsticks no longer.

These New Testament writers were engaged in forming a community based on values and on an ideology wholly other from that of the society. This leads us to consider how to create effective, energizing congregations and support groups that enable individuals to remain faithful to the life and witness to which God has called them, and how to defuse the messages they receive from other members of the society that dissuade them from wholehearted commitment to this "outdated" or "impractical" religion and seduce them into caring first for the things of this life. This is especially insidious in twentieth-century American culture, where the dominant culture speaks the language of Christianity and where many churches function basically as proponents of a Christianity wholly adapted to the needs of the dominant culture. Pastors and lay leaders will need to grow in their awareness of social engineering, as it were, if they are to see vital communities of disciples following the call of Jesus and not the call of society.

The New Testament authors provide us with many resources for building up congregational and individual resistance to society's aggressive promotion of its own values and its marginalization of historic Christian values. They model effective strategies for neutralizing the power of non-Christians' evaluations of "successful" and "valuable," particularly as this acts to dissuade single-minded pursuit of discipleship and commitment to do what God values. They underscore the importance of and model how to go about forming and activating the church as the alternate "court of reputation," in which the members reinforce for one another the centrality of God's values and the meaning of success in terms of Christlikeness, obedience to the New Testament teachings and serving God's agenda.[50]

One significant challenge here is for the church to act reliably and consistently as this court of reputation, not continuing to be or allowing itself to become a mirror of society's values. This was the problem in the Corinthian celebration of the Lord's Supper or in the "ushers' guild" depicted by James, which seated the rich in the best seats and pushed the poor to the corners. Do we or do our churches show partiality along similar lines, importing into the church the persistent tendency in American culture to honor the rich and despise the poor? Do our interactions with others show that we reflect God's valuing of the heart, or are we, like our culture, attentive to beauty and fine dress and disdainful of the plain and ill-clad? Do we harbor ethnic, regional, class or cultural prejudices that override our respect for and solidarity with our sisters and brothers in Christ? Self-examination of this kind is a process to be undertaken by every believer and group of believers. Guidance for this process can be found in the New Testament, as Jesus, Paul, James and others all address intrusions of the world's criteria of personal worth into the Christian community. Authentic discipleship means discerning and leaving behind those alien values and prejudices that prevent us from honoring, respecting and loving each other—and ourselves!—as God calls his family to do.

As we analyze the way in which the New Testament constructs Christian honor and mobilizes communities of faith to reinforce the pursuit of honor in terms of discipleship, we have the opportunity to become more

---

[50]Christians and the leaders of congregations will need to take care not to stamp out the diversity that enriches our worship life or our experiences of God. The aim is not creating uniformity but holding one another to the core values and ethos of the Christian culture while being generous in the toleration of "indifferent matters" (see Rom 14).

aware of the ways in which individual discipleship depends on the support of a Christian community. We can observe and adapt the strategies used by the first-century congregations and their leaders to reinforce each believer's honor and self-respect in ways that promote the embodiment of specifically Christian values and commitments. The result will be a stronger community of disciples, a clearer awareness of the values that distinguish Christian culture from other groups. This in turn will enable a clearer prophetic voice for the church in its critique of society as well as radical commitment to seek honor in God's eyes, resisting the gravity of society's affirmations of what makes a life worthwhile.

Finally, we cannot fail to observe the connections between the early church and the situation of Christians in many parts of the non-Western world (e.g., India, China, Indonesia, Nigeria, many Islamic countries and the former Soviet Union), where society is frequently overtly hostile toward Christians in their midst and use all the deviancy-control techniques at their disposal to "correct" Christians. Reading the New Testament with a sensitivity to the needs and strategies explored above opens valuable resources for Christians in such circumstances to understand the significance of the opposition they encounter in such a way as to be empowered to endure society's rejection, insult, scorn and even violence if the path of obedience to Jesus' teachings and God's vision leads in that direction. Such a reading also educates Christians in the West concerning our responsibility to encourage, affirm and extend spiritual and material support to those sisters and brothers who face hostile shaming and physical abuse for the faith. We can investigate and tell the stories about the persecuted, spreading the fame of these heroes of faith, and let those needing support know that their struggle does not go unnoticed but rather brings them the admiration of their sisters and brothers. This may be more meaningful than many Westerners would imagine, since many persecuted churches are also embedded in honor and shame cultures very much like the first-century Mediterranean. We can seek out means of communicating with the persecuted, encouraging them in their noble contest, making the reality of the church as a "body of significant others" felt more keenly through prayer, material support (particularly when the primary supporter of a family is jailed or removed, or when economic privations are a principal means of coercion) and working toward the alleviation of the persecution. We can let them know how valued they are by their sisters and brothers worldwide and seek out ways to affirm their dignity and to help them to face the harsh deviancy-control measures imposed on them. Their own harsher contest can in turn embolden us, in a spirit of positive and brotherly emulation, to face our own bloodless contests here with greater courage and commitment.

Growing in sensitivity to the cultural context of honor, to the social dynamics at work where a minority culture is shamed into conformity, and to the strategies developed by the leaders of the minority culture takes us to the New Testament with a distinctive agenda. This agenda opens us up to the ways in which the New Testament can help us (and help us help one another) to set aside any ambition to be recognized as honorable (to be approved) by the worldly minded on their own terms and to set our hearts fully on living so as to hear those two words that only Jesus can speak at the last day: "Well done."

Excursus: A Word About Shame

Shame has become something of a buzzword in psychology—both in professional and popular publications, and so we will give some attention to the intersection of honor and shame in the church with shame in the psychological disciplines. One psychologist who has brought the academic discussion of shame in psychology to popular attention, Robert Karen,[51] distinguishes between three kinds of shame. The first is the "feeling" or "experience" of shame (the warmth under the skin and extreme self-consciousness that overtakes an individual when he or she has done something that provokes public disapproval or ridicule); the second is a "sense" of shame, the "healthy attitudes that define a wholesome character," the predilection for avoiding certain behaviors that bring shame.[52] The first two meanings are very much in line with the definition of shame at the opening of chapter one. The third kind of shame, however, is what Karen describes as "repressed but hounding shame, something activated to the level of gnawing self-doubt, occasionally reaching the intensity of fully inflamed self-hatred," a kind of shame about who we are that "drives people toward perfectionism, withdrawal, diffidence, combativeness," "a festering negative self-portrait against which one is repeatedly trying to defend."[53]

---

[51]Robert Karen, "Shame," *The Atlantic Monthly*, February 1992, pp. 40-70.
[52]Ibid., p. 42.
[53]Ibid., pp. 42, 58.

This third kind of shame is clearly pathogenic. It is the kind of shame that the church should heal rather than reinforce. It means hiding part of who we are because we are sure we will be rejected and loathed because of that part, a commitment to repression that spawns all manner of dysfunctional and inauthentic behaviors, relational patterns and self-image. It is this vague, self-hating shame that is the target of psychologists, who rightly affirm that this kind of shame is prevalent even in a time when shame in its other senses appears to be so much in a recession (witness the immodesty that leads people to "expose their sexuality on TV, howl obscenities at those who would once have been considered their betters, cling to elective office despite the revelation of serious breaches of public trust, and greedily pen books about their misdeeds").[54]

The discoveries of psychologists with regard to the presence and impact of this kind of shame on the human psyche lead me to suggest that while we can be quite avid and broad in our honoring those who embody Christian ideals and commitments, shaming techniques must be employed only with great care in the church. The church must be committed to becoming a place where people are healed of that which causes them to hide away some part of themselves, for as they hide it from fellow Christians, they also tend to push it back past the reaches of God's power to cure. How can we begin, then, to reinforce group values and curtail non-Christian behaviors without reinforcing the hold of pathological shame on the individual?

First, if we are to recover the mechanisms by which the early Christians helped one another stay on course in the "race set before us," we need to break through the modern lie that one's life is one's own business, encourage people to talk about their struggles as they seek to walk in line with the gospel, and elevate the importance and value of struggling courageously and diligently to fight the good fight for the Lord who redeemed them and the God who delights in the ethical victories of God's children. We also need very much to increase our conversation with one another concerning what God does value and what values God hopes will direct his children—this is vital, since there is so much conversation happening about what is valuable to and valued by the secular society. When we do not speak out to one another, we by our silence collude with society's indoctrination of the values of pluralism, the privatization of

---

[54]Ibid., p. 57.

religion, the importance of the bottom line, the eschatological ideal of financial wealth, the promotion of consumerism to the point of a virtual return to debt slavery.

I would dare to suggest, however, that we also need to break through our discomfort with confrontation and recover a certain level of "situational" shame—the kind of shame that keeps us from behaving inappropriately, from giving free reign to aggression or lust and so forth. Remaining silent about behaviors that run counter to what the New Testament teaches and the church has passed on throughout the centuries has a great and dangerous potential for reinforcing pathological shame. We can remain silent, we can avoid confronting a sister or brother, but we cannot hide our aversion. As this is translated into nonverbal communication and eventually into unmistakable patterns of relational avoidance, we can easily convey the impression that we reject the person who has transgressed Christian values. Thus we impose the kind of shame that leads to pathology. Ironically, then, as we shy away from speaking about behaviors that are shameful (from the viewpoint of the New Testament and Christian ethics) out of a desire not to promote psychological dis-ease, we end up being more prone to do what we would avoid.

If we were to be bold to speak as a group about the behavior, however, our aversion would be clearly and precisely focused. The transgressor would know that it was the behavior and not his or her person that did not find acceptance. The recipient of this censure would have the opportunity to divorce him- or herself from the dishonorable behavior (repent), as well as the opportunity to choose perseverance in what the Christian culture calls sin, knowing that he or she would thus continue to bring grief to the sisters and brothers. Either way, however, the church would not be reinforcing the dangerous, self-hating shame. Karen writes that guilt is about doing, shame about being. "We say, I am ashamed of *myself*. I am guilty *for* something."[55] This distinction, however, is too clean and simple. In the Greco-Roman world (including the Jewish subculture), being is reflected in doing: one is what one does; a tree is known by the nature of its fruits; good people do virtuous acts; the one who does what is shameful is a shameful and base person (Mt 7:16-20). In that world, people are made to feel

---

[55]Ibid., p. 47.

ashamed of doing certain things, and that kind of shame remains a helpful safeguard against the dangers of sin. Only when a person is made ashamed of "being" does shame become destructive.

Psychologists have studied twelve-step groups intently from the perspective of shame, something closely connected with addiction. Karen levels the critique that these groups deal with "secondary shame," the shame of being addicted to something, but not the "core feelings of shame that may have caused one to become an addict in the first place."[56] A room full of alcoholics can quickly dissipate the stigma of being an alcoholic. What is most needed, however, is to get at the root of what drove a person to alcoholism, to touch and heal that shame or disorder.

How can we apply this apt critique so as to improve the mission of the church? We would do well to begin to see ourselves as a sort of "sinners anonymous." This means, rather straightforwardly, admitting rather than suppressing the truth of our fallenness, ceasing our efforts to create and preserve a perfect image (that is, a mask—and our commitment to our own mask reinforces everyone else's commitment to their own masks) and refocusing our churches healthfully on the restoration of God's image in us. Admitting our solidarity in this regard removes the sense of being a shameful person[57] because of some sin. This is the kind of shame that prevents a person from confessing, discussing, becoming open about who he or she really is—a silence that proves the best breeding ground for sin fully to conceive and bear fruit. Removing the secondary shame makes it possible for the person to expose the sin, to discover what motivates the sin, and to pursue release from the power of that sin in an atmosphere of prayer, mutual honesty and mutual support. The Christian learns that he or she fights a common enemy who works best by alienating our secret obsessions with sin from our healing community. Disarming the enemy's strategy and sharing our temptations make it all the less likely that we will follow through on,

---

[56]Ibid., p. 55.

[57]Ibid., p. 70. Karen recognizes the healing potential of what he calls "universal shame," which he links with medieval Christendom but really could have linked with its source, the apostle Paul (see Rom 1—3). This is the shame inherent in being human: falling short of God's glory. "The belief that all people were sinners" was "used to bind the community, to maintain a spiritual focus and, perhaps incidentally, to drain off some shame that might otherwise have become individual and narcissistic [i.e., pathogenic]."

or persist in, the sin. If we are honest as a believing community about who we are and with what we struggle, we can also support one another as a family of faith on the way to becoming what the power of God seeks to make of us.

Three

PATRONAGE & RECIPROCITY

The Social Context of Grace

P *eople in the United States and northern Europe may be culturally condi*tioned to find the concept of patronage distasteful at first and not at all a suitable metaphor for talking about God's relationship to us. When we say "it's not what you know but who you know," it is usually because we sense someone has had an unfair advantage over us or over the friend whom we console with these words. It violates our conviction that everyone should have equal access to employment opportunities (being evaluated on the basis of pertinent skills rather than personal connection) or to services offered by private businesses or civic agencies.[1] Where patronage occurs (often deridingly called nepotism: channeling opportunities to relations or personal friends), it is often done "under the table" and kept as quiet as possible.[2]

---

[1]See Halvor Moxnes, "Patron-Client Relations and the New Community in Luke-Acts," in *The Social World of Luke-Acts*, ed. Jerome H. Neyrey (Peabody, Mass.: Hendrickson, 1991), pp. 242-44.
[2]John H. Elliott, "Patronage and Clientism in Early Christian Society," *Forum* 3 (1987): 40.

We tend to get what we need or want by means of buying and selling, where exchange is precisely measured out ahead of time. You do not leave a department store owing the sales person a favor, nor does the cashier at a restaurant owe me a good turn for the money I gave after dinner. When we seek employment, most often we are hired on the basis of our skills and experience by people we do not know. We prepare for employment not so much by cultivating connections (although this is still useful!) as by equipping ourselves with the knowledge and skills that, we hope, a potential employer will recognize as giving us the necessary resources to do the job well. When we fall into hard times, there is a massive public welfare system in place, access to which is offered not as a personal favor but as a bureaucratized right of the poor or unemployed. If an alien wants citizenship and the rights that go along with it, he or she applies and undergoes the same process as every other naturalized citizen—it is not a favor granted personally by an individual in power.

The world of the authors and readers of the New Testament, however, was one in which personal patronage was an essential means of acquiring access to goods, protection or opportunities for employment and advancement. Not only was it essential—it was expected and publicized! The giving and receiving of favors was, according to a first-century participant, the "practice that constitutes the chief bond of human society" (Seneca *Ben.* 1.4.2). To enter their world and hear their words more authentically, we have to leave behind our cultural norms and ways of doing things and learn a quite different way of managing resources and meeting needs.

Patronage and Friendship

For everyday needs there was the market, in which buying and selling provided access to daily necessities. For anything outside of the ordinary, the person sought out the individual who possessed or controlled access to what the person needed and received it as a favor. The ancient world from the classical through the Roman periods was one of significantly limited access to goods. The greater part of the property, wealth and power was concentrated into the hands of the few, and access to these goods was through personal connection rather than bureaucratic channels. The kinds of benefits sought from patrons depended on the needs or desires of the petitioner. They might include plots of land or distributions of money to get started in business or to supply food after a crop failure or failed business venture. Other benefits might include protection, debt relief or an appointment to some office or position in government. "Help one person with money, another with credit, another with influence, another with advice, another with sound precepts" (Seneca *Ben.* 1.2.4, LCL). If the patron granted the petition, the petitioner would become the client of the patron and a potentially long-term relationship would begin.[3] This relationship would be marked by the mutual exchange of desired goods and services, the patron being available for assistance in the future, the client doing everything in his or her power to enhance the fame and honor of the patron (publicizing the benefit and showing the patron respect), remaining loyal to the patron and providing services whenever the opportunity arose.

Sometimes the most important gift a patron could give was access to (and influence with) another patron who actually had power over the benefit being sought. For the sake of clarity, a patron who provides access to another patron for his or her client has been called a "broker"[4] (a classical term for this was *mediator*). Brokerage was commonplace and expected in public life. Sophocles (*Oed.* 771-774) provides a fictional example of this in the words of Creon, who defends himself with these words against Oedipus' charge of conspiracy to usurp the kingship:

> I am welcome everywhere; every man salutes me,
> And those who want your favor seek my ear,
> Since I know how to manage what they ask.

Creon enjoys high esteem and displays of public reputation on the

---

[3]Bonds of reciprocity (whether between social equals, called "friends," or between patrons and their clients) could continue across the generations. A child inherits, as it were, his or her parents' networks of friends and enemies. Ben Sira bears witness: "He has left behind him an avenger against his enemies, and one to repay the kindness of his friends" (Sir 30:6), as does Isocrates: "It is fitting that a son should inherit his father's friendships even as he inherits his estate" (*Ad Dem.* 2, LCL). See also Seneca *Ben.* 2.18.5: "I must be far more careful in selecting my creditor for a benefit than my creditor for a loan. For to the latter I shall have to return the same amount that I have received, and, when I have returned it, I have paid all my debt and am free; but to the other I must make an additional payment, and, even after I have paid my debt of gratitude, the bond between us still holds; for, just when I have finished paying it, I am obliged to begin again, and friendship endures; and, as I would not admit an unworthy man to my friendship, so neither would I admit one who is unworthy to the most sacred privilege of benefits, from which friendship springs" (LCL).
[4]Jeremy Boissevain, *Friends of Friends: Networks, Manipulators and Coalitions* (New York: St. Martin's, 1974), p. 148.

basis of his ability to grant or withhold his primary resource: access to King Oedipus and thus to royal favors.

Numerous examples of brokerage can be found in the letters of Cicero, Pliny the Younger and Fronto, correspondence providing windows into public policy from the late republic through the second century of the empire.[5] Pliny's letters to the emperor Trajan (dating from A.D. 111-113, the time during which Pliny was governor of Bithynia) contain attempts by Pliny to procure imperial favors for his own friends and clients. In one such letter (*Ep.* 10.4), Pliny introduces a client of his, named Voconius Romanus, to Trajan with a view to getting Voconius a senatorial appointment. He addresses Trajan clearly as a client addressing his patron and proceeds to ask a favor for Voconius. Pliny offers his own character as a guarantee of his client's character, and Trajan's "favorable judgement" of Pliny (not Voconius, whom he does not know) would become the basis for Trajan's granting of this favor. Should the favor be granted by the emperor, Voconius would be indebted not only to Trajan but also to Pliny, who will, in turn, be indebted further to Trajan.[6] The broker, or mediator, at the same time incurs a debt and increases his own honor through the indebtedness of his client. Brokerage—the gift of access to another, often greater patron—was in itself a highly valued benefit. Without such connections the client would never have had access to what he desired or needed. This is especially apparent in the case of Pliny's physical therapist, Arpocras, who gains both Roman and Alexandrian citizenship by means of Pliny, who petitions Trajan on his behalf (*Ep.* 10.5-7, 10). Pliny gives this local physician access to the emperor, the fount of patronage, which he would never have enjoyed otherwise. Brokerage could even intervene in the judicial process. Both Cicero[7] and Marcus Aurelius (*Ad M. Caes.* 3.2) use their connections of friendship with a judge to secure favorable outcomes for their clients, on whose behalf they write.

So far we have been discussing personal patronage as it occurred

---

[5] A fuller analysis of these can be found in Geoffrey E. M. de Ste. Croix, "Suffragium: From Vote to Patronage," *British Journal of Sociology* 5 (1954): 33-48.

[6] See also Richard Saller, *Personal Patronage Under the Early Empire* (Cambridge: Cambridge University Press, 1982), p. 75 n. 194: "That the mediators would have received the credit and gratitude from the ultimate recipient of the favor is clear from the last sentence of Pliny *Ep.* 3.8, where Pliny secures a tribunate for Suetonius who passes it on to a relative, with the result that the relative is indebted to Suetonius who is in turn indebted to Pliny."

[7] *Ad Familiares* 13, cited in Andrew Wallace-Hadrill, "Patronage in Roman Society: From Republic to Empire," in *Patronage in Ancient Society* (London: Routledge, 1989), p. 77.

between people of unequal social status: someone of lesser power, honor and wealth seeks out the aid of a person of superior power, honor and wealth. The kinds of benefits exchanged between such people will be different in kind and quality, the patron providing material gifts or opportunities for advancement, the client contributing to the patron's reputation and power base. Relationships of reciprocity also occur between social equals, people of like means who can exchange like resources, neither one being seen by the other or by society as the inferior of the other. Such relationships went by the name of "friendship."[8] The basic ethos undergirding this relationship, however, is no different from that of the relationship of patrons and clients; the same principle of reciprocity and mutual fidelity is the bedrock of both. Moreover, because patrons were sensitive to the honor of their clients, they rarely called their clients by that name. Instead, they graciously referred to them as friends, even though they were far from social equals. Clients, on the whole, did not attempt to hide their junior status, referring to their patrons as "patrons" rather than as "friends" so as to highlight the honor and respect with which they esteemed their benefactors.[9] Where we see people called "friends" or "partners," therefore, we should suspect that we are still looking at relationships of reciprocity.

Patronage Among the Poor

The greater part of the ancient population has left no written legacy for us to study. Observation of modern agrarian societies leads scholars to believe that all classes participated, in their own ways, in forming relationships of reciprocity. One such cultural anthropologist, Julian Pitt-Rivers, studied the rural communities of southern France,[10] noting that neighbors are always ready to help one another at harvest or sheep-shearing time, not for money or for specific returns. While the helper would even publicly deny that he or she has placed the helped party under obli-

---

[8]See Saller, *Personal Patronage*, pp. 8-11. Cicero provides this testimony: "Another strong bond of fellowship is effected by mutual interchange of kind services; and as long as these kindnesses are mutual and acceptable, those between whom they are interchanged are united by ties of enduring intimacy" (*De Offic.* 1.56, LCL).

[9]Saller, *Personal Patronage*, pp. 8-11; see also Carolyn Osiek and David Balch, *Families in the New Testament World* (Louisville: Westminster John Knox, 1997), p. 49.

[10]Julian Pitt-Rivers, "Postscript: The Place of Grace in Anthropology," in John G. Peristiany and Julian Pitt-Rivers, *Honor and Grace in Anthropology* (Cambridge: Cambridge University Press, 1992), pp. 215-46.

gation, should the latter refuse to help others, it would be remembered and become a blot on that farmer's reputation as a good neighbor:

> Great prestige attaches to a good reputation as a neighbor. Everyone would like to be in credit with everybody and those who show reluctance to lend a hand when they are asked to do so soon acquire a bad reputation which is commented on by innuendo. Those who fail to return the favor done to them come to be excluded from the system altogether. Those of good repute can be sure of compliance on all sides.[11]

Even in the rural areas, there are those who do more favors than receive favors, and these become local patrons of a sort. This situation bears remarkable resemblance to the discussion of reciprocity among farmers in Hesiod's *Works and Days*, written in the sixth century B.C.[12]

Pitt-Rivers advances that another motive for helping when help is needed is as "insurance" against the time when one might need to rely on the neighbors to get through a difficult crisis, to which "a single family farm is particularly vulnerable."[13] Seneca had seen this as an essential aspect of the system of reciprocity two millennia before: "How else do we live in security if it is not that we help each other by an exchange of good offices? It is only through the interchange of benefits that life becomes in some measure equipped and fortified against sudden disasters. Take us singly, and what are we? The prey of all creatures" (*Ben.* 4.18.1). We may conclude then, that those who left us no direct testimony—namely, peasant farmers and local artisans—also entered into relationships of reciprocity and sought to fulfill their part of the relationship nobly as the means both to local honor and security.

Public Benefaction

Personal patronage was not the only form of beneficence in the ancient world. Most public entertainments, whether religious festivals and feasts or local celebrations of athletic competitions, were "given" to the inhabitants of the city by wealthy benefactors. Moreover, most civic improvements, whether temples or theaters, pavements or porticoes, were also

---

[11]Ibid., p. 233.
[12]See especially lines 342-51; 401-4. These are ably discussed in Paul Millett, "Patronage and Its Avoidance in Classical Athens," in *Patronage in Ancient Society*, pp. 15-48, especially pp. 19-20.
[13]Pitt-Rivers, "Postscript," p. 233.

the gifts either of local elites or wealthy persons abroad who wished to confer benefits on a famous city (as Herod the Great provided the money for buildings not only in Jerusalem but also Rhodes, Athens and Sparta).[14] In times of crisis, wealthy benefactors would come to the aid of the public, providing, for example, famine or disaster relief. Public benefaction was an arena open to both men and women of means.[15]

Such public gifts did not make every recipient a client of the benefactor,[16] for lines were drawn between personal patronage and public munificence, but the public as a whole was nevertheless still indebted to that benefactor.[17] In general, the response of the grateful city would consist of the conferral of public honors (like crowning at a prominent public festival, special seating at games) and the provision for a permanent commemoration of the generosity of the giver in the form of honorary inscriptions or, in special cases, statues. Inscriptions across the Mediterranean from North Africa to Greece, Asia and Egypt bear witness to the phenomenon of both personal patronage and public benefaction.[18]

The most powerful figures in the ancient world, namely, kings and emperors, frequently granted public benefactions to cities or even whole provinces in addition to the numerous personal benefactions by which they bound to themselves their client base. Relief from oppression, whether from an extortionate local official, from pirates on the sea or from a hostile force from outside would be a benefaction especially well-suited for an emperor to give. Pardon for crimes committed was reserved for kings and emperors to grant, who were also credited with doing the broad public a great service if peace and stability characterized their rule. The extreme form of response to benefactions from rulers was the offering of worship—those who gave gifts usually besought from the gods were

---

[14]Josephus *J.W.* 1.21.11-12.

[15]Osiek and Balch, *Families*, p. 50.

[16]In Seneca's words, "There is a great difference between not excluding a man and choosing him" (*Ben.* 4.28.5). Personal patronage involves a choice and a commitment to an ongoing relationship with a client.

[17]See Seneca *Ben.* 6.19.2-5.

[18]See Richard P. Saller, "Patronage and Friendship in Early Imperial Rome: Drawing the Distinction," in *Patronage in Ancient Society*, ed. Andrew Wallace-Hadrill (London: Routledge, 1989), pp. 54-55; especially important is the collection of fifty-one inscriptions analyzed in Frederick W. Danker, *Benefactor: Epigraphic Study of a Graeco-Roman and New Testament Semantic Field* (St. Louis: Clayton Publishing, 1982).

judged to be worthy of the honors offered the gods. When the Athenians greeted their general, Demetrius Poliorketes, who had just freed them from foreign domination in 307 B.C., they used cultic language: "Other deities are far away, or have no ears, or are not, or have no care for us at all: but you we see here present—not shaped by wood or stone but in reality. And so to you we pray: First bring us peace, for you possess the power."[19]

A similar picture emerges from the first-hand observations of Nicolaus of Damascus concerning the origin of the cult of Augustus: "All people address him [as Augustus] in accordance with their estimation of his honor, revering him with temples and sacrifices across islands and continents, organized in cities and provinces, matching the greatness of his virtue and repaying his benefactions towards them."[20] The "peace of Augustus" was viewed as relief of divine proportions, and the return of thanks must be equal to the gift. Augustus thus succeeded in the East to the tradition of according divine honors to benefactors, generals and, during the Roman Republic, governors. The imperial cult also provided people in the province with a bridge of access to their ultimate patron. Provinces sought imperial aid (benefactions) through the mediation of the priests of the imperial cult, who both officiated in the province and became the official ambassadors to Rome on behalf of the province. Sending the priests of imperial cultic honors to Rome put the province in the most positive light. The priest was an image of the province's uncompromising loyalty and gratitude, so that the province could be assured of ongoing favor.

Patronage in Greek and Roman Settings

Patronage is not strictly a Roman phenomenon, even though our richest discussions of the institution were written by Romans (Cicero in *De Offic.* and Seneca in *Ben.*). Both public benefaction and personal patronage are well-attested in both Greek and Roman cultures. Only during the time of the Athenian democracy is there an attempt to move away from patronage as the basic model for structuring society.[21] From before the demo-

---

[19]Athenaeus *Deipnosophists* 6.253e-f; quoted in Danker, *Benefactor*, pp. 202-3.
[20]Quoted in Simon R. F. Price, *Rituals and Power: The Roman Imperial Cult in Asia Minor* (Cambridge: Cambridge University Press, 1984), p. 1.
[21]See Paul Millett, "Patronage and Its Avoidance in Classical Athens," in *Patronage in Ancient Society*, ed. Andrew Wallace-Hadrill (London: Routledge, 1989), pp. 15-48.

cratic revolution of 462 B.C., we have the example of Cimon of Athens, whose provision of personal patronage to needy suppliants as well as gifts to the city in general win him the status of "first citizen" and result in his election to the generalship for seventeen consecutive years.[22] Throughout the period of the democracy itself, the avoidance of open patronage applies only between citizens, whose freedom should not be compromised out of a need to gratify a potential or past benefactor. The noncitizens (called "metics," or "resident aliens") are *required* to have a sponsor or patron (a *prostatēs*) who would provide access to the institutions of the city for the noncitizen.[23]

By the time that Philip of Macedon and his son, Alexander, rise to prominence, however, personal patronage is once again openly spoken of in Athens. Demosthenes, an orator who died in 322 B.C., speaks openly both of his public benefactions (fortification of the city walls), which he deems worthy of gratitude and public honor, and his private acts of patronage to the distressed and financially challenged (*De Corona* 268-69, 299). Aristotle speaks in his *Nicomachian Ethics* (1163b1-5, 12-18) of the type of friendship in which one partner receives the larger share of honor and acclamation, and the other partner the larger share of material assistance—clearly a reference to personal patronage between people of unequal social status. By the first century A.D., the attempt at Athens to restrict personal patronage is but a distant memory, an exception to an unobjectionable rule.

Greek and Latin authors from the Hellenistic and Roman periods express a shared ethos where friendship, patronage and public benefaction are concerned. Aristotle and Seneca, Dio Chrysostom and Cicero, agree concerning what guidelines the giver and recipient should follow. Moreover, as the Greek world is transformed into the provinces of the Roman Empire, Greek cities become acquainted with patronage as the means by which the whole city gets connected with the center of power and resources, namely, the emperor and Senate of Rome. A Greek statesman like Plutarch, instructing aspiring politicians, discusses the advisability of having well-placed friends who can support and advance one's political agenda (*Mor.* 814C). The main difference between personal patronage in the Greek and Roman cultures is the formalized etiquette

---

[22]Ibid., pp. 23-25.
[23]Ibid., p. 34.

surrounding the latter in the morning greeting of the patron by his or her clients. The *salutatio* displays the relationship of patron and clients visibly and publicly, a display that would continue throughout the day as some number of clients accompany the patron in public places, displaying the patron's prestige and power with a visible entourage at home and in the public spaces.[24] With this one difference (a difference that disappears as Roman customs spread throughout their empire), patronage and benefaction proceed in Greek and Roman circles with much the same ethos and expectations.

The Social Context of Grace

We have looked closely and at some length at the relationships and activities that mark the patron-client relationship, friendship and public benefaction, because these are the social contexts in which the word *grace (charis)* is at home in the first century A.D. Today, *grace* is primarily a religious word, heard only in churches and Christian circles. It has progressed through millennia of theological reflection, developments and accretions (witness the multiplication of terms like "justifying grace," "sanctifying grace" and "prevenient grace" in Christian theology, systematizing the order of salvation). For the actual writers and readers of the New Testament, however, *grace* was not primarily a religious, as opposed to a secular, word. Rather, it was used to speak of reciprocity among human beings and between mortals and God (or, in pagan literature, the gods). This single word encapsulated the entire ethos of the relationships we have been describing.

First, *grace* was used to refer to the willingness of a patron to grant some benefit to another person or to a group. In this sense, it means "favor," in the sense of "favorable disposition." In Aristotle's words (*Rhetoric* 2.7.1 [1385a16-20]), "Grace *[charis]* may be defined as helpfulness toward someone in need, not in return for anything, nor for the advantage of the helper himself [or herself], but for that of the person helped."[25] In this sense, the word highlights the generosity and disposition of the patron, benefactor or giver. The same word carries a second sense, often being used to denote the gift itself, that is, the result of

---

[24]Saller, "Patronage and Friendship," pp. 57-58.
[25]See the discussion also in Hans Conzelman and Walther Zimmerli, "χάρις κτλ," in *TDNT* 9:373-76.

\

the giver's beneficent feelings.[26] Many honorary inscriptions mention the graces *(charitas)* of the benefactor as the cause for conferring public praise, emphasizing the real and received products of the benefactor's goodwill toward a city or group.[27] Finally, *grace* can be used to speak of the response to a benefactor and his or her gifts, namely, "gratitude." Demosthenes provides a helpful window into this aspect in his *De Corona* as he chides his audience for not responding honorably to those who have helped them in the past: "But you are so ungrateful *(acharistos)* and wicked by nature that, having been made free out of slavery and wealthy out of poverty by these people, you do not show gratitude *(charin echeis)* toward them but rather enriched yourself by taking action against them" *(De Corona* 131).[28] *Grace* thus has very specific meanings for the authors and readers of the New Testament, meanings derived primarily from the use of the word in the context of the giving of benefits and the requiting of favors.

The fact that one and the same word can be used to speak of a beneficent act and the response to a beneficent act suggests implicitly what many moralists from the Greek and Roman cultures stated explicitly: grace must be met with grace; favor must always give birth to favor;[29] gift must always be met with gratitude. An image that captured this for the ancients was the picture of three goddesses, the three "Graces," dancing hand in hand in a circle. Seneca's explanation of the image is most revealing:

---

[26]It is in its meaning as "gift" that *grace* also referred to the qualities of "poise," "charm" or "beauty" and that the adjective *graceful* was, and is, applied to "charming, beautiful, skilled" people. In these cases *graceful* means "graced" or "gifted," that is, "having received positive endowments from God or nature."

[27]See the frequent occurrence of the plural *graces* ("gifts," *charitas*) in the inscriptions collected in Danker, *Benefactor* (as well as the discussion on p. 328); Conzelman and Zimmerli *(TDNT* 9:375) also cite the customary formula: "On account of the gifts, the χάριτας, of so-and-so we proclaim these honors." The Latin term *beneficium* is defined by Seneca as the equivalent of these first two meanings of *charis* (*Ben.* 2.34.5). The Latin word *gratia*, moreover, shares the three meanings wedded within the Greek *charis*.

[28]See, further, Conzelman and Zimmerli *(TDNT* 9:376): "In relation to the recipient of grace χάρις means 'thanks' to the benefactor." The following passages also use the expression "have grace" in the sense of "show thanks": Luke 17:9 and Hebrews 12:28; on "grace" as "thanks," see the expression "thanks *(charis)* be to God" in Romans 6:17; 7:25; 2 Corinthians 8:16; 9:15.

[29]Hence the saying of Sophocles *(Ajax* 522): "Favor *(charis)* is always giving birth to favor *(charin)*."

Some would have it appear that there is one for bestowing a benefit, one for receiving it, and a third for returning it; others hold that there are three classes of benefactors—those who receive benefits, those who return them, those who receive and return them at the same time. . . . Why do the sisters hand in hand dance in a ring which returns upon itself? For the reason that a benefit passing in its course from hand to hand returns nevertheless to the giver; *the beauty of the whole is destroyed if the course is anywhere broken,* and it has most beauty if it is continuous and maintains an uninterrupted succession. . . . Their faces are cheerful, as are ordinarily the faces of those who bestow or receive benefits. They are young because the memory of benefits ought not to grow old. They are maidens because benefits are pure and holy and undefiled in the eyes of all; [their robes] are transparent because benefits desire to be seen. (*Ben.* 1.3.2-5; LCL, emphasis added)

From this and many other ancient witnesses, we learn that there is no such thing as an isolated act of *grace*. An act of favor and its manifestation (the gift) initiate a circle dance in which the recipients of favor and gifts must "return the favor," that is, give again to the giver (both in terms of a generous disposition and in terms of some gift, whether material or otherwise). Only a gift requited is a gift well and nobly received. To fail to return favor for favor is, in effect, to break off the dance and destroy the beauty of the gracious act.

In what follows, we will look closely at how Greek and Roman authors conceived of well-executed grace exchanges, first in relation to the giver and then in relation to the recipient.

Showing Favor (Grace)

Generosity was a highly valued characteristic in people in the Hellenistic and Roman periods. Most public works, public festivals and entertainments, and private aid to individuals or groups came through the willingness of generous people of means to spend their wealth on others. Because their assistance was essential in so many ways, there were strong social sanctions against violating the expectations of gratitude (see below), violations that threatened to cut off the source of aid or redirect that aid in more promising directions.

There were also clear codes of conduct for the giver as well, guidelines that sought to preserve, in theory at least, the nobility and purity of a generous act. First, ancient ethicists spoke much of the motives that should guide the benefactor or patron. Aristotle's definition of *grace* in its first sense (the generous disposition of the giver), quoted above, also under-scores the fact that a giver must act not from self-interest but in the inter-est of the recipient.[30] If the motive is primarily self-interest, any sense of "favor" is nullified and with it the deep feelings and obligations of grati-tude (Aristotle *Rhetoric* 1385a35-1385b3). The Jewish sage Yeshua Ben Sira lampoons the ungraceful giver (Sir 20:13-16). This character gives not out of the virtue of generosity but in anticipation of profit, and if the profit does not come immediately, he considers his gifts to be thrown away and complains aloud about the ingratitude of the human race. Seneca also speaks censoriously of this character: "He who gives benefits imitates the gods, he who seeks a return, money-lenders" (*Ben.* 3.15.4).[31] The point is that the giver, if he or she gives nobly, never gives with an eye to what can be gained from the gift.[32] The giver does not give to an elderly person so as to be remembered in a will, or to an elected official with a view to get-ting some leverage in politics. Such people are investors, not benefactors or friends.

Gifts are not to be made with a view to having some desired object given in return, but gifts were still to be made strategically. According to Cicero, good gifts badly placed are badly given (*De Offic.* 2.62). The shared advice of Isocrates, Ben Sira, Cicero and Seneca is that the giver should scrutinize the person to whom he or she is thinking of giving a gift.[33] The recipient should be a virtuous person who will honor the gen-

---

[30]Seneca allows the giving of a benefaction to be profitable both to the giver and the recipi-ent, stressing that the recipient is not released from showing gratitude: "I am not so unjust as to feel under no obligation to a man who, when he was profitable to me, was also profit-able to himself . . . nay, I am also desirous that a benefit given to me should even be more advantageous to the giver, provided that, when he gave it, he was considering us both, and meant to divide it between himself and me. . . . I am, not merely unjust, I am ungrateful, if I do not rejoice that, while he has benefitted me, he has also benefitted himself" (*Ben.* 6.13.1-2, LCL).

[31]Throughout his book, Seneca stresses that benefactors and friends give "for the sake of giv-ing" and not for the sake of any return (*Ben.* 1.2.3; 4.29.3).

[32]Pitt-Rivers points out that the typical responses to thanks in English, French, Italian and German-speaking countries involve some equivalent of "it was nothing" or "it was a plea-sure," sayings that, in denying that obligation has been incurred, stress the purity of the motive of the giver (without nullifying any obligation—in fact, only making that obligation felt more strongly by the recipient of favor since the motives are seen to have been pure). It is astounding that the moral ideal of giving "purely" for the sake of the recipient has per-sisted intact across the millennia ("Postscript," pp. 217-18).

[33]Ben Sira advises: "If you do a kindness, know to whom you do it, and you will be thanked for your good deeds" (Sir 12:1), advice that was remembered in the early church (see

erosity and kindness behind the gift, who would value more the continuing relationship with the giver than any particular gift. Especially poignant is Isocrates' advice: "Bestow your favors on the good; for a goodly treasure is a store of gratitude laid up in the heart of an honest man. If you benefit bad men, you will have the same reward as those who feed stray dogs; for these snarl alike at those who give them food and at the passing stranger; and just so base men wrong alike those who help them and those who harm them" (*Ad Dem.* 29, LCL). An important component in deciding who will be a worthy recipient of such gifts is the person's track record of how he or she has responded to other givers in the past.[34] Has the person responded nobly, with gratitude? He or she will probably be worthy of more favors. A reputation for knowing how to be grateful was, in effect, the ancient equivalent of a credit rating.

Giving without advance calculation of a return and selecting one's beneficiaries carefully may appear to be contradictory principles. When Seneca writes that gifts given to the ungrateful are "thrown away" (*Ben.* 1.1.2), he may appear to intensify this contradiction. Aware of this potential misunderstanding, he writes: "I choose a person who will be grateful, not one who is likely to make a return, and it often happens that the grateful man is one who is not likely to make a return, while the ungrateful man is one who has made a return. It is to the heart that my estimate is directed" (*Ben.* 4.10.4). The noble giver evaluates his or her potential beneficiaries not in light of any actual return they might make—not in terms of the value of the gifts or services they might give in exchange in the future—but in light of the disposition of the recipient's heart toward feeling gratitude, appreciating and remembering the gift and making whatever return the person is able, given his or her means. The patron's motive must be kept pure, that is, not sowing benefits for the sake of material gains or other temporal advantages, but looking only for the grateful heart irrespective of the means possessed

---

Didache 1.5-6) as a good rule for giving alms (an important form of benefaction, which, though personal, did not initiate the ongoing relationship of patron and client). Cicero affirms that "our love [a common way to refer to beneficence] must be shown to the worthy," urging his reader to consider the potential recipient's "character, his regard for us, his closeness to us, his usefulness to us in former services" when weighing the decision to give or not to give (*De Offic.* 1.45). The need to select beneficiaries and clients with great care is a frequent theme in Seneca (*Ben.* 1.1.2; 3.11.1; 3.14.1; 4.8.2).

[34]Thus Isocrates: "Make no man your friend before inquiring how he has used his former friends; for you must expect him to treat you as he has treated them" (*Ad Dem.* 24, LCL).

by the potential recipient to be of service in the future.

The benefactor's favor was not, however, to be limited by the potential beneficiary's virtue (or lack thereof). Even while advising his readers to channel their resources first toward the deserving (that is, those who have given signs of a grateful character),[35] Seneca urges givers to remain as free as the gods in terms of their generosity. Benefaction was the initiation of the dance of grace, an action rather than a response, a perfect and self-contained act rather than an act that depended on anything beyond the virtue and goodwill of the giver. Therefore, Seneca advises his readers, the human benefactor should imitate the gods, by whose design "the sun rises also upon the wicked" and "rains" are provided for both good and bad (*Ben.* 4.26.1, 4.28.1), who follow the leading of their own generous and kind hearts in their dealings with human beings, both the grateful and the sacrilegious (*Ben.* 1.1.9).

A virtuous human patron or benefactor, then, will be willing to grant public benefactions even though he or she knows that the ingrates will also derive enjoyment from the games, the public meals, the construction of a new theater. Seneca's lofty code for givers, however, applies also to personal patronage. A generous-hearted patron may even choose a known ingrate—even someone who has previously failed to show gratitude for a previous gift granted by this same patron—to receive a favor (*Ben.* 1.10.5; 7.31.2, 4). Repeated acts of kindness, like a farmer's ongoing labor over difficult soil, may yet awaken a slow heart to show gratitude and respond nobly (*Ben.* 7.32).

Responding with Grace

As we have already seen in Seneca's allegory of the three Graces, an act of favor must give rise to a response of gratitude—grace *must* answer grace, or else something beautiful will be defaced and turned into something ugly. According to Cicero, while initiating a gift was a matter of choice, gratitude was not optional for honorable people, but rather an absolute duty (*De Offic.* 1.47-48). Receiving a favor or kindness meant incurring very directly a debt or obligation to respond gratefully, a debt on which one could not default.[36] Seneca stresses the simultaneity of receiv-

---

[35]See Seneca *Ben.* 1.10.5.

[36]See Seneca *Ben.* 2.35.3-4; 5.11.5; 1.4.3 (which uses the expression "debt of gratitude"). Aristotle (*Nic. Eth.* 8.14.3 [1163b12-15]) also speaks of the necessity of repaying a gift, even

ing a gift and an obligation: "The person who intends to be grateful, even while she or he is receiving, should turn his or her thoughts to returning the favor" (*Ben.* 2.25.3). Indeed, the virtuous person could seek to compete with the giver in terms of kindnesses and favor, trying not merely to return the favor but to return it with interest like the fruit-ful soil that bears crops far more abundant than the seeds that were scat-tered on it.[37]

Gratitude toward one's patrons (or toward public benefactors) was a prominent example in discussions of what it meant to live out the cardi-nal virtue of justice, a virtue defined as giving to each person his or her due. It ranked in importance next to showing the gods, those supreme benefactors, the proper honor and services.[38] Failure to show gratitude, however, was classed as the worst of crimes, being compared to sacrilege against the gods, since the Graces were considered goddesses.[39] It was censured as an injury against the human race, since ingratitude discour-ages the very generosity that is so crucial to public life and to personal aid. Seneca captures well the perilous nature of life in the first-century world and the need for firm tethers of friendship and patronage to secure one against mishap:

> Ingratitude is something to be avoided in itself because there is nothing that so effectually disrupts and destroys the harmony of the human race as this vice. For how else do we live in security if it is not that we help each other by an exchange of good offices? It is only through the interchange of bene-fits that life becomes in some measure equipped and fortified against sud-den disasters. Take us singly, and what are we? The prey of all creatures. (*Ben.* 4.18.1, LCL)[40]

The ingrate committed a crime against the gods, humanity and ulti-

---

though the kind of gifts may be vastly different (e.g., a "friend" of lesser means returns intangible goods like honor and fame for material goods received from a "friend" of greater means, i.e., a patron).

[37] Cicero *De Offic.* 1.48; Seneca *Ben.* 1.4.3; see also Isocrates *Ad Dem.* 26: "Consider it equally disgraceful to be outdone by your enemies in doing injury and to be surpassed by your friends in doing kindness (*tais euergesiais*)" (LCL). See also Pseudo-Phocylides (*Sentences*, 80): "It is proper to surpass benefactors with still more."

[38] Thus Dio Chrysostom *Or.* 31.7. Ben Sira goes so far as to suggest that the requital of favors counts as an offering to God: "The one who returns a kindness (*antapodidous charin*) offers choice flour" (Sir 35:3).

[39] Seneca (*Ben.* 1.4.4) and Dio Chrysostom (*Or.* 31.37) both call ingratitude an assault on the honor of the three Graces, and thus a wicked act of sacrilege.

[40] See also Cicero *De Offic.* 2.63.

mately himself or herself, while the person who returned grace for grace embodied the highest virtues of piety and justice and was valued for contributing to the forward movement of the dance of grace on which so much depended.

Responding justly to one's benefactors was a behavior enforced not by written laws but rather "by unwritten customs and universal practice," with the result that a person known for gratitude would be considered praiseworthy and honorable by all, while the ingrate would be regarded as disgraceful.[41] There was no law for the prosecution of the person who failed to requite a favor (with the interesting exception of classical Macedonia), but, Seneca affirmed, the punishment of shame and being hated by all good people would more than make up for the lack of official sanctions.[42] Neglecting to return a kindness, forgetfulness of kindnesses already received in the past, and, most horrendous of all, repaying favor with insult or injury—these were courses of action to be avoided by an honorable person at *all* costs.[43] Rather, gifts were always to be remembered, commemorated first of all in the shrine of one's own mind, and always to be requited with gratitude. The social sanctions of honor and shame, therefore, were important bulwarks for the virtue of gratitude and exerted considerable pressure in this direction.

Practically speaking, responding with gratitude was also reinforced by the knowledge that if an individual has needed favors in the past, he or she most assuredly will still need favors and assistance in the future. As we have seen already, a reputation for gratitude was the best credit line a person could have in the ancient world, since patrons and benefactors, when selecting beneficiaries, would seek out those who knew how to be grateful. Even though benefactors might be moved to risk giving to a per-

---

[41]Quote from Anaximenes (frequently attributed to Aristotle), *Rhetorica ad Alexandrum* 1421b3-1422a2. Seneca appeals to unanimity of human opinion in this regard: "What is so praiseworthy, upon what are all our minds so uniformly agreed, as the repayment of good services with gratitude?" (*Ben.* 4.16.3); "Not to return gratitude for benefits is a disgrace, and the whole world counts it as such" (*Ben.* 3.1.1).

[42]Seneca *Ben.* 3.6.2; 3.17.1-12.

[43]On the shamefulness of forgetting benefactions, see Cicero *De Offic.* 2.63; Seneca *Ben.* 3.1.3; 3.2.1; on the even greater dangers of insulting one's benefactors, see Aristotle *Rhetoric* 2.2.8 and Dio Chrysostom *Or.* 31. Such courses of action do not only destroy a patron's benevolent disposition toward one—they can turn benevolence into virulent anger and the desire for revenge (see also Pitt-Rivers, "Postscript," p. 236).

son whose reputation had been marred by ingratitude, since most benefactors' resources were limited, they would seek out the worthy recipients
first.[44] The person who "requites favors," then, is commended by Ben Sira
for his foresight, since he will not fail to find aid when needed in the
future (Sir 3:31).

An extreme yet surprisingly common example of showing gratitude
with an eye to future favors came to expression in honorary inscriptions. Several inscriptions proclaiming honors to public benefactors
contained in Danker's collection make explicit the motive behind the
inscription, namely, "that all might know that we express appropriate
appreciation to those who . . . make us the beneficiaries of their philan-
thropies," and that other benefactors may confer their benefits in the
assurance that "they shall receive appropriate gratitude" as well.[45] Seeing that these cities or groups provided for the honor and remembrance
of their benefactors, other benefactors would be encouraged to channel
their resources in their direction as well (even as the honored benefactor
would be positively inclined to continue his or her beneficence).[46] The
opposite would also be true, namely that those who have shown ingratitude to their patrons or benefactors should expect to be excluded from
future favors, both by the insulted benefactor and by other potential
patrons as well. Just as no one goes back to a merchant who has been

---

[44]See, again, Seneca *Ben.* 1.10.5; Isocrates *Ad Dem.* 24, 29. Wallace-Hadrill ("Patronage in
Roman Society," pp. 72-73) suggests, astutely in light of the perception of limited goods
that marked the ancient world, that a patron's power came not from being able to give
whatever was needed to whomever asked but from the impossibility of bestowing favors
on all who needed them. The finitude of beneficence made jockeying for limited resources
all the more intense and enhanced the willingness of clients or would-be clients to vie with
one another to attain the patron's favor through services, honors and the like: "Their success in control lay as much in their power to refuse as in their readiness to deliver the
goods." This certainly played out in the scene of provinces and cities vying for a special
place in the emperor's eye, so that scarce resources would be diverted one way and not
another. At this point an important distinction between human patronage and God's
patronage emerges, for the latter is proclaimed as the giver of boundless benefits to whomever asks (Lk 11:9-13; Jas 1:5).

[45]Five out of fifty-one inscriptions collected and translated by Danker contain these expressions or their near equivalents (see Danker, *Benefactor,* pp. 57, 77-79, 89-91, 152-53, 283-85).
Cicero (*De Offic.* 2.70) also attests that showing gratitude to present patrons attracts the
positive attention of potential future patrons as well.

[46]Dio Chrysostom bears witness to the truth of these dynamics: "For those who take seri-
ously their obligations toward their benefactors and mete out just treatment to those who
have loved them, all men regard as worthy of favour [*charitos axious*], and without exception each would wish to benefit them to the best of his ability"(*Or.* 31.7).

discovered to cheat customers, and as no one entrusts valuables to the safekeeping of someone who has previously lost valuables entrusted to him or her, so "those who have insulted their benefactors will not be thought worthy of a favor *(charitos axious)* by anyone" (Dio Chrysostom *Or.* 31.38, 65).

As we consider gratitude, then, we are presented with something of a paradox. Just as the favor was freely bestowed, so the response must be free and uncoerced. Nonetheless, that response is at the same time necessary and unavoidable for an honorable person who wishes to be known as such (and hence the recipient of favor in the future). Gratitude is never a formal obligation. There is no advance calculation of or agreed on return for the gift given.[47] Nevertheless the recipient of a favor knows that he or she stands under the necessity of returning favor when favor has been received. The element of exchange must settle into the background, being dominated instead by a sense of mutual favor, of mutual goodwill and generosity.[48]

Manifestations of Gratitude

"Returning a favor" could take on many forms, depending on the nature of the gift and the relative economic and political clout of the parties concerned. Cities or associations would show their gratitude for public benefactions by providing for the public recognition (honoring and increasing the fame) of the giver and often memorializing the gift and the honors conferred by means of a public inscription or, in exceptional cases, a statue of the giver or other monument.[49]

Even in personal patronage (in which the parties are not on equal footing), however, public honor and testimony would comprise an important component of a grateful response. An early witness to this is Aristotle,

---

[47]Seneca *Ben.* 3.7.2

[48]Seneca *Ben.* 6.41.1-2. Once again, Pitt-Rivers's observations of reciprocity in the modern Mediterranean (rural) context resonate deeply with their ancient counterpart: "A gift is not a gift unless it is a free gift, i.e., involving no obligation on the part of the receiver, and yet . . . it nevertheless requires to be returned" ("Postscript," p. 233); "You cannot pay for a favor in any way or it ceases to be one, you can only thank, though on a later occasion you can demonstrate gratitude by making an equally 'free' gift in return" (ibid., p. 231).

[49]See Dio Chrysostom *Or.* 31.17, 20; 51.9. The first half of Danker, *Benefactor,* consists of translations and analyses of such honorary inscriptions. In *Oration* 66, Dio Chrysostom lampoons the "glory seeker" who spends all his fortune on public benefactions just to receive crowns, special seating and public proclamations—"lures for the simpletons."

who writes in his *Nicomachean Ethics* that "both parties should receive a larger share from the friendship, but not a larger share of the same thing: the superior should receive the larger share of honor, the needy one the larger share of profit; for honor is the due reward of virtue and beneficence" (*Nic. Eth.* 8.14.2 [1163b1-5]). Such a return, though of a very different kind, preserves the friendship. Seneca emphasizes the public nature of the testimony that the recipient of a patron's gifts is to bear. Gratitude for, and pleasure at, receiving these gifts should be expressed "not merely in the hearing of the giver, but everywhere" (*Ben.* 2.22.1): "The greater the favour, the more earnestly must we express ourselves, resorting to such compliments as: . . . 'I shall never be able to repay you my gratitude, but, at any rate, I shall not cease from declaring everywhere that I am unable to repay it'" (*Ben.* 2.24.4). Increasing the fame of the giver is part of the proper return for a benefit, and a gift that one is ashamed to acknowledge openly in the hearing of all, one has no business accepting in the first place (*Ben.* 2.23.1).

These dynamics are also at work in Jewish literature with regard to formulating a proper response to God's favors, that is, with regard to answering the psalmist's question "What shall I give back to the LORD for all his gifts to me?" (Ps 116:12, my translation). The psalmist answers his own question by enumerating the public testimonies he will give to God's fidelity and favor. Similarly, after God brings a happy ending to the many dangers and trials faced by Tobit and his family, the angel Raphael enjoins such public testimony to honor God as a fitting response: "Bless God and acknowledge him in the presence of all the living for the good things he has done for you. . . . With fitting honor declare to all people the deeds of God. Do not be slow to acknowledge him. . . . Reveal the works of God, and with fitting honor . . . acknowledge him" (Tob 12:6-7).[50]

A second component of gratitude that comes to expression in relationships of personal patronage or friendship is loyalty to the giver, that is, showing gratitude and owning one's association with the giver even when fortunes turn, and it becomes costly. Thus Seneca writes about

---

[50]Aristotle regards human patronage and the favor of the gods to be of one kind, different merely in terms of degree, with the result that, in the case of the gods, an individual cannot ever repay their favors and a person "is deemed virtuous if he pays them all the regard he can" (*Nic. Eth.* 8.14.3-4 [1163b12-18]).

gratitude that "if you wish to make a return for a favor, you must be willing to go into exile, or to pour forth your blood, or to undergo poverty, or,
. . . even to let your very innocence be stained and exposed to shameful
slanders" (*Ep. Mor.* 81.27). Wallace-Hadrill writes that despite the fact
that, in theory, clients were expected to remain loyal to their patrons, in
practice, if a patron fell into political trouble or if his or her fortunes
began to wane, the patron's entourage of clients would evaporate.[51]
Such practice, however, was contrary to the ideal of gratitude, according to which a person would stand by (or under) the person's patron
and continue to live gratefully even if it cost the individual the future
favors of others, or brought him or her into dangerous places and
worked contrary to self-interest.[52] The person who disowned or dissoci-
ated himself or herself from a patron because of self-interest was an
ingrate.

It is worth noting at this point that *faith* (Lat *fides*; Gk *pistis*) is a
term also very much at home in patron-client and friendship relations,
and had, like *grace,* a variety of meanings as the context shifted from
the patron's faith to the client's faith. In one sense, *faith* meant
"dependability." The patron needed to prove reliable in providing the
assistance he or she promised to grant. The client needed to "keep
faith" as well, in the sense of showing loyalty and commitment to the
patron and to his or her obligations of gratitude.[53] A second meaning
is the more familiar sense of "trust": the client had to trust the goodwill and ability of the patron to whom the client entrusted his or her
need, that the patron would indeed perform what he or she promised,[54] while the benefactor would also have to trust the recipients to
act nobly and make a grateful response. In Seneca's words, once a gift
was given there was "no law [that can] restore you to your original
estate—look only to the good faith *(fidem)* of the recipient" (*Ben.*
3.14.2).

---

[51]Wallace-Hadrill, "Patronage in Roman Society," p. 82.
[52]Seneca *Ben.* 4.20.2; 4.24.2.
[53]This is the sense of *faith (pistis)* in 4 Maccabees 13:13; 16:18-22. Seven Jewish brothers have
  the choice laid before them by the tyrant Antiochus IV: transgress Torah and assimilate
  wholly to the Greek way of life or die miserably. The brothers choose to brave the tortures,
  keeping "faith" with the God who gave the brothers the gift of life.
[54]See, again, 4 Maccabees 8:5-7, where King Antiochus urges the young Jewish brothers to
  trust, or have faith in, him for their future well-being and advancement, abandoning their
  current alliances and associations in favor of a new attachment to him.

The principal of loyalty meant that clients or friends would have to take care not to become entangled in webs of crossed loyalties. Although a person could have multiple patrons,[55] to have as patrons two people who were enemies or rivals of one another would place one in a dangerous position, since ultimately the client would have to prove loyal and grateful to one but disloyal and ungrateful to the other. "No one can serve two masters" honorably in the context of these masters being at odds with one another, but if the masters are "friends" or bound to each other by some other means, the client should be safe in receiving favors from both.

Finally, the grateful person would look for an occasion to bestow timely gifts or services. If we have shown forth our gratitude in the hearing of the patron and borne witness to the patron's virtue and generosity in the public halls, we have "repaid favor [the generous disposition of the giver] with favor [an equally gracious reception of the gift]," but for the actual gift one still owes an actual gift (Seneca *Ben.* 2.35.1). Once again, people of similar authority and wealth ("friends") can exchange gifts similar in kind and value. Clients, on the other hand, can offer services when called on to do so or when they see the opportunity arise. Seneca especially seeks to cultivate a certain watchfulness on the part of the person who has been indebted, urging him or her not to try to return the favor at the first possible moment (as if the debt weighed uncomfortably on the person's shoulders), but to return the favor in the best possible moment, the moment in which the opportunity will be real and not manufactured (*Ben.* 6.41.1-2). The point of the gift was not, after all, to obtain a return but to create a bond that "binds two people together."

The Dance of Grace

The careful reader may already have observed some apparent contradictions in the codes of grace. Rather than make the system fall apart, these contrary principles result in a creative tension between the mindset that must guide the giver and the mindset that should direct the recipient of favor. As a pair of dancers must sometimes move in contrary directions for the dance to be beautiful (and to avoid crashing into one another), so the patron and client are each given his or her own chart of steps to follow

---

[55]See Saller, "Patronage and Friendship," pp. 53-56.

in the dance of grace. Sometimes they move together, sometimes in contrary ways, all for the sake of preserving the freedom and nobility of the practice of giving and receiving benefits. Seneca is especially fond of bringing contrasting rules of conduct together, only to tell each party to forget that it knows, in effect, what the other party is thinking. Clients are advised to think one way, patrons another—and if these mindsets get mixed up or crossed, the beauty of reciprocity, the gracefulness of grace, becomes irreparably marred.

Speaking to the giver, Seneca says that "the book-keeping is simple—so much is paid out; if anything comes back, it is gain, if nothing comes back, there is no loss. I made the gift for the sake of giving" (*Ben.* 1.2.3). While the giver is to train his or her mind to give no thought to the return and never to think a gift lost, the recipient is never allowed to forget his or her obligation and the absolute necessity of making a return (*Ben.* 2.25.3; 3.1.1). The point is that the giver should wholly be concerned with giving for the sake of the other, while the recipient should be concerned wholly with showing gratitude to the giver. If the recipient should say to himself, "She gave it for the sake of giving; I owe nothing," then the dance has turned sour, and one partner has trampled the other's toes.

Many other examples of this double set of rules exist. The giver is told "to make no record of the amount," but the recipient is "to feel indebted for more than the amount" (Seneca *Ben.* 1.4.3); the giver should forget that the gift was given, the recipient should always remember that the gift was received (*Ben.* 2.10.4; see Demosthenes *De Corona* 269); the giver is not to mention the gift again, while the recipient is to publicize it as broadly as possible (*Ben.* 2.11.2). In cases where a recipient has taken great pains to try to return a benefit, being watchful and thoughtful for the opportunity but simply not finding a way to help one who is far greater than himself, "the one should consider that he has received the return of his benefit, while the other should know that he has not returned it; the one should release the other, while the other should feel himself bound; the one should say, 'I have received,' the other, 'I still owe' " (*Ben.* 7.16.1-2).

The most dramatic contradiction exists between the denial that the ingrate can again hope to receive favors (Dio Chrysostom *Or.* 31.38, 65) and the exhortation of patrons to imitate the gods and give even to the unworthy and ungrateful (Seneca *Ben.* 1.10.5; 7.31.2, 4; 7.32). What

accounts for the contradiction? Simply, the different audience and situation. Seneca speaks to patrons in these passages, discoursing about the
loftiest ideals for generosity. Dio speaks to recipients of favor, urging
them to cease a specific practice that shows ingratitude toward their benefactors. The recipients of favor should not dwell too long on the possibility (perhaps even the obligation) of benefactors giving even to the ingrate,
lest this lead them to excuse themselves from showing gratitude (especially when costly) and to presume on the favor of the giver, favor that is
never to be taken for granted. The patron should not, on the other hand,
dwell too long on the impossibility of restoring the ingrate to favor, for
different considerations are to guide him or her, namely generosity even
to the undeserving.

Such mutually contradictory rules (forgetting and remembering, being
silent and bearing witness, and the like) are constructed so as to keep the
giver's mind wholly on what is noble about patronage (generosity, acting
in the interest of others) and the recipient's mind wholly on what is noble
for the client (namely making a full and rich return of gratitude for favors
conferred). They are devised in order to sustain both parties' commitment
to acting nobly within the system of reciprocity. The ultimate goal for
these ancient ethicists, after all, was not perfect systematization but virtuous conduct.

Grace, then, held two parties together in a bond of reciprocal
exchanges, a bond in which each party committed to provide what he or
she (or they) could to serve the needs or desires of the other. Public
benefactions were frequent, particularly as a means by which local elites
reaffirmed or increased their stature in the public eye. Such graces did
not form long-lasting bonds of mutual commitment, but friendship relations and personal patronage did. In the case of social equals, this
amounted to an exchange of like goods and services, always within the
context of mutual loyalty and commitment. Between a social or political
superior and his or her juniors, goods and opportunities were channeled down from above, and respect, public praise and loyal service
were returned from below, again within the context of mutual commitment. Giving was to be done for the sake of generosity and bringing
another benefit, and not with a view to material profit from returns.
Receiving, however, was always to be accompanied by the desire and
commitment to return grace for grace. Though often profitably compared to a dance that had to be kept "grace-full" in a circle of giving and

receiving, these relationships were far more than ornamental or recreational (as dances are). They formed the bedrock of society, a person's principal assurance of aid and support in an uncertain and insecure world.

Four

PATRONAGE & GRACE
IN THE NEW TESTAMENT

I*n the previous chapter we explored the first-century Greco-Roman world as* one in which many relationships would be characterized in terms of patronage and friendship, in which the wealthy were indeed known as "benefactors" (Lk 22:25), and in which there was a clearly articulated code that guided the noble exchange of graces. It was within this world that Jesus' message took shape and throughout this world that the good news of God's favor was proclaimed. Not all relationships fell under this heading of "grace relationships," since there were many "contractual" relationships (e.g., between tenants and landlord, merchants, and the like) in which the return for goods, services or privileges was spelled out in advance and not left to goodwill. Nevertheless, Jesus and his first disciples moved among and within patronage and friendship networks, for patronage was as much at home on Palestinian soil as in Greece, Asia Minor, Egypt, Africa and Rome. Centuries of living under Greek, Ptolemaic, Seleucid[1] and

---

[1]During this period we have clear evidence of the intentional and aggressive Hellenizing of Jerusalem and Judea, led by priestly and other aristocratic Jewish families (see 1 Macc 1; 2 Macc 3—4).

finally Roman domination[2] obliterated any hard and fast boundaries between Palestinian and non-Palestinian culture.

Moreover, after just a few years of incubation in Judea, Christianity began to spread through the urban centers of the Mediterranean world, where there would have been a consistently high level of exposure among all the Christians to public benefaction and public responses of gratitude, and among many Christians to personal patronage. These would have been prominent aspects of the world that they inhabited and even of the experiences they personally enjoyed. As Jews and Gentiles came to hear Paul or other missionaries celebrate the marvels of God's grace made available through Jesus, the sole mediator between God and humanity, they would have heard it in the context of so many inscriptions and other public declarations of the beneficence of great figures.[3] For such converts, God's grace *(charis)* would not have been of a different kind than the grace with which they were already familiar; it would have been understood as different only in quality and degree. Moreover, they would have known that the reception of gifts "given freely" laid the recipients under obligation to respond with grace to match (insofar as possible), with the result that

---

[2]Especially during the period of Roman rule we find Judean monarchs like Herod the Great continuing a strong Hellenizing and Romanizing program both in Jerusalem and in the creation of new cities in Galilee and the coastlands. See Martin Hengel, *Judaism and Hellenism,* 2 vols. (Philadelphia: Fortress, 1977), the groundbreaking study of how fully Hellenized Judea and Jerusalem were by the time of Christ. The mindset that somehow Palestine maintained an "Old Testament" or Hebrew culture while the rest of the world went on its Hellenized way persists even in the work of otherwise excellent scholars (see Randall Gleason, "The Old Testament Background of the Warning in Hebrews 6:4-8," *BSac* 155 [1998]: 62-91, esp. p. 63 and n. 4), but looking to Jewish backgrounds (themselves quite Hellenized, if one considers intertestamental literature) to the exclusion of or in preference to Greco-Roman backgrounds is not consistent with what we know about the Hellenization of Palestine and the Jews' creative use of Hellenistic thought and culture as they reformulated their own culture and religion during the centuries before Christ.

[3]Frederick W. Danker draws a correct and perceptive conclusion: "It is not probable that Greek or Roman bakers and shoemakers bothered to read the words of every dedicatory stele. Yet there would be far more acquaintance on the part of the general public with the themes and formulations of these documents than with the works of literary figures. People who had never heard of Herodotos or Sophokles would certainly have opened their eyes or ears when a Caesar proclaimed relief from oppressive legislation. . . . To do hermeneutical justice, then, to public documents like those in the Pauline corpus—including even the Letter to Philemon—it is necessary to interpret them first of all in the light of linguistic data that would have been available to the larger public and which would have provided the necessary semantic field for understanding the argument of a versatile communicator like Paul" (*Benefactor: Epigraphic Study of a Graeco-Roman and New Testament Semantic Field* [St. Louis: Clayton, 1982], pp. 28-29).

much exhortation in the New Testament falls within the scope of directing believers to a proper, "grateful response" to God's favor.[4]

Luke 7 provides us with a place to start as we consider the networks of grace relationships in operation within the pages of the New Testament:

> A centurion there had a slave whom he valued highly, and who was ill and close to death. When he heard about Jesus, he sent some Jewish elders to him, asking him to come and heal his slave. When they came to Jesus, they appealed to him earnestly, saying, "He is worthy of having you do this for him, for he loves our people, and it is he who built our synagogue for us." And Jesus went with them, but when he was not far from the house, the centurion sent friends to say to him, "Lord, do not trouble yourself, for I am not worthy to have you come under my roof; therefore I did not presume to come to you. But only speak the word, and let my servant be healed. For I also am a man set under authority, with soldiers under me; and I say to one, 'Go,' and he goes, and to another, 'Come,' and he comes, and to my slave, 'Do this,' and the slave does it." When Jesus heard this he was amazed at him, and turning to the crowd that followed him, he said, "I tell you, not even in Israel have I found such faith." When those who had been sent returned to the house, they found the slave in good health. (Lk 7:2-10)

The centurion is presented as a local benefactor, doing what benefactors frequently do—erecting a building for public use (here, a synagogue). Faced with the mortal illness of a member of his household, and made aware of Jesus' reputation as a healer (thus himself a broker of God's favors), he seeks assistance from Jesus, whom he knows has the resources to meet the need. He does not go himself, for he is an outsider—a Gentile (and a Roman officer, at that). Instead, he looks for someone who has some connection with Jesus, someone who might be better placed in the scheme of things to secure a favor from this Jewish healer. So he calls upon those whom he has benefited, the local Jewish elders, who will be glad for this opportunity to do him a good service (to do a favor for one who has bestowed costly favors on the community). He knows they will do their best to plead his cause and thinks that their being of the same race and, in effect, extended kinship group as Jesus will make success likely. Thus the centurion's beneficiaries return the favor by brokering access to someone who has what the centurion needs. When

---

[4]For example, wherever reception of gifts or promises from God is used as the motivation for some act or behavior (the frequent use of "therefore" to connect exhortation to a prior discourse on God's grace or favors and kindnesses is far from accidental or cosmetic).

the Jewish elders approach Jesus, they are, in effect, asking for the favor. As mediators, they also provide testimony to the virtuous character of the man who will ultimately be the recipient of favor. Jesus agrees to the request. Then the centurion does something surprising. He sends some of his friends (either people of like status with whom he shares benefits or people of lesser status that are attached to him as their personal patron) to intercept Jesus. A local benefactor shows astonishing humility in his dealings with a transient Jewish healer, and he shows exceptional trust in Jesus' ability to grant God's favors. The end result is that the Roman centurion receives from Jesus the gift he needed.[5]

Another text that prominently displays the cultural codes and dynamics of reciprocity is Paul's letter to Philemon, which speaks of past benefits conferred by Paul and Philemon and calls for a new gift, namely freeing Onesimus to join Paul. Although Paul lacks both property and a place in a community, he nevertheless claims to be able to exercise authority over Philemon on the basis of having brought Philemon the message of salvation, thus on the basis of having given a valuable benefit (Philem 8, 18). Philemon himself has been the benefactor of the Colossian Christians, seen in his opening up of his house to them (Philem 2) and in the generosity that has been the means by which "the hearts of the saints have been refreshed" (Philem 7), perhaps including material assistance offered Paul during the time of their acquaintance and after.

We find a mixture of grounds on which Paul bases his request: on the one hand, Paul claims authority to command Philemon's obedience as Paul's client (Philem 8, 14, 20);[6] on the other, he voices his preference to address Philemon as friend, coworker and partner (Philem 1), and only actually makes his request on that basis (Philem 9, 14, 17, 20), hoping now to benefit (Philem 20) from Philemon's continued generosity toward the saints, which has earned him much honor in the community. The gift (really, the "return") that Paul seeks is the company and help of Onesimus, Philemon's slave. Paul presents Onesimus as someone who can give Paul the kind of help and service that Philemon ought to be providing

---

[5]See also the treatment of this passage in Halvor Moxnes, "Patron-Client Relations and the New Community in Luke-Acts," in *The Social World of Luke-Acts*, ed. Jerome H. Neyrey (Peabody, Mass.: Hendrickson, 1991), pp. 252-53.

[6]This may be a bold move on Paul's part, for his claim to being Philemon's patron is far less visible (in terms of actual, visible favors) than Philemon's claim on the church and, quite likely, on Paul.

Paul (Philem 13), and Paul's mention of his own need (his age and his imprisonment, Philem 9) will both rouse Philemon's feelings of friendship and desire to help as well as make failure to help a friend in such need the more reprehensible.

The situation is somewhat complicated by the fact that Onesimus has estranged himself from Philemon, running from his master and lodging with Paul.[7] This means that Paul must act first as mediator for Onesimus, first seeking to gain a benefit from his friend Philemon for his own client. Paul's mediation means that Philemon will no longer treat Onesimus as Onesimus deserves (that is, as a disobedient and troublesome slave), but will treat him as his patron, Paul, deserves. Any injury committed by Onesimus is to be written on Paul's account, which shows a very wide credit margin (Philem 18-19).[8] Paul's decision to return Onesimus with the letter allows Philemon to act nobly and charitably toward both his new brother in the faith (Philem 16) and toward his partner and spiritual patron, first by welcoming Onesimus on Paul's merits (Philem 17) and then by releasing him to help Paul (Philem 13-14).

Philemon really does appear to be in a corner in this letter—Paul has left him little room to refuse his request! If he is to keep his reputation for generosity and for acting nobly in his relations of reciprocity (the public reading of the letter creates a court of reputation that will make this evaluation), he can only respond to Paul's request in the affirmative. Only then would his generosity bring him any credit at all in the community. If he refuses and Paul must command what he now asks, Philemon will either have to break with Paul or lose Onesimus anyway without gaining any honor as a benefactor and reliable friend.

Many other examples of favors being granted by local patrons or human benefactors being acknowledged exist in the New Testament.[9] These pro-

---

[7]Onesimus, who was now lodged with Paul, might not legally have been considered a runaway slave. Slaves who were experiencing difficulty in their masters' homes were known to leave the master in search of one of the master's "friends," who could plead the slave's case, acting as a broker between slave and master, in the hope of the slave's returning to a more endurable situation. Such a slave remained, in effect, within the master's household by fleeing to a friend of the master—making him disobedient, perhaps, but not a runaway.

[8]This is strikingly similar to the case of Voconius Romanus in Pliny's letter to the emperor Trajan, discussed in chapter three.

[9]Just considering Luke-Acts, we have the following examples. Acts 10:2, 22 presents a second centurion, one who "gave alms generously," that is, committed himself to public benefaction, particularly of the poor (providing sustenance rather than entertainments or

vide us with but a starting point for discovering the social codes of grace within the text. Of greater import is the manner in which New Testament authors conceptualize the involvement of God in human affairs as the involvement of a benefactor and a personal patron, how they understand Jesus' role within the framework of God's beneficence, and how they direct the recipient of God's gifts to respond to such "amazing grace." To these we now turn, concluding with an examination of how patronage within the Christian community is transformed into stewardship, so that God remains, in fact, "all in all."

God the Benefactor and Patron
The opening and closing wishes in New Testament epistles are consistently for God's "grace" (favor) to be on the recipients of the letter. God's grace *(charis)* would have been understood by the recipients of those epistles within the context of the meaning of usage of grace in everyday parlance. It is not a different species of *charis* but rather derives its meaningfulness as a kind of *charis*—one in which certain surprising qualities are displayed but also one with some important areas of continuity with grace in general.[10]

God has indebted all living beings by virtue of being the creator and

---

buildings—but still a form of public benefaction), with the result that he was "well spoken of by the whole Jewish nation," the recipients and observers of his beneficence. The opening of the speech of Tertullus before Felix (Acts 24:2-4) is filled with the customary praises of a beneficent ruler who has maintained peace through his foresight, a profession of gratitude before a new request for a favor is made. Acts 24:27 and 25:9 show again how manipulation of the judicial process could be construed as a "favor" done to benefit someone or some group (recall the discussion of Cicero's and Marcus Aurelius's attempts to secure favorable verdicts for their friends and clients). In the parable of the prudent steward (Lk 16:4-9), the soon-to-be-unemployed steward provides relief from substantial amounts of debt to the master's debtors as a benefaction, anticipating (indeed, counting on) the recipients showing their gratitude when he will need aid in the near future. In the middle of Luke's passion narrative, we find a new friendship relationship being formed (replacing former mistrust and rivalry) as Pilate and Herod exchange mutual courtesies (Lk 23:6-12), honoring one another by giving the other the right to decide a case. Finally, I would mention the prologues to Luke and Acts (Lk 1:1-4; Acts 1:1-2) as quite probably the literary dedication of a work to the patron whose support had made the leisure for research and writing possible (which would be in keeping with the many other dedications beginning works of literature in Greek or Latin).

[10]There is a peculiar tendency in scholarship (particularly among those claiming the title evangelical) to drive wedges between the New Testament texts or early Christianity and the Greco-Roman culture within which it grew up and formulated its conception of the work of God and human response (within which, for that matter, Judaism continued to

sustainer of all life (Acts 14:17; 17:24-28; 1 Cor 8:6; Rev 4:9-11). From the moment a person draws breath, he or she is bound to revere the God who gives breath (Rev 14:6-7).[11] Paul reminds his readers that no human being has ever made God a debtor. God is always the first giver who obligates us "for from him and through him and to him are all things" (Rom 11:35-36). This is why Jew and Gentile have exactly the same standing before God, namely recipients of the favor of the Gracious One, neither with a claim on God's return of favor but both obligated to respond to God's favor. It is precisely here, however, that humanity has failed. Neither Gentile nor Jew returned to God the reverence and service God merited but even went so far as to insult God through blatant disobedience (Rom 1:18—2:24). Meeting God's favor with insult, humanity incurred the anger of the one who had sought to benefit them.[12]

The New Testament authors, however, announce a new manifestation of God's favor, an opportunity for deliverance from experiencing his wrath made available to all through Jesus the Christ (1 Tim 4:10). This beneficent act is presented as God's fulfillment of longstanding promises

---

take shape both in Palestine and, let us not forget, in the Diaspora). This is evident, for example, when scholars insist without defense that Old Testament backgrounds are "closer" to the New Testament and on that basis exclude other backgrounds (as in Gleason, "Old Testament Background," p. 63), or when scholars affirm differences without allowing themselves to acknowledge or "see" similarities (a recurring problem in Don N. Howell Jr., "Review of *Despising Shame: Honor Discourse and Community Maintenance in the Epistle to the Hebrews*," *JETS* 42 [1999]:161-63). This ideological trend has been helpfully demonstrated and criticized in Vernon Robbins, *The Tapestry of Early Christian Discourse: Rhetoric, Society and Ideology* (London: Routledge, 1996), pp. 232-35. The result is a skewed presentation of the sources that informed and were transformed within early Christian culture. Paul, for example, appears to have used whatever material would help convey the significance of Jesus Christ to shape and motivate a faithful response within a community of disciples, whether that material was drawn from the Jewish Scriptures, Greek poets or philosophical ethicists. Holding the text up against a variety of backgrounds, rather than choosing one to the exclusion of all others, will result in a more richly nuanced understanding of how the text was heard by its (largely) Greco-Roman audience and how it sought to persuade them. Do we believe that Christianity is "more legitimate" if its ideas can be traced back to Jewish (or, more specifically, Hebrew) sources than if we find Greek or Roman ideas informing Paul or Luke?

[11]In this regard, the fact that Greek and Latin authors classify people's obligations to God (or in some authors, the gods) under the rubric of returning just thanks and honor is significant. Long before the birth of Christianity, the ancients knew the divine to be the supreme benefactor of humanity and thus upheld the virtue of piety as an essential obligation (see Aristotle *Nic. Eth.* 8.14.4 [1163b16-18]).

[12]Aristotle, for example, notes among the things that rouse anger and desire for vengeance, insulting or mistreating a benefactor (*Rhetoric* 2.2.8).

made to Israel, presenting God as a reliable benefactor who has "kept faith" with his historic body of clients (Lk 1:54, 68-75; Acts 3:26; Rom 15:8). The songs of Mary and Zechariah in Luke's infancy narratives are especially noteworthy as testimonies to God's fidelity with regard to delivering the grants he had promised to Abraham and Abraham's descendants, expressed in terms familiar from decrees honoring contemporary emperors (bringing peace, deliverance from oppression and the like).[13] Christians are repeatedly made aware that they are specially privileged to witness the working out of God's provision for deliverance in Jesus—many great people of the past looked forward to the day when that gift would be given (Mt 13:16-17; Lk 10:23-24; 1 Pet 1:10-12).

An important component of the New Testament message about God's beneficence is that while having kept faith with Israel, God now invites all people to stand in his favor and enjoy his patronage. Recognition for God's inclusion of the Gentiles within the sphere of his favor was not easily won in the early church, but eventually the church came to realize the breadth and scope of God's generosity in this new act of favor. The specific gift of God in bestowing the Holy Spirit even on Gentiles was the decisive proof of God's acceptance of the non-Jew into God's favor (Acts 11:15-18; Gal 3:1-5; 3:28—4:7).[14] The experience of the Holy Spirit in the lives of the believers was understood as a gift from God that signified adoption into God's family (Gal 4:5-6), the fulfillment of the promise made to Abraham (Gal 3:14), the restoration of peace and favor with God (Rom 5:5), and a pledge of the future benefits God has prepared and will confer at the return of Jesus or after the believer's death (2 Cor 1:22;

---

[13]Mary's song also highlights God's interest in benefiting and protecting the poor and humble, often to the exclusion of the rich and powerful (Lk 1:48, 51-53; see also Jas 2:5). Jesus also presents himself as the agent of God's beneficence toward the poor and marginal (Lk 4:18-19), and Paul interprets the Corinthians' reception of favor along similar lines (1 Cor 1:26-31). In this way, God subverts the "food chain" in normal patron-client relationships, taking on as his clients not those closer up in rank and status (hence possessing greater potential for returning favors) but reaching down to those who lack rank and status. Humility rather than upward climbing is the way to get close to this patron, to "find favor" from God (see Sir 3:18; Jas 4:10; 1 Pet 5:5-6).

[14]See also Luke 4:25-30, in which Jesus reminds the hearers of God's previous benefactions bestowed specifically on Gentiles—and who at times when there were many Jews in need of such a favor but who received none. Ephesians 1:3—3:21 is in many respects a lengthy public decree honoring God for his immense generosity, and prominent within this paean is the celebration of God's favor extending to Gentiles as well as Jews. It is noteworthy that the New Testament authors consider even repentance to be not a human act but a gift bestowed by God (Acts 11:15-18; 2 Tim 2:25).

5:5; Eph 1:13-14). The vibrant and vital presence of the Spirit was thus an important assurance to the church of God's favor toward them.

We come at last to what is surprising about God's grace. It is not that God gives "freely and uncoerced." Every benefactor, in theory at least, did this.[15] God goes far beyond the high-water mark of generosity set by Seneca, which was for virtuous people to consider even giving to the ungrateful[16] (if they had resources to spare after benefiting the virtuous). To provide some modest assistance to those who had failed to be grateful in the past would be accounted a proof of great generosity, but God shows the supreme, fullest generosity (not just what God has to spare!) toward those who are God's enemies (not just ingrates, but those who have been actively hostile to God and God's desires). This is an outgrowth of God's determination to be "kind"[17] even "to the ungrateful [acharistous] and the wicked" (Lk 6:35). God's selection of his enemies as beneficiaries of his most costly gift is one area in which God's favor truly stands out.[18]

A second aspect of God's favor that stands out is God's initiative in effecting reconciliation with those who have affronted God's honor. God does not wait for the offenders to make an overture or to offer some token acknowledging their own disgrace and shame in acting against God in the first place. Rather, God sets aside his anger in setting forth Jesus, providing an opportunity for people to come into favor and escape the consequences of having previously acted as enemies (hence the choice of

---

[15]The distinction made by Howell to the effect that God's grace is unmerited and unconstrained (while somehow Pliny's favors are consistently merited and constrained?) is thus a false one ("Review of Despising Shame," p. 163). Grace always looks to the needs of the recipient, remains free and can be granted to the meritorious and the notorious by human patrons as well.

[16]The Greco-Roman world, too, understood the difference between merited favors and unmerited favors, both of which exhibited the generosity of the giver (but the latter even more so). While we are not deserving of God's favor (thus favor remains unmerited), the fact that God does extend such favor to us communicates to us our worth in God's estimation. God shows not only his love for us but also his regard for us in the quality of the gifts he gives (most poignantly in the laying down of the life of his Son for our sake). It is this communication of both love and esteem that should wash over the hardest heart and dissolve it in a return to God. "A gift is not a benefit if the best part of it is lacking—the fact that it was given as a mark of esteem" (Seneca Ben. 1.15.6; also 4.29.3)

[17]Kindness (chrēstotēs or its adjectival form) is an important descriptor of benefactors in Danker's collection of inscriptions (see Benefactor, pp. 325-37).

[18]Read Romans 5:6-10 now in this light: God does for enemies what even a virtuous person would hesitate to do for a friend (see also Eph 2:1-6; Tit 3:3-7).

"deliverance," *sōtēria*, as a dominant image for God's gift). We will see below that Jesus is primarily presented in terms of a mediator or broker of access to God's favor, since he connects to another patron those who make themselves his clients. Nevertheless, those images cannot make us ignore that even such a mediator is God's gift to the world, hence an evidence of God's initiative in forming this relationship (Rom 3:22-26; 5:8; 8:3-4; 2 Cor 5:18, 21; 1 Jn 4:10). The formation of this grace relationship thus runs contrary to the normal stream of lower-echelon people seeking out brokers who can connect them with higher patrons.

God is guided in this generosity by the consideration of "his own reputation and *aretē*" (2 Pet 1:3), a phrase that resonates again with honorary inscriptions, in which benefactors are said to demonstrate their virtuous character, or live up to their forebears' reputation for virtue, through their generosity.[19] The death of Jesus on behalf of humankind thus becomes a "demonstration of God's righteousness" (his character and virtue, Rom 1:16-17; 3:25-26), showing that God's generosity exceeds all expectations and upper limits and that God needs nothing from the sinner still to act in accordance with his own generous character. The early Christians are repeatedly admonished, however, to take such a demonstration of boundless generosity as God's single call to humankind at last to respond virtuously and whole-heartedly (most eloquently, 2 Pet 1:3-11), and never as an excuse to offend God further (Rom 6:1; Gal 5:1, 13).

God not only dispenses general (rather than personal) benefactions like the grant of life to all creatures (Acts 14:17) or gifts of sun and rain (Mt 5:45),[20] but he becomes a personal patron to the Christians who receive his Son. These believers become part of God's own household (see, e.g., Gal 3:26—4:7; Heb 3:6; 10:20-21; 1 Jn 3:1) and enjoy a special access to divine favors. The rich and well placed were careful in their choice of friends and clients—while they might provide meals, games or buildings for the public (benefaction), they did not accept any and all as clients (personal patronage). Rather distinctive about God's favor is that he

---

[19]Danker draws a comparison with an inscription from Priene, which declares that a certain benefactor named Moschion has proven "worthy of the arete and reputation of his ancestors" (*Benefactor*, p. 457).

[20]A comparison between Jesus' words in Matthew 5:45 and Seneca's words on the gods' beneficence toward good and wicked alike (see discussion of *Ben.* 4.26.1, 4.28.1 in chapter three) is striking indeed, particularly considering that both use the model of divine beneficence as an impetus to be generous to the good and ungrateful alike.

offers to any who will come (thus in the form of a public benefaction), without prior scrutiny of the character and reliability of the recipients, the assurance of welcome into God's own extended household (thus into a relationship of personal patronage)—even to the point of adoption into God's family as sons and daughters and to the point of sharing the inheritance of the Son (which is exceptional even in personal patronage).[21] The authors of the New Testament therefore offer attachment to God as personal patron, something that would be considered highly desirable for those in need of the security and protection a great patron would provide.[22]

As God proved reliable in his promises to Israel, so he will prove reliable toward the Christians who have trusted his promises and welcomed his invitation to become God's clients (1 Thess 5:23-24; 2 Tim 1:12; Tit 1:2; Heb 10:23). Paul speaks thus about God being responsible for rescuing him from past distress, about his confidence of personal help in future trials, about God assisting and multiplying his labors, and the like.[23] Each Christian also enjoys assurance that God is open to hearing specific petitions from individuals or local communities of faith, and the privilege of access to God for such timely and specific help (Eph 3:20; Phil 4:6-7, 19; 2 Thess 3:3; Heb 4:14-16; 13:5-6; 1 Pet 5:7). Christians need never falter in their commitment to Jesus or release their grasp on God's final rewards because of the hostility or pressures applied by unbelievers. Rather, they may "hold fast to [their] confession" as they "approach the throne of favor with boldness," so as to "receive mercy and find favor for timely help" (Heb 4:14-16, my translation).[24]

Christian Scriptures are unanimous in affirming that God's favor and

---

[21]This statement needs to be tempered, however, in light of statements like "many are called, but few are selected." The New Testament does not speak of universal incorporation into the household of God but only of *potential* universal incorporation. Many recipients of God's beneficence remain quite dead to their obligations of gratitude and persist in their rejection of the divine patron and his invitation to become a part of his household (see, e.g., 2 Cor 4:3-4)

[22]Christians were not alone in this view of God; the Stoic philosopher Epictetus also suggested that a person could find no better patron to whom to attach oneself than God—not even Caesar could compare (*Diss.* 4.1.91-98).

[23]Look closely at Acts 26:22; 2 Corinthians 1:9-11; Philippians 4:13; 2 Thessalonians 3:1-2; 1 Timothy 1:12-15; 2 Timothy 3:11; 4:16-18 from this perspective.

[24]Seneca (*Ben.* 4.4.2) speaks in similar terms of divine benefits: people are "conscious of their benefits that sometimes are presented unasked, sometimes are granted in answer to prayer—great and timely gifts, which by their coming remove grave menaces."

help are assured, so that trust is justified and only appropriate. Romans 8:32 is perhaps the most poignant assurance of ongoing favor: What assistance or favor would God withhold from us, after having given up his Son on our behalf even before we were reconciled?[25] Jesus taught that God had knowledge of his clients' needs and exercised forethought to provide both for their physical and eternal well-being (Mt 6:7-8, 25-33).[26] Jesus did not, however, discourage prayer in spite of God's knowledge, and the rest of the New Testament authors either promote prayer as the means to securing divine favors or display prayer as effective (e.g., Lk 1:13). Why pray if God already knows our needs? Because God delights to grant favors to those who belong to his household. When we ask, we also have the opportunity to know the "blessed experience" of gratitude[27] and live out our response (in fact, be ennobled by feeling grateful and responding to God's grace). The result of the offering of prayers and God's answering of petitions is thanksgiving "from many mouths," the increase of God's honor and reputation for generosity and beneficence (2 Cor 1:11). Prayer becomes, then, the means by which believers can personally seek God's favor, and request specific benefactions, for themselves or on behalf of one another (see 2 Cor 1:10-11; Eph 6:19; Phil 1:19; 4:6-7; Col 1:3; 4:12; 1 Thess 5:17, 25; 2 Thess 3:1-2; 1 Tim 2:1; Jas 5:15-16; 1 Jn 5:14-16).

God's patronage of the Christian community is also evidenced in the growth and building up of the churches and their members. The thanksgiving sections of Paul's letter attribute all progress as disciples and as communities of faith to God's gifting and equipping (1 Cor 1:5-7; Col 1:3-4; 1 Thess 1:2; 2 Thess 1:3; 1 Tim 1:3-6). As churches or their leaders "take stock" of what has been accomplished in their midst, it becomes a time to return thanks and honor to the God who accomplishes every good work. God bestows spiritual and material endowments on individual believers

---

[25]See also such texts as Matthew 7:7-11; 11:22-24; 21:21-22; Luke 11:9-13 (with regard to the granting of the Holy Spirit); Romans 8:32; James 1:5-8 (with regard to the specific gift of wisdom); 1 John 5:14-16.

[26]An interesting development of the belief that God has created and provided all manner of foods for human consumption is that receiving food with thanksgiving (gratitude) to the creator and giver nullifies concerns over defilement or pollution from foods (Rom 14:6; 1 Cor 10:30-31; 1 Tim 4:3-4). Convictions about God as giver override pollution taboos—indeed those very taboos legislated in Torah.

[27]Thus Seneca (*Ep. Mor.* 81.21): Gratitude is "a great experience which is the outcome of an utterly happy condition of soul."

to be used for the health and strengthening of the whole church (1 Cor 12:1-11, 18; 14:12; Eph 4:1-12). Even monetary contributions made by Christians to churches or other works of charity are now seen as God's provision for the body and not the means by which local patrons (or would-be patrons) can make a power base out of the church (the recipients of their favors).

God is presented in the New Testament, then, as the source of many gifts (indeed, of "every good and complete gift," Jas 1:17, my translation) in connection with Jesus. From the gift of life and provision of all things needed for the sustaining of life, to the provision for people to exchange enmity with God for a place in God's household and under God's personal patronage, God is the one who supplies our lack, who gives assistance in our need. Nor does God's favor exist for this life only. The announcement of God's "year of favor" includes being chosen by him and being made holy (2 Thess 2:13; 1 Pet 1:1-2), given a new birth into a new family and heritage (Jn 1:12-13; Jas 1:18), and qualified to share in an eternal inheritance (Col 1:12), which is deliverance itself (Col 1:13). When the day of God's reckoning arrives, God will vindicate his clients in the face of all the shame and abuse they suffered at the hands of those who refused God's favor, for God protects the honor of his household by avenging wrongs done to them (Lk 18:1-8; 2 Thess 1:6), but those who have committed themselves to God in trust and gratitude will receive their unshakable kingdom (Heb 12:28).

Jesus, the Mediator of God's Favor

While Jesus is "put forward" by God (Rom 3:25) as a provision for reconciliation, and thus a gift from God, he is cast more frequently in the New Testament in the role of mediator of God's favors and broker of access to God. From an early point in the developing reflection on Jesus' significance, that mediation was seen to have begun in the act of creation itself as the preincarnate Son was assigned the role of God's coworker in creation,[28] indeed the agent through whom God fostered creation (Jn 1:3, 10; 1 Cor 8:6; Col 1:16; Heb 1:2-3).

Luke sums up the earthly ministry of Jesus as follows: "he went about doing good *(euergetōn)* and healing" (Acts 10:38). Luke has chosen the

---

[28] A role formerly ascribed to Wisdom in Jewish literature: Proverbs 8:27-31, 35-36; Wisdom of Solomon 9:1-2, 9.

verb form of the noun *benefactor (euergetēs)* to characterize Jesus' activity, which was "benefiting" others. Indeed, the second verb reveals the principal kind of benefaction bestowed by Jesus throughout his ministry, namely healing disease or infirmity and delivering from demonic oppression,[29] even the restoration of the dead to life (Mt 9:18-25; Lk 7:11-17). Jesus' ministry of teaching could also be considered a gift (and not something the crowds endured in order to receive gifts!), since good advice and guidance were valued and valuable commodities. Seneca (*Ben.* 1.2.4), for example, includes "advice" and "sound precepts" amidst the various kinds of assistance a friend or patron would give. Jesus' provision of simple meals for his vast entourage of five thousand and four thousand also resembles (with the important difference of the miraculous element; Mt 14:14-21; 15:32-38) the Roman *sportulae* (akin to our modern "boxed lunch") provided by patrons for the clients who attended them at their doorstep. This connection is especially apparent in John, where Jesus chides the crowds for following after him (joining his entourage) for the sake of a handout of food rather than for the spiritual food he has to offer (Jn 6:11, 15, 26-27, 34-35).

Jesus' ability to confer benefits of such kind derives from his relationship with God, specifically as the mediator of favors that reside in the province of God's power and prerogatives to grant or withhold. One episode that brings this to the fore poignantly is the healing of the paralytic who was let down through Peter's roof (Mt 9:2-8; Mk 2:3-12; Lk 5:20-26). Jesus first grants the man forgiveness of his sins, a bold act that prompts the religious experts sitting in the crowd to criticize him for presuming upon God's prerogatives (Mk 2:7), namely pardon for crimes committed against God. Jesus successfully defends his claim to be able to confer divine favors (like pardon), however, as he heals the paralytic and allows him to walk away. The visible benefit proves the unobservable one, demonstrating that his declaring forgiveness is not blasphemy but the real conferral of God's gift.[30]

The response to Jesus during his earthly ministry bears the stamp of responses typical of beneficiaries to their benefactors. Notable is the

---

[29]Physicians and healers were considered a kind of benefactor in the Greco-Roman world, as the inscriptions honoring physicians included by Danker (*Benefactor*, pp. 57-64) attest (see Mt 4:23-25; 8:5-17; 9:18-35, etc; Mk 1:34, 39; 3:10; Lk 4:40; 5:15; 6:18; 7:21; 9:11).

[30]See also John 9:30-33; 11:22; 14:6, 13-14; 16:23-27 for passages emphasizing Jesus' mediation of God's favors.

spread of Jesus' fame, the result of public testimony being given to the benefactor's generosity (Mt 9:26, 31; Mk 5:19-20; 7:24; Lk 5:15; 7:17; 8:39). Even those who are commanded to be silent cannot refrain from spreading his fame, so ingrained is public praise of one's benefactor (Mt 9:30-31; Mk 1:45; 7:36-37; Lk 13:17).[31] It is possible that those healed understood Jesus' commands against publicizing it as signs of the genuineness of Jesus' motives in healing—he was not a "glory seeker" but a sincere benefactor. Ironically, this would have the effect of making them feel gratitude even more deeply, and thus more apt to declare Jesus' *aretai*, his demonstrations of his virtue in well doing. The result of this spread of the report of his well doing is the collection of vast entourage (in essence, a *clientela*; Mt 4:25; Lk 5:15) who are clearly presented as seekers or recipients of his favors. The mass of followers is the visible representation of Jesus' fame and a potential power base for any public agenda he might entertain, hence the cause of the arousal of envy (Jn 12:19) and possibly the source of the fear that led to his execution by the Romans as a political enemy.

In addition to the increase of his reputation by his clients and those who approve his beneficent acts, Jesus personally receives the thanks and reverence due a patron. The story of the ten lepers (Lk 17:11-19) especially highlights the appropriateness of such expressions of gratitude at the reception of a benefit.[32] Jesus is approached by suppliants in an attitude of trust that he could provide access to divine favor and benefits (Mt 8:8-10; 9:18, 28). When one suppliant expresses an ounce of doubt about Jesus' ability in this regard, Jesus takes issue with him (Mk 9:22-24). When encountering the trust of the Syro-Phoenician woman, Jesus even alters

---

[31]Recall Aristotle's dictum that well-doers merit honor and Seneca's directions to testify publicly to benefits received as a prime ingredient of gratitude.

[32]So, rightly, Danker, *Benefactor,* p. 441. Bruce J. Malina offers a peculiar analysis of this passage. From his observations of modern Mediterranean culture, Malina claims that saying thank you to a social equal means a breaking off of relations of reciprocity, whereas one does still give thanks to social superiors for their gifts. He suggests that Mediterranean people might empathize more with the nine lepers who do not thank Jesus, who leave the relationship open in case they have needs in the future (*Windows on the World of Jesus: Time Travel to Ancient Judea* [Louisville: Westminster John Knox, 1993]). Such a reading, however novel, cannot be supported from the text. Jesus is addressed as a social superior ("Master"), and the petition is cast in terms suggestive of the suppliants' awareness of social inferiority ("have mercy on us"). Jesus' response to the one leper who did return suggests the expectation that the other nine ought to have returned to express gratitude to God for their healing in the presence of the mediator of God's favor. Were Malina correct, we should have found Jesus saying to this Samaritan leper: "You dolt! You think that's the last favor you're going to need from me?!"

his determination to channel God's favors to the people of Israel (the stated mission of his earthly ministry) since his generous character compels him to respond graciously to such trust (Mt 15:22-28). Some who have been benefited by Jesus find ways to offer him a service in turn. For example, Peter's mother-in-law responds to Jesus' healing by taking the lead in offering hospitality (Lk 4:38-39), and the women who have been healed or exorcised now support financially the ministry of the one who benefited them (Lk 8:1-3). Finally, Jesus' benefactions motivate praise of God, showing people's awareness of the ultimate source of these benefits, as of all good gifts (Lk 7:16; 17:15-18; 18:43; 19:37; Acts 4:21).[33]

The crowning benefaction conferred by Jesus is, of course, his voluntary death by means of which he grants deliverance from sin, death and the power of Satan (see, among many other passages, Mt 1:21; Jn 1:29; Acts 5:31; 1 Cor 15:3; 2 Cor 5:21; Gal 1:4; Col 1:19-20, 22; 2:13-14; Heb 2:14-15; 1 Pet 3:18.). A prominent feature of passages speaking about this deliverance is the great cost that Jesus incurred on himself ("gave himself for us," "died on our behalf" and the like) to bring us these benefactions.[34] It often happened that a benefactor would put himself at risk and even incur great personal loss to bring benefits to others. Paul articulates the model as it would be practiced by the "best" or most generous of people (Rom 5:6-8; see also Jn 15:13), and indeed it was considered the height of generosity to give one's life for the good of another (hence the extreme honor showed to those who died in battle to protect a city). Jesus, then, is primarily celebrated as one who spent his all bringing us good: "You know the generous act of our Lord Jesus Christ, that though he was rich, yet for your sakes he became poor, so that by his poverty you might

---

[33]This, too, is not wholly unparalleled in the Greco-Roman world, as inscriptions give credit not only to the immediate benefactor but also to divine providence for providing such a virtuous person for the benefit of humankind (see, e.g., the famous inscription from Priene celebrating the benefits conferred on the whole world through Augustus by the divine; translation given in Danker, *Benefactor*, pp. 215-18).

[34]Danker calls this the "endangered benefactor" motif and documents that it is was widely applied to those who braved dangers, incurred risks or shouldered inordinate expenses for the public good or the good of others (*Benefactor*, pp. 417-35). "He gave himself for others" is common diction honoring such a benefactor (pp. 321-23). In the New Testament see 1 John 3:16-17 (which also expresses the appropriate response to such beneficence); the words of institution at the Last Supper (e.g., Lk 22:19-22); also Mt 20:28; 26:26-28; Mk 10:45; Lk 22:19-20; Jn 6:51; 10:11, 15, 17-18; 15:13; 2 Cor 8:9; Gal 1:4; 3:13; Eph 5:2; 1 Tim 2:6; Tit 2:14; Heb 2:9; 7:27; 13:12; Rev 1:5; 5:9-10.

become rich" (2 Cor 8:9);[35] "He it is who gave himself for us that he might redeem us from all iniquity and purify for himself a people of his own who are zealous for good deeds" (Tit 2:14). This topic is widely utilized by New Testament authors to explain how a degrading execution was in reality a noble, beneficial death, and to stimulate our gratitude and sound the depths of the return we are to make by underscoring the costliness of Jesus' act of favor. Most poignant in this regard is 2 Corinthians 5:15: "He died *for all*, so that those who live might live no longer for themselves, but for him who died and was raised *for them*" (my emphasis).

By means of his death, by which the memory of our sins is wiped away (in our conscience as well as in the mind of God, Heb 9:9-14; 10:17), and now by means of his ongoing priesthood,[36] Jesus has opened up for his clients access to God the Father, the great patron. He achieves for those who rely on him what neither angels nor Moses nor generations of Levitical priests had been able to provide,[37] namely, direct access to God's "throne of favor," giving human beings the boldness to enter that holy space in the assurance of finding "mercy and favor for timely help" (Heb 4:14-16, my translation), having effectively removed all that stood in the way of God's favor, namely sins (Heb 10:1-14). Many passages of the New Testament emphasize that Jesus is the sole grantor of access to the Father (see Mt 11:27; Jn 14:6; 1 Tim 2:5), placing him in the familiar role of broker, whose principal gift is connection with another patron (the whole work of reconciliation is an aspect of securing this relationship and a prerequisite to conferring the access the Christian now enjoys).[38]

---

[35]The decision of the NRSV translators to render *charis* here as "generous act" is most astute, combining an emphasis both on the giver's disposition and the resulting benefaction.

[36]Priests were seen in general as the parties who managed relationships with the divine, restoring favor, mediating thanks and securing gifts from the divine. Hebrews 5:1 captures, by way of general definition, the essence of priesthood as standing before God on behalf of human beings. The Latin word for priest, *pontifex*, or "bridge-maker," also underscored the mediatorial (=brokering) nature of the priest's role.

[37]Hebrews 1—10 contains many topics geared to amplify the favor (gift of access) conferred by Jesus (thus amplifying also the corresponding sense of indebtedness to the giver). Aristotle wrote that a favor "is great if shown to one who is in great need, or who needs what is important and hard to get, or who needs it at an important and difficult crisis; or if the helper is the only, the first, or the chief person to give the help" (*Rhetoric* 2.7.1). Jesus is consistently celebrated in Hebrews as the "first" and "only" broker (mediator) to succeed in conferring the gift of direct access to God (see, e.g., Heb 7:11-28; 9:6-15; 10:1-14).

[38]Other texts emphasizing Jesus' gift of a new access to God's favor and assistance include John 16:26-27; Romans 8:34; Ephesians 2:18; 3:11-12; 1 Timothy 2:5-6; Hebrews 10:19-23; 1 Peter 1:21; Revelation 1:6 (making us priests means bestowing access to God).

In the Gospels, Jesus makes his disciples mediators of divine favor as well, conferring on them the grant of authority to do the things he had been doing (healing, exorcizing, teaching). After his ascension his benefaction continues through the work of his apostles, who publicly attest that Jesus' "beneficence" *(euergesia)* stood behind the healing of the lame man in the Temple (Acts 4:9-10). The disciples appear at first to have understood their role as analogous to other middle-level brokers of access to a great person: they are the gate-keepers (note how they attempt to regulate the flow of access to Jesus in Mk 10:13-14), and jealously guard that privilege (Mk 9:38-39). Jesus must teach them that, in the kingdom God is building, being a mediator of the great patron's favor is not to become the means to build up one's own power base or enhance the perception of one's importance as a channel of divine favor, monopolizing access to Jesus and God's favor (Lk 9:49-50). Instead, although they do go out as brokers of Jesus (Mt 10:40; Jn 13:20), they are not giving with a view to receiving honor or thanks or service from the recipients of the favors they mediate but are to give as a response to having received themselves from God (Mt 10:1, 8). As if by way of extreme lesson, teaching those who enter into Christ's service that they do so not to enhance their own prestige and power through collecting clients, Jesus elevates those with whom no worldly minded person would think it advantageous to "network," namely the weak, the little ones, as also his brokers, and thus brokers of the one who sent Jesus (Mt 18:5; Mk 9:37; Lk 9:46-48). Not only does this remedy the wrong view of our brokering role as disciples, but it points us ever against our cultural wisdom to network with the needy—the unconnected!—as the way to connect with Jesus.

Reception of "power from on high" after Jesus' ascension (Lk 24:49; Acts 1:8), which continues to place the apostles in a mediatorial role, stands in parallel with the authority and offices sought for as favors by local elites or semi-elites from those above them in the political chain of command. Such a gift brought with it both the obligations of the office (which could be quite burdensome) and the power and prestige of the office (from which angle it was indeed a benefit). Paul views his own apostleship this way as well: it is a great honor (hence a great favor from God, as in Rom 1:5; and "the grace that had been given to me," [Gal 2:9]) that has at the same time obligated him to serve people (Rom 1:14), to discharge an office zealously and at great expense to himself for the good of others. Being granted a privileged office, Paul becomes the mediator himself of divine favor, if only as the one who brings the announcement (the good news) about Jesus the one mediator who reconciles us to God. He presents himself consistently as acting on behalf of the believers, bringing them spiritual blessing, and often incurring great costs and braving great dangers and pains to bring them these benefits.[39] The believers are thus obligated to Paul,[40] even as God obligated Paul to execute his office. They are not to despise his sufferings and his manual labor, since it is all "for them" (see especially 2 Cor 1:3-7; 4:7-15).

Jesus' favor is certainly not presented in terms of past generosity only. Hebrews, as we have noted, underscores his present mediatorial assistance in securing access to God for us, to which one may add his ongoing intercession on behalf of his own before the Father (Rom 8:34; Heb 7:25; 1 Jn 2:1). This is presented primarily in terms of the removal of sins and their potential damage to the relationship of favor, but one suspects that the author of Hebrews has in mind Jesus' interest in securing for the believers all the divine assistance they need to arrive at the end of their journey. In the midst of their trials and temptations (not just wrestling with particular sins but wrestling with finding the strength to continue to endure society's insults and abuse for their association with Jesus), Jesus lays hold of and "helps" the believers (Heb 2:16-18). Through his intimate acquaintance with their condition, he knows what specific assistance they will need from the "throne of favor."

This continued intercession and assistance itself points to the great gifts that are yet to come. We need Christ's assistance in overcoming those obstacles that threaten to despoil us of that prize. The New Testament authors point the believers consistently forward to the future benefaction, promised, awaited now in trust ("faith") and hope. Through Jesus, believers look forward to receiving the redemption of their bodies, which Paul equates with the realization of their adoption as sons and daughters (Rom 8:23), namely, the transformation of the mortal body (Phil 3:20-21) into the resurrection body, the "house not made with hands"

---

[39]Second Corinthians 1:3-7; 4:7-15; 6:4-10 (esp. 6:10); Ephesians 3:1-2, 13; Colossians 1:24-25; 2:1; 1 Thessalonians 2:8-9 (where he emphasizes that he has not been a burden on the "public" in the execution of his office).

[40]Paul does not use this to lord it over his converts (and he takes explicit pains to avoid giving this impression; 2 Cor 1:24), but he does remind his addressees of their debt to him at times when he is uncertain of their response and needs to use his trump card (as perhaps in Philem 18-19) or when fidelity to Paul is at stake (as in 2 Cor).

(2 Cor 5:1-5; 1 Thess 4:14). This is the "promise of life" (2 Tim 1:1) that we await in hope (Tit 1:2). Having been made heirs (Tit 3:7; 1 Pet 3:7), believers do not yet possess, so that they still await reception of the promised inheritance (Eph 1:13-14; 1 Pet 1:4). Other images used to describe this future, impending grant from God are deliverance effected at Jesus' return (1 Thess 1:10; 5:9; Heb 9:28; 1 Pet 1:5, 9, 13); entrance into "rest" (Heb 4:1-11), our heavenly city (Heb 11:16; 13:14), namely, New Jerusalem (Rev 21:2-7) a share in Christ's honor ("glory," 2 Thess 2:14; Heb 2:10; 1 Pet 5:10); and reign (Rev 5:10). When the Christian enjoys these benefactions, he or she has at last received the "hope" laid up for God's faithful clients in heaven (Col 1:5).

Mindful of the many benefits God has already conferred in Christ and that Christ has secured for the Christians, the believers are left by the New Testament authors in a posture of hope and anticipation: "Set all your hope on the grace [*charin*, better rendered "gift" in this context] that Jesus Christ will bring you when he is revealed" (1 Pet 1:13). The history of God's generosity toward the Christian community gives strong assurance that these future gifts will not fail to be granted, hence bolsters faith or trust.[41] The hope of this gift of unending life in God's realm becomes the "anchor of the soul" (Heb 6:19-20): as the addressees of these texts keep their hope and yearning for this gift strong, the authors know, the Christians' own firmness and reliability in their loyalty toward Jesus and their orientation toward their divine patron will be similarly strong.

The tendency of New Testament authors to speak of Jesus as "Savior" is also in keeping with his role as benefactor, for the term was applied as an honorary term to great and powerful figures who brought a city deliverance from an enemy, provided famine relief and removed other threats

---

[41]Seneca speaks of the tendency of human patrons to give repeatedly to those they have helped in the past: "How often will you hear a man say: 'I cannot bear to desert him, for I have given him his life, I have rescued him from peril. He now begs me to plead his cause against men of influence; I do not want to, but what can I do? I have already helped him once, no, twice.' Do you not see that there is, inherent in the thing itself, some peculiar power that compels us to give benefits, first, because we ought, then, because we have already given them? . . . We continue to bestow because we have already bestowed" (*Ben.* 4.15.3). The investment God and Christ have already made in us becomes a cause for confidence of their continued favor and investment in the faithful, an assurance of future help. In Paul's words, "He who did not withhold his own Son, but gave him up for all of us, will he not with him also give us everything else?" (Rom 8:32).

to the well-being and stability of a group of people.[42] The believers have
already experienced many aspects of his saving activity, namely, deliverance ("salvation") from sin (Mt 1:21; Acts 5:31) or from the godlessness
and slavery to the passions of the flesh that characterized their life prior
to experiencing God's kindness (Tit 3:3-5). This Savior (or Deliverer) has
conquered death and opened up the way to unending life (2 Tim 1:10); his
beneficiaries, however, still await other aspects of this act of deliverance
("salvation," Heb 1:14; 1 Pet 1:5, 9): deliverance from the wrath of God on
the Day of Judgment (Rom 5:9); the final deliverance from mortality that
will come on that anticipated day when the Savior "that we are expect-
ing" returns (Phil 3:20-21).

Making a Gracious Response

"Since we are receiving an unshakable kingdom, let us show gratitude"
(*echōmen charin*, Heb 12:28, my translation). One of the more important
contributions an awareness of the ethos of grace in the first-century world
can make is implanting in our minds the necessary connection between
giving and responding, between favor and gratitude in the fullest sense.
Because we think about the grace of God through the lens of sixteenth-
century Protestant polemics against "earning salvation by means of pious
works," we have a difficult time hearing the New Testament's own affirmation of the simple, yet noble and beautiful, circle of grace. God has
acted generously, and Jesus has granted great and wonderful gifts. These
were not earned, but grace is never earned in the ancient world (this
again is not something that sets New Testament grace apart from everyday grace). Once favor has been shown and gifts conferred, however, the
result must invariably be that the recipient will show gratitude, will
answer grace with grace. The indicative and the imperative of the New
Testament are held together by this circle of grace. We must respond generously and fully, for God has given generously and fully.[43]

How are Christians directed to respond to the beneficence of God in

---

[42]See Danker, *Benefactor*, pp. 324-25.

[43]The objection is raised by Howell that somehow in contrast to "the giving and receiving
of benefactions in the patronal society of Greece," Christians realize that they can never
repay the favors of God ("Review of *Despising Shame*," p. 163). Far from being a point of
contrast, this is a point that resonates strongly and specifically with Greco-Roman patronage. The client, being a social inferior to the patron, was not in a position to "repay" the
patron, hence expressed his or her gratitude by some other means than offering an equally
valuable gift in the future. Aristotle (*Nic. Eth.* 8.14.4 [1163b15-18]) knew that the favors of

Christ? The first component of a fulsome response of gratitude is simply giving thanks to the Giver. "When we have decided that we ought to accept, let us accept cheerfully, professing our pleasure and letting the giver have proof of it in order that he may reap instant reward. Let us show how grateful we are for the blessing that has come by pouring forth our feelings" (Seneca *Ben.* 2.22.1). Exuberant thanksgiving characterizes the worship of Israel (see Ps 92:1-4; 95:1-2; 103; 138; Sir 51:1-12), and was to mark the lives and gatherings of Christians as well (Eph 5:4, 19-20; Col 3:15, 17; 4:2; 1 Thess 5:18). Paul provides his churches with a remarkable model for thanksgiving, rendering praise to God for all progress in the churches (evidence to him of God's nurturing and equipping: Rom 1:8; 1 Cor 1:4-7; Col 1:3-4; 1 Thess 3:9), for every deliverance from hardship or trouble (2 Cor 1:9-11), and for the work that God was accomplishing through him (2 Cor 2:14). Paul's example teaches us to be mindful ever of God's past gifts and watchful for the signs of God's continued assistance and gifting at work in our lives and in our churches, so that we can give God thanks as the firstfruits, as it were, of grateful hearts (Col 1:12; 2:7).

"Let us bear witness to them, not merely in the hearing of the giver, but everywhere" (Seneca *Ben.* 2.22.1). Recipients of God's favor should therefore zealously seek the increase of God's honor or, better, the increase of the recognition of God's honor and generosity. The author of Ephesians shares the assumption of Aristotle and Seneca, namely, that beneficence rightly results in the augmented renown and praise of the giver. So also God's generosity revealed in Jesus flows "unto the praise of the honor of his generosity *(charis)* with which he graced *(echaritōsen)* us in the Beloved" (Eph 1:6, my translation; see also 1:12, 14). It falls to the recipient of favor to testify to the favor and bring honor to the giver: the believers are now "to announce the virtuous deeds *(aretai)* of the One who called you out of darkness into his marvelous light" (1 Pet 2:10, my translation).[44] Showing gratitude to God

---

the gods and of parents can never be adequately repaid, with the result that the person who pays them all the regard he or she can is deemed virtuous. With regard to human patrons, Seneca envisions the situation where a recipient shows his gratitude thus: "I may not be able to repay you, but at the least I shall not refrain from declaring everywhere that I cannot repay you" (*Ben.* 2.24.4). He discourses also at some length (*Ben.* 7.16.1-4) about the recipient who has taken great pains to try to return a benefit, being watchful for the opportunity but simply not finding a way to help one who is far greater than himself or herself: "The one should say, 'I have received,' the other, 'I still owe.'"

[44]The declaration of God's *aretai* resembles the use of this term in honorary inscriptions,

in the first instance means proclamation of God's favors and publicly acknowledging our debt to (and thus association with) Jesus, the mediator through whom we have access to God's favor (Lk 12:8-9).[45] A grateful heart is the source of evangelism and witness, which is perhaps most effectively done as we simply and honestly give God public praise for the gifts and help we have received from God. Perhaps some shrink from evangelism because they think they need to work the hearer through Romans, or discourse on the two natures of Christ. Begin by speaking openly, rather, about the favor God has shown you, the positive difference God's gifts have made in your life: tell other people facing great need about the One who supplies every need generously.

Words are not the only medium for increasing God's honor. Jesus directed his followers to pursue a life of good works that would lead those seeing them to "give honor to your Father who is in heaven" (Mt 5:16, my translation).[46] As believers persist in pursuing "noble deeds," those who now slander them will come to glorify God at the judgment (1 Pet 2:11-12). A particular "good work" and "noble deed" is benefaction; abundance in this ministry "overflows with many thanksgivings to God" (2 Cor 9:11-12). Living worthily of God's call, that is, walking in the life of virtue made possible through God's gift of the Spirit, also results in the increase of the honor given Jesus' name (2 Thess 1:11-12). By telling others of God's gifts, and by being zealous for virtue and well-doing, we have opportunity to advance our great patron's reputation in this world, possibly leading others in this way to seek to attach themselves to so good a benefactor.

---

where it means not just virtue but "demonstration of character and exceptional performance" (Danker, *Benefactor*, p. 318). This aspect of response to divine benefits is deeply rooted in the worship of Israel (see Ps 96:1-4; 105:1-2; 107; 116:12-18).

[45]Early Christians frequently had reason to hide their attachment to Jesus and his followers, since association with that group brought suspicion, reproach, physical abuse and financial ruin (see Heb 10:32-34; 1 Pet 4:14-16). Keeping silent about one's patron and denying his gifts through their silence was not an option for virtuous recipients of favor. Recall Seneca's admonition: "As the giver should add to his gift only that measure of publicity which will please the one to whom he gives it, so the recipient should invite the whole city to witness it; a debt that you are ashamed to acknowledge you should not accept" (*Ben.* 2.23.1).

[46]In John 15:8, Jesus says that the Father is glorified when Jesus' followers "bear much fruit and become my disciples." The vagueness of this expression (the "fruit" is never specified in John) may have been quite intentional, alerting the readers to watch for all possible opportunities to "be fruitful" to the increase of God's honor, whether that be in good works that point to the source of all goodness, in making new disciples, or simply in internalizing ever more fully the life of discipleship as taught by Jesus and his apostles.

Besides bringing honor to a patron, it was also a vital part of gratitude to show loyalty to the patron. Attachment to a patron could become costly[47] should that patron have powerful enemies. Being grateful—owning one's association and remaining committed to that patron—could mean great loss (Seneca *Ep. Mor.* 81.27). True gratitude entails, however, setting the relationship of grace above considerations of what is at the moment advantageous.[48] First-century Christians often faced, as do so many international Christians in this century, choosing between loyalty to God and personal safety. For this reason, several texts underscore the positive results of enduring hostility and loss for their commitment. First Peter 1:6-9 interprets the believers' present experiences of testing as an opportunity for them to demonstrate the firmness of their commitment to their divine patron. Even though the mediator of their salvation, Jesus, is presently unseen, they love him and persist in trust toward him. The end result of keeping this trust firm is the preservation of their souls. Their joy in this interim is an outward witness to their confidence in their patron to deliver what has been promised.

Suffering on account of association with the name of Jesus is considered a gift from God (Phil 1:29-30; 1 Pet 2:18-21).[49] Loyalty to God even in the face of suffering is a gift insofar as it brings one in line with Christ's example, so that "you may follow in his footsteps" (1 Pet 2:21, my translation). It is the ultimate destination of that path that makes suffering for the name of Christ a gift now, namely the deliverance and honor that God will give to those who commit themselves to him, trusting him (1 Pet 3:14; 4:13, 19; cf. Jesus' posture in 2:23). Given the cost Jesus was willing to incur in bringing us into God's favor, the believer should be emboldened to make a like return, leaving behind worldly comfort, honor and safety for the sake of responding to Jesus (Heb 13:12-13). Loyalty to God means

---

[47]Although I deeply appreciate Dietrich Bonhoeffer's challenging words on cheap grace and costly grace in *The Cost of Discipleship* (New York: Collier, 1959), the concept of "costly gratitude" might have served his point better (avoiding any misunderstandings that grace could be acquired or purchased). His argument is, of course, that gifts costing the Son so dearly must rouse us to make a like return.

[48]Recall Seneca: "It is the ungrateful man who thinks· 'I should have liked to return gratitude, but I fear the expense, I fear the danger, I shrink from giving offense; I would rather consult my own interest" (*Ben.* 4.24.2).

[49]First Peter 2:19-20 contains the enigmatic phrases *touto gar charis* and *touto charis para theō(i)*. The NRSV renders these "it is a credit to you" and "you have God's approval," but in both obscures the more immediate impression of the words "this is a gift," "this is a gift from God" (or "this is [the manifestation of] favor before God").

being careful to avoid courting God's enemies as potential patrons as well. In the first century this meant not participating in rites that proclaimed one's indebtedness to the gods whose favor non-Christians were careful to cultivate, whether the Greco-Roman pantheon or the emperor (1 Cor 10:14-21; Rev 14:6-13). If avoidance of such rituals meant losing the favor of one's human patrons, this was but the cost of loyalty to the great patron. One could not be more concerned with the preservation of one's economic and social well-being than living out a grateful response to the one God (Mt 6:24; Lk 12:8-9).

The other side of loyalty is trust (quite literally, since *pistis* referred to both). As seen already in 1 Peter 1:6-9, believers endured society's hostility not only out of gratitude for God's past gifts but out of firm trust in the future benefactions of God, specifically the deliverance about to be revealed at the second coming (1 Pet 1:5, 13). At stake in Galatia, from Paul's perspective, was the Christian community's trust in Jesus' ability to secure God's favor for them. If they were to seek to secure God's favor for themselves on the basis of works of Torah, this would now amount to a vote of no confidence in Jesus' mediation, to which they had previously committed themselves (and by means of which they had already received the Holy Spirit, Gal 3:1-5). The result would be alienation from Jesus, who would no longer benefit those who distrusted, and ultimately from God's favor itself (Gal 2:20-21; 5:2-4). Firm trust in God becomes a source of stability for the believer, allowing him or her, in turn, to be a reliable client of God and friend of fellow believers (Col 1:5). Jesus' own stability—the fact that he is the same person today as yesterday and will still remain such tomorrow—provides the suitable platform for a stable trust (Heb 13:7-8).[50]

Clients would return gratitude in the form not only of honor and loyalty but also in services performed for the patron. It is here that good works, acts of obedience and the pursuit of virtue are held together inseparably from the reception of God's favor and kindnesses. A life of obedience to Jesus' teachings and the apostles' admonitions—in short, a life of good works—are not offered to gain favor from God, but nevertheless

---

[50]In an oration on the reasons for distrust, Dio Chrysostom points out that "what someone has said about Fortune might much rather be said about human beings, that no one knows about anyone whether he will remain as he is until the morrow," changing his word and breaking agreements as his advantage leads (*Or.* 74.21-22). There is no such lack of "constancy" (*Or.* 74.4) in the Christian's patron, Jesus, affirms the author of Hebrews.

they *must* be offered in grateful response to God. To refuse these is to refuse the patron (who gave his all for us) the return he specifically requests from us. Paul well understands how full our response should be: if Jesus gave his life for us, we fall short of a fair return unless we live our lives for him (2 Cor 5:14-15; Gal 2:20).

God's acts on our behalf become the strongest motivation for specific Christian behaviors. For example, Paul reminds the Corinthian church that, since they were ransomed for a great price, they are no longer their own masters; they owe it to their Redeemer to use their bodies now as it pleases him (1 Cor 6:12-20).[51] In more general terms, he reminds the Roman Christians that their experience of deliverance from sin and welcome into God's favor leaves them obliged now to use their bodies and lives to serve God, as once they served sin. They are "debtors," not to the flesh, but to the God who delivered them and will deliver them (Rom 8:12).[52] Such righteous conduct is always itself the result of God's enabling, God making us able even to offer a suitable response to his favor (Rom 8:2-4; Phil 1:11; Heb 13:20-21; 2 Pet 1:3-4). The fact that such resources are provided, however, makes it all the more incumbent on the Christians to avail themselves of God's abundant supply and to make use of them rather than neglect them.

A prominent kind of exhortation in the New Testament promotes imitation of the virtues and generosity displayed by God and Jesus. First, Jesus enjoins the recipients of God's favor to imitate God's beneficence (see Mt 5:43-48; Lk 6:27-36). He challenges normal limits of reciprocity and generosity, setting rather as the standard God's own

---

[51]Consider the similar logic in 1 Peter 1:17-21: the believers have an obligation to conduct themselves in such a way as shows reverence for God (1 Pet 1:17) because of the acts of beneficence already performed for them by God in Jesus, namely being ransomed at no less a price than Jesus' own lifeblood—a price foreseen before creation itself (the topic of forethought in beneficence was common: see Acts 24:2-4 for but one example). They thus owe God more than they would owe any human benefactor who effected their deliverance through the paying of a ransom in gold or silver (already a staggering debt of gratitude). The beneficent intent of God in the incarnation and passion of Jesus is underscored again as "on your account" (δι' ὑμᾶς, 1:20).

[52]See, rightly, Danker, *Benefactor,* p. 451. Other passages deserving attention in this context are Romans 12:1 and Ephesians 4:1 (which begin to outline the proper response to the beneficence celebrated in Rom 1—11 and Eph 1—3) and Hebrews 13:15-16, which describes the proper demonstration of "gratitude" and "reverent service" (Heb 12:28) to be rendered to God by those his Son has cleansed, to whom he gave access to God's favor and presence, whom he will yet perfect by leading them into the unshakable realm.

example.[53] Christians are directed to be benefactors to their non-Christian neighbors (1 Thess 3:12; 5:15), especially in the face of antagonism, so as to silence slander by "doing good" (1 Pet 2:15, my translation). The logic of these exhortations is consistently to respond in accordance with what benefactions one has received, whether pardoning (or "forgiving," Mt 6:14-15; 18:23-35; Eph 4:32; Col 3:13) as we have been pardoned; Jews and Gentiles extending welcome and acceptance within the church since they have each been welcomed freely by Christ (Rom 15:7); loving one another as Christ had shown love for us (Eph 5:2; 1 Jn 4:11); being more mindful of the interests of others than our own interests and recognition, as Christ gave example when he poured himself out for our benefit (Phil 2:1-11); or laying down our lives to help one another, and this often in very practical and material demonstrations, because Jesus laid down his life to help us (1 Jn 3:16-18).

Another angle from which New Testament authors approach this response of service is calling Christians to be mindful of fulfilling God's purposes for us in giving us what he has given and doing for us what he has done—that is to say, using God's gifts rightly and to their proper end.[54] God's patience toward the sinner is a gift meant to lead the sinner to repentance, "the riches of his kindness" to bring about a change of heart (Rom 2:4). Failure to use this gift correctly shows that one "despises" God's kindness and results in wrath. God's gift of freedom in Christ is neither to be set aside (Gal 5:1) nor used for purposes that do not honor or please God (Gal 5:13). Rather, this freedom is an opportunity for love and service to fellow believers. Both Titus 2:11-14 and 2 Peter 1:4 focus on the transformation of our lives from lives marked by "the corruption that is in the world because of lust" or by "impiety and worldly passions" into "lives that are self-controlled, upright, and godly," reflecting our participation in "the divine nature." Sanctification, in essence, is simply a right response to God's gifts, putting the resources God has made available for holiness in Christ to good and proper use.

---

[53]Recall Seneca's attempt to do the same, directing patrons and benefactors to imitate the gods, who lavish their gifts on the sacrilegious and indifferent as well as the pious (*Ben.* 1.1.9; 4.25.1; 4.26.1; 4.28.1), acting ever in accordance with their own character and virtue, even in the face of lack of virtue.

[54]Failure to do so inevitably insults the giver, who gives in the expectation that a gift will be utilized and used in a manner suitable to its worth (the person given a precious artifact should not put it in the attic, nor use it for a cuspidor, for example).

Similarly, Paul and the author of 1 Peter speak frequently of the ways in which God has gifted individual believers for the good of the whole church. Divine endowments of this kind (whether teaching, prophetic utterance, wisdom, tongues or even monetary contributions) become opportunities and obligations for service. The proper response to receiving such gifts is not boasting (1 Cor 4:7), which in effect suppresses the acknowledgment that these qualities stem from God's endowment, but sharing God's gifts with the whole church and the world. We are to exercise stewardship of the varied gifts that God has granted with the result that the honor and praise offered to God increases (1 Pet 4:10-11; see also Rom 12:3-8; 1 Cor 12:4-11; Eph 4:7-16).

Commitment to respond as grateful recipients is reinforced throughout the New Testament by the assurance that such a response keeps one centered in God's favor and leads to future benefactions from God. "You are my friends if you do what I command you. . . . I appointed you to go and bear fruit, fruit that will last, so that the Father will give you whatever you ask him in my name" (Jn 15:14, 16). Obedience leads to a friendship relationship with Jesus and access to and assurance of God's personal patronage (God's willingness to hear and answer believers' petitions; see also Jn 14:14-17). Jesus is the "source of eternal salvation for all who obey him" (Heb 5:9); the author of Hebrews especially motivates perseverance in gratitude by means of keeping the addressees focused on salvation as something they are "to inherit" (Heb 1:14) at Christ's second coming (Heb 9:28). Both 1 Peter 3:12 (quoting Ps 34:16) and 1 John 3:21-22 affirm that "obey[ing] his commandments" brings assurance that God remains favorable to the Christians' petitions. In a passage that has been helpfully compared with the very form of the honorary decree commemorating benefactors,[55] the author of 2 Peter suggests that responding properly to God's ample provision for godliness involves the believers' supplying alongside God's provision our own zeal to bear the most fruit with the seed God plants within us (2 Pet 1:3-10). Such a lifestyle, demonstrating mindfulness of God's past benefactions of cleansing from sin and God's "precious and great promises" (meant to give us the impetus to rise above worldly corruption), leads to the final benefit: "entrance into the eternal kingdom" will "be abundantly supplied to you" (2 Pet 1:11, my translation).[56]

---

[55]Danker, *Benefactor,* pp. 453-66.

[56]On the frequent occurrence of the verb *epichorēgeō* in reference to the activity of benefactors, see Danker, *Benefactor,* pp. 331-32.

Ungraceful Responses to God's Beneficence

The Christian Scriptures also present the danger of failing to attain God's gift (Heb 12:15), of "receiving God's gift in vain" (2 Cor 6:1, my translation). Just as living out a response of gratitude assures the believer of God's favor in the future, so responding to God's favor with neglect, ingratitude or even contempt threatens to make one "fall from favor" (Gal 5:4, my translation), resulting in the danger of exclusion from future benefactions. When attempting to dissuade their audiences from a particular course of action, the New Testament authors show the hearers how such a course of action is inconsistent with the obligations of gratitude and how such a course threatens to turn the affronted patron's favor into wrath.

In effect, refusal or neglect of the sorts of acts described above as constituting a response demonstrating gratitude would mean that the recipient of priceless favors broke the circle of grace and brought the dance to a strident halt. Disowning Jesus (Mt 10:32-33), failing to honor God or return reverence (Rom 1:21; Rev 9:20-21; 16:9, 11), failing to use God's gifts for their intended purposes (Rom 2:4-5; Jude 4), showing distrust toward God or Jesus, faltering rather than acting on their promises (Gal 1:6; 2:21; 5:2-4; Heb 3:12, 19; Jas 1:6-7), showing disloyalty by making alliances with God's enemies (Jas 4:4; Rev 14:9-11), and responding to the divine patron's call for service with disobedience (Heb 3:18-19), such as brings God's name into dishonor (Rom 2:17-24), are all ugly and unsuitable courses of action in light of the generosity and favor God has lavished upon the Christians. Such actions show gross forgetfulness of these benefits[57] and provoke God by meeting his favor and kindness with insult and abuse.

The sermon "to the Hebrews" provides strong examples of these topics at work.[58] Here was a congregation that had faced a time of painful hostil-

---

[57]Forgetfulness of benefits is strongly censured by Seneca (*Ben.* 3.1.3-3.3.2), as also in Cicero *De Offic* 2.63: "All people hate forgetfulness of benefactions, thinking it to be an injury against themselves since it discourages generosity and thinking the ingrate to be the common enemy of the needy." We should expect 2 Peter 1:9 to arouse similar disgust and shame, leading the hearers to take care to pursue the course recommended by the author that shows mindfulness of God's favors.

[58] For a close analysis of patron-client and grace scripts at work in the pastoral strategy of this text, see David A. deSilva, "Exchanging Favor for Wrath: Apostasy in Hebrews and Patron-Client Relations," *JBL* 115 (1996): 91-116; on Hebrews 6:4-8 specifically, see David A. deSilva, "Hebrews 6:4-8: A Socio-Rhetorical Investigation," *Tyndale Bulletin* 50.1 (1999): 33-58; and 50.2 (1999): 225-35.

ity, reproach, abuse and marginalization (Heb 10:32-34). Some members were finding their association with the Christian group less valuable than returning to the good favor of society (Heb 10:25). The author strongly urges the believers to resist any pull that leads them to "drift away" from a straight course toward the good goal that God has set for them. They must "go on toward perfection" (Heb 6:1), since

> it is impossible to restore again to repentance those who have once been enlightened, and have tasted the heavenly gift, and have shared in the Holy Spirit, and have tasted the goodness of the word of God and the powers of the age to come, and then have fallen away, since on their own they are crucifying again the Son of God and are holding him up to contempt. Ground that drinks up the rain falling on it repeatedly, and that produces a crop useful to those for whom it is cultivated, receives a blessing from God. But if it produces thorns and thistles, it is worthless and on the verge of being cursed; its end is to be burned over. (Heb 6:4-8)

The audience is described as having received several important gifts from God (enlightenment, the Holy Spirit, the unspecified heavenly gift) as well as foretastes of the benefactions yet to come. How then could they think of falling away? Such an act would display contempt for the gifts and the Giver, bringing public disgrace on Jesus rather than enhancing his honor as they testify to their neighbors: "You were right. Jesus' favor is not worth the cost of remaining associated with his name." The agricultural illustration that closes the paragraph teaches that God's gifts (here, rain) look for a return, a suitable crop; if the land bears instead what is unpleasant and unprofitable, it has only the fire to look forward to.[59] The author asserts that God has carefully cultivated the believers through abundance of gifts to be "fruitful soil" for him, to bear "suitable vegetation for those on whose behalf [they] were cultivated," namely, acts of love and service for their fellow believers (Heb 6:9-10), remaining reliable and faithful supports to one another in the face of society's shaming techniques. How could they, then, think of bearing the prickly thorns of defection or shirking their responsibilities to help one another and support one

---

[59]Agricultural images are common in classical texts on patronage and reciprocity. Seneca frequently compares giving to sowing seed, grateful clients to good soil, ingrates to wornout soil (*Ben.* 1.1.2; 2.11.4-5; 4.8.2; 4.33.1-2). Pseudo-Phocylides (the real name of the author of this Jewish collection of wise advice is unknown) similarly writes: "Do no good to a bad man; it is like sowing into the sea" (*Sentences* 152).

another through their common pilgrimage?[60]

This very passage has stood at the center of the theological controversy of eternal security as opposed to the possibility of believers committing an unpardonable sin. The author of Hebrews moves in a social ethos in which recipients of benefactions are led to act with one set of considerations in view (namely, the importance of maintaining a response of gratitude and avoiding any course which would show ingratitude toward a patron), while benefactors are led to act with another set of considerations in view (with an emphasis on exercising generosity and magnanimity). Most poignant in this regard is Seneca's advice to the patron who has met with ingratitude not to be afraid to give a second gift, in the hope that, as the farmer works the unproductive soil, this new gift will awaken gratitude and loyalty in all their fullness (*Ben.* 7.32). The doctrine of eternal security threatens to distract us, who are clearly in the role of clients, from focusing on what is our proper business, namely maintaining our commitment to return grace for grace. Attempts to set limits on God's generosity, on the other hand, also impinge on what is not properly ours, namely God's freedom to give even to one who has proven ungrateful in the extreme. The scriptural witness creates the same sort of tension discovered in Greco-Roman texts on patronage—warning clients about the grave perils of ingratitude and the exclusion from favor it brings, but also extolling the patron whose generosity is greater than the ingratitude of some recipients. It is a healthy tension, and choosing one side to the exclusion of the other would be a misstep in the dance of grace.

Christian Giving

It seems appropriate to give some space in this chapter to the topic of Christian giving and to the New Testament interpretation of acts of benefaction and patronage within the new community. Jesus had much to say about beneficence toward the poor. Charity leads to lasting (eternal) wealth (Lk 2:33; 14:12-14; 16:9; 18:22), with the result that Jesus urges all his hearers, "Sell your possessions, and give alms. Make purses for yourselves that do not wear out, an unfailing treasure in

---

[60]Hebrews 10:26-31 offers an even more intense depiction of the significance of withdrawing from open association with the Christian community in the hope of getting back in the good graces of society. The value of the gift and what it cost the Giver are despised by such life choices, and the honor of Jesus, whose favor has been trampled, is avenged by God the Judge in the punishment of the ingrates.

heaven" (Lk 12:33).[61] The concept that a person's true possessions are
what he or she gives away was known to Seneca,[62] although Seneca
would have advised a more judicious (from a worldly point of view)
deployment of benefits than Jesus, who tells us to seek out those who
have no means of repayment, so that God will repay us "at the resurrection of the righteous" (Lk 14:12-14). The striking vision of Matthew 25:31-
46, in which the righteous are separated from the wicked on the basis of
beneficence toward the needy, surprises the hearers and readers by asserting that providing food and clothing and comfort to the needy is the way
to return the favor to the one who has given us all we need for our well-
being and survival (gifts of food and clothing, for example; Mt 6:11, 25-
33). We have the opportunity to make a gracious return to our Lord and
benefactor in the person of the poor or the oppressed.

Especially in the letters of Paul we find a remarkable transformation of
the cultural code of patronage. Monetary contributions and other forms
of assistance or beneficence within the local church or between cells of the
church universal remains a source of recognition and honor. Paul honors
the Macedonian Christians for their generosity by praising them to the
Corinthian congregations (2 Cor 8:1-5; 11:9), amplifying their virtue by
stressing that they did not let their own poverty hinder their generosity.[63]
Paul includes in his letters remembrances of individuals who have under-

---

[61]Luke lays special emphasis on this point: only in his Gospel are we told how to provide
ourselves with these "treasures in heaven," namely by charitable giving, and only in his
Gospel is the challenge poised at the young rich man also poised to all who would follow
Jesus (see especially Lk 14:33). This conviction is developed in the second-century Christian text *Shepherd of Hermas*, similitude 1.

[62]" 'Whatever I have given, that I still possess!' . . . These are the riches that will abide, and
remain steadfast amid all the fickleness of our human lot; and, the greater they become,
the less envy they will arouse. Why do you spare your wealth as though it were your own?
You are but a steward. . . . Do you ask how you can make them your own? By bestowing
them as gifts! Do you, therefore, make the best of your possessions, and, by making them,
not only safer, but more honorable, render your own claim to them assured and inviola-
ble" (*Ben.* 6.3.1, 3).

[63]Compare Seneca: "Sometimes we feel under greater obligations to one who has given
small gifts out of a great heart, who 'by his spirit matched the gift of kings', who bestowed
his little, but gave it gladly, who beholding my poverty forgot his own"(*Ben.* 1.7.1). Also
striking is the similarity between Seneca's and Jesus' evaluations of gifts from the rich and
from those of poor means. "A gift has been made by someone of a large sum of money, but
the giver was rich, he was not likely to feel the sacrifice; the same gift was made by
another, but the giver was likely to lose the whole of his patrimony. The sum given is the
same, but the benefit is not the same" (*Ben.* 3.8.2). Compare this with the story of the
widow's mite (Lk 21:1-4).

gone expense or exercised beneficence for his good or the good of the church. He announces that he is himself, together with "all the churches of the Gentiles," indebted to Prisca and Aquila, who "risked their necks for [Paul's] life," thus who displayed the greatest generosity (Rom 16:3-4). Paul calls for public honors to be given Stephanas, Fortunatus and Achaicus for their service ("So give recognition to such persons" [1 Cor 16:17-18]). He makes special mention of the service of Epaphroditus, a person who, acting as the agent or vehicle of the Philippian church's support of Paul, spends himself to the uttermost (he endures illness even almost to death). Such a person, Paul declares, merits honor in the community (Phil 2:29-30). Since the letters are public documents, read before the gathered assembly of believers, such mention amounts to a public announcement of the individual's generosity and brings him or her honor in the congregation.

Nevertheless, benefaction within the church is a specific gift of God. It is a manifestation of God's patronage of the community, mediated through its members (Rom 12:6-8; Eph 4:7, 11-12).[64] Alongside and among spiritual endowments and edifying services like prophecy, tongues, teaching and words of knowledge, God also bestows the gift of giving to achieve God's purposes in the family of God. God supplies all things, so that Christians are called to share on the basis of their kinship responsibilities toward one another in the church rather than use gifts of money and hospitality to build up their client base (the source of local prestige and power).[65] This is a bold transformation of patronage into stewardship.

Patronage and benefaction are therefore removed from the realm of

---

[64] This theme will recur throughout early Christian literature. *The Acts of Peter,* for example, promotes the awareness that the benefactions of wealthy Christians are presented as examples "of Christ's care for his own" (Robert F. Stoops Jr., "Patronage in the *Acts of Peter,*" *Semeia* 38 [1986]: 94) that result in praise and thanks to Jesus rather than act as the means by which rich people enhance their own prestige in the community. Their gifts are not to advance their own personal power but are given on the basis of their loyalty to Jesus ("Patronage," p. 98; *Acts of Peter* 19); see also Clement of Alexandria's sermon "On the Rich Man Who Enters Heaven."

[65] Another model used to communicate the ideal of Christian giving is that of friendship. Luke presents the earliest community of believers fulfilling the ancient ideal of friendship, where friends, united by a common commitment to virtue, "hold all things in common" (Aristotle *Nic. Eth.* 8.9.1 [1159b31]). No one considered his or her property to be "his own" but rather treated it as the common property of all the believers and used his or her property to relieve need wherever it arose (Acts 4:32-35). Within this relationship there was sharing without power plays.

competition among humans for honor and accumulation of power—a message as relevant today as ever. Indeed, participating in relief efforts is presented as much as a favor granted the givers as a favor done by the givers. The collection for the poor in the Judean churches is perhaps the most prominent act of beneficence among the churches in the New Testament (Acts 11:29; Rom 15:26-27; 2 Cor 8—9). Paul views this, however, not as an act of human patronage, but as God's beneficence working itself out through responsive Christians (2 Cor 9:8-15; God "supplies" *(epichorēgeō)* the resources that meet the needs of the Corinthians fully and give them "abundance for every good deed," so that ultimately God rightly receives the thanks for the donation (2 Cor 9:11-12; my translation). Participation in the relief effort is a "favor" for which the Macedonian Christians earnestly "begged" Paul (2 Cor 8:4). The Judean Christians reciprocate with prayer on behalf of the Gentile Christians (2 Cor 9:14).[66] An important motive for giving is supplied by Paul in his interjection of Christ's generous example, who "though he was rich, yet for your sakes he became poor" (2 Cor 8:9). Participating in the relief effort is a means of honoring the divine benefactor (2 Cor 9:13) by imitating his generosity. Christ's example should spur them on in this endeavor. Moreover, since the Corinthians have been enriched by Christ (2 Cor 8:9) and by God (2 Cor 9:10-11) in so many ways, they are honor bound to use the riches entrusted to them for God's purposes, namely relieving the needs of the saints.

Much tension within contemporary churches could be relieved if we took to heart Paul's paradigm shift for patronage. Those who contribute to the local church do not lay the minister or the congregation under obligation but are enacting faithfully their service to God (and ought to be honored on that basis). They give not in order to secure a return (usually in the form of power and influence within the local church), but because God has given.

Conclusion

Growing in our understanding of the social contexts of grace contributes to our reading of the New Testament in several ways. We become

---

[66]Spiritual favors and material favors can be exchanged in the reciprocal relationships between believers and churches: the latter is certainly not more "real" than the former, and even less glowing (see Rom 1:11-12; 15:26-27; 1 Cor 9:11; Gal 6:6).

more attuned to the gifts God has granted to those who approach him through his Son and are reminded of the favors God has promised for the future. It keeps our focus returning to these, so that God's benefits remain always on our minds (rather than neglected or forgotten as we go about our daily lives). Paul prays in the opening of Ephesians that Christians be made mindful of the magnificence of God's generosity (Eph 1:3, 7-11, 17-19). Indeed, we should return frequently to meditate upon the immensity of God's favor both in terms of his general benefactions (life, salvation, a future of hope) as well as in terms of his personal patronage, the ways in which his favor has entered into our own lives at our points of need. Our awareness of God's generosity and our indebtedness to him will in this way become the focal points for our understanding of our lives, with the result that the cares of the world, as well as its promises, are less likely to distract and entangle us.

The fundamental ethos governing relationships of patrons and clients, benefactors and beneficiaries, and friends is that grace must answer grace. The receiving of favor must lead to the return of gratitude, or else the beauty and nobility of the relationship is defaced (dis-graced). As we grow in our appreciation of God's beneficence, we are thereby impelled to energize our commitment to make an appropriate response of gratitude to God. When the magnitude of God's generosity is considered, gratitude and its fruits must of necessity fill our speech, attitudes and actions.

The New Testament authors outline what a just and suitable response would entail, guiding us to act as honorable recipients of favor and averting us from making an ugly response of ingratitude, neglect or disloyalty, which would also lead to the danger of exclusion from future favors yet to be conferred. We come to engage evangelism more naturally (but also necessarily) not now as a contest for winning souls, but as an opportunity to spread the fame of God and testify to the good things God has done in our behalf. The obligations of gratitude demand that we not hold our tongue in this regard! We begin to understand that obedience to God—throwing ourselves and our resources into the work of caring for the global church—is not something we might do over and above the demands of everyday life. Rather, these pursuits are placed at the center of each day's agenda. As God did not bestow on us what was merely left over after he satisfied himself, so we are called on to make a like exchange by giving our all and our best to God's service first. Moreover, we discover that loyalty to such a patron must be preserved without wavering. This can embolden us in our struggles with our own sins, as we consider how indulging them enacts disloyalty toward the one we should only please. It can also embolden our confrontations with an unbelieving world that finds wholehearted loyalty to this God and his ways a threat and reproach to its way of life. Gratitude provides a clarifying focus to the Christian for his or her life, a single value that, lived out as the New Testament authors direct, will result in a vibrant, fruitful discipleship.

Finally, as we read the pages of the New Testament with an eye to promises of favor, we become more highly sensitized to the way these authors seek to instill in us such a hope for, and trust in, God's promised benefactions that we will have firmness and fixedness in the midst of this life's chances and changes. Such an undivided hope provides an anchor for the soul and the means for stability and reliability in our Christian commitment. As our ambitions are all channeled toward the good gifts that God has prepared for us, we, like the early Christians, will find it easier to detach ourselves from the trivial pursuits and rewards promoted by the society around us and remain constant in our orientation toward the divine patron.

Five

KINSHIP

Living as a Family
in the First-Century World

One thing that all human beings share in common is that they are born into families. Even where parents die shortly after the baby's birth, the remaining natural relatives, a foster family or the fictive family of a state institution will surround the infant, or else the infant will not survive. Unlike many creatures, who need merely to procreate, we need to nurture our young or else they—and with them, our species—will die. But "family" can be constructed in a great variety of ways, can mean vastly different things, can act in a diversity of ways across cultures and centuries, so we will need to think carefully about what family meant for those early Christians who lived both within natural families as well as within the "family of faith." What was significant about belonging to a certain natural family? What were the everyday realities of family life? What were the expectations one had of other members of a household? Why were adoption by God and incorporation into Abraham's family such vitally important symbols for the early Christians? What did it mean for them to call one another and hear themselves called "brother" or "sister"? Immersing ourselves in the ethos of the Greco-Roman and Jewish households will help us recapture the richness of the New Testament vision for communities of faith as the "household of God," as well as allow us an insider's view of texts that speak about family, lineage and the assumptions about how kin interact.

Kinship and Identity

A person's family of origin is the primary source for his or her status and location in the world and an essential reference point for the person's identity. People are not just free-floating individuals out in the world but are located within the larger constellations of "family" in a very broad sense (like clan). Location in a larger family—an ancestral house—is critical not only for the person's self-perception but also for the perception and expectations others will have of him or her. In the ancient world, people are not just "taken on their own merits." Instead, their merits begin with the merits (or debits) of their lineage, the reputation of their ancestral house. Greeks and Romans receive a basic identity from their larger family: for Romans this takes the form of including the clan name in the name of each individual.

This is even more pronounced in Jewish culture. Priests and Levites assume their roles in the temple based solely on their lineage. The "sons of Aaron," themselves from the tribe of Levi, serve as priests (1 Esd 1:14); the remainder of the descendants of Levi are arranged according to their "ancestral houses" (1 Esd 1:5, 10) to perform their various ministries in the temple worship (some of these special functions are listed at 1 Esd 5:26-28: the functions of "doorkeepers" and "sacred singers" are fulfilled by certain families). The care with which priests and other members of the tribe of Levi kept track of their lineage (and, indeed, with which official registries kept track of lineage) is shown in the lists preserved in 1 Esdras 5:24-40 and 8:28-40 (1 Esd 5:9-23 preserves the lineage of the rest of the Israelites in the assembly of the returnees). Those priests and Levites among the returnees from the Babylonian exile whose lineage could not be verified were excluded from temple service until such time as a high priest could cast Urim and Thummim to determine the truth about their place in the tribe (1 Esd 5:36-40).

A person's lineage, therefore, gave him or her a specific location in the vastly extended kinship group of the descendants of Abraham. Thus when Luke introduces Zechariah as belonging to "the priestly order of Abijah" and Zechariah's wife, Elizabeth, as also "a descendent of Aaron" (Lk 1:5), Joseph as "from the house and family of David" (Lk 2:3-4), and the prophetess Anna as "the daughter of Phanuel, of the tribe of Asher"

(Lk 2:36), he gives important information about their status and place in the nation of Israel, as well as the status and identity of those sons born into these families (i.e., John the Baptist and Jesus).

Historical dimension: Genealogy and lineage. Perhaps the least appealing passages of Scripture to modern Western readers are the genealogies, which are often skipped as hopelessly boring. But to the writers and hearers they contained important information and could be constructed in a variety of different ways to convey a variety of meanings. Genealogies are, simply, lists of relatives. They can be linear, tracing the contemporary generation back to a founding or especially noteworthy ancestor, or segmented, going back perhaps a few generations only but including more than one member of each generation (listing siblings and even the descendants of each sibling).[1] Genealogies encode important claims about the people in the text whose genealogies are being developed. R. R. Wilson comments that the linear genealogy serves to "ground a claim to power, status, rank, office, or inheritance in an earlier ancestor."[2] Thus Ezra is introduced into the story of 1 Esdras with his genealogy (1 Esd 8:1-2), tracing his lineage through the celebrated Phineas to "Aaron the high priest." This presents him as one occupying the highest honor and status in Israel by birth, as well as legitimizing the role he is about to play in the reconstitution of the Torah and the ethnic purging of Israel. The general-turned-historian Josephus uses genealogy to open his autobiography (the *Vita*, or "Life") to prove his nobility. Aware that some slander him, he retorts that he is of the priestly line (the way, he says, Jews reckon nobility among them); indeed, he even comes from the first of the twenty-four priestly families (courses) and from the chief family within that course.

With this in mind, read the two genealogies of Jesus in Matthew 1 and Luke 3. The differences between these two genealogies are readily apparent, first insofar as Matthew traces Jesus' genealogy only from as far back as Abraham (Mt 1:2), while Luke works backwards as far as Adam and God himself (Lk 3:38). Matthew presents three groups of fourteen generations each between significant milestones in Israel's history (Abraham, David, exile to Babylon, Jesus) and talks about these numbers. He also includes notice of five mothers in his genealogy. Luke attends to nothing

---

[1]Genesis 5 provides our earliest linear genealogy; Genesis 10 the first segmented genealogy; Genesis 11:10-30 mixes the types.
[2]Robert R. Wilson, "Genealogy, Genealogies," *ABD* 2.929-32, p. 931.

other than the naming of the successive fathers. He has fifty-six generations between Jesus and Abraham, which clashes with Matthew's forty-
two for the same span.[3] What are the two evangelists attempting to communicate by means of these lists?

First, the differences show us that there are a variety of options for the
person composing a genealogy. Where one begins and ends is clearly a
choice. One may also skip generations if the author's purpose is something other than completeness. Who is included and excluded are
choices, not necessities, so that these decisions should be viewed as carrying significance.[4] Both Matthew and Luke demonstrate that Jesus has a
pure Israelite lineage, a true descendent of Abraham. Matthew is interested in two principal ancestors, announced in the first verse of his Gospel: "Jesus the Messiah, the son of David, the son of Abraham" (Mt 1:1).
"Son of David," the brief notice of lineage indicating a claim to be a
potential heir of David's throne throughout the Gospel (Mt 9:27; 20:30-31;
21:9), is an important genealogical claim made for Jesus. Matthew highlights this in two ways. First, Jesus is of the royal line of David through
David's royal successor Solomon and through the kings of Judah whose
names and deeds are known from 1 and 2 Kings (this is different from
Luke); second, Matthew has constructed the genealogy so that all significant events in the history of Israel fall fourteen generations apart, and
fourteen is the sum of the Hebrew letters in the name David.[5] Jesus' birth
at a fourteen-generation interval is a way of highlighting his significance
for the house of David, a restoration after its demise in the exile. Additionally, Matthew's inclusion of four women from the premonarchial and
monarchial period (significantly focusing down on David)—four women
whose place in the genealogy was most questionable, either because
they were Gentiles or because the circumstances of their union with the
father was abnormal (to say the least)—provides important precedent
for the abnormal nature of Jesus' conception as well. Jesus' descent

---

[3]The commonly attempted solution to read one genealogy as Joseph's and the other as
Mary's flies in the face of both evangelists' explicit naming of Joseph as the one through
whom each genealogy is being traced. Such "solutions" betray a greater commitment to
harmonizing the Gospels than to hearing what each has to say.
[4]Kenneth C. Hanson, "*BTB* Reader's Guide: Kinship," *BTB* 24 (1994): 187.
[5]In Hebrew, as in Greek and Latin, letters were also used for numerals. The interchangeabil-
ity led to the practice of *gematria,* adding up the letters of a name and then using that as a
code for the name itself. Thus for "David," *dwd:* daleth = 4, waw = 6, daleth = 4: the sum
being 14.

from David and Abraham is thus able to be held in tension with his special descent from God (see Mt 1:20).[6]

Luke's interest is shown in his simple tracing of the line from Joseph back to Adam and thus to God. It is a genealogical argument for the universality that Luke will claim for Christ's rule (begun in the scope of the church's mission, uniting into one body all the nations of the earth, all the descendants of Adam and, ultimately, God who made all nations "from one" (Acts 17:26). Pushing past Abraham to Adam and God is a way of claiming that the scope of the gospel reaches far beyond the boundaries of the Jewish nation. This may be a significant way to introduce Jesus in a two-volume work that takes up the question of the relevance of being Jewish to being Christian (see Acts 15). It is also a genealogical defense of the title "Son of God," a claim that will be put to the test in the immediately following passage (Lk 4:1-13).

Segmented genealogies can serve to "defend a claim to honor (articulating the web of significant family relationships), identify social roles and obligations, establish inheritance rights, identify eligible marriage partners or actual exogamous partners, and within the family to indicate birth order, honor order, or motherhood (important in polygynous families)."[7] That is to say, segmented genealogies attempt to lay out something of the horizontal dimension of a person' kinship, perhaps in an attempt to evaluate the collective honor of the individual's siblings and their families, or to determine seniority or precedence within a family. The segmented genealogy of Genesis 10 serves, among other purposes, to locate the indigenous occupants of Canaan most unfavorably: they are descendants of Ham, who dishonored his father, Noah, and whose son Canaan was specifically cursed by his own grandfather to be the slave of the other nations that would spring up from these primeval ancestors. The genealogy legitimates the contempt and enmity between Israel and the peoples it displaced and continued to be at odds with during the period of the judges and the early monarchy.

We will not encounter many polygynous families (that is, polygamy—multiple wives or concubines) in Scripture after the patriarchal period. Multiple marriage is thereafter confined to royalty. Neverthe-

---

[6]Jesus' question to the scribes in Matthew 22:41-46 is designed to prove from Scripture that God's Messiah must be more than merely Son of David.
[7]Hanson, "*BTB* Reader's Guide: Kinship," p. 187.

less, Jews did pay attention to maternity in genealogies of the tribes of
Israel. The twelve sons of Jacob did not consistently exemplify the best
of kinship ethics, and their stories are retold and even greatly expanded
in the *Testaments of the Twelve Patriarchs*, an astounding piece of Jewish
literature from the intertestamental period, as a means of teaching the
dangers of competition, division and rivalry within the family of Jacob
(the "house of Israel"). Brothers in a polygynous family sharing a common mother are depicted banding against or fearing some deceit and
harm from their half brothers by a different mother. Whether or not one
is born of a free woman (Leah and Rachel) or one of their maidservants
(Zilpah and Bilhah) also becomes a determinant of a sort of intra-family
status ladder. Wherever their stories are told, it seems, being wary of
repeating their breaches of the ethos of kinship appears to be a dominant purpose.

As Jesus' audience in the synagogue of Nazareth struggles to make
sense of the wisdom of his preaching and the miraculous deeds attributed
to him, they make use of a segmented genealogy: "Is not this the carpen-
ter, the son of Mary and brother of James and Joses and Judas and Simon,
and are not his sisters here with us?" (Mk 6:3).[8] The status that Jesus is
claiming by means of his actions and words, and the role he has begun to
play as teacher, prophet and miracle worker is dissonant with the status
ascribed him by birth. The way he is located in Judean culture becomes
problematic for the acceptance of his message. The segmented genealogy
the audience has constructed conflicts with the message of the linear
genealogy that begins Matthew's Gospel and appears later in Mark's
Gospel as well (the connection of Jesus with the lineage of David at Mk
10:47-48; 11:9-10).

Ascribed honor and dishonor. The importance of one's ancestry for one's
own honor is amply demonstrated from the fact that rhetorical handbooks all prescribe beginning the encomium (the commemorative funerary speech) with a discussion of the praiseworthy ancestors of the subject
of the speech and then the virtues and accomplishments of the immediate
progenitors. The reputation of the family of origin sets up the expecta-

---

[8]The Marcan form of this question may contain an added barb—in referring to Jesus as the
son of Mary rather than the son of Joseph in a culture in which everyone is named by his
paternity, we may have an implication being made of his questionable legitimacy. Matthew
and John (Mt 13:55-57; Jn 6:42) do not have this implication here, although John may refer
to it elsewhere (Jn 8:41: "We are not illegitimate children").

tions for what the progeny will be like, whether noble or shameful, virtuous and reliable or base and unreliable. His study of honorary
inscriptions leads F. W. Danker to speak of the "genetic consistency" in
the manifestation of virtue, beneficence and the like.[9] One of the inscriptions he includes—the Lycian League's decree in honor of Opramoas—
bears eloquent witness to this phenomenon. It begins by setting out the
noble acts that brought honor to his ancestors, then the generosity and
virtue of his immediate parents, and finally, now, the ways in which
Opramoas has lived up to the mark of his ancestors.

People are known first of all by their father's name in Jewish culture,
hence Bar-Abbas, Bar-Timaeus (Mk 10:46), Bar-Jesus (Acts 13:6), Bar-
Jonah (Mt 16:17; Jn 1:42; 21:15), Bar-Sabbas (Acts 1:23). The father's reputation becomes the starting place for the reputation of the children. If they
come from a good, reliable father, it will be taken as a given that they will
be good and reliable unless they prove otherwise. Conversely, a father in
disgrace is a hard legacy to overcome: "Children will blame an ungodly
father, for they suffer disgrace because of him" (Sir 41:7).[10] Family honor
is an essential part of the inheritance given to children.[11] The importance
of honor derived from birth is reflected in the tendency to insult other
people by questioning their parentage or by providing them with an
unflattering genealogy (some things change very little over the centuries).
We must recognize that the epithet "offspring of snakes" ("brood of
vipers") in Matthew 3:7; 12:34; 23:33; or the descriptions of adversaries as
descendants of murderers (Mt 23:31-33; Acts 13:10), who will act out the
same vices of their forebears are the most virulent of insults available to
people in the ancient world.

---

[9]Frederick W. Danker, *Benefactor: Epigraphic Study of a Graeco-Roman und New Testament
Semantic Field* (St. Louis: Clayton, 1982), pp. 348-49.

[10]See, at greater length, Wisdom of Solomon 3:16-19; 4:3, 6 on the children of adulterous
unions, who will "be held of no account" and whose old age will even "be without honor."
Tobit (Tob 3:5) assumes that punishment for the sins of forefathers can be exacted from the
descendants (as in Ex 20:5-6); the stain of the progenitors clings to the offspring. The
Greco-Roman world shared this view, as in the Oedipus saga, where Oedipus suffers as
part of the unfolding of the curse on the house of Cadmus for a primeval sin. In both traditions, however, there are voices that question the justice of blaming children for the parents' misdeeds and vice versa.

[11]Hanson, *"BTB Reader's Guide: Kinship,"* p. 185. The relationship between the honor of
parents and the honor of children is reciprocal: the parents provide the starting place for
the children's honor, but dishonorable children can also soil the honor of the parent (see Sir
22:3-5).

The horizontal dimension: The living kinship group. "Kin" are those who are "kind" in the sense of "being of the same sort as oneself, being like oneself." There is a certain connection established between kin in their nature, rather than in their deliberate choice. How wide a person's conception of his or her kin was in the first-century world, however, is impossible to determine with precision. To my knowledge, a thorough study of this question—that is, where the line of kin or family is drawn for the average Jew or Greek—has not been undertaken. Indeed, it appears that the width of an individual's conceptual circle of kin varied greatly depending on his or her situation or context, as well as on his or her ideological convictions about what defined kinship.

While some philosophers attempted to draw the circle of kinship so broadly as to embrace the entire human species,[12] the widest functional definition of kinship in the ancient world appears to have been ethnicity. Jews, of course, claimed to be one large kinship group descended from Abraham through Isaac and Jacob (in contrast to the other descendants of Abraham through Ishmael and Esau). Hence the expressions "house of Jacob," "house of Israel," "children of Jerusalem" (the latter being frequent in literature deriving from, or looking back on, the exile) and the like were verbalizations of the corporate solidarity of the Jews on the basis of a notion of extended kinship. All Jews are ultimately "brothers" (Tob 2:2; 2 Macc 1:1) despite the careful tracing of precise lineage and relationships that exists alongside this concept. Greeks also recognized their essential kinship with one another—their likeness and solidarity—in opposition to every barbarian race, concerning which Aristotle could say that "they are a community of slaves, male and female. Wherefore the poets say—'It is meet that Hellenes should rule over barbarians'; as if they thought that the barbarian and the slave were by nature one" (*Pol.* 1.2 [1252b7-10]).

The level at which ideas of kinship operated depended, in large measure, on the context. In the Diaspora communities, Jews, knowing themselves to be a largely unprotected minority, tended to see and treat each another as kin simply on that basis, being bonded together in the midst of a dominant, non-Jewish culture. Complaints made by non-Jews about the

---

[12]Marcus Aurelius is a striking, though by no means an early, example of this: he speaks of a fellow human being as his brother by virtue not of blood but by sharing reason and the spark of the divine mind (*Meditations* 2.1; see also 3.11).

way in which Jews were always willing to help each other but seemed reluctant to help non-Jews bear indirect testimony to the tendency to draw kinship lines quite broadly in such settings (based on common descent from the twelve patriarchs and common commitment to an inherited way of life).[13] In Palestine, however, one encountered a lot more competition between Jews who, now being the majority culture, were free to define their kinship circles more narrowly. From *ethnos* a person could move down to "tribe" (a meaningful designation both in Roman and Jewish culture) and "clan," and eventually down to those who were close blood-relatives (parents and grandparents; siblings of parents and their children; a person's own siblings and their conjugal families; a person's own spouse and children, and children's conjugal families). Where kinship was invoked or established between two people, however, competition and distrust could quickly give way to cooperation and trust.

One can discern in the teachings of Jesus (and as early as the preaching of John the Baptist) a definite attempt to recover among Palestinian Jews a larger sense of kin and cooperation on the basis of shared lineage with Abraham. Thus Jesus will shame the synagogue officials by reminding them that the woman whom he has healed is "a daughter of Abraham," a sister to those who would water their animals on the sabbath but deny her relief from her crippled, wretched state (Lk 13:16). He declares that the despised Zacchaeus is "also a son of Abraham" (Lk 19:9) to be brought back to the family rather than hated as a "sinner," with kinship bonds and affections denied (Lk 19:7). Luke 15:1-32 forms an extended address relevant to this problem, particularly the parable of the two sons. Jesus criticizes the scribes and Pharisees for acting as loveless brothers toward their wayward kin, those who respond to Jesus' call to repent and return to righteous conduct. It is they, the Pharisees, who should be ashamed of their breach of the kinship ethic, including their refusal to show the love for their sisters and brothers that would delight the heart of their Father, and their lack of concern for working together to redeem their kin from the dishonorable lifestyles into which they had fallen.

The Ethos of Kin

Those who were family behaved in certain ways toward one another—

---

[13]See Tacitus *Hist.* 5.5; Diodorus of Siculus *Bib. Hist.* 34.1-4; 40.3.4; Juvenal *Sat.* 14.100-104; Apion's charge in Josephus *Ag. Ap.* 2.121.

ways that were frequently quite different from their behavior toward those outside the kinship group (however that group is being defined at a given time). Behaving toward your kin as you would toward outsiders was reprehensible, a mark of dishonor in the family. If we are to understand the exhortations in the New Testament about living together as the "family of God," we must first grasp the essential contours of what it meant to be family at all for those authors and their congregations.

Cooperation, not competition. The Greco-Roman and Jewish environments were competitive. People outside of an individual's kinship group, or outside an individual's extended household (which would include friends and clients or patrons) were viewed as potential rivals and sometimes even antagonists. Honor and its various components (wealth, fame, positions of influence, acknowledged precedence) were the prizes for which people competed with one another. It was essential, however, that this ethic of competitiveness be reserved for encounters outside of the kinship group. Such behavior within a family would erode its strength, its unity, its viability. Thus, while it would be perfectly acceptable to gain honor by successfully challenging and disgracing a rival, Ben Sira would write "Do not glorify yourself by dishonoring your father, for your father's dishonor is no glory to you" (Sir 3:10).

Special attention is given in this regard to siblings by classical, Hellenistic and Greco-Roman ethicists. The relationship between siblings is the closest, strongest and most intimate of relationships in the ancient world. Aristotle considers brotherly love to be a special and augmented form of friendship: "Brothers love each other as being born of the same parents; for their identity with them makes them identical with each other (which is the reason why people talk of 'the same blood', 'the same stock', and so on). They are, therefore, in a sense the same thing, though separate individuals" (*Nic. Eth.* 8.12.3 [1161b30-35]). The friendship of siblings is enhanced by "a common upbringing," a sentiment echoed four centuries later by Plutarch: "In so far as Nature has made [siblings] separate in their bodies, so far do they become united in their emotions and actions, and share with each other their studies and recreations and games" ("On Fraternal Affection" 5 [*Mor.* 480B-C]).[14]

---

[14]See also Xenophon: "Those from the same seed, nurtured by the same mother, grown up in the same house, loved by the same parents . . . how should they not be close to one another?" (*Cyr.* 8.7, 14). See also the Jewish author of 4 Maccabees 13:23-26.

We are accustomed to speak in America of sibling rivalry as a natural phenomenon but should be aware that such rivalry was a great evil in the classical world, to be guarded against completely or defused as soon as possible. Plutarch advises that "it is . . . of no slight importance to resist the spirit of contentiousness and jealousy among brothers when it first creeps in over trivial matters, practicing the art of making mutual concessions, of learning to take defeat, and of taking pleasure in indulging brothers rather than in winning victories over them. For the men of old gave the name 'Cadmean victory' to no other than that of the brothers at Thebes, as being the most shameful and the worst of victories"[15] ("On Fraternal Affection" 17 [*Mor.* 488A]).

Solidarity and cooperation, rather than competition, should be the hallmark of the interactions between siblings: "Nature from one seed and one source has created two brothers, or three, or more, not for difference and opposition to each other, but that by being separate they might the more readily co-operate with one another," even as multiple fingers of a single hand work together to accomplish a task ("On Fraternal Affection" 2 [*Mor.* 478E]). Rivalry, competition and working against a brother or sister's advantage would be as unnatural and as dysfunctional as for one hand to break what the other hand builds, or for one foot to trip up the other. Plutarch, in fact, spends the greater part of this essay giving advice concerning how to avoid competition and envy between brothers and engender a spirit of cooperation and unity.

A brother who is considered superior in some respects is to make his other siblings partners with him in that excellence in some way, "adorning them with a portion of his repute and adopting them into his friendships"[16] ("On Fraternal Affection" 13 [*Mor.* 484D]). The good sibling does not "thrust [his brother], as though in athletic competitions, from the first places always, but yields in his turn and reveals that his brother is better and more useful in many respects," thus promoting his brothers' honor as his own rises in his proper field. In so doing "he deprives himself of nothing, but adds a great deal to his brother" ("On Fraternal Affection" 13 [*Mor.* 485B-C]). A principle Plutarch advances is that, where inequalities

---

[15]The two sons of Oedipus, namely, Eteocles and Polyneices, killed each other in a battle for the throne of Thebes (see Sophocles *Antigone* and Aechylus *Seven Against Thebes*).
[16]This probably means including them into the circle of strategic contacts he makes by virtue of that excellence.

are unavoidable (for example, in age and thus seniority), the brother in the senior position must downplay his advantage out of sensitivity to the junior, while the brother in the "inferior" position should respect the difference in status ("On Fraternal Affection" 16 [*Mor.* 487A-B]). In so doing, each honors the other and unity is preserved.[17]

Trust. Where kin understood themselves to be in cooperation with one another—partners in a common quest to advance the family's honor and its components, to advance one another's interests—there could be trust, a commodity rarely extended to those outside of one's family (friends and patrons or clients were also expected to be reliable and therefore trustworthy). "Because the household [here we should read "household" as "kinship group" rather than people in a common dwelling] conceptually constituted the limits of trust and loyalty, business and long-term financial arrangements rarely expanded beyond it."[18]

The Jewish romance Tobit (written perhaps during the third century B.C.) exhibits the principle that only kin are ultimately reliable:

> [Tobias] went in and said to his father, "I have found some one to go with me." He said, "Call him to me, *so that I may learn to what tribe he belongs, and whether he is a reliable man to go with you.*" So Tobias invited him in; he entered and they greeted each other. Then Tobit said to him, "My brother, to what tribe and family do you belong? Tell me." But he answered, "Are you looking for a tribe and a family or for a man whom you will pay to go with your son?" And Tobit said to him, "I should like to know, my brother, your people and your name." He replied, "I am Azarias the son of the great Ananias, one of your relatives." Then Tobit said to him, "You are welcome, my brother. Do not be angry with me because I tried to learn your tribe and family. *You are a relative of mine, of a good and noble lineage.* For I used to know Ananias and Jathan, the sons of the great Shemaiah, when we went together to Jerusalem to worship and offered the first-born of our flocks and the tithes of our produce. They did not go astray in the error of our brethren. My brother, you come of good stock." (Tob 5:8-14, emphasis added)

In this episode Tobit tests Raphael (disguised as Azarias) by his lin-

---

[17]It might not be out of place to read 1 Corinthians 12:22-26 at this point. The reader will find that this is also the ethos we find Paul promoting as he considers the various gifts (even degrees of giftedness) within the church—those visibly more gifted must compensate by bestowing honor of those less gifted in order "that there may be no dissension."

[18]Lin Foxhall and Keith R. Bradley, "Household," in *The Oxford Companion to Classical Civilization,* ed. Simon Hornblower and Antony Spawforth (Oxford: Oxford University Press, 1998), p. 359.

eage, which will tell Tobit everything he needs to know about Azarias' character. Once he learns that Azarias is "part of the family," and that his father Ananias is an honorable person, Tobit knows all he needs to trust Azarias and to accept him for an important business venture.

Harmony: Sharing ideals and sharing possessions. Essential words in the discussion of kinship ties were *harmony, concord* and *unity* (in expressions like "being of one soul," "one mind" and the like). Again focusing on the relationship of siblings, Plutarch writes that "through the concord of brothers both family and household are sound and flourish, and friends and intimates, like a harmonious choir, neither do nor say, nor think, anything discordant" ("On Fraternal Affection" 2 [*Mor.* 479A]). Such an ideal is just as widely cherished in Jewish culture, from the famous opening of Psalm 133, which declares "How good, how pleasant it is for brothers and sisters to live in unity" (Ps 133:1, my translation)[19] to the celebration in 4 Maccabees of the unanimous decision of seven brothers to accept martyrdom for the sake of keeping Torah: "O sacred and harmonious concord of the seven brothers on behalf of religion! . . . Just as the hands and feet are moved in harmony with the guidance of the mind, so those holy youths . . . agreed to go to death for [piety's] sake. O most holy seven, brothers in harmony!" (4 Macc 14:3, 6-7).

Such mutual love, harmony and unity is lauded as an appropriate and gratifying display of reverence and gratitude toward parents, who seek nothing more than for a sibling to show "steadfast goodwill and friendship toward a brother" (Plutarch "On Fraternal Affection" 4 [*Mor.* 480A]). "Fathers do not find such pleasure in seeing their sons gaining a reputation as orators, acquiring wealth, or holding office as in seeing that they love one another" ("On Fraternal Affection" 5 [*Mor.* 480C]). Love of one's siblings is "a proof of [one's] love for both mother and father" ("On Fraternal Affection" 6 [*Mor.* 480F]).[20]

This harmony manifests itself in numerous ways, a prominent one being the sharing of a common religion. Plutarch will advise a young bride thus to share her husband's religion and pursue no cult on her own ("Advice on Marriage" 19). Greeks and Romans both had a well-developed domestic religion, binding the members of a household together in

---

[19]Noteworthy is the way this psalm extends the applicability of the term *siblings* to all Jews, the common descendants of Abraham.
[20]John will put this maxim to extensive use in his first epistle (see 1 Jn 4:7-8, 20-21).

a common piety. At the center of these family devotions was Hestia (or Vesta), the goddess of the hearth. In Greece, worship of Hestia was joined to worship of Zeus Herkeios (Zeus, guardian of the home), and in Roman families to the *genius* (the protective spirit of the head of the household), *di penates* (spirits of the pantry, hence of the provision of sustenance), and the family *lares* (spirits of departed ancestors).[21] No less would Jewish households be united in a common religious observance, for whom the central code of fathers and mothers passing on the religion of Moses to their children was written into the Shema itself (the twice-daily recitation of Deut 6:4-9), among other passages. This religious identity in the Jewish family is even more thoroughly reinforced thanks to distinctive dietary practices, the family observance of the sabbath and of major identity-defining feasts like Passover.[22]

The unity of kin was also expressed through their attitudes toward their wealth. Since friends were held to "own all things in common" (Aristotle *Nic. Eth.* 8.9.1 [1159b31-32]), the same was all the more to be expected of close kin. Brothers are "to use in common a father's wealth and friends and slaves" just as "one soul makes use of the hands and feet and eyes of two bodies," as in the case of Siamese twins (Plutarch "On Fraternal Affection" 1 [*Mor.* 478C-D]). Plutarch was acutely aware that money was a potent, divisive force.[23] When it comes time to divide an inheritance, therefore, he urges siblings to allow one another to take what is preferable and suitable to each, considering that "it is the care and administration of the estate that is being distributed, but that its use and ownership is left unassigned and undistributed for them all in common" ("On Fraternal Affection" 11 [*Mor.* 483D]). To outmaneuver a brother out of something he treasured is to gain a trifle but lose "the greatest and

---

[21]See Everett Ferguson, *Backgrounds of Early Christianity* (Grand Rapids, Mich.: Eerdmans, 1993), pp. 166-70; Carolyn Osiek and David L. Balch, *Families in the New Testament World: Households and House Churches* (Louisville: Westminster John Knox, 1997), pp. 81-97; John M. G. Barclay, "The Family as the Bearer of Religion in Judaism and Early Christianity," in *Constructing Early Christian Families: Family as Social Reality and Metaphor,* ed. Halvor Moxnes (London: Routledge, 1997), pp. 66-80, especially pp. 67-68.

[22]See David A. deSilva, "Giving Rebirth for Immortality," *Preaching* 14, no. 6 (May-June 1999): 32-37; Barclay, "Family as Bearer," pp. 68-72.

[23]See also the *Sentences* of Pseudo-Phocylides, a collection of advice by an unknown Hellenistic-era Jew, which speaks of the danger posed by "love of money" to the harmony of kin: "For your sake there are battles and plunderings and murders, and children become the enemies of their parents, and brothers of their kin" (*Sentences* 46-47); "Do not . . . permit yourself strife with your kinsfolk about possessions" (*Sentences* 206).

most valuable part of their inheritance, a brother's friendship and confidence" *(Mor. 483E)*.[24] With regard to the family estate, they are to "abolish, if possible, the notion of 'mine' and 'not mine' " ("On Fraternal Affection" 12 [*Mor. 484B*]).

First Timothy 5:4, 8 offers some indirect testimony to the ideal of sharing material resources among kin. The pastor asserts that charity (here, the relief of widows in need) must begin among the natural kin if any exist. Those who fail to provide for their natural kin in need, especially for parents and grandparents, effectively deny the faith. That such a one would be counted "worse than an unbeliever" (1 Tim 5:8) indicates that even outside the Christian group such sharing of possessions and coming to the aid of kin in need would be the expected norm.

Hiding the shame of kin. Closely related to the banishment of rivalry and competition between kin and the promotion of cooperation for the sake of advancing the mutual interests and honor of family members is the tendency to cover up any disgrace or dishonor that kin may have incurred rather than parade the failings of a person's family members.

The *Testament of Joseph* offers a fine testimony to this value among kin. According to this expansion of the biblical narrative, Joseph might have saved himself from being sold into slavery if he had revealed his identity as a son of Jacob, the head of a large and powerful Bedouin tribe. Instead, Joseph remained silent and even twice disclaimed any kinship with Jacob as a means of not impugning his own brothers for having acted disgracefully in selling their own flesh and blood into slavery.[25] The moral of this story comes from the lips of Joseph to his own sons on his deathbed: "My children, look at what I endured in order to keep my brothers from shame. You, too, must love one another and patiently hide one another's faults" (Testament of Joseph 17.1-2).

Similar dynamics stand behind Jesus' father's reluctance to expose

---

[24]Luke 12:13-15 affords a window into the very real strife and division that "dividing the inheritance" can bring to siblings, a divisiveness into which Jesus refuses to be drawn.

[25]We should notice that "lying" to outsiders in order to protect the honor of kin is presented in at least a neutral, if not a positive, light in this story. See further John J. Pilch, "Lying and Deceit in the Letters to the Seven Churches," *BTB* 22 (1992): 126-35. Philo also knows of this tradition (see his *Joseph,* § 247-48), adding that for the duration of his captivity and even of his tenure as administrator of the land of Egypt, he never spoke of what his brothers had done to him, but maintained that he was a slave from birth (contradicting Genesis directly at Gen 40:15, where Joseph claims to be a victim of kidnapping, hence a freeborn person illegally subjected to slavery).

Mary to public humiliation (Mt 1:19). It is a manifestation of justice or righteousness that Joseph instead seeks to keep the shame of his fellow Jew as hidden as possible. Paul also shows concern for this as he disclaims having any complaint against his nation, his kinship group taken as a whole (Acts 28:19). It is important to his reception by the Jews in Rome for him to clarify that he comes not as a plaintiff out to discredit his kinship group: airing any dirty laundry in the eyes of Gentiles would harm the collective honor of the Jewish people. Mark 3:21, 31-35 also shows a family guarding its collective honor when one of its members appears to be endangering it. In this case it is most clear that they are hiding what they perceive to be the censurable conduct of a family member not simply in the interest of his reputation but for the sake of the reputation of the whole family (on which so much in village life depends).

Forgiveness, reconciliation, patience. Finally, ancient moralists stress the importance of practicing forgiveness within the kinship group, of bearing patiently with one another and seeking reconciliation wherever a breach occurs. Plutarch advises that a brother ought to rebuke a brother with all frankness when he errs, "but should apply his admonition as one who cares for his brother and grieves with him" ("On Fraternal Affection" 10 [*Mor.* 483B], LCL). Gentleness and forbearance are to characterize a sibling's approach to the fault or injury caused by another:

> We should make the utmost use of these virtues in our relations with our families and relatives. And our asking and receiving forgiveness for our own errors reveals goodwill and affection quite as much as granting it to others when they err. For this reason we should neither overlook the anger of others, nor be stubborn with them when they ask forgiveness, but, on the contrary, should try to forestall their anger, when we ourselves are time and again at fault, by begging forgiveness, and again, when we have been wronged, in our turn should forestall their request for forgiveness by granting it before being asked. ("On Fraternal Affection" 18 [*Mor.* 489C-D], LCL)

The similarities between this ethic and the practice of mutual forgiveness (and, indeed, of forestalling anger by going ourselves to those we have hurt or provoked) enjoined by Jesus and Paul cannot escape notice (see Mt 5:23-24; 18:15, 21-22; Col 3:12-13). Plutarch finally holds up the Pythagoreans as exemplary for kin: even though they are not related by birth, they still make it a firm rule that "if ever they were led by anger into recrimination, never [to] let the sun go down before they joined right hands, embraced each other, and were reconciled" ("On

Fraternal Affection" 17 [*Mor.* 488B-C], LCL).

From the collection of the *Testaments of the Twelve Patriarchs* comes very similar advice: "Now my children, each of you love his brother. Drive hatred out of your hearts. Love one another in deed and word and inward thoughts. . . . If anyone sins against you, speak to him in peace. . . . If anyone confesses and repents, forgive him. If anyone denies his guilt, do not be contentious with him. . . . In a dispute do not let an outsider hear your secrets. . . . Even if he is devoid of shame and persists in his wickedness, forgive him from the heart and leave vengeance to God" (T. Gad 6:1-7).[26] The gentle confrontation, the quick acceptance of the penitent, and the confidence in the reliability of the sibling shown by not questioning a denial of wrongdoing[27] are again all present, together with the important addition that airing family disagreements in the sight of outsiders is a detriment to the standing and well-being of the family.

The Household
While family or kin encompasses far more than the people living in the same dwelling, the "household" is an important kinship unit in the ancient world. According to Aristotle, "A complete household consists of slaves and freemen. . . . The first and fewest possible parts of a family are master and slave, husband and wife, father and children" (*Pol.* 1.3 [1253b2-7]).[28] In this description, the terms *master, husband* and *father* describe the same individual, who is thus placed at the hub of the family unit, the "head" in relation to whom the other members of the family take their bearings. Most discussions of duties within the household will focus on these relationships (as will the household codes found in the New Testament), although in practice a household frequently consisted of both more and less than Aristotle's formula.

---

[26]Quoted in Dennis C. Duling, "Matthew 18:15-17: Conflict, Confrontation, and Conflict Resolution in a 'Fictive Kin' Association," *BTB* 29 (1999): 4-22. This is an exceptionally well-documented article on the subject.

[27]See also Wisdom of Ben Sira 19:13-15 on the possibility that the friend or family member has been slandered and is not truly guilty of the offense of which one suspects him or her.

[28]See also 1 Esdras 5:1, which speaks of the male heads of households returning to Israel with their wives, sons and daughters, male and female slaves, and livestock. In Arius Didymus' summary of Aristotle (Arius was a contemporary and friend of Augustus), this household is reduced to the husband and wife joined for the purpose of begetting and raising children (although most of the households of Arius' circle would have included impressive numbers of slaves as well).

One might find more blood kin living in a household. Lin Foxhall describes the possibility of the "stem family" (the nuclear family plus a grandparent) as well as the extended family, incorporating unmarried sisters or aunts.[29] Simon Bar-Jonah's living situation may not have been atypical: he lives with his mother-in-law (Mt 8:14) and his (unmarried?) brother (Mk 1:29); probably his wife is alive as well, though unmentioned; he may very well also have children by her. Jesus certainly assumes that some of his disciples have left behind wives and children as well as parents and siblings (Mt 19:27, 29). This household appears also to have less than Aristotle's ideal household, since slaves are not mentioned. In the households of the wealthy, however, one finds not only parents with married sons and their children (or eldest married son and unmarried siblings) but also slaves, frequently in some number. Guests and clients would also be considered part of the household, even though the former would not necessarily ever live under the same roof. Clients were, nevertheless, conceptually under the same roof, even as they maintained their own households.

Marriage and Divorce

The study of marriage practices and regulations of divorce in the ancient world, like the New Testament teachings on divorce and remarriage, is extensive. Since excellent treatments already exist, it will not be my goal to reproduce the entire discussion here, giving instead only a primary orientation to the subject.[30]

Marriage among Jews in the Greco-Roman era tended still to follow an endogamous strategy. That is to say, Jews sought to marry close kin without getting so close as to violate incest laws (Lev 18:6-17; see John the Baptist's criticism of Herod Antipas and Herodias in Mt 14:3-4). At the very least, it was expected that a Jewish male would marry a Jewish female. Marrying within the *ethnos* was an essential means of preserving its values and its commitment to the distinctive way of life prescribed by

---

[29]Foxhall and Bradley, "Household," p. 354.
[30]See, for example, the following monographs: Percy E. Corbett, *The Roman Law of Marriage* (Oxford: Clarendon Press, 1930); Will Deming, *Paul on Marriage and Celibacy: The Hellenistic Background of 1 Corinthians 7* (Cambridge: Cambridge University Press, 1995); Craig Keener, *And Marries Another: Divorce and Remarriage in the Teaching of the New Testament* (Peabody, Mass.: Hendrickson, 1991).

Torah. Marriage to Gentile women was considered a serious breach of the holiness of Israel and the surest path to promoting national apostasy and assimilation to the Gentiles (along the lines of the bad precedent set in Num 25:1-18).

This commitment to endogamy was reinforced strongly by Ezra's reforms (Ezra 9:1—10:19), in which those Israelites that had married non-Jewish wives divorced them en masse and disowned the children they had had by such unions. The continuing relevance of this story may be seen from its being retold in the final chapters of the apocryphal 1 Esdras, which serves as a sort of reminder in the Greek period of the nation's commitment to endogamy. "The holy seed has mixed itself with the peoples of the land" lament some of the leaders of Israel (Ezra 9:2 NRSV; see 1 Esd 8:70), resulting in Ezra's creation of a pastiche of Mosaic sayings about marriage into a clear law: "The land that you are entering to possess is a land unclean with the pollutions of the peoples [1 Esd: "aliens"] of the lands, with their abominations. . . . Therefore do not give your daughters to their sons, neither take their daughters for your sons, and never seek their peace or prosperity,[31] so that you may be strong and eat the good of the land and leave it for an inheritance to your children for ever" (Ezra 9:11-12 NRSV; see 1 Esd 8:83-85). Endogamy within one's own tribe was prescribed by Moses where a man's only heirs were daughters, so that the ancestral inheritance would remain intact for each tribe (Num 36:5-9).

The author of Tobit, a romance from the third-century B.C. that was probably written in the Diaspora, shows a great deal of interest in endogamy. The main characters model endogamy, and their conversations and instructions present this as the only pious and prudent policy for Jews. Tobit, who "married Anna, a member of our family" (Tob 1:9), thus advises his son Tobias: "Beware, my son, of all immorality. First of all take a wife from among the descendants of your fathers and do not marry a foreign woman. . . . Love your brethren, and in your heart do not disdain your brethren and the sons and daughters of your people by refusing to take a wife for yourself from among them" (Tob 4:12-13). Some Jews in the Hellenistic period might indeed "disdain" endogamous marriage, since marrying into the dominant culture might make

---

[31]The non-Jews are thus to remain outside the kinship group, outside the sphere of cooperation.

for a more prosperous and prestigious future.[32]

In Jewish custom, marriage was preceded by a lengthy betrothal, which itself could only be broken by divorce. A marriage contract would be filled out in length (final negotiations could occur on the night before the wedding!) specifying terms of marriage, mutual obligations, moneys exchanged and amount due the woman in the event of divorce or her husband's death (probably reflecting the return of her dowry, which was, in effect, her paternal inheritance).[33] The new couple tended to locate itself in or near the groom's father's house (the technical term is *patrilocal* marriage), particularly if the groom were the eldest son. The book of Tobit, again, provides an example of this, since Sarah returns with Tobias to the home of Tobit (which Tobias will eventually inherit). This was not necessarily a universal custom among Jews: the maxim used both at 1 Esdras 4:20 and Matthew 19:5, both of which depend on Genesis 2:24, assumes a neolocal family, that is, a "man leaving his parents" and finding a new home with his wife.

Within the New Testament we see a variety of marriage practices. Zechariah and Elizabeth have followed a traditional endogamy, all the more as both belong to the line of Aaron (Lk 1:5). Acts brings us into contact with two mixed marriages of Jewish women marrying Gentile males (Acts 16:1; 24:24). There is no likelihood that Felix was a proselyte, nor Timothy's father since he left his son uncircumcised. S. C. Barton analyzes the marriages of Josephus from the perspective of honor. For Josephus, marriage was a means of increasing his status. His first wife was a gift from the emperor Vespasian. It was a symbol of Josephus' bond with the emperor and thus his honor in the Roman world. The fact that the wife was a Jewish virgin, moreover, preserves his honor in Jewish eyes, since he has followed the tradition of endogamy. His third wife is mentioned as

---

[32]The heroine, Sarah, also provides an important model in this regard, since, after the demon Asmodeus has killed her seventh husband, she assumes her marriage choices are exhausted since her father "has no near kinsman or kinsman's son for whom I should keep myself as wife" (Tob 3:15). See also Tobit 6:10-12, where the angel arranges the marriage of Tobias and Sarah, since their fathers are kin, and their union will keep the inheritance within the same ancestral tribe. Other intertestamental literature reinforces endogamy as well. Judith 9:4, for example, speaks of the zeal of the sons of Jacob to take vengeance on the Shechemites: they "abhorred the pollution of their blood." Endogamy ensures pure blood; exogamy pollutes the people—dilutes the family—of Israel.

[33]Ferguson, *Backgrounds*, p. 68.

being of well-born parents, thus again contributing to his rising status.[34]

The Roman marriage practice of exogamy, marrying outside of one's kinship group (though not, in this case, ethnicity), was based more on interest in creating strategic alliances between different families. Legally the woman was under the guardianship of some male. Roman marriage *cum manu* meant that the wife would live under the authority of her husband, effected either in an ornate ceremony, by "sale" of the woman to the husband or by cohabitation for more than one year. Marriage *sine manu* meant that the wife remained a part of the father's household and under his ultimate jurisdiction.[35] Only Roman citizens could contract legal marriages (in the eyes of Rome, that is), but, of course, marriage flourished throughout the empire as local law regulated. Slaves had no legal basis for marriage, yet raised families anyway (despite the fact that no inheritance could be left to children and that owners could break up families by sale).[36]

The purpose of marriage was chiefly provision for the future (see Aristotle *Pol.* 1.2 [1252a25-31]), both in terms of progeny and inheritance.[37] It was not the result of a process of dating, falling in love, talking about compatibilities and the like. Rather, it was arranged by parents (or by bride's parents and groom) with a view to the future of their families and their honor. The importance of procreation, of keeping family lines alive, provided the rationale for levirate marriage—that is, when the brother of a man who died childless undertook to provide a child in the dead man's name with the widow. A man's family line must not be allowed to die, if at all preventable (see the case presented to Jesus in Mt 22:23-27). The survival of households was sufficiently in jeopardy among Roman aristocracy for Augustus to pass legislation providing incentives for multiple childbirth and restrictions on those who did not marry or produce children. Childbirth was a dangerous enterprise: infant mortality ran about 40 percent, and many women died giving birth. Augustus' incentives did

---

[34]Stephen C. Barton, "The Relativisation of Family Ties in the Jewish and Graeco-Roman Traditions," in *Constructing Early Christian Families: Family as Social Reality and Metaphor*, ed. Halvor Moxnes (London: Routledge, 1997), p. 89.

[35]Ferguson, *Backgrounds*, pp. 66-67.

[36]See Osiek and Balch, *Families in the New Testament World*, p. 62. This sad reality figures in one of Jesus' parables (see Mt 18:23-35).

[37]This is also assumed to be the main purpose of marriage in Pseudo-Phocylides *Sentences* 175-76: "Do not remain unmarried, lest you die nameless. Give nature her due, you also, beget in your turn as you were begotten."

not, in the end, convince many more aristocratic women to place themselves in that danger.

Marriage was not a provision for the fleshly desires: "Do not surrender wholly to unbridled sensuality toward your wife. For eros is not a god, but a passion destructive of all" (Pseudo-Phocylides *Sentences* 193-94). Unrestrained lust in marriage was considered dishonorable to such an extent that it might be considered a sign of honoring the marriage bed for a husband to seek debauchery elsewhere. Plutarch ("Advice on Marriage" 16) even tells a bride to think it a compliment to her if her husband uses some other woman for his lustful passions—although he does directly advise that husbands and wives take care not to seek extramarital unions that could result in embarrassing offspring ("Advice on Marriage" 42). In Paul's world, marriage did not make indulgence any more acceptable for Christians than it was among Greco-Roman moralists (see 1 Thess 4:3-6, according to one line of interpretation).

Then, as now, not all persevered in a marriage. In the event of divorce, which was rather easy to accomplish then, the woman would return to her father's family (or brother's house if the father is dead), along with her dowry.[38] Greek and Roman law allowed either partner to initiate; among Jews, only the husband had this prerogative. Divorce was a common recourse for infertility (particularly if a woman had not borne sons) and for adultery. Ben Sira advises his students to divorce a wife "if she does not go as you direct" (Sir 25:26) and comments that barrenness in a woman is a cause of anxiety to the father (Sir 42:9-10). We can now understand the rationale behind his proverb, since this was a common cause for divorce. Jesus is notably more austere on this point than his contemporaries and the traditions of both Jewish and Greco-Roman cultures (Mt 5:31-32; Mk 10:2-12).

Management of and Behavior Within the Household
Several classical ethicists have written extensively about the science of household management, focusing their attention on the "rule of a master over slaves, . . . of a father, and . . . of a husband" (Aristotle *Pol.* 1.12

---

[38]The dowry might be so substantial as to prevent a man from divorcing a wife. Pseudo-Phocylides cautions against the potential of a large dowry to undermine the husband's authority and freedom: "Do not bring as a wife into your home a bad and wealthy woman, for you will be a slave of the wife because of the ruinous dowry" (*Sentences* 199-200).

[1259a36-39]), and the duties of slaves, children and wives. The head of a household "is the master and acts on behalf of the household," representing it to the outside world.[39] These ethicists, however, do not paint a picture of a tyrant who exploits the members of his household so that he may enjoy a life of ease. With his rule comes heavy moral responsibility. He "ought to have moral virtue in perfection," since he must supply the "rational principle" for his wife (who possesses the rational faculty, but without authority), children (who possess but an immature rational faculty), and slaves (who possess none; Aristotle *Pol.* 1.13 [1260a17-18]). Seneca (*Ben.* 2.18.1-2) also speaks of the reciprocal and equal obligations of parents to children, and husbands to wives. These writers already understand quite well that a husband's authority means "duty," "responsibility" and "care."

One important aspect of household life that will be unfamiliar to many readers in the Western world is that the household was a producing unit as well as a consuming unit. The members of a household would work together in some trade or craft for the purpose of income.[40] This could be as simple as selling surplus crop production as grain in the market, or might involve a trade like leather-working, pottery or even surgery. For the purpose of the trade, a room of a house in a city or village would be allowed to open onto the street and serve as a shop. For upper-class families, an individual's own home and the homes of others were places for networking with friends and supporters. The household for people of the upper strata of the Greco-Roman world embraced the staff (mostly freedpersons and slaves) of country estates as well as a mansion in the city.[41] These estates could produce vast amounts of wine, oil, grain and the like, serving as the source of the family's wealth. In the Gospels we find the two brothers, Peter and Andrew, sharing a house and a business, as do Zebedee and his two sons (the presence of hired servants suggests a rather good trade, too). Their wives might participate in this business (preparing the fish by salting or drying, and the like), and might engage also in "women's work," usually some kind of textile industry.

Ancient authors see a close correspondence between the household

---

[39]Moxnes, *Constructing Early Christian Families*, p. 25.

[40]See Osiek and Balch, *Families in the New Testament World*, p. 54; Moxnes, *Constructing Early Christian Families*, p. 23.

[41]Such estates might also be leased out to tenant farmers for rent or a percentage of the harvest. Such a scenario is envisioned in Mark 12:1-12.

and the state, such that the former is a kind of microcosm of the latter
(Aristotle *Pol.* 1.1 [1252a7-17]; Philo *Jos.* 37-39).[42] Only those men who
could exercise proper oversight in their own households were seen to be
fit to exercise authority in the state. Thus Plutarch ("Advice on Marriage"
43) writes: "A man who proposes to produce harmony in the city or in the
market-place or among his own friends, must have harmony at home."[43]
The same presupposition is at work in 1 Timothy 3:4-5 concerning those
who wish to be bishops.

Husbands and wives. The Jewish and Gentile worlds were agreed on at
least one thing: the household was organized hierarchically with the hus-
band/father/master exercising authority over the other members of the
household. Aristotle holds this to be inherent in the nature of the two gen-
ders, just as it is inherent in human nature to mate in the first place (*Pol.*
1.2 [1252a25-32]). The male is the "natural ruler," and the female is the
"natural subject." Greco-Roman authors especially are careful to qualify
the nature of the husband's authority over his wife. While the father's
rule over children and slaves is absolute (Aristotle likens it to a monarch's
power), the husband's rule over his wife is more like "constitutional
rule." Aristotle moves to the sphere of politics to explain what he means:
"The idea of a constitutional state implies that the natures of the citizens
are equal, and do not differ at all. Nevertheless, when one rules and the
other is ruled we endeavor to create a difference of outward forms and
names and titles of respect. . . . The relation of the male to the female is of
this kind, but there the inequality is permanent" (*Pol.* 1.12 [1259b6-10]). In
effect, he avers that husband and wife are equal in nature, but perma-
nently unequal in the roles they play in the government of the household.[44] Plutarch provides an even more nuanced picture of this authority
at work in the everyday life of the household: "When two notes are

---

[42]See further, John H. Elliott, *A Home for the Homeless: A Sociological Exegesis of 1 Peter, Its Situation and Strategy* (Philadelphia: Fortress, 1981), pp. 171-73, who shows how the language
for regional and civic government and the different offices and groups therein, most thoroughly in Egypt, is derived from the *oik-* ("pertaining to a house") root.

[43]Plutarch, *Selected Essays & Dialogues*, trans. Donald Russell (Oxford: Oxford University
Press, 1993), p. 294.

[44]Neo-Pythagorean ethicists are also careful to define the precise nature of the husband's
authority: "He does not rule over her with a despotic power: for he is diligently attentive
to her welfare. Nor is his government of her entirely of a guardian nature; for this is itself a
part of the communion" (Callicratidas *On the Happiness of Households* 106.1-5, quoted in
David Balch, *Let Wives Be Submissive: The Domestic Code in 1 Peter,* SBLMS 26 (Missoula,
Mont.: Scholars Press, 1981], pp. 56-57).

struck together, the melody belongs to the lower note. Similarly, every action performed in a good household is done by the agreement of the partners, but displays the leadership and decision of the husband" ("Advice on Marriage" 11).[45]

Jewish authors, it appears, are more sweeping in their claims about the relationship of husband and wife. Josephus, for example, passes down the following instruction: "The woman, says the law, is in all things inferior to the man. Let her accordingly be submissive, not for her humiliation, but that she may be directed, for the authority has been given by God to the man" (Josephus *Ag. Ap.* 2.199, LCL). Similarly, Philo writes: "Wives must be in servitude to their husbands, a servitude not imposed by violent ill-treatment but promoting obedience in all things" (Philo *Hypoth.* 7.3, LCL). These two authors agree with their Gentile counterparts that women are not under a husband's authority for her harm. It is notable, however, that "inferiority in all things" is not a description that Xenophon or Aristotle attaches to woman.[46]

The common stereotype that the ancients regarded women as chattel is our modern interpretation of the immense power and control males (chiefly the father, secondarily the husband) had over the women in their families. Russ Dudrey is correct to say that "functionally most women were treated as property"[47] insofar as they were given in marriage or could even be sold as slaves by their fathers (but similar power was wielded over sons, whose marriages were arranged and who, like their infant sisters, could be exposed at birth if unwanted) and insofar as they were under "lifelong guardianship" by a male throughout the classical and Hellenistic periods. This resulted in the provisions for women to be given to other males for guardianship in the will of a head of household. That they were treated in ways similar to property is undeniable; that

---

[45]This tells us how different Greek music was from most Western music, since we tend to assign the melody to the upper voices, harmony to lower voices.

[46]Xenophon, in fact, sees male and female strengths and weaknesses as complementary one to another. God made women more affectionate for children, since nursing would fall to them, more fearful by nature, since protection of the stores would fall to them. God made men more courageous, since they would have to be the defender of the household. "And just because both have not the same aptitudes, they have the more need of each other, and each member of the pair is more useful to the other, the one being competent where the other is deficient" (*Oec.* 7.28).

[47]Russ Dudrey, " 'Submit Yourselves to One Another': A Socio-Historical Look at the Household Code of Ephesians 5:15—6:9," *RQ* 41 (1999): 37.

they were regarded as property is less clear. Telling in this regard is the openness with which Aristotle or Roman legists call slaves "chattel" or "property," while these same authors do not refer to freeborn women as such. We may be guilty of reading into the construction of the hierarchy of a household a devaluing (or even depersonalization) of women that the Greco-Roman world would not have thought a necessary corollary of their authority structures.

An important source for information about the ideal of the household in classical Greece is the *Oeconomicus* (the "Householder") by Xenophon. The picture of the relationship between husband and wife that he develops is very much one of partnership, with the husband being the "senior" partner. Husbands are responsible for training their wives in the management of a household, especially since the women marry so young.[48] This training is all the more essential, however, because husbands entrust more to their wives than to anyone else. While under the husband's authority and tutelage, she nevertheless contributes equally to the successful running of the household (*Oec.* 3.10-15). Xenophon, in fact, stresses the authority that the wife has over the rest of the household, entrusted with enforcing the laws and agenda given by the husband, with rewarding "the worthy with praise and honour" and not sparing "rebuke and punishment when they were called for" (*Oec.* 9.14-15). Related to this is the comment by Dionysius of Halicarnassus that "if a wife was virtuous and in all things obedient to her husband, she was mistress of the house to the same degree as her husband was the master of it" (*Rom. Ant.* 2.25.5, LCL).[49] In a large household this could mean considerable authority and even influence well beyond the confines of the household. Such women had the potential for indebting males outside the household through patronage and thus gaining unofficial but potent political clout.

---

[48]Ischomachus, Socrates' conversation partner in Xenophon's dialogue, confesses that his wife was not yet fifteen when they married (*Oec.* 7.5). More than four centuries later, Pliny the Younger laments the death of the daughter of his good friend Fundanus just a short while before her wedding—all before she was fourteen (*Ep.* 5.16, helpfully cited in Albert A. Bell Jr., *Exploring the New Testament World* [Nashville: Thomas Nelson, 1998], p. 231). In the Greek and Jewish cultures, men tended to be ten to fifteen years older than their (first) wives.

[49]This text is helpfully cited in Balch, *Let Wives Be Submissive*, p. 55. His monograph contains a very rich collection of ancient texts relating to the role of women in the Greco-Roman and Jewish households, as well as a thorough exploration of the instructions for wives in 1 Peter 3.

The husband and wife were partners in labor as well: a woman is to adorn herself with industriousness in the oversight of the house and with the healthy blush of domestic exercise like making bread rather than with paints and other external adornments (*Oec.* 10.2-13; see Sir 26:16). The wife acts as a queen bee in the hive, overseeing the servant bees in their tasks, caring for her young, putting away the supplies and distributing the food and clothing as needed. She tends the sick in the household and teaches young slave girls the arts of weaving and the like.

The ethos of the ideal woman. Jewish and Greco-Roman authors also agree to an astonishing extent on the ideal they hold up for women to emulate.[50] In addition to acceptance of, and submission to, the authority of the male head of the household, silence is prominent among the virtues prized in women. Thus in fourth-century B.C. Athens, Aristotle writes: "All classes must be deemed to have their special attributes; as the poet says of women, 'Silence is a woman's glory', but this is not equally the glory of men" (*Pol.* 1.13 [1260a28-31]). He chooses "silence" here as the core virtue for women, and the use of the poet's maxim suggests that all his readers would take this for granted as well. Ben Sira would write in second-century B.C. Jerusalem: "A silent wife is a gift from the Lord, and nothing is so precious as her self-discipline" (Sir 26:14 NRSV). The persistence of this ideal well into the Roman imperial period is shown by Plutarch's advice to a young couple in the second century A.D.: "A wife should speak only to her husband or through her husband, and should not feel aggrieved if, like a piper, she makes nobler music through another's tongue" ("Advice on Marriage" 32).[51] The words of an honorable woman, like her very body, must never become public property: "She should be shy with her speech as with her body, and guard it against strangers" ("Advice on Marriage" 31).[52]

Another very prominent facet of this ideal is that the woman keeps herself as much as possible to private spaces. Xenophon (*Oec.* 7.16-41) provides a lengthy discussion of the divinely ordained and perfectly complementary division of labor between husband and wife, according to

---

[50]We will not speak here of the ideological critique of this ideal, except to say that the ideal held up for women does very obviously serve the interests of the males in the culture; the males' competition in the public sphere is immediately cut in half, and challenges in the private sphere are sharply curtailed.

[51]Plutarch, *Selected Essays*, trans. Robin Waterfield (London: Penguin, 1992), p. 291.

[52]Ibid.

which order the husband engages activity in the open air, to which his physiognomy is better suited, for the acquisition of what is needful, and the wife occupies the closed spaces for the preservation of what is needful. It is honorable for each to be in the proper sphere, and as unseemly for a man rather "to stay indoors than to attend to the work outside" as for a woman to "abide in the fields." Philo of Alexandria, the first-century A.D. Jewish author, fully concurs with this picture: "Women are best suited to the indoor life which never strays from the house, within which the middle door is taken by maidens as their boundary, and the outer door by those who have reached full womanhood" (Philo *Spec. Laws* 3.169-71, LCL).[53] She is encouraged to "seek seclusion" rather than "show herself off in the streets," save for visits to the temple in Jerusalem. Finally, Plutarch reaffirms this ideal: "A good woman . . . should be seen most when she is with her husband, and stay at home and be hidden when he is away" ("Advice on Marriage" 9).[54]

Jewish women appear to have had greater dealings in public (e.g., in the market and by the well, the latter coming to be considered part of the "private" sphere of women since the women of a village would all meet there early in the morning to draw water for the family's use that day) than their Greek and Roman counterparts, but actually less legal freedom.[55] Most women engaged in work in the home, being highly skilled in certain crafts that they would employ not only to provide for the needs of the household but to sell in the attached shop or in the market for the profit of the household. Among the elite it became more and more customary for Roman husbands (and those imitating Roman practice) to take their wives to dinner banquets, although in Greece women would not tend to leave their own homes even with their husbands. Instead, *hetairai*—cultured conversation partners but capable of other entertainments as well—would be invited to Greek banquets to provide a female presence.[56] Rome continued to be more progressive in this regard, while the East had difficulty parting with its tradition.

---

[53]Again, I am indebted to Balch (*Let Wives Be Submissive*, p. 53) for this testimony. Pseudo-Phocylides adds yet another witness to this consensus: "Guard a virgin in firmly locked rooms, and do not let her be seen in front of the house until her wedding day" (*Sentences* 215-16).

[54]Plutarch, *Selected Essays*, p. 28.

[55]Ferguson, *Backgrounds*, p. 71.

[56]Osiek and Balch, *Families in the New Testament World*, p. 69.

To submission, silence and seclusion would be added modesty and chastity.[57] Ben Sira thus writes: "A modest wife adds charm to charm, and no scales can weigh the value of her chastity" (Sir 26:15 NRSV). The author of 4 Maccabees, who has praised the mother of the seven martyrs for her courage (her "manliness," literally), concludes his work by reaffirming the importance of her female virtues as well: she "was a pure virgin and did not go outside my father's house; but I guarded the rib from which woman was made. No seducer corrupted me on a desert plain, nor did the destroyer, the deceitful serpent, defile the purity of my virginity. In the time of my maturity I remained with my husband" (4 Macc 18:6-9).[58]

As a final sign of her submission to her husband and embeddedness in him, a wife is to share her husband's religion. "A wife ought not to have friends of her own, but use her husband's as their common stock. And the first and most important of our friends are the gods. A married woman should therefore worship and recognize the gods whom her husband holds dear, and these alone. The door must be closed to strange cults and foreign superstition. No god takes pleasure in cult performed furtively and in secret by a woman" (Plutarch "Advice on Marriage" 19).[59] The husband's circle of friends, including the gods, became the woman's circle, and her willingness to limit herself to these bound her all the more closely in partnership with her husband (though, again, an obviously unequal partnership).

The raising of children. Based on the fact that parents had given the gift of life itself to their children, they (particularly the father) also had great, legitimate authority over their lives. Aristotle compares it to the authority of a monarch over his subjects (Aristotle *Pol.* 1.12 [1259b10-12]). Philo creates an even fuller description of the standing of parents and children

---

[57]The feminine ideal is succinctly captured in many funerary inscriptions. See, for example, the epitaphs for Turia and Aurelia (first century B.C.), quoted in Dudrey, " 'Submit Yourselves,' " p. 34: "Why recall your inestimable qualities, your modesty, deference, affability, your amiable disposition, your faithful attendance to the household duties, your enlightened religion . . . your affection for your family—when you respected my mother as you did your own parents and cared for her tomb as you did for that of your own mother and father"; "I was chaste and modest; I did not know the crowd; I was faithful to my husband. . . . He, through my diligent performance of duty, flourished at all times."

[58]Dudrey (" 'Submit Yourselves,' " p. 29) cites a text from a Neo-Pythagorean ethicist: "A woman's greatest virtue is chastity," which is taken to be a "more appropriately female" virtue than courage or reason.

[59] Plutarch, *Selected Essays*, p. 288.

with regard to one another: "Parents are . . . seniors and instructors and benefactors and rulers and masters; sons and daughters are . . . juniors and learners and recipients of benefits and subjects and servants" (*Spec. Laws* 2.226-27, LCL).[60] Thus in every respect, children are seen as obligated to their parents, particularly obligated to honor and obey them. The comparison of parents as benefactors is especially poignant and is one also used by Aristotle. Children are held to have incurred a debt to their parents that they can never repay, so that the virtuous person will honor the parents, and "return the favors" bestowed by the parents throughout childhood, for the remainder of the parents' lives (*Nic. Eth.* 8.14.4 [1163b14-27]). Rome legislated this ethic, such that the male head of a family had authority even over his adult and married sons until his death.

Thus it would be expected that children should become "the very best of allies and the very best of support in old age" for their parents (Xenophon *Oec.* 7.12).[61] Children are to honor their parents in word and deed, and especially to be loyal and serviceable to them in the parent's old age:

> O son, help your father in his old age, and do not grieve him as long as he lives; even if he is lacking in understanding, show forbearance; in all your strength do not despise him. For kindness to a father will not be forgotten, and against your sins it will be credited to you; in the day of your affliction it will be remembered in your favor; as frost in fair weather, your sins will melt away. Whoever forsakes his father is like a blasphemer, and whoever angers his mother is cursed by the Lord.[62] (Sir 3:12-16)

Children are never to despise the old age and feebleness of their parents but to continue to honor and serve them at that stage in life when they most need their children. It is the mark of piety to use that stage of life as an opportunity most fervently to "repay the favors" of early childhood nurture.

---

[60]Quoted in Balch, *Let Wives Be Submissive*, p. 53. See also Sir 3:2, 6-7: "The Lord honored the father above the children, and he confirmed the right of the mother over her sons. Whoever glorifies his father will have long life, and whoever obeys the Lord will refresh his mother; he will serve his parents as his masters."

[61]See also *Oec.* 7.19; Plato *Laws* 717C.

[62]Similar sentiments are uttered by the Neo-Pythagorean ethicist Perictione: "Parents ought not to be injured either in word or deed; but it is requisite to be obedient to them, whether their rank in life is small or great. . . . It is necessary to be present with, and never to forsake them, and almost to submit to them even when they are insane" (*On the Harmony of a Woman* 145.8-13; quoted in Balch, *Let Wives Be Submissive*, p. 57).

Plutarch, however, insists that parental care must not be given solely, or even chiefly, in the anticipation of receiving one's investment back again at a later date, since even animals offer such care to their young as a "gift" *(charis)*.[63] Plutarch thus brings parenting further into the ethos of patronage "done right" (see chapter three), seeking to preserve the proper purview and the purity of intention of each party. Giving must be free and done in the interest of the recipient, not the interest of the giver, to be noble. The recipient is, however, still obligated to show gratitude.

Like parent, like child. Both Greek and Jewish writers stressed the likeness between parents and their children, a "wondrous likeness both of mind and of form" (4 Macc 15.4). This likeness was held to extend beyond physical appearance to emotions, predispositions and moral character.[64] An important element of this likeness was the children's adoption of the parents' traditions, especially their religious observances (see Sir 41:14). This presumed likeness in all essential aspects of life leads to the topic one frequently finds in the New Testament (and, of course, its contemporary texts) that one's behavior reflects on one's parentage. This can be applied in several ways. An honorable child may be said to bring honor to one's parents and vice versa (see Sir 22:3-5). A person's conduct, however, may also be censured by calling him or her the child of some dishonorable or vice-ridden character (like the devil, in Christian literature).

John 8:31-47 contains a conversation between Jesus and "the Jews who had believed in him," which utilizes the topic of likeness extensively and combatively. Jesus claims that following his word will make these Jews free, but that implies that they are currently slaves. They invoke their noble ancestry from Abraham to deflect this implication. Jesus explains that their innate drive to sin—in particular, to kill Jesus because his word has no place in them—reveals their slavery to sin and alienation from "the Father." Here again the Jews rest on the claim: "Abraham is our

---

[63]See Plutarch "On Affection for Offspring" 2 (*Mor.* 495A-B); "On Affection for Offspring" 4 (*Mor.* 496C).

[64]Moses Hadas provides two helpful quotations. The first is from Nemesius *De natura hominum:* "Cleanthes . . . declares that we are similar to our parents not only in respect to body but also in respect to soul, in emotions, morals, dispositions"; the second is from Plutarch *Plac. Philos.* 7.11.3: "The Stoics maintain that seed derives from the entire body and from the soul and that likeness in form and character is moulded from the same origins, appearing to the beholder like an image painted with the same colors"(*The Third and Fourth Books of Maccabees* [New York: Harper and Brothers, 1953], p. 220).

Father," to which Jesus responds: "If you were Abraham's children, you would be doing what Abraham did, but now you are trying to kill me, a man who has told you the truth that I heard from God. This is not what Abraham did. You are indeed doing what your father does" (Jn 8:39-41). The Jews claim now that God is their father, but Jesus refutes it. Their rejection of God's emissary shows that they are not of God's household. Rather, "You are from your father the devil, and you choose to do your father's desires. He was a murderer from the beginning and does not stand in the truth, because there is no truth in him. When he lies, he speaks according to his own nature, for he is a liar and the father of lies" (Jn 8:44). The Jews' rejection of Jesus and his word of truth thus shows them to be offspring of the liar. Throughout this exchange, then, claims to a certain parentage and attributions of alternative parentage encode challenges and defenses about behavior and honor.

The education of children. For most people, education was received from the parents in the home. Since all would participate in some form of business (even women, within the home), some grasp of writing, reading and counting would be essential. This is not to say that the majority of people were literate, since so few had leisure or resources for expensive books or extended hours in libraries, but a rudimentary education in these areas would be in keeping with the needs of running a household.[65] Mothers had primary care during the first few years. After the children had reached five or six years of age, the father would take a more active role in the education of the children. In 4 Maccabees 18:10-19 we find a fine window into the moral and religious instruction the seven brothers received at the feet of their father while he was still alive, as he fulfilled the central command of Torah to pass on instruction in the law of Moses to his children (Deut 6:6-9). Plutarch ("On the Education of Children" [*Mor.* 13D]) gives fathers the same advice as does Paul in Ephesians: to avoid harshness and restrain anger in the upbringing of their children.[66]

Those who had the means would employ a pedagogue for the early years of a child's education. The pedagogue was a combination of disci

---

[65]Osiek and Balch, *Families in the New Testament World,* p. 67.
[66]Quoted in Osiek and Balch, *Families in the New Testament World,* p. 70. See also Pseudo-Phocylides *Sentences* 207: "Do not be harsh with your children, but be gentle."

plinarian and elementary educator.[67] Mothers would continue to teach
their daughters the skills necessary for managing a household. Daughters
were raised solely to be married (Sir 7:25), and parents were deeply concerned to preserve their chastity so as to preserve their marriageability
(Sir 7:24). A daughter's sexuality was seen to pose a severe threat to a
father's honor and peace of mind (Sir 42:9-14), since any breach there
would be a serious stain upon the household.

An essential element of the last years of home schooling included
reading the poets and singing the hymns that cultivated piety toward
the gods and the ethics of the dominant culture.[68] This level of education
was apparent in Corinth, as Paul expects some members to come with a
hymn—either a memorized or a composed poetical and musical piece in
honor of the deity. Paul expects the same to be a part of the assemblies
of believers in Colossae, with the expected repertory of "psalms, hymns,
and spiritual songs" (Col 3:16). Schools existed in both Greek and Jewish contexts to provide advanced education for the aristocratic families,
training the next generation of statesmen and leaders of the community.
Every important city had public institutions of learning—public, that is,
for those enrolled as citizens of the city, which was frequently limited to
an upper class—where adolescent boys would be trained in elementary
rhetorical exercises, composition and classical philosophy, and would
exercise voice and body as well. The *progymnasmata* would lead to
advanced training in rhetoric and to the skills needed for public life (for
which public speaking was the most visible part). Jewish communities,
and particularly the city of Jerusalem, had schools specifically geared to
training the elite Jewish male youth in the Torah, but also in the rules for
interpreting and applying Torah, in the art of argumentation and in the
art of communication. One might say that, while the textbooks differed
in Greek and Jewish schools, the basic curriculum was remarkably similar.

Ancient ethicists were deeply concerned that the young would pursue

---

[67]The pedagogue plays an important role in the metaphor Paul uses for salvation history
  itself in Galatians 3:23-25, suggesting that his readers would have widespread familiarity,
  if not direct experience, with such a figure.

[68]Osiek and Balch, *Families in the New Testament World*, pp. 70-71. In Jewish homes, of course,
  the tendency would be to train children in reading the Jewish Scriptures (in Greek, of
  course, throughout most of the Mediterranean Diaspora; in Aramaic, most likely, and possibly Hebrew, in Palestine).

education not only in rhetorical skill but also in virtue. In "On Listening to Lectures" 1 (*Mor.* 37D), Plutarch counsels young people who have reached majority and left the oversight of the pedagogue to obey reason rather than use their freedom from human oversight as an opportunity to give free reign to desire:

> When some young people shed the mantle of childhood, they simulta-
> neously shed inhibition and caution, and no sooner have they divested
> themselves of restrictive clothing, than they overflow with self-indulgence.
> You, on the other hand, have often been told that following God and listen-
> ing to reason are identical; so bear in mind that for intelligent people the
> passage from childhood to adulthood is not an abandonment of rules, but a
> change of ruler: instead of someone whose services are hired and bought,
> they accept in their lives the divine leadership of reason—and it is only
> those who follow reason who deserve to be regarded as free.[69]

The goal of education was thus the development of an inner pedagogue, an internalized commitment to virtue as the proper goal of one's freedom as a full citizen.[70]

Slavery in the ancient world. Approximately one in five people living within the city of Rome was a slave,[71] and the overall slave population of the empire ran even higher. Slavery in the ancient world was consider-ably different from the Western experience of the sixteenth through nine-teenth centuries and the aftermath of that legacy (the "futile ways inherited from our ancestors" [to borrow from 1 Pet 1:18]). Most impor-tantly, no single race was consigned to slavery by virtue of being part of that race. Slave and free were frequently indistinguishable in appearance and even clothing (rich and poor were, of course, immediately distin-guishable), especially in the cities. A person might become a slave by mil-itary conquest, as a penalty in a criminal proceeding, by birth into a slave family or by defaulting on debts (especially in Egypt).

Aristotle's notorious definition of a slave is that of a "living tool," the chattel of the master (*Pol.* 1.4 [1253b27-33]). He defends the notion that

---

[69]Quotations from Plutarch's "On Listening to Lectures" are taken from Plutarch, *Selected Essays*.

[70]Compare this with Paul's exhortations in Galatians 3:23—4:7; 5:1, 13-25. He too urges Christians, released from the pedagogue of the Torah, to make use of their freedom for the achievement of virtue, following God's leading ("walking by the Spirit") rather than obey-ing the passions of the flesh.

[71]Ferguson, *Backgounds,* p. 56.

there are people who are slaves "by nature": "From the hour of their birth, some are marked out for subjection, others for rule" (*Pol.* 1.5 [1254a23]). For such sets of people "it is expedient and right for the one to be slaves and the others to be masters: the one practising obedience, the others exercising the authority and lordship which nature intended them to have" (*Pol.* 1.6 [1255b7-9]). He goes on, however, to indicate that masters have to exercise that authority judiciously and virtuously: "The abuse of this authority is injurious to both; for the interests of part and whole, of body and soul, are the same, and the slave is a part of the master, a living but separated part of his bodily frame" (*Pol.* 1.6 [1255b9-13]).[72] Similarly, in his *Ethics* (5.6 [1134b8-12]), he says: "There can be no injustice in the unqualified sense towards things that are one's own, but a man's chattel [that is, his slave], and his child until it reaches a certain age and sets up for itself, are as it were a part of himself, and no one chooses to hurt himself."[73] In practice, however, punishment of slaves could be quite severe and harsh.[74]

The conditions of slavery were wholly dependent on the virtue, or lack of virtue, of the master. Greco-Roman philosophers, Jews like Philo and early Christians like Paul all sought to foster a benevolent relationship between masters and slaves and to balance the complete imbalance of power in the relationship by nurturing reciprocity. Thus Philo claims that the Torah gives instructions "to servants on rendering an affectionate loyalty to their masters, to masters on showing the gentleness and kindness by which inequality is equalized" (*Decal.* 167, LCL). Similarly, the Neo-Pythagorean Ecclus "makes a remarkable reference to 'the benevolence *(eunoia)* [cf. Eph 6:7] of the servant towards the master, and the anxious care of the master for the welfare of the servant' (*On Justice* 78, 10-11)."[75] The centurion whose trust in Jesus becomes exemplary for the early church (see Lk 7:2-10) also embodies this kind of "anxious care" for the welfare of his slave—not just as an investment in jeopardy but as a member of his household, under his care, requiring assistance.

---

[72]There are also those who are not slaves by nature but are slaves by law or convention, such as prisoners of war. In such cases slavery can be inexpedient both for those forced into slavery and those who are their masters (*Pol.* 1.6 [1255a4-10; 1255b12-15]).

[73]This comes very close to the rationale Paul will give for the considerate and loving treatment of wives by husbands, "for no one ever hates his own body" (Eph 5:29).

[74]See Osiek and Balch, *Families in the New Testament World*, pp. 79-80.

[75]Quotes from Balch, *Let Wives Be Submissive*, pp. 53, 58.

Both Xenophon (*Oec.* 13.6-13) and Aristotle (*Pol.* 1.13 [1260b3-7])
advise masters to take an interest in the training of their slaves, and
even through frequent conversations to be "the source of excellence
[virtue]" in them. Xenophon provides a picture of using status-markers
(like quality of clothing and shoes) within the household as a means of
rewarding (and thus promoting) obedience and diligent performance
of duties. Those duties were amazingly varied in the ancient world.
Imperial slaves (the "household of Caesar" spanning the empire) were
used as bureaucrats and civil servants at every level, performing
important services like accounting, overseeing imports and exports,
and assisting the appointed governors and their staffs. Temples owned
slaves, who were mainly responsible for groundskeeping and maintenance. The senatorial and equestrian families (the upper class of
Rome), and their counterparts across the Mediterranean, would deploy
scores or even hundreds of slaves as fieldworkers on the estates, fore-
men and managers, artisans, and domestic servants. Many families of
even modest means had at least one slave. Finally, slaves could be
found in the most abject and degrading of employments, as in the gal-
leys or the mines.

The family life of the slave was precarious and completely under the
master's control. Slaves had no legal standing and therefore contracted
no legal marriages (though slaves would "marry" each other and often
remain lifelong companions). Xenophon (*Oec.* 9.5) shows a certain ambiguity about slaves and families: the loyal slave is rendered more stable
if he has a family, but the rogue is only made worse. Xenophon is clear
on one point, however: "breeding" is to happen only with the master's
consent. The children born to a male slave were the property of that
slave's master. Most often, those children would remain a part of the
master's estate, to be passed on to the heirs ad infinitum. It was always
a possibility, however, that a slave would suffer seeing his family broken up if the master decided to give away or sell any of them. Whether
employed as a foreman or field hand, a scribe or scrubber, this lack of
autonomy made slavery an evil for those unfortunate enough to be born
or fall into it. Slaves of private individuals, however, did have the hope
of manumission. Sometimes they could purchase their own freedom
from money they squirreled away in the course of doing business on
their master's behalf. Most often they were freed by the master in his or
her will as a gift for decades of faithful service and as a sign of a gener-

ous spirit. Freedmen were expected to remain loyal to the house of their master.[76]

Architecture and activity. Both Greek and Italian houses tended to be arranged around a partially covered inner courtyard or atrium. The rooms of the house opened onto this courtyard. A number of rooms would have been reserved for private use (i.e., sleeping quarters), but a sizeable part of the house would be geared toward entertainment and production. A notable room in Greek houses was the dining room, called the *andrōn*, the "place of men," often with a raised floor around the sides for the dining couches, present in modest as well as wealthy homes. Greek homes would also be equipped with a large living room (either enclosed or an open porch) spanning one side of the house, suitable for receiving guests. Italian homes also had a formal dining room called a *triclinium*, after the three dining couches placed in it, as well as ancillary rooms for the entertaining of guests.

In cities and villages, both styles of house could (and often would) have one room open onto the street to serve as a shop. Particularly in urban areas, the one-level plan would be altered to include a second story. The amount of space within a house dedicated to the manufacturing of goods (the "women's work" of weaving, for example), to the conducting of business, and to networking with friends and associates is truly striking given the basically private orientation of the modern, Western home. In Xenophon's *Oeconomicus* (9.2-5), Ischomachus speaks of his house having a storeroom (a room that is difficult of access, hence the most secure space), a dry, covered room for a pantry, a cool storage area for wine and a decorated living room. The women's (sleeping) quarters were separated from the men's sleeping quarters by a bolted door "so that the servants may not breed without our leave." [77]

---

[76]An excellent resource for further study is S. Scott Bartchy, *First-Century Slavery and 1 Corinthians 7:21,* SBLDS 11 (Missoula, Mont.: Scholars Press, 1973). See also William L. Westermann, *The Slave System of Greek and Roman Antiquity* (Philadelphia: American Philosophy Society, 1955).

[77]For further reading, see Michael H. Jameson, "Houses, Greek," pp. 359-60, and Nicolas Purcell, "Houses, Italian," pp. 360-62 in *The Oxford Companion to Classical Civilization,* ed. Simon Hornblower and Antony Spawforth (Oxford: Oxford University Press, 1998). On Palestinian homes, see Santiago Guijarro, "The Family in First-Century Galilee," in *Constructing Early Christian Families: Family as Social Reality and Metaphor,* ed. Halvor Moxnes (London: Routledge, 1997), pp. 42-65.

Fracturing and Remaking Kinship Ties

The nature of kinship—that is, what really constitutes kinship—was a frequent topic of debate in the Hellenistic and Roman periods. It became commonplace to place more emphasis on the similarity of character that bound siblings together rather than relationship merely by blood (see 4 Macc 13:24-26), from which it became an easy step to claim that such kinship of character was enough to create kinship. Thus Philo (*De Nobilitate* 195) could claim that "kinship is not measured only by blood, but by similarity of conduct and pursuit of the same objects." Natural kinship (kinship by blood or marriage) might not be considered an ultimate or unbreakable bond if important components of what made people "kin" were missing.

Departure from the religion and values of the family could prompt the natural family to exert pressure on the individual to return to a respectable way of living, to be loyal to the family. In extreme cases, however, an unbelieving head of a household might divorce or disown the disloyal, so as to preserve the solidarity and the public honor of the family. Ancestral values and public opinion would be, in such cases, rated higher than family ties. For example, Philo claims that if any family member attempts to lead his or her family toward apostasy or transgression of Torah, that family will "punish him as a public and general enemy, taking little thought for the ties that bind us to him" (Philo *Spec. Leg.* 1.316). Philo, in fact, is willing both to dissolve kinship by blood where shared religion is absent *and* to take a common devotion to Torah as sufficient basis to make people kin:

> For we should have one tie of affinity, one accepted sign of goodwill, namely the willingness to serve God, and that our every word and deed promotes the cause of piety. But as for these kinships, as we call them, which have come down from our ancestorx s and are based on blood-relationship, or those derived from marriage or similar causes, let them all be cast aside if they do not seek earnestly the same goal, namely the honour of God, which is the indissoluble bond of affection which makes us one. For those who are so minded will receive in exchange kinships of greater dignity and sanctity. (Philo *Spec. Leg.* 1.316-17, LCL)[78]

---

[78]See Stephen C. Barton, *Discipleship and Family Ties in Mark and Matthew* (Cambridge: Cambridge University Press, 1994), pp. 23-56, for a masterful collection of texts from Josephus, Philo, the Qumran and Greco-Roman philosophers attesting to the phenomenon of reconstructing one's family based on moral or religious values. Among this latter group, the

Non-Jews who leave behind "their country, their kinsfolk and their friends for the sake of virtue and religion" are to find a welcome into a new family, namely the Jewish community (Philo *Spec. Leg.* 1.52). Philo's words are stunningly close to Jesus' thought on the subject, down to the promise of a replacement family for those whose natural ties are severed (compare with Mt 12:46-50; 19:27-29). Jesus' words about the relativization of natural kinship ties and the family created by commitment to a common way of life have multiple resonances and strong precedents throughout the Greco-Roman world.

Because family relations and the bonds of kin were so powerful and pervasive, these aspects of life provided a potent set of metaphors for binding people who were not related by blood together in new configuration, as well as cultivating an ethos of support and appropriate ways of relating. The application of the roles and ethos of family to people who are not related is called "fictive kinship." This was prominently at work, for example, in Roman imperial ideology, according to which the whole empire was a household with the emperor as the *pater patriae*, the "father of the country," the head of a vastly extended family. The importance of this title for Augustus' own construction of the ideology of his rule is seen in the fact that the award of this title is the climax of his catalog of his many services to the Roman people, the *Res Gestae Divi Augusti*.[79] As an extension of being under the "Father of the Country," the emperor's own household slaves— imperial slaves and freedmen across the empire—served as the civil servants and bureaucracy of empire. Thus the "household of Caesar" spanned the Mediterranean, referring to this infrastructure of persons directly attached to the imperial family administering the empire.[80]

This brings us to the movement begun by Jesus, a movement that Jesus himself says will result in the breaking apart and remaking of families. In the Synoptic Gospels, Jesus is very forceful about the threat that association with him poses to natural kinship. It threatens to bring strife and division to the household (see Mt 10:21; 10:34-36). We now well under-

---

Cynics stand out as particularly significant. Cynics require detachment from family and property to pursue their vocation without distraction or hindrance (Epictetus *Diss.* 3.22.69-72); as they pursue philosophy, all humanity becomes their family, specifically children to be cared for and admonished (3.22.81-82). The Greek philosophical principle that all humanity is kin, being children of the gods, appears in Acts 17:26-29.

[79]Edwin A. Judge, *The Social Pattern of the Christian Groups in the First Century* (London: Tyndale Press, 1960), pp. 32-33.

[80]Elliott, *Home for the Homeless*, p. 177.

stand the reasons: the Christian will be seen as a disloyal deviant, rejecting the family's values and threatening its honor if his or her presence is countenanced without censure and, if that fails, expulsion.[81] For this reason, Jesus emphatically relativizes family ties where these threaten loyalty to him and his teaching: "Whoever loves father or mother more than me is not worthy of me; and whoever loves son or daughter more than me is not worthy of me" (Mt 10:37; see the stronger form in Lk 14:26). Loyalty to him even outweighs the most sacred duty to parents (Mt 8:21-22), but notably only when these conflict. Otherwise, Jesus upholds traditional obligations of children to parents (see Mt 15:4-6; Mk 7:10-12 on the practice of Corban).

A transition between natural kinship and the fictive kinship of the community of disciples is facilitated by the concept of God as Father. This is a topic with strong roots in Jewish and Greco-Roman philosophical literature. For but one example, we may turn to the Wisdom of Solomon, in which the righteous Jew claims to be a child of God and claims God as Father (Wis 2:12-13, 16, 18), a claim that the impious test by assaulting the honor of the righteous person through insult, physical abuse and degrading execution. Additionally, "Solomon" refers to Israel as God's "sons and daughters" (Wis 9:7), speaking of the land of Canaan receiving "a colony of God's children" (Wis 12:7). Jesus draws on the conception of the godly as "children of God" frequently in the sayings collected in the Sermon on the Mount. The "peacemakers" will be acknowledged the children of God, and those who do "good works" will promote the praise of the progenitor who begat such virtuous offspring, the principle of "like father, like children" being operative here. An even more overt application of this principle occurs in Matthew 5:44-48 (and the parallel saying at Lk 6:35-36): those who imitate the Father's generosity toward both good and bad people, loving both the just and the unjust, become God's own children.

---

[81]That a person's natural kin would respond so vehemently was a possibility only, not a rule. We more frequently find family ties continuing after one member has become a believer. See, for example, the believing wife of the unbelieving husband in 1 Corinthians 7:12 16 and 1 Peter 3.1-6. Paul advises a believing spouse to remain in the marriage unless the other will not have it. Slaves of unbelieving masters likewise might meet with punishment "for the name of Christ," but were otherwise enjoined to seek to serve their masters well and overcome the breach by virtuous conduct if possible. Conversely, not every believing head of household would force conversion on the whole household (as in 1 Cor 7:12; Philem 10, 16).

The possibility of becoming part of God's family provides the basis for the alternative kinship group that Jesus begins to create within his own ministry. The most well-known passage in this regard is Matthew 12:46-50 (see also Mk 3:31-35; Lk 8:19-21), in which he redefines his own kin not as those born into his father Joseph's household but rather as "whoever does the will of my Father in heaven," that is, whoever is born into his heavenly Father's household. Many of his first disciples did, in fact, leave their natural families behind. Jesus replies to their perceived loss by assuring them that "everyone who has left houses or brothers or sisters or father or mother or children or fields, for my name's sake, will receive a hundredfold, and will inherit eternal life" (Mt 19:27, 29). The emerging community of disciples becomes this hundredfold family, a body of people united by a common devotion to Jesus and his teaching, committed to love, support and help one another as completely as any natural family.

Six

KINSHIP &
THE "HOUSEHOLD OF GOD"
IN THE NEW TESTAMENT

Kinship language, household relations and adopting a kinship ethos as the standard for interpersonal relations within the group dominate the descriptions of, and prescriptions for, the church in the New Testament. Immersing oneself in the everyday world that gives meaning to kinship language is therefore a necessary preparation to hearing what the New Testament authors seek to create in the new world of the church using this realm of language and social relations. We turn now to consider how the early Christian leaders constructed this new family (chiefly through the attention they gave to creating a lineage), used this family's lineage to promote perseverance in the family of faith, adapted the ethics of kinship to the new community, and finally held together the fictive kinship of the whole church with the setting of the church within natural households. As with the other contexts we have explored, the goal of this inquiry is to stimulate our thinking about what it means to be the church of God and how we can recover more fully the New Testament's vision for our congregations and our global Christian community, as well as rediscover its resources for building up strong disciples and communities of faith.

Creating a New Family

Christians were heirs to the Jewish conception of the people of God as "brothers and sisters," which was for Israel merely an exaggeration of natural genealogical proximity (they were, ideally at least, all actually related as descendants of Jacob). This conception of people of God as kin takes a particularly Christ-centered focus. It is now attachment to this Jesus that determines whether or not a person is in the family, rather than the person's bloodline or natural lineage. Discussions in the New Testament of the formation of this family focus on determining "the true descendants of Abraham" as well as adoption into God's own family. The purpose of such discussion is manifold: it gives the early church a sense of shared identity and binds the members together in the solidarity of the kinship bond; it provides them with a legitimate connection to the promises of God recounted in the Jewish Scriptures; it speaks of the profound honor and privilege that has come to them by virtue of attachment to the Christian community, and the coming manifestation of that honor, such that perseverance with the group remains an attractive option even when the pressure to defect is high.

Jesus' sonship. The critical link in the construction of this family is Jesus, who enjoys a double lineage (see Rom 1:3-4). First, he is a legitimate descendant of Abraham, but he is also the Son of God, the "heir of all things" (Heb 1:2). Both aspects of this lineage are highly significant for the presentation of the Christian family as the true "descendants of Abraham" as well as "children of God," the many siblings of the "firstborn of many sisters and brothers" (Rom 8:29, my translation). The "Son of God" title appears to be more frequently affirmed across the New Testament, perhaps because of the power of this concept to create the relationship between Christians and God as children and Father through faith in the Son par excellence.[1]

As Son, Jesus becomes the most effective and important mediator between humanity and God (see chapter four). On the basis of his filial

---

[1]The Synoptic Gospels depict Jesus' status as "Son of God" being ascribed directly by God (Mt 3:17; 17:5). This is a claim immediately challenged by Satan and successfully defended in that context (Mt 4:1-11) and affirmed thereafter throughout Matthew's Gospel (Mt 14:25-33; 16:16; 27:54). John's Gospel is even more interested in the significance of Jesus as the "Son of the Father" (Jn 1:14, 34; 3:16, 18; 5:18) and thus the revealer of the Father (Jn 1:18; on the principle of "like father, like child," see also Jn 14:8-9), and the agent and proxy of the Father (Jn 5:19-20, 26, 36-37, 43; 6:27). Paul and his circle also appeal frequently to this description of Jesus (e.g., 1 Cor 1:9; 2 Cor 1:3, 19; Heb 1:2, 5-6).

closeness to the Father, Jesus becomes a better mediator than the many priests who inherit that status through their Levitical lineage. The author of the epistle to the Hebrews can now therefore reject physical descent as a basis for priesthood in the case of Jesus (Heb 7:3, 5-6, 13-16). This most central defining feature of priestly status is overturned on the basis of Jesus' divine appointment. Just as Jesus is named "Son" by God (Heb 1:5 and 5:5, both quoting Ps 2:7), so he is named "priest forever" by God (Heb 5:5-6).

Jesus as Son is thus the bridge between those who are made the many children and the Father, the one who knits together this family and brings the believers to their inheritance as children of God. Hebrews 2:5—3:6 develops this link at some length, starting with an interpretation of Psalm 8:4-6. Jesus is the only human being in whom the glorious vision of that psalm has been fulfilled, but he has made it possible for all to arrive at glory. The Son is the pioneer who leads the "many sons and daughters" to their destiny (Heb 2:10). His incarnation—his sharing in flesh and blood—becomes a witness to his kinship with us, his willingness to call us his sisters and brothers, as well as the cause of his sympathetic mediation on our behalf. This trustworthy Son has made all the believers part of his household (Heb 3:6), and as we remain attached to Jesus, we retain our grasp on our promised inheritance in glory.

Descent and lineage. It is noteworthy, however, that even in Hebrews 2:5—3:6 it is not sufficient to describe the Christians as the "many sons and daughters" of God (Heb 2:10, my translation). They are also specifically identified as "the children of Abraham" (Heb 2:16, my translation). Abraham's story is the beginning of the story of redemption. God promised blessing to Abraham: the gift of a homeland, an innumerable progeny and, through him, blessing to "all the families of the earth" (Gen 12:3). He was the channel through whom God's promise would flow and to whom the fulfillment would come. His family thus had a unique and matchless heritage: his descendants were the people of God's promise and possessors of a great inheritance. This was a heritage that the early Christians would claim as their own. In the birth pangs experienced by the movement as it separated from the parent body, the claim to be the true descendants of Abraham gave the church the assurance that it was the God-approved continuation of the faith of the patriarchs, the strength to withstand the censure of non-Christian Jews, and the ability to persevere in trust that it would receive the promised blessings of God. The particular way in which kinship with Abraham was redefined within the Christian movement allowed Gentiles and Jews to enter the family on an equal basis, eliminating the ethnic particularities attached to conversion. In effect, it turned the God of Israel, a tribal deity, into the God of all the nations (Rom 3:28-30).

Redefining Descent from Abraham

The process of reassessing kinship with Abraham begins with John the Baptist and Jesus, as they question the meaningfulness of physical descent from Abraham on its own. In light of the coming judgment of God, there can be no resting on the merits of that honorable ancestor, or automatic reception of the promises given to Abraham (Mt 3:9; Lk 3:8). Instead, it is necessary to bear good fruit oneself, in effect to show one's kinship with Abraham by living righteously as he did. Genealogy is no insurance against the Day of Judgment: "I tell you, many will come from east and west and will eat with Abraham and Isaac and Jacob in the kingdom of heaven, while the heirs of the kingdom will be thrown into the outer darkness, where there will be weeping and gnashing of teeth" (Mt 8:11-12; see Lk 13:28). Jesus strikes at the heart of Jewish doctrines of election as he claims that Gentiles will enter the kingdom of heaven while the blood relations of Abraham find themselves excluded.[2]

Paul develops this even further, prompted in no small part by the disturbances that erupted in the Galatian churches. After Paul had evangelized that region and set up a number of house churches, other teachers came to those Christians, who were mostly Gentiles, telling them that they had to accept circumcision (and perhaps the dietary and calendrical laws of Torah as well) in order truly to belong to the people of God. Paul had given them a good beginning, but they needed to seal their place in the family of Abraham by accepting the mark of circumcision as Abraham had done.[3] In this way, Jews and Gentiles could enjoy table fellowship in the new community without leading the Jewish Christians into breaches

---

[2]See also the parable of the rich man and Lazarus, in which the rich man repeatedly calls Abraham "Father Abraham" (Lk 16:24-25, 27, 30), but from the flames of hell. Again Jesus insists that kinship with Abraham has no bearing on eternal destiny but rather fulfilling God's commands (here, caring for the poor).
[3]On the crisis in Galatia and the response of Paul, see the excellent work of John M. G. Barclay, *Obeying the Truth: Paul's Ethics in Galatians* (Minneapolis: Fortress, 1991); James D. G. Dunn, *The Theology of Paul's Letter to the Galatians* (Cambridge: Cambridge University Press, 1993); Ben Witherington III, *Grace in Galatia* (Grand Rapids, Mich.: Eerdmans, 1998).

of Torah. That Paul attributes the Judaizers' main motive to be avoidance of persecution may not be entirely untrue; if they could make it plain that Christianity both kept Jews Torah-observant and made Gentiles into Torah-observant proselytes, their non-Christian Jewish neighbors would no longer have cause for censuring or opposing the movement.

Paul's response to the persuasive arguments of the Judaizers centers on what makes one a descendant of Abraham. In Galatians 3:16, he notes that the promise of God is "to Abraham and his seed" (KJV). In a twist of linguistic legerdemain, Paul points out that "seed" is in fact a singular, not a plural, word (it would normally be read as a collective noun, much like our word "offspring"). Paul argues that Jesus was *the* seed, and that all who belong to this seed, to Christ, belong to the family and inheritance of Abraham: "In Christ Jesus you are all children of God through faith. . . . And if you belong to Christ, then you are Abraham's offspring, heirs according to the promise" (Gal 3:26, 29). According to Paul, birth into this family happened at baptism, in which the baptized "clothed [themselves] with Christ" (Gal 3:27). As they dress themselves with the Son, they become sons and daughters themselves. Embeddedness in Christ is the way to be embedded both in the family of God and the family of Abraham—anything else is meaningless; anything less leaves a person outside the inheritance.

In Galatians 4:21-31 Paul effects an exegetical coup by crossing the natural lineage of Jews (traced through Isaac) with the lineage of those nations that would end up being counted among the Gentiles (the descendants of Ishmael). In this argument, "flesh" serves as a metaphor broad enough to link Abraham's natural power to beget a child (Ishmael) and the Judaizers' emphasis on circumcision as the physical sign of belonging to Abraham's family and the people of God (a mark in the flesh). Because they rely on a mark of the flesh and on physical descent for their place in Abraham's family, Paul is able to identify the non-Christian Jews as children born according to the flesh and the Christians, whether Jewish or Gentile, as children born according to the promise. Because they are born by trusting God's promise (in Jesus), the Christians emerge as the true descendants of Isaac, while the Judaizers and the non-Christian Jews are disinherited as children of Hagar![4] The relative honor

---

[4]In less polemical circumstances, Paul can affirm Abraham's paternity of both lines without devaluing one in favor of the other: in Romans, Abraham is presented as the ancestor both to

of these two lines—one born of a slave into slavery, a most dishonorable condition, and the other born free—would not be missed by Paul's readers. The Christians would be confirmed not only in their legitimacy as children of Abraham and therefore children of God but also in their higher place of honor in Abraham's family. Paul prepares thus a potent remedy to the doubts raised in the Christians' minds about belonging to the family of God, removing any advantage to be gained by accepting the Judaizers' proposal.

Paul's definition of kinship with Abraham and belonging to the line of promise eventually wins in this debate. Looking back on this argument, Luke presents the Jerusalem Council of Acts 15 as a decisive turning point in the construction of the "family of God" and "family of Abraham." In Acts 15:23, a clear note is sounded as the Jewish brothers send greetings to the believers of Gentile origin with the report of the Jerusalem Council about circumcision. This is an incredibly significant step in the Christian movement since it has at least been decided that a believer does not have to join the "house of Israel" through circumcision and proselytization in order to join the "household of God"—these two houses being one and the same for the non-Christian Jew.

Paul has far greater sympathy for his "kin according to the flesh" than one gleans from Galatians alone. In Romans 9—11, he struggles at length over the place of non-Christian Jews and Christians in the "household of God." He is keenly aware of the tension between the promises made to Abraham's posterity and the response of Israel (defined as Israel "according to the flesh" to distinguish it from the church, called "Israel of God" in Gal 6:16) to the work of Jesus and the proclamation of the gospel, the good news of how God is fulfilling those promises given to Abraham so long ago.[5] In Romans 9:3-5 he states the problem: the Jews,

---

those who are circumcised and those who "follow the example of the faith that our ancestor Abraham had before he was circumcised" (Rom 4:11-12), to both "adherents of the law" and those who "share the faith of Abraham" (Rom 4:16). Paul finds in this wider paternity of Abraham the fulfillment of God's promise that he would be "the father of many nations" (Rom 4:17-18; see Gen 15:5; 17:5).

[5]A similar ambiguity about non-Christian Jews is present in Acts. The non-Christian Jews can be called brothers by the Jewish apostles (Acts 2:29, 37; 3:17; 7:2, 11, 12; 13:15, 17, 26, 38; 22:1; 23:1, 5, 6; 28:17). Jews are the "descendants of the prophets and of the covenant," and the seed in which all will be blessed (Acts 3:25), but ultimately it is only those Jews who heed the "prophet like Moses" that will remain part of the "people" (Acts 3:22-23). A most telling scenario is where the "Jews" are ranged against (and are thus outside) "the brothers,"

his "kindred according to the flesh" (note again how Paul qualifies their kinship as at the level of the flesh), had the advantage by birth of possessing the adoption as sons and daughters, the patriarchs who had received the promises, as well as "the glory [or honor], the covenants, the giving of the law, the worship, and the promises," and even the Messiah, who was born into their extended family. Why then did they not embrace the inheritance when it appeared? This question is even more pressing because it is ultimately God's faithfulness to the promises that is at issue—whether or not "the word of God had failed" (Rom 9:6).

In a first argument, Paul makes the case that genealogical descent does not equal kinship (a stunning claim, to be sure): "Not all Israelites truly belong to Israel, and not all of Abraham's children are his true descendants; but 'It is through Isaac that descendants shall be named for you.' This means that it is not the children of the flesh who are the children of God, but the children of the promise are counted as descendants" (Rom 9:6-8). He uses the historical precedents of Isaac and Ishmael, and then Jacob and Esau, to demonstrate the claim he makes, a claim that turns out to be supported by Scripture itself. When God declares that only the children of Isaac will be counted as Abraham's descendants with regard to the promise, God himself initiates the relativization of natural kinship that Paul continues in his interpretation: it is the children of promise (those born of trusting) rather than the children of flesh (those born of natural descent) that are ultimately "Israel."

Isaiah 10:22 lends further scriptural authority to Paul's arguments: the oracle declares that only a remnant of God's people will be saved, that is, receive what had been promised (Rom 9:27). Paul then points to the presence of Jews among the new people of God, the church. A remnant exists in whom God's fidelity to God's promises is demonstrated. Paul offers himself, a Jewish Christian, as exhibit A (Rom 9:27; 11:1). His own words about his descent—"an Israelite, a descendant of Abraham, a member of the tribe of Benjamin"—anchor him in the natural kinship group of Israel. God's faithfulness to him becomes therefore one example among many of God's faithfulness to the promises made to that kinship group. Paul's last words on the subject extend strong hope for the remainder of the natural kinship group of Israel: with regard to "the gospel they are enemies of God for your sake; but as regards election they are beloved, for the sake of their ancestors" (Rom

---

showing how they stand outside the family at least wherever one finds them opposed to the church (Acts 14:2; 17:5-6).

11:28). He refuses at the end to allow his relativization of natural kinship to override the rules of natural kinship. John would later express the maxim, "whoever loves the parent loves the one begotten of the parent" (1 Jn 5:1, my translation), and Paul shows that he shares in this conviction as well. God's love for Abraham would not permit him to exclude Abraham's children, even though they bitterly opposed Paul's gospel now.

Adoption into the Family of God

Those who join themselves to the Christian family do not merely gain the honor of being born into the family of a noble and widely celebrated progenitor (Abraham). They become the children of no less a father than God himself. We have already found a strong Jewish precedent for understanding the righteous as children of God in Wisdom of Solomon 2:12-18. Also prevalent throughout the Hellenistic period is the Greek philosophical concept—certainly in keeping with the unifying aims of Hellenism—that the fatherhood of God transcends limitations of ethnic and tribal kinship, binding all people together into a common humanity (see Acts 17:26-29; Eph 3:14-15). This becomes a very serviceable and high-minded concept for the negation of the boundaries surrounding the Jewish *ethnos* and its claim on being the gateway to belonging to God's family.

That God "destined us for adoption as his children through Jesus Christ" (Eph 1:5) is a frequent topic in the New Testament, since it stands at the heart of what makes Christians kin one to another—adoption into a single family under a shared Father. Both Paul and John find in the promise made by God to David with regard to his successor (2 Sam 7:14) a promise that now applies in the plural (see Hos 1:10 as a possible bridge) to the new community of faith: "I will be your father, and you shall be my sons and daughters, says the Lord Almighty" (2 Cor 6:18);[6] "Those who conquer will inherit these things, and I will be

---

[6]The inclusivity of "sons and daughters" here is Paul's own intentional addition to his pastiche of Old Testament texts. Verses like this undermine extreme readings of Paul in which women have no place in the "brotherhood" of the Christian community (the thesis of Lone Fatum, "Brotherhood in Christ: A Gender-Hermeneutical Reading of 1 Thessalonians," in *Constructing Early Christian Families: Family as Social Reality and Metaphor,* ed. Halvor Moxnes [London: Routledge, 1997], pp. 183-200). While we cannot make Paul more liberated than he is (1 Cor 11:2-16 with its theological rationales for headdresses is a perpetual stumbling block here), we cannot on the other hand make him more androcentric than he is, as Fatum does. His use of the term *brother* must be taken not as an exclusively male term of reference but as a generic use of a male term for a male and female body of siblings.

their God and they will be my children" (Rev 21:7).

Our place in God's household is the result of the beneficence of the Son, Jesus, whose death redeemed us "so that we might receive adoption as sons" (Gal 4:4-5, my translation), an adoption effected, as we have seen, through trusting in Christ (Jn 1:12) and symbolically enacted in baptism (Gal 3:26-29). The Christians thus become heirs of what God has promised, and the Holy Spirit within them bears witness to their place in God's family (Gal 4:6-7; see also 3:1-5). Gentile Christians are no longer "aliens" *(paroikoi)* to God, but members of the family *(oikeioi)*: "So then you are no longer strangers and aliens, but you are citizens with the saints and also members of the household of God" (Eph 2:19). Paul uses references to God as the Father of believers at the start of many of his letters, showing the prominence and almost "givenness" of this new household and its *paterfamilias* within Christian culture, and thus its availability as a foundational principle from which to derive ethical exhortations, explanations of the believers' condition in the world and encouragements from their hope for the future (see Gal 1:3, 4; Eph 1:2; Phil 1:2; 1 Thess 1:3; 2 Thess 1:1; 2:16).

Johannine literature speaks of this as being "born of the Spirit," which is required for entering God's kingdom (Jn 3:3-8). Those outside the group are thus outside God's family, the disprivileged and unhappy ones. Just as a natural father's "seed" constitutes his offspring, so God has planted his "seed" in the Christian (1 Jn 3:9), whether this is conceived of as the word (as in 1 Pet 1:23) or the Spirit (as is probably the case in Johannine literature). This new birth—this new imprinting of God's spirit on our spirit—makes it possible for the believer to forsake sin and pursue love of the brothers and sisters (1 Jn 3:9; 4:7). "Walking in the Spirit" or being "led by the Spirit" is, in effect, living out the new constitution, dispositions and morals implanted in us by our new birth (to speak of a new genetic predisposition would be an anachronism, but it comes close to the point).

New Testament authors frequently find it useful to draw sharp contrasts between the believers' natural birth and heritage and their adoptive birth and heritage. Birth into God's family signals the potential for a radical break with everything connected with one's natural birth and becomes a powerful image with which to drive ethical exhortation and to reinforce group integrity and solidarity. John is especially strong in this regard. The new birth is not added to an individual's former birth and heritage but replaces it. Christians are "born, not of blood or of the will of the flesh or of the will of man, but of God" (Jn 1:13). A person's birth "of the flesh" is of incomparably less value than being born "of the Spirit" (Jn 3:3-8). Being born of the spirit means being born "from above" (ironically, the beloved expression "born again" represents more Nicodemus' misunderstanding than Jesus' meaning), a birth of a higher order than that which belongs to the physical realm. First Peter makes the difference in value clearer: "You have been born anew, not of perishable but of imperishable seed, through the living and enduring word of God. For 'All flesh is like grass and all its glory like the flower of grass. The grass withers, and the flower falls, but the word of the Lord endures forever.' That word is the good news that was announced to you" (1 Pet 1:23-25). Natural birth is what ultimately gives a person the inheritance of death; mortality is the only result of human seed. Birth into God's family, however, means that a believer has been born into eternal life beyond death. The Christians are thus no longer subject to going the "way of all flesh," to perishing as swiftly and meaninglessly as the grass of the field.

Along with the dissolution of one's first birth comes redemption from the heritage of that birth. As we have seen, the ultimate heritage therefrom is death, but the author of 1 Peter recognizes that the convert has also inherited much else from his or her earthly parents: "You know that you were ransomed from the futile ways inherited from your ancestors" (1 Pet 1:18). These "futile ways" refer to the primary socialization of the believers before their conversion into the values, the worldview and the religion of the dominant culture. This former way of life is most negatively portrayed as an inheritance of dishonorable vice: "You have already spent enough time in doing what the Gentiles like to do, living in licentiousness, passions, drunkenness, revels, carousing, and lawless idolatry" (1 Pet 4:3). The believers, who are experiencing society's pressure to return to that way of life inherited from their ancestors (see 1 Pet 2:12, 15; 4:4, 12-16), are urged to keep themselves distanced from that way of life—to consider it now alien and foreign to them: "I urge you as aliens and exiles to abstain from the desires of the flesh that wage war against the soul" (1 Pet 2:11). The reason for persevering in their new, secondary socialization into the values, worldview and ethos of the Christian community is the surpassing value of the new inheritance that attachment promises to bring: "By his great mercy he has given us a new birth into a living hope through the resurrection of Jesus Christ from the dead, and into an inheritance that is imperishable, undefiled, and unfading, kept in heaven for you" (1 Pet 1:3-4; see also Eph 1:11, 14; Col 1:12). Language of birth into God's family can thus become a strong incentive to ethical behavior, to solidarity among the Christians and to separation from those activities that, though they would reduce the tension between church and society, nevertheless would blur the distinctive witness of the Christian way of life.[7]

An important issue is the "status inconsistency" experienced by Christians. On the one hand, they enjoy the great honor of being children of no less distinguished a Parent than the God of the universe.[8] On the other hand, that status is hardly manifested in the world as they variously experience insult, reproach, physical abuse, financial hardship and ruin, even imprisonment and, occasionally, lynching. This is dealt with in a number of ways.

First, the experience of Jesus provides an important lens for integrating these two opposing points. The early Christians knew what honor Jesus had as God's Son, but also what slander, abuse and degradation he suffered at the hands of people. They also know that God vindicated Jesus' honor by raising him from the dead and seating him at his right hand. Based on this precedent, the Christian may begin to make sense of the dishonor that falls to him or her in the world on account of attachment to the household of Jesus (see Mt 10:25; Jn 15:18-20), sharing in his rejection by the "wicked and perverse race," knowing that God will manifest their honor to the world even as God manifests Jesus' honor at the second coming (see chapter two). Hebrews 2:5-18 is again relevant here: the bond of

---

[7]Another example of the parallels between natural parenthood and God's parenthood being used to promote perseverance in Christian commitment in the face of a hostile world appears in the concept of God's educative discipline of the believers in Hebrews 12:5-11 (see discussion of this text in chapter two). The exercises God provides for the training of their virtue and character—their firmness in trust, loyalty, hope and love—in the form of opposition and hostility from outsiders actually becomes an assurance of their legitimacy as God's children, hence their honorable status in God's household and their claim on the inheritance.

[8]See John H. Elliott, *A Home for the Homeless: A Sociological Exegesis of 1 Peter, Its Situation and Strategy* (Philadelphia: Fortress, 1981), p. xxiii, which correctly observes the importance of "having a home in the family of God" in 1 Peter's strategy for combating the erosive force of the pressures of the outside world on Christian commitment, an image that includes the affirmation of their honorable status despite their lack of status and honor in the eyes of society. The image of the church as "household of God" provided the "most effective means for . . . reinforcing a sense of the distinctive and prestigious character of their communal identity" (pp. 229-30).

unity between Jesus and the "many sons and daughters" assures them that the honor he enjoys now, namely, the exaltation over creation celebrated in Psalm 8, will be theirs at the completion of their pilgrimage as well (Heb 2:10).

This conviction leads directly to promises about the day when the inconsistency will be resolved finally in the Christians' favor, a second resource for making the tension more endurable in the interim. The opening benediction of 1 Peter (1 Pet 1:3-9), for example, addressed to the Christians throughout Asia Minor suffering reproach and rejection from their non-Christian neighbors, strategically begins by talking about this very hope, the imperishable inheritance reserved in heaven (1 Pet 1:4), the "deliverance that is about to be revealed" (1 Pet 1:5, my translation). The believers' perseverance in their love for Christ in the midst of their trials will mean "glory and honor when Jesus Christ is revealed" (1 Pet 1:7). They are the recipients of all the wondrous gifts of God that the prophets foresaw (1 Pet 1:10-12), and so are encouraged to lift their eyes away from the present situation, in which their honor is assaulted and challenged, to the "gift that is coming to you at the revelation of Jesus Christ" (1 Pet 1:13, my translation), the final manifestation of their "glory and honor" in the eyes of their detractors.

Romans 8:14-23 is a particularly rich discussion of the believers' place in God's family, the tension they experience as God's children in this age, and the inevitable resolution of that tension:

> For all who are led by the Spirit of God are children of God. For you did not receive a spirit of slavery to fall back into fear, but you have received a spirit of adoption. When we cry, "Abba! Father!" it is that very Spirit bearing witness with our spirit that we are children of God, and if children, then heirs, heirs of God and joint heirs with Christ—if, in fact, we suffer with him so that we may also be glorified with him. I consider that the sufferings of this present time are not worth comparing with the glory about to be revealed to us. For the creation waits with eager longing for the revealing of the children of God; for the creation was subjected to futility, not of its own will but by the will of the one who subjected it, in hope that the creation itself will be set free from its bondage to decay and will obtain the freedom of the glory of the children of God. We know that the whole creation has been groaning in labor pains until now; and not only the creation, but we ourselves, who have the first fruits of the Spirit, groan inwardly while we wait for adoption, the redemption of our bodies.

Paul begins by pointing to the Spirit as the proof of their share in Christ's inheritance. That Spirit, and the assurance it brings them, should enable great boldness in the face of whatever opposition or suffering the world brings to bear on the believer—it is the Spirit of a freeborn child of God, who should exhibit courage and confidence rather than cowering slavishly. Enduring the hostility of unbelievers means solidarity with the one who is now seated at God's right hand and thus means, in the end, honor. They are assured that the cost they pay now is but pennies on the dollar compared to the inheritance they will enjoy at the consummation. Moreover, the Christians are not alone in their groaning for the manifestation of their full honor and their glorified existence in the resurrection; all creation feels the tension as well, groaning to God to bring resolution. The hearers are encouraged to persist in solidarity with the name of Christ, associated closely with him even though it means some degree of deprivation or even suffering now, because that association is their claim on the inheritance. The Spirit that bears witness to them about their adoption is merely the firstfruits of their promised crop.

Finally, the believers do experience their favored status as sons and daughters in the assembly and in their enjoyment of God's gifts. This includes first and foremost the gift of the Holy Spirit as the internal witness to the Christians' place in God's family (Rom 8:14-17; Gal 4:6-7), the pledge of our full adoption, and as the seed planted in us that enables us to live as Jesus lived, to love as God loves—in short, to resemble our new family. It also means assurance of God's provision for his daughters and sons (Mt 17:24-27, for example, is a story that leads to this expectation), and of God's assistance in answer to the requests of his household (Mt 7:7-11). While the non-Christians may thus challenge the believers' honor, God himself, in the fellowship of the family of faith, continuously affirms the believers' honor as his own children.[9] As we will see below, the "many sons and daughters" also play an important role in affirming one another's worth as God's children, countering the power of society's resistance with mutual support, encouragement and affirmation.

Having God as Father becomes a source of ethical exhortation throughout the New Testament. The character of God must be reflected in

---

[9]Hebrews 12:5-11 is again a potent passage in this regard, since it transforms the very attempts of the outside world to degrade the Christians into a sign of God's provision for his true children's training and equipping.

his children and can indeed be reflected in us since "God's seed abides in them" (1 Jn 3:9). We have already observed how Jesus used this topic of "like father, like child" in his exhortation to be generous of heart and spirit toward the just and the unjust, toward those who do good to us and those who do ill (Mt 5:44-48; Lk 6:35). Just as God's favor is not bounded by the gratitude or ingratitude of the recipients, but flows and blesses strictly according to God's good will, so are his children to exercise utter freedom in their own ability to love the undeserving and the deserving alike. This is to be "perfect, therefore, as your heavenly Father is perfect" (Mt 5:48).

Other New Testament voices echo Jesus' teaching in this regard. The author of 1 Peter, for example, writes: "Like obedient children, do not be conformed to the desires that you formerly had in ignorance. Instead, as he who called you is holy, be holy yourselves in all your conduct; for it is written, 'You shall be holy, for I am holy'" (1 Pet 1:14-16). Here the injunction to be like their new Father (using Lev 19:2 as a resource) strengthens the exhortation against melting back into the dominant culture and the kinds of behaviors they would approve. In Ephesians Paul uses the topic to cultivate an ethos of mutual forgiveness and love within the Christian community. Since God forgave, they are to forgive; since Christ loved, they are to love. In this way, they are to "be imitators of God, as beloved children" (Eph 4:31—5:2; see also 1 Jn 3:1-3).

Paul brings another dimension to this in Romans 8:29: Christians are being "conformed to the image of his Son, in order that he might be the firstborn of many brothers and sisters" (my translation). Thus the Christians seek in all things to imitate not only the Father but also their senior brother. Answering the question "What would Jesus do?" (and then doing it) is not just a clever gimmick—it is the distinguishing mark of Jesus' kindred.

The Ethos of the "Household of Faith"

The Christians are explicitly instructed to treat one another as family: "Do not speak harshly to an older man, but speak to him as to a father, to younger men as brothers, to older women as mothers, to younger women as sisters—with absolute purity" (1 Tim 5:1-2). Fostering an ethos of kinship within the Christian group was a widespread technique of the group, grounded in the conviction that believers have become kin by the blood of Christ, being adopted into the one household of God as the many sons and daughters.

Of all the possible family relationships from which to choose, however, it is the sibling relationship that emerges as prominent. *Philadelphia* ("the love of brothers and sisters") becomes the central topic for shaping relationships with one another in the church. Believers are often specifically exhorted to embody this particular species of love toward one another (Rom 12:9-10; 1 Thess 4:9-10; Heb 13:1; 1 Pet 1:22; 3:8; 2 Pet 1:7), and their fellowship is called a "brotherhood" by one author (*adelphotēs*, 1 Pet 2:17; 5:9).[10] Use of the terms *brother, sister* and *brethren* for the community of disciples from the very beginning (see Mt 18:15; 28:10; Lk 22:32; Jn 20:17-18; 21:23; Acts 1:15; 9:30; 10:23; 15:1, 3, 22, 32-33, 36, 40; 21:17; 28:15; by far the most common way of referring to fellow Christians) facilitates the adoption of a sibling ethic for the Christian church. The New Testament authors consistently come back to this kinship ethic to evaluate what behaviors are compatible and what behaviors are incompatible with living together as the household of God.

Mutual love. First, Christians are repeatedly urged to love one another (Jn 13:34; 15:17), specifically after the example of Jesus, who valued the well-being of his sisters and brothers above his own life (Jn 15:12-13). Just as it would be disgraceful for a person to love his or her natural kin only as long as that love cost nothing, so people joined by the blood of Jesus are to "go the distance" in loving each other. Putting one another ahead of our comfort level, our attachment to our money, even our personal safety—this was the kind of love that, for John at least, sums up all of Jesus' teaching. This is to be the church's essential mark, so that the world will recognize their connection with Jesus by the love they show one another (Jn 13:35).

Love of the brothers and sisters is an essential characteristic of those

---

[10]Although I value the NRSV and have adopted it as the standard for my classes, its commitment to inclusive language has led the translators in far too many places to replace strategically chosen kinship terms like *brothers, brotherly love* and the like with *believers, mutual love* and so forth. This practice derives from the translators' desire for arriving at a smoothly flowing translation, and retaining "brother and sister" in every instance would admittedly prove cumbersome. For example, 1 Peter 3:8 reads "have . . . love for one another," for *philadelphoi [ginesthe].* To preserve both the sense of the word and a gender-inclusive translation would require the following: "be filled with brotherly and sisterly love." While layreaders throughout the English-speaking world will appreciate the translators' commitment not to allow their desire for gender inclusivity to result in awkward and long phrases, it will be a detriment to us here in this specific investigation. The NASB or NIV, for some of the purposes of this chapter, may be of greater service.

HONOR, PATRONAGE, KINSHIP & PURITY

who are "in the light"; without such love, one is "still in the darkness" (1 Jn 2:9-11). Loving the family of God is the indication of being "born of God" (1 Jn 4:7) and also of loving God. As for Plutarch, so for John, love for siblings is the best proof of love for one's parents. Those without such love for the fellow believers show themselves to be "children of the devil" (1 Jn 3:10), as were the schismatics who broke off relations with those whom John consoles in his letter.

Love must be practically demonstrated. John provides a simple way in which "laying down one's life for the sisters and brothers" can be enacted: "We ought to lay down our lives for one another. How does God's love abide in anyone who has the world's goods and sees a brother or sister in need and yet refuses help? Little children, let us love, not in word or speech, but in truth and action" (1 Jn 3:16-18). So also for Paul, love and its practical manifestation in mutual service go hand in hand: "You were called to freedom, brothers and sisters; only do not use your freedom as an opportunity for self-indulgence, but through love become slaves to one another" (Gal 5:13). Christian freedom is a very different thing from modern, Western notions of freedom. We celebrate our freedom to speak our mind in public (no matter whom we hurt), to do with another consenting adult whatever we might wish (no matter what time-honored values and teachings we arrogantly trample) or to pursue wealth and luxury (no matter how many poor and hurting people we neglect along the way). The Christian's freedom is always directed by love for the other, not concern for our own rights and desires. It seeks opportunities to serve in the name of Jesus, not to indulge oneself in the name of rights.

An important manifestation of mutual love is the staunch refusal to do what will bring harm to one's kin (all the more as this, ultimately, is to harm oneself). Thus Paul in two places forcefully urges believers to put the spiritual well-being of the sister or brother ahead of the exercise of the believers' freedom in Christ. Abstaining from hurting the sister or brother takes the highest priority: "So by your knowledge those weak believers for whom Christ died are destroyed. But when you thus sin against members of your family, and wound their conscience when it is weak, you sin against Christ. Therefore, if food is a cause of their falling, I will never eat meat, so that I may not cause one of them to fall" (1 Cor 8:11-13) To injure a brother or sister is to cease "walking in love" (Rom 14:15, 21). Such concern for what is in the interest of one's sisters and brothers becomes the primary guide to conduct (both abstention and positive pursuit): "Let each of you look not to your own interests, but to the interests of others" (Phil 2:4). In the "rights culture" of modern America, this is definitely a countercultural way of life. Nevertheless, Paul's standard of love means abstaining from one's rights if the full exercise of one's freedom will offend and tear down a sister or brother. Most ecclesiastical debates I have witnessed tend to pursue an alternative strategy, namely, forcing one's perceived freedom on the rest of the family of faith, trying to maneuver one's way into making them "live with it" and "accept it." Our commitment to enjoying and enforcing our rights inevitably results in shattering the body of Christ into ever more splinters. It is an American way but not a Christian way.

The following three topics develop a richer New Testament picture of what it means to have "fellowship" (*koinōnia*) in the body. Where fellowship means less than this, the church is missing out on the full enjoyment of its inheritance in this life.

Sharing of resources. The conviction that siblings are to make use in common of their inherited goods undergirds the exhortation to benefit and share with one another within the community (Heb 13:16; cf. 6:9-10; 10:24-25). Lucian bears witness that this attitude is thoroughly established among Christians by the second century in one of his satires: "Their first lawgiver persuaded them that they are all brothers of one another. . . . Therefore they despise all things [i.e., material goods] indiscriminately and consider them common property" (*Peregr.* 13). As siblings in Christ, the believers are to pool their resources in every way so that each member of the family knows the love of this family at his or her point of need and so that all arrive safely at the heavenly goal.

The picture of the earliest community of disciples painted by Luke is one in which the ideal of friendship is fully lived out: "No one claimed private ownership of any possessions, but everything they owned was held in common" (Acts 4:32). As the need to care for the poor in their midst made itself felt, the Christians of means would sell their houses and lands, and bring the proceeds to the apostles for distribution (Acts 4:34-35). The aversion of democratic and socialist countries to communism need not dull our appreciation of this picture. What we witness in the early church is not an attempt to create a system of government and economics enforced through terror but rather an attitude that each believer has toward fellow believers—"love for the brothers and sisters"—and lives out without reservation. The realization of kinship through the sharing of possessions continues in the famous collection project for the poor in the Judean churches (Acts 11:29), which is also a prominent topic of Paul's letters as he actually carries out that project. Such an attitude toward possessions was not a historical curiosity of the first decade of the church but continued to be a prominent aspect of its living out of the new relationships God had forged, as well as a proof of the genuineness of Christian faith (Rom 12:13; Gal 6:9-10; Jas 2:15-17; 1 Jn 3:16-18). Believers are called on throughout the New Testament to fulfill the ideal for the people of God promised by God in Deuteronomy: "There will . . . be no one in need among you" (Deut 15:4); "there was not a needy person among them" (Acts 4:34).

No single group of Christians was permitted to lose sight of the fact that it was part of the vastly extended and ever-growing global family of God. Thus while they are urged to hold each other's need in remembrance and to supply one another with material help, they are also enjoined to open up the resources of one Christian center to sisters and brothers from other centers (see, e.g., Rom 12:13; 2 Tim 1:16; Tit 1:8; Heb 13:2; 1 Pet 4:9; 3 Jn 5-10). The relationship of hosts and guests was long considered a sacred bond, the preservation of which is a facet of being a just person (Pseudo-Cicero *Rhetorica ad Herennium* 3.3.4). Within the Christian culture, hospitality was also an important expression of the love of believers one for another, a living out of the ethos of kinship within the translocal Christian community:

> In addition to the poor, the outcasts, the dispossessed, the imprisoned and the widows and orphans who had to be cared for, there were, according to Hatch, "the strangers who passed in a constant stream through the cities of all the great routes of commerce in both East and West. Every one of those strangers who bore the Christian name had therein a claim to hospitality. For Christianity was, and grew because it was, a great fraternity. The name 'brother' . . . vividly expressed a real fact . . . a Christian found, wherever he went, in the community of his fellow-Christians a welcome and hospitality."[11]

The importance of hospitality toward visiting brothers and sisters carrying on the work of the church is apparent throughout the New Testa-

---

[11]Elliott, *Home,* p. 146, citing Edwin Hatch, *The Organization of the Early Christian Churches* (Oxford and Cambridge: Rivingtons, 1881), pp. 43-44.

ment. Itinerant teachers, missionaries and leaders of the movement were especially dependent on the hospitality of their fellow believers along the way. Third John, for example, praises Gaius for his hospitality toward visiting Christians (3 Jn 5-8) but censures Diotrephes for his refusal to extend hospitality and his attempts to prevent others from exercising this ministry (3 Jn 9-10). Paul, similarly, depends on the hospitality of converts for his travels (see 1 Cor 16:5-6; Philem 22). Hospitality is also an aspect of sharing one's resources with the local Christian community, since the houses of the better-endowed believers became the meeting places for the local Christian community, which sustained the "constant intercourse and meeting . . . essential to preserve the Church's cohesion and distinctive witness," as well as providing the place where the distinctive Christian worship could be practiced[12] (see Rom 16:3-5, 23; 1 Cor 16:19; Col 4:15; Philem 2; 1 Pet 4:9). Both for the ongoing nurture of the local community and for the sake of ongoing connectedness with the larger Christian culture—the supra-local family of God—hospitality was a core value of the early church.[13]

Unity, harmony, concord. The author of 1 Peter writes: "Finally, all of you, be of one mind, sympathetic, filled with brotherly and sisterly love *(philadelphoi)*, compassionate, humble" (1 Pet 3:8, my translation). The first two words *(homophrones, sympatheis)* are, as we saw above, very common in discussions of the third word, "fraternal love." Being "of one mind" or "of one heart and soul" (Acts 4:32), is the source of the Christian movement's strength in the face of strong opposition—a witness, as it were, to the ultimate victory of Jesus over the world: "You are standing firm in one spirit, striving side by side with one mind for the faith of the gospel, and are in no way intimidated by your opponents. For them this is evidence of their destruction, but of your salvation" (Phil 1:27-28).

In 1 Corinthians 1:10-11, having opened the letter with friendly words of greeting and praise, Paul turns to an area of deep concern to him: "Now I appeal to you, brothers and sisters, by the name of our Lord Jesus Christ, that all of you be in agreement and that there be no divisions

---

[12]Edward G. Selwyn, *The First Epistle of Peter,* 2d ed. (London: Macmillan, 1955), p. 218.
[13]See further Wayne A. Meeks, *The First Urban Christians: The Social World of the Apostle Paul* (New Haven, Conn.: Yale University Press, 1983), pp. 16-23, 107-10; Michael B. Thompson, "The Holy Internet: Communication Between Churches in the First Christian Generation," in *The Gospels for All Christians: Rethinking the Gospel Audiences,* ed. Richard Bauckham (Grand Rapids, Mich.: Eerdmans, 1998), pp. 55-56.

among you, but that you be united in the same mind and the same purpose. For it has been reported to me by Chloe's people that there are quarrels among you, my brothers and sisters." The repetition in each sentence
of the address "brothers and sisters" is strategic, as Paul holds before
them the disgraceful inconsistency between their identity in Christ (their
close kinship) and their behavior (divisions, quarrels). The words *schis-
mata* and *erides* conjure up images of factions, of ugly rivalry, of breaches
of the unity and harmony that is the ideal state of an honorable family.
The Corinthians are confronted at the outset with the ugliness and inappropriateness of their behavior toward one another. They should be
defusing rivalries and partisanship rather than fostering it.

A fine study in the application of the ethos of unity and harmony to
life in the church is Paul's letter to the Philippian Christians. Two prominent women in the church, Syntyche and Euodia, whom Paul calls his
colaborers in the gospel, are at odds with one another (Phil 4:2-3), and this
rivalry threatens to undermine the unity and strength of the congregation
at a time when pressures from without are also high (Phil 1:29-30). The
nature of their quarrel is forever lost to us, but knowing the specifics
would probably only move us to take sides, as it was doing within the
Philippian church. Paul addresses this situation by censuring all rivalry,
all selfish ambition and everything else that contributes to disunity as out
of place in the church. It is a violation of the "mind of Christ" that believers are to have toward one another:

> If then there is any encouragement in Christ, any consolation from love, any
> sharing in the Spirit, any compassion and sympathy, make my joy com-
> plete: be of the same mind, having the same love, being in full accord and of
> one mind. Do nothing from selfish ambition or conceit, but in humility
> regard others as better than yourselves. Let each of you look not to your
> own interests, but to the interests of others. (Phil 2:1-4)

Paul discerns that the self intrudes mightily wherever division and
strife emerge, and this promotion of the self is exactly what Christ refused
to consider as he ran the course of obedience unto greatest honor. So also
we as sisters and brothers in the church are enjoined to keep our focus on
the work of God, on the larger vision of God in which we can cooperate
and which we will only serve effectively as we put the needs and worth
of one another ahead of our own, even as Jesus did.

One specific breach of unity brought out by Paul, and quite relevant for the American scene, was the tendency of the Corinthian Christians to continue to raise lawsuits against one another: "Can it be that there is no one among you wise enough to decide between one believer and another, but a believer goes to court against a believer—and before unbelievers at that? In fact, to have lawsuits at all with one another is already a defeat for you. Why not rather be wronged? Why not rather be defrauded? But you yourselves wrong and defraud—and believers at that" (1 Cor 6:5-8). Lawsuits were just one more facet of their preconversion life that the Corinthian believers thought nothing of continuing. Paul argues, however, that the new relationship between the parties makes court cases inappropriate. It is better to suffer injury or loss than to seek to hurt or avenge yourself on your kin. An important aspect of this for Paul is the public that will view the suit—"and that before unbelievers." In Paul's eyes, such lawsuits are a stain on the honor of the family of God as well as an excellent cause for unbelievers to question the virtue and value of this group that calls itself family.

How can Paul's ideal of unity—or Jesus' for that matter (see Jn 17:11, 21)—ever be realized in our fragmented and polarized church? It will not be realized as long as we insist that unity be achieved by "accepting me on my terms." Only a spirit of humility, a willingness to sacrifice what we may hold dear for the sake of love for the other, a willingness to "die to self" will contribute to restoring unity in the church where it has been breached and to preserving it where it is now threatened. When each of us ceases to demand of others that they recognize and accept us, and instead shows a willingness to abstain from that which gives offense—not out of fear, nor out of hopelessness, but out of love, regarding the other as more important than ourselves—then we may see a transformation of Western Christendom.

Unity as befits sisters and brothers will also not be achieved as long as we in our various Christian denominations cling to our differences as if these were issues that truly separated the saved from the lost. We have too long and too often taken the words "be of the same mind" to mean, functionally, "if you agree with me on these points of doctrine, then we can be sisters and brothers, have fellowship and experience God together." As Paul has structured Philippians 2:1-4, the experience of God is primary: since you have received encouragement from Christ, since you have shared in the one Spirit of God, live in full accord with one another, being of one mind. We are prone to be disputatious and to place victory in theological debates higher than the bond of unity. This is not Paul's way except in issues that truly cut to the core of being Christian (and most issues, let us be honest, do not). Rather than seek to "have it our way" in terms of every dispute, we again find an opportunity for laying down our lives, or at least our egos, for our sisters and brothers as we put love, peace and unity with one another ahead of being right all the time. Paul makes it clear that no one has *all* the facts (1 Cor 13:12-13 is strong and necessary medicine for our conceited race), and therefore disagreements are not ultimate. Our agreement—our common experience of God through the Spirit—is of greater importance than our disagreement based on finer points of theology, liturgical practice and interpretation. Our agreement is founded on God's act on our behalf; our disagreements on our own thoughts, minds and hearts. To place greater importance on the latter than the former is an act of pride, of *hybris*, an affront to God. To be "like-minded" is not to agree on everything; it is to put foremost in our minds what is central and common to the believing community in every place, what makes for building up the church of God in the bond of love.

Cooperation and mutual honoring, not competition for precedence. Given what we have learned about the cultural context of honor, it is not surprising to find that early Christians approached life in the church and discipleship as another arena for the competition for honor and winning precedence and distinction. What New Testament authors keep emphasizing—and this with astonishing frequency and unanimity—is the inappropriateness of viewing one another in this fashion as competitors, which is essentially to view one another as outsiders to one's own honor and family. Instead, Christians are to view one another as partners, cooperating for and contributing to one another's honor and success.

Mark 10:35-45 provides a helpful study in this regard. James and John come to Jesus seeking advancement together: "Grant us to sit, one at your right hand and one at your left, in your glory" (Mk 10:37). They are acting as natural kin ought to do, cooperating with each other in the quest for honor.[14] It is probably of no importance to them which is granted the seat at the right hand over the left. Nevertheless, their request is not in keep-

---

[14]We may also note here the way in which Andrew immediately seeks out his brother, Peter, to share the good news of the Messiah's arrival and to include Peter on the ground floor of this movement in John 1:40-41.

ing with the ethos Jesus seeks to create among all his disciples. The two natural brothers have made a distinction between themselves and the other ten and see themselves in competition with the other disciples. The response of the ten here, who are "angry with James and John" (Mk 10:41), as well as their previous argument with one another concerning "who was the greatest" (Mk 9:33-34), shows that all twelve were still thinking in terms of competition for precedence within the group. Jesus declares that such an attitude must yield to the kinship values of cooperation and seeking how to be most of service to the brothers and sisters, rather than seeking how to achieve the greatest precedence and distinction among them. That is what will make for honor within the Father's household—acting honorably as family rather than competitively.

Jesus' criticism of the scribes and Pharisees in Matthew 23:5-9 addresses this rather directly. These figures are censured for seeking precedence over their brothers and sisters (i.e., other Jews), seeking to distinguish themselves above their fellow Jews so as to become a class of religious "leaders" (Rabbim). Jesus' followers are not to do this: "You are not to be called rabbi, for you have one teacher, and you are all brothers and sisters. And call no one your father on earth, for you have one Father" (Mt 23:8-9, my translation). They are to maintain the bond of unity as siblings under one Father—namely, God—and not create hierarchies that divide.

Paul also seeks avidly to replace competition for honor with cooperation and mutual honoring within the church, countering a primary aspect of their socialization into the dominant cultural values of seeking precedence over those who are not blood relations. Thus in Romans 12:10 he advises: "Try to outdo one another in showing respect."[15] Throughout the hortatory section of Galatians (Gal 5:13-6:10), Paul weaves in terms of sibling relationship ("brothers," Gal 5:13; "household of faith," Gal 6:10, my translation) to create an ethos of cooperation, love and solidarity within the church.[16] The works of the flesh are heavily weighted with descrip-

---

[15]This is how the early translations of the New Testament into Latin, Armenian and Syriac read the passage. Another possibility would be "as far as honor is concerned, let each one esteem the other more highly" (see entry "proēgeomai," in Walter Bauer, William Arndt and F. Wilbur Gingrich, *A Greek-English Lexicon of the New Testament and Other Early Christian Literature* [Chicago: University of Chicago Press, 1952], pp. 712-13).

[16]See the detailed discussion of this passage by Philip F. Esler, "Family Imagery and Christian Identity in Galatians 5:13 to 6:10," in Moxnes, *Constructing Early Christian Families*, pp. 121-49, esp. pp. 134-43.

tions of behaviors specifically inappropriate for kin: "enmities, strife, jealousy, anger, quarrels, dissensions, factions, envy" (Gal 5:20-21). Similarly,
Paul proscribes boasting, challenging and envying (Gal 5:26) for members
of the household of faith, who should instead serve one another and protect (rather than challenge) one another's honor. Since Christians are not
in competition but in a joint venture together, they are free to "practice
the art of making mutual concessions, of learning to take defeat, and of
taking pleasure in indulging brothers rather than in winning victories
over them," as Plutarch puts it ("On Fraternal Affection" 17 [*Mor.* 488A],
LCL).

Paul skillfully uses the metaphor of the body, the living organism composed of many parts, in 1 Corinthians 12 to reinforce the ethos of family
within the church—and this in a historical context in which competition
and claims of precedence in honor were a besetting problem in so many
areas of the church's life: "But God has so arranged the body, giving the
greater honor to the inferior member, that there may be no dissension
within the body, but the members may have the same care for one
another. If one member suffers, all suffer together with it; if one member
is honored, all rejoice together with it" (1 Cor 12:24-26). Paul articulates a
principle, derived from the metaphor of the physical body, that holds true
for the social body of the household as well. As J. D. M. Derrett rightly
observes, "The advance of one member of an agnatic family would
advantage all his kindred," as the reverse would be to the detriment of
the whole family.[17] This means that the honor or loss experienced by one
member of the household is the honor or loss felt by the whole kinship
group. Aristotle's description of siblings as being "identical with each
other" since they share a common identity with their parents and are
therefore "in a sense the same thing, though in separate individuals,"
(*Nic. Eth.* 8.12 [1161b31-33]) confirms Derrett's observations about the
way close kin respond to one another's successes and losses.[18] This sense

---

[17]J. Duncan M. Derrett, *Jesus' Audience: The Social and Psychological Environment in Which He Worked* (New York: Seabury, 1973), p. 38.

[18]It was, of course, not unthinkable for a brother to rejoice in a brother's defeat and even for such a brother to think that a sibling's loss would be his gain. The example of Eteocles and Polyneices (see Aeschylus *Seven Against Thebes*, and Sophocles *Oedipus at Colonus* and *Antigone*) teaches us this. But the way in which these two brothers are remembered and held up throughout the classical and Hellenistic periods as disgraceful, deluded people caught up in a self-destructive feud also shows the majority culture's rejection of competition between close kin as an acceptable attitude.

of sharing completely in one another's fortunes, then, is precisely the solidarity that Christians are to embody. It is also a sure path to fulfill the command to "love your neighbor as yourself."

The author of Hebrews uses this same rationale in his appeal to the hearers to "remember the imprisoned, as being imprisoned together with them, the mistreated as being yourselves in their skin" (Heb 13:3, my translation). They are, as kin, "the same thing, through separate individuals," so they should feel and respond to one another's needs in that spirit—the free believer must regard the sufferings of another as his or her own sufferings and alleviate them as wholeheartedly and bravely as a person would relieve his or her own distress. In this manner, the Christians not only reassure those who are experiencing the most pressure from outside the group but also reassure one another that this new family will never desert them in their time of need. Rather, they will be for one another the visible and active manifestation of the promise of God never to forsake or leave the believer (Heb 13:5).[19]

The specific focus on reorienting the believers' attitudes toward one another away from competition for honor and toward celebrating and building up one another's honor and self-respect serves the goal of promoting unifying behavior and averting divisive competition. It is thus effectively a subset of the values of unity and concord among kin.

Reconciliation in the family. Also in keeping with the ideal of unity and concord is the emphasis in the New Testament, as in non-Christian texts about brotherhood, on seeking reconciliation where an injury has

---

[19]Solidarity with believers who are victimized by the outside society became a prominent feature of the Christian counterculture. The journey of Ignatius from Antioch to his martyrdom at Rome, visited, attended and given hospitality by Christians along the way, shows the willingness of the believers to "remember those who are in prison as though you were in prison with them" (Heb 13:3). The martyr himself testifies to their familial loyalty to him (*Smyrn.* 10): "My life is a humble offering for you; and so are these chains of mine, for which you never showed the least contempt or shame." Lucian's famous satire on the charlatan Peregrinus also provides a window into the Christian community in the mid-second century:

The Christians . . . left nothing undone in the effort to rescue [Peregrinus]. Then, as this was impossible, every other form of attention was shown him. . . . From the very break of day aged widows and orphan children could be seen waiting near the prison, while their officials even slept inside with him after bribing the guards. Then elaborate meals were brought in, and sacred books of theirs were read aloud. . . . Indeed, people came even from the cities in Asia, sent by the Christians at their common expense, to succour and defend and encourage the hero. *They show incredible speed whenever any such public action is taken; for in no time they lavish their all.* (*Peregr.* 12, LCL, emphasis mine)

occurred. The urgency with which Plutarch advises forgiving the penitent brother and making amends with the injured brother is present in the teachings of Jesus, who declares that reconciliation with an offended sister or brother takes precedence before offering gifts at the altar (Mt 5:22-34).[20] Forgiving the penitent is not optional but necessary since both parties have been adopted into God's family and made siblings by God's prior forgiveness of much weightier offenses (Mt 18:21-35; see Lk 17:3). Rather than complain or murmur against a fellow Christian (see Jas 4:11; 5:9), which advertises rather than hides the shame of one's kin and contributes to an atmosphere of division, the believer is to seek reconciliation one-on-one with a sibling in Christ. The procedure outlined in Matthew 18:15-17 shows a great deal of sensitivity to keeping the disagreement as private as possible, so that reconciliation can be effected without at the same time damaging the honor of a sister or brother.[21]

It is noteworthy that both the Matthean and Lucan sayings on this matter lay responsibility on the offended sister or brother to tell the offender that an injury has been done, rather than merely to wait for the other person to make the overture, during which time grudges can grow, unkind thoughts and words multiply, and breaches widen. This was also the command of Leviticus and the advice of Plutarch and the author of the *Testament of Gad.*[22] Within Matthew alone, both the one who has been hurt and the one who has caused hurt are separately exhorted to drop everything and seek reconciliation. The two should run toward each other and remove the threat to unity as quickly as possible (even if that means dropping this book for a brief span).

Within the family, siblings may need to be reconciled not only to each other but also to the values of the group and to their parent. Plutarch creates a picture of a sibling who stands as an advocate for the errant brother or sister in the presence of the father of the house, and who gently rebukes his or her wayward sibling so as to bring that person back to

---

[20]Jesus here speaks of fellow Jews as siblings but, of course, his words will be heard quite differently by the early Christian readers and hearers, for whom Matthew writes his Gospel, in the context of calling one another brother and sister.

[21]See the rich study of Dennis C. Duling, "Matthew 18.15-17. Conflict, Confrontation, and Conflict Resolution in a 'Fictive Kin' Association," *BTB* 29 (1999): 4-22, for a thorough investigation of this passage, particularly in its Jewish context.

[22]"You shall not hate in your heart your brother, but you shall surely reprove your neighbor, lest you bear a grudge against him" (Lev 19:17, my translation); "If anyone sins against you, speak to him in peace. . . . If anyone confesses and repents, forgive him" (T. Gad 6.1-3).

a commitment to act nobly (see "On Fraternal Affection" 9-10 [*Mor.* 482E-483B]). This picture is precisely what New Testament authors construct for the Christian family. Believers are to stand before the Father in prayer on behalf of the sibling who sins, with the result that the sin will in most cases be forgiven, covered over by God (1 Jn 5:16). They are to rebuke the wrongdoer and restore him or her to the spirit-led way "in a spirit of gentleness" (Gal 6:1-2), grieving with the wrongdoer rather than using it as an occasion to put him or her down. As we have seen (see chap. two), the Christian family, like any natural family, can apply pressure to keep its wayward members in line with the family values. The relevant point here, however, is that even in the midst of applying such corrective procedures, the community is to remember that the offender is a brother or sister *first*, and not an enemy and outsider: "Do not regard them as enemies, but warn them as sisters and brothers" (2 Thess 3:15, my translation).

The parable of the two sons (Lk 15:1-32) and the restoration of Zacchaeus (Lk 19:1-10) model for the Christian community how they should treat wayward members of the household of faith and how they should extend that gentle spirit of restoration to those outside the community of faith. Jesus sees Zacchaeus as "a son of Abraham" (Lk 19:9) whose restoration ought to be sought after diligently, whereas his neighbors see only "one who is a sinner" (Lk 19:7) and exclude him on that account. But the sinner, Jesus shows us, is first a sibling in God or at least a potential sibling in God, and it is on that basis that we must reach out to him or her in welcoming love. The parable of the two sons is directed primarily at the scribes and Pharisees, whose criticism of Jesus' willingness to meet sinners where they are opens the chapter (Lk 15:1-2). That parable places the sinner and the Pharisee in the relationship of brothers, reorienting the latter toward the former and showing how ugly a spirit of exclusivity and condemnation is in the eyes of a father who longs for the return of all his children. If we look upon outreach to the "undesirables" of our community as did Luke's Pharisees, Jesus' criticism of the scribes and Pharisees will be his criticism of us as well.

New Family, New "Not-Family"
The Christian movement holds in creative tension its commitment to the conversion of people outside the movement with its commitment to draw clear boundary lines between what belongs to the group and what

belongs to the world outside the group. These boundary lines are important for the preservation of the distinctive values, ethos and witness of the group, for the focusing of each member's commitment and devotion to fellow Christians, and for reinforcing each member's commitment to the new family and the way of life it has adopted.

Jesus' parable of the weeds distinguishes between two families inhabiting the world—the "children of the kingdom" and "children of the evil one" (Mt 13:38)—and Paul will use similar designations to distinguish his converts from outsiders, the "children of light" and "of the day" from the children "of the night" and "of darkness" (1 Thess 5:8). Paul's purpose in drawing these family lines is to underscore the difference in lifestyles between the two families (and the disgraceful conduct of those children "of darkness"), such that his converts should not succumb to the pressure of outsiders to conform again to the way of life they left behind. The two families also display different levels of awareness—as different as "sober" from "drunk," "awake" from "asleep"—which places the children "of night" at a distinct disadvantage vis-à-vis the coming judgment of God. Similarly in Ephesians, Paul distinguishes the converts from the "sons and daughters of disobedience" (Eph 5:6-8, my translation), the family of which Christians used to be part, but from whose way of life they are now, as part of God's family, to distance themselves. They can no longer act in ways that suggest fundamental partnership with the pagan society or that suggest affirmation of the values of that society.

The purpose of such images is not to exclude outsiders as the object of Christians' care and beneficence, since Paul will also enjoin this explicitly in the same letter (see 1 Thess 3:12; 5:15). Rather, they are always used in the service of maintaining the commitment of Christians to continue in the way of life into which God has called them, particularly in the face of pressures from outside to conform.

"Natural" Households and Early Christianity

Early Christianity was basically a "household" movement first in that it sought after the conversion of heads of households, whose dependents would follow them into the new faith. The unnamed official in John 4:53 believes "along with his whole household." Cornelius, who had previously committed to semi-attachment to Judaism along with his household as "God fearers" (Acts 10:2) also converts to Christianity with his whole household (Acts 10:24, 44-48). The same pattern of conversion along with the head of a household is evidenced in the stories of Lydia (Acts 16:14-15), the Philippian jailor (Acts 16:31-34) and Crispus in Corinth (Acts 18:8). Entire households are greeted as part of the church in several Pauline letters: "the family of Aristobulus" in Romans 16:10, the "family of Narcissus" in Romans 16:11, the "household of Stephanas," baptized together by Paul (1 Cor 1:16; see 16:15), and the "household of Onesiphorus" in 2 Timothy 4:19. In Titus 1:10-11, false teachers are "upsetting whole families" with their doctrine, another testimony to this prominent (though by no means consistent) tendency.[23] From the beginning of the Jesus movement itself, we find ties of natural kinship within the group of disciples, working alongside the ties of fictive kinship. Thus we have two pairs of brothers at the center of the movement, exemplifying the tendency of siblings to make such decisions together. Jesus' own natural family is part of the movement by the period after the resurrection (Acts 1:14). The mother of the sons of Zebedee appears to have followed her sons, appearing finally at the foot of the cross in Matthew 27:56. We also find frequent references to "relatives" *(syggenēs)* in Romans 16:7, 11, 21. The new household of faith does not abolish or suspend natural kinship relations within it; rather, these natural ties strengthen the group as a whole, as families or parts of families commit to the larger Christian family together.

Second, it was a household movement insofar as it depended on the hospitality of its member householders not only for the regular assemblies of the church (see Acts 5:42; 12:12; 20:20; the house of Aquila and Prisca in Rom 16:3-5 and 1 Cor 16:19; the house of Gaius, host to the whole church in Corinth, Rom 16:23; the house of Nympha, Col 4:15; the house of Philemon, Apphia, and Archippus, Philem 1-2) but also for the travels and visits of its itinerant leaders and teachers (see Mt 10:11-13; Acts 16:15, 40; 21:8, 16; 28:14; 2 Tim 1:16; Philem 22), as well as lay Chris-

---

[23]The household codes, particularly the addresses to children and their parents in Ephesians 6:1-4 and Colossians 3:20-21, also indicate the presence of whole families in the church, and the possibility now for parents (especially fathers) to bring up their young "in the discipline and instruction of the Lord" (Eph 6:4). John M. G. Barclay comments that the fact that these codes address children directly reveals an assumption on the part of the writer that children will be present in the assembly, being introduced from early on to the mysteries of God just as their Jewish and pagan counterparts would be ("The Family as the Bearer of Religion in Judaism and Early Christianity," in *Constructing Early Christian Families: Family as Social Reality and Metaphor*, ed. Halvor Moxnes [London: Routledge, 1997], p. 77).

tians serving as messengers and couriers in the work of the church (2 Cor 8:23; see 3 Jn 5-8). Hospitality withdrawn or refused was a powerful means of limiting or even quashing the influence of "deviants" within the Christian movement (2 Jn 10), but those who would come to be regarded as the legitimate bearers of the gospel also encountered this form of social control within the group (3 Jn 10). Elliott rightly adds that the household base also made possible the charitable relief of the sisters and brothers in need or in prison, "the economic self-sufficiency of the movement," and the provision of a "sense of belonging" to the "rootless, the aliens, the deprived and the dispossessed."[24]

Because the household became the center of the new religion, the structures of the household affected the structures of the new religion. This is seen most prominently in the Pastoral Epistles, in which house-holders emerge as the only likely candidates for bishop and deacon. According to Titus 1:6 (see also 1 Tim 3:5), only heads of Christian house-holds, with obedient Christian children, are allowed to serve as bishops. These local leaders are to have been married only once (just as true widows are those who have had only one husband according to 1 Tim 5:9-14, 16) and able to manage their own natural households (especially their children) well as proof of their ability to manage the household of God (1 Tim 3:2-5, 12).

Managing the Christian (natural) household. The survival of a group propagated through households and supported in households depends ultimately on the survival of households: "The household as a religious and social unit offered the Christians the best possible security for their existence as a group. Any weakening here would thus be a potentially devastating blow to their own cohesion."[25] The extensive overlap between the expectations of each member of a household (and the quali-ties to be embodied, for example, by women and children) in the domi-nant culture and in the emerging Christian culture reveals the importance of the continuation of households as the early Christians had known them for the survival of the movement. Moreover, overt attacks on house-hold economy would be regarded by outsiders—particularly those in power as subversive tendencies requiring corrective measures. New

---

[24]Elliott, *Home*, p. 198.
[25]Edwin A. Judge, *The Social Pattern of the Christian Groups in the First Century* (London: Tyn-dale Press, 1960), pp. 75-76.

motivations for old behaviors (e.g., now anchoring them in the example of Christ or the will of God) stand alongside startling modifications of old behaviors necessitated by the example of Christ. These give the Christian (natural) household a distinctive identity and internal dynamic while at the same time maintaining a positive stance toward the maintenance of family units, with the result that the movement would not be branded as a subversion of the social order by the dominant culture (particularly by its officials).

Marriage and Remarriage

Paul urges against the dissolution of existing marriages between an unbeliever and a believer unless the former wishes to break up the union (see 1 Cor 7:10-15). New marriages, however, are to follow the endogamous strategy—only fellow Christians form the pool of eligible spouses (1 Cor 7:39; 9:5). Marriage is not to be forbidden (1 Tim 4:3).

Christians are enjoined to preserve their marriages inviolate: "Let marriage be held in honor by all, and let the marriage bed be kept undefiled; for God will judge fornicators and adulterers" (Heb 13:4). While the dominant culture might be more tolerant of sexual desire flowing beyond the marital relationship (as long as it did not mean the pollution of aristocratic family lines, by involving men of low status with women of high status, for example), the Christian culture drew an impassible line. Such a stance, on the one hand, creates an important difference in values that reinforces the boundaries of the Christian community. On the other hand, it wards off injury to those intimate relationships between people who should rather be supporting one another in the Christian enterprise. Anyone who has witnessed the damage that adultery (particularly when committed by people in the same church) can do to the Christian walk of the individuals involved and to the vision and mission of the whole church will understand at once.

Household Codes

Three New Testament texts contain blocks of instructions, called "household codes" (the German word, *Haustafeln*, became a technical term encountered even in many English studies on the New Testament), directed at the different members of the household, following the pairs laid out as early as Aristotle to such a degree as to suggest that these were standard topics in ethical instruction. Thus in Ephesians 5:22—6:9 and

Colossians 3:18—4:1 we find instructions to wives and husbands, children and fathers, slaves and masters (the same male being potentially husband, father and master in a household); a truncated version of this form is found in 1 Peter 2:18-3:7, with instructions to slaves, wives and husbands.

These are among the less popular passages in the New Testament epistles, mainly on account of the facility with which they are employed to affirm patterns of intrafamilial relationship that degrade the female partner in favor of the male or the children in favor of the parent. I remember, as a child, being present in the home of some family friends when the husband was using the texts about wives being submissive to get his own way and keep his wife under his thumb (a union that ultimately ended, by the way, in divorce). The authoritarian aspect of these texts can be very appealing for males, especially, as they initiate or counter power plays in the home.

Abuses of this kind have, however, no place in the Christian home, since these passages are but a small part of the larger enterprise of the great household code being formed throughout the New Testament, teaching "how one ought to behave in the household of God, which is the church of the living God" (1 Tim 3:15). The more universal rules explored above as aspects of the ethos of honorable kin apply all the more within the Christian natural household. This is something that Paul brings out forcefully in Ephesians 5:21, the preface to the entire household code: "Be subject to one another out of reverence for Christ." Mutual love, unity, cooperation for one another's good, putting the interests of the other ahead of one's own—all these form the relational context in which these household codes are to be enacted and the interpretive lens through which they are to be understood and applied.

Although 1 Corinthians 14:34-35 is not part of a household code, we should observe that the blanket command to women to speak in private is very similar to Plutarch's view that women should not speak in public but only "to and through their husbands." That is to say, Paul attempts to maintain the conventional ethos of the ideal wife among the Corinthian believers. This passage, together with 1 Timothy 2:8-15, has been the mainstay of arguments against the ordination of women and the perpetuation of gender as a qualification for ministry (despite other texts, like Gal 3:28, that declare qualifications of race, social status and gender to be dissolved in Christ). The space and scope of this volume prohibit a full sortie into this minefield, except to point out at least how this passage stands in tension with Paul's matter-of-fact description of women participating in worship with words of prophecy and prayer (1 Cor 11:5), where Paul's only complaint is the absence of a headdress for the women.

We may never satisfactorily resolve this tension, since we will never know what specific kind of behavior prompted Paul's strong words in 1 Corinthians 14 save that it was disruptive to the orderliness of the worship service. Since "asking questions" is the only specific hint given, it seems more prudent, however, to limit Paul's prohibition to speech that happens alongside and about the worship service but does not contribute to the worship service. At the very least, Paul is seen to permit a woman to speak God's words in the church meeting as prophecy, or to speak words to God in prayer, even if there is still reluctance to let them speak their own words. We will return briefly to this vexed question at the end of this section.

First Corinthians 14:34 also speaks of the subordination of woman, presumably to the husband, (as does 1 Tim 2:6-15 explicitly) as the proper ethos for Christian women, just as it had been the ethos for these wives in their pre-Christian enculturation, whether Jewish or Greco-Roman. This theme also comes out forcefully in 1 Corinthians 11:2-16 as the rationale for head coverings: "Christ is the head of every man, and the husband is the head of his wife, and God is the head of Christ" (1 Cor 11:3). However one chooses to translate *kephalē* ("head") here, the firstness indicated by this term is difficult to avoid.[26] Submissiveness as a wifely virtue also receives affirmation in Ephesians 5:22-24 and 1 Peter 3:1-6, where the example of the church's relationship to Christ is invoked as a model and rationale for marital relationships. We begin to see how the church is modifying and qualifying these traditional values in Paul's preface to his own household code in Ephesians 5:21: "Be subject to one another out of reverence for Christ." However much we may find the New Testament authors upholding the subordination of wives to their husbands, we cannot then ignore the distinctively Christian addition they bring to this

---

[26]The pattern of subordination is reinforced through a reading of the creation story in 1 Corinthians 11:7-10.

arrangement: husbands are to be subject to their wives as well.[27] In this way, the household hierarchy is not eliminated, any less than the celestial hierarchy of the supreme servant is diminished, but as the instructions to husbands make clear, it is to be lived out in such a way as manifests the essential and paradoxical nature of authority as servanthood (personified in Christ).

The distinctive Christian modifications are most apparent in discussions of the husband's role and the ethos he is to embody in Ephesians 5:25-33 and 1 Peter 3:7. That husbands are to care for their wives "as for their own flesh" will probably be familiar from Greco-Roman ethics, since the same thing had been said even of slaves four centuries before, and since the female's honor was embedded in the honor either of her father or husband. The model for loving now available to the Christian, however, is the self-sacrificial love of Jesus, who gave himself for the church. This certainly raises the level of nourishing and tender caring for the wife to a new height. Indeed, this specifies the way in which a husband is to be subject to his wife, as he recalls the Lord who came "not to be served but to serve, and to give his life" (Mk 10:45). To this, the author of 1 Peter adds the following advice, which has been consistently mistranslated in English versions: "Likewise the husbands are to live together with their wives considerately as with the weaker vessel, giving honor also

---

[27]Russ Dudrey correctly finds this general, overarching qualifier to the household code to be the touchstone for the interpretation of the whole. The point of these codes is not mainly to urge women, slaves and children to be submissive but rather to set this submission (which was a given in the Greco-Roman and Jewish cultures) within the context of the distinctively Christian ethos of mutual submission ("'Submit Yourselves to One Another': A Socio-Historical Look at the Household Code of Ephesians 5:15—6:9," *RQ* 41 [1999]: 27-44). Thus "husbands are no longer to view their wives as their possessions [here I suspect Dudrey is perpetuating a stereotype, given the careful nuancing of the husband's authority we see in Xenophon, Aristotle and Plutarch]; rather they are to love them as Christ loved the church and to lay down their lives for them. Christ transforms marriage into a relationship of reciprocity. . . . Fathers are to involve themselves personally in training their children in the teachings of Christ [although this is already quite familiar in the Jewish context, and also in Greek and Roman houses of more limited means]. . . . Masters are no longer to view their slaves as their possessions [here the term is accurate]; rather, they are to view themselves as fellow slaves in Christ and to treat their slaves as Christ treats them [or perhaps as they hope to be treated?]" (p. 41, with my comments in brackets). His conclusionis most provocative, challenging both supporters of "traditional" patriarchalism and liberationists: "Our Father calls all members of his household, not to misuse and abuse others, but to submit ourselves to one another; and he calls us not to seek empowerment, but to live out our lives in the moral and spiritual equivalent of martyrdom: to die with Christ, to lay down our lives in service to one another" (p. 44).

as to fellow heirs of the gift of life in order that your prayers may not be hindered" (1 Pet 3:7, my translation).[28] Again, the first rationale will be familiar from Greco-Roman ethicists, who also would frown upon inconsiderate domination of the wife. The great dignity conferred on the woman by God, however, as a fellow heir of the same gift of life for which the husband hopes necessitates holding her in honor—indeed, in equal honor as he might hold himself. This is the principle that is to guide him in his relationship with her.

Children, in keeping not only with the Greco-Roman ethic but also the Mosaic Decalogue, are still to obey their parents (Eph 6:1-3, which explicitly refers to Deut 5:16). Fathers are urged to train their children gently, specifically "in the discipline and instruction of the Lord" (Eph 6:4). The father's role in education is not new (see Deut 6:4-8; 4 Macc 18:6-19; fathers were also involved in Greek and Roman education), but the curriculum is specifically a Christian one. The father is charged with the momentous responsibility of making disciples here not of all nations but of his own children. Again, the specific injunction not to "provoke your children to anger" (and, in Col 3:21, not to bear oneself in such a way that the children lose heart) guards against a pre-Christian or non-Christian equation of the *paterfamilias* with monarchical ruler of a household. He is here cast as a patient pedagogue, a servant of the household educating the children.

Finally, these household codes turn their attention to the attitudes that slaves and masters are to have toward one another. Slaves are predictably enjoined to "obey [their] earthly masters in everything," not only when their work is being scrutinized but at all times (Col 3:22; Eph 6:5). So far, this is standard. The rationale offered by Paul, however, is wholly new. They are not to work in this manner out of a desire to please their earthly masters but are offering service in their appointed tasks to their

---

[28]The NRSV, for example, renders this: "Husbands, in the same way, show consideration for your wives in your life together, paying honor to the woman as the weaker sex, since they too are also heirs of the gracious gift of life—so that nothing may hinder your prayers." The problem here is that the Greek text links the rationale "as the weaker sex" with the first instruction ("live considerately") and the rationale "as fellow heirs" with the second instruction ("show honor"). The way the RSV and NRSV handle it, "showing honor" to the wife can be seen as a magnanimous gesture by the male toward the "weaker vessel," whereas it is really a necessity, being what is due the Christian wife as an equal heir. The NIV and NKJV link both rationales with the second instruction as equal reasons for showing honor; the NASB, however, translates it accurately, and the NJB is a close second.

heavenly Lord (Eph 6:6-7; Col 3:22-24). They are called to be exemplary slaves out of faithfulness to Jesus, the one who will bestow on the slave his or her inheritance, which we recall to be the inheritance not of slaves but of children of God. Ephesians makes this all the more clear: "Whatever good we do, we will receive the same again from the Lord, whether we are slaves or free" (Eph 6:8). Before the judgment seat of Christ, when "each will receive his or her reward for deeds done in the body, whether good or evil" (2 Cor 5:10, my translation), such earthly status markers as "slave" and "free" have no meaning—a brilliant insight declared in Galatians 3:28, but awaiting the passing of centuries and millennia to be worked out in practice.

The author of 1 Peter also offers instructions for slaves, going so far as to enjoin them to show deference even to bad and unjust masters (whom, one would hope, would have been found only outside the Christian community), never committing a crime such as would merit punishment, but enduring undeserved punishment, if it comes, assured of God's favor and approval of their upright character (1 Pet 2:18-20). The Christian slaves are to imitate Christ, who also endured undeserved suffering, did not sin, offered no insult or abuse in return, entrusting himself instead to God (1 Pet 2:21-24). What is most striking about this author's instructions, however, is that the exhortations to slaves become the prism through which he develops his instructions to the whole body. After giving instructions to slaves (1 Pet 2:18-25), wives (1 Pet 3:1-6) and husbands (1 Pet 3:7), the author turns to the whole Christian community. Now he enjoins all to endure any suffering incurred on account of their attachment to Jesus, knowing that they have God's approval (1 Pet 3:14, 17; 4:14, 16), to avoid criminal entanglements and sin (1 Pet 3:10-12, 17; 4:15), to refuse to retaliate (1 Pet 3:9), to entrust themselves to God (1 Pet 4:19), all with an awareness of Christ's own example (1 Pet 3:18; 4:1). It is the slaves and not the masters who become the model for the behavior of all Christians.

Masters of slaves receive specific instructions in the household codes of Ephesians and Colossians. The instructions are brief, making the distinctively Christian rationales and modifications stand out all the more:

> Masters, treat your slaves justly and fairly, for you know that you also have a Master in heaven. (Col 4:1)

> Masters, do the same to them. Stop threatening them, for you know that both of you have the same Master in heaven, and with him there is no partiality. (Eph 6:9)

The way a master or mistress treats his or her slaves must be governed at all times by an awareness of their mutual Master in heaven, who will judge both master and slave without partiality (see Job 31:13-15, a clear piece of evidence that Christianity builds on Jewish ethics at this point). The Ephesians text is even more striking, first in openly challenging the meaningfulness of human-made distinctions between slaves and masters—a distinction that does not exist in the eye of God, with whom "there is no partiality." The equality of persons before the heavenly Master is presented as a check to the inherent *hybris* of the masters, who must not lord it over the slave with threats and force. The master must remember that he or she too is but a human being like the slave and that the human-made labels of "slave" and "free" merely reflect a temporary and passing order rather than the absolute value of two classes of people. Second, the instruction to masters opens very strangely, calling on the masters to "do the same" toward their slaves as Paul has enjoined on the slaves to do for their masters, namely to "render service with enthusiasm, as to the Lord . . . knowing that whatever good we do, we will receive the same again from the Lord, whether we are slaves or free" (Eph 6:7-8). This is a most stunning return to the topic of mutual subjection that opened Paul's "household code" at Ephesians 5:21, showing that it is unavoidably the guiding principle for the Christian master as well as the slave (just as it was for husband and wife).

From the perspective of twentieth-century America, one can say that it is indeed a great calamity that the authors of the New Testament did not say that slavery as an institution was reprehensible and contrary to God's order. Instead, its injunctions to slaves and masters were read by slaveholders and their pastors in antebellum America as a sign of God's approval of this institution (and it is all too apparent that they did not read everything that the New Testament had to say about how masters were to treat slaves). The liberating word was thus made an unwilling partner in the systematic debasement of a race—many of whom had become sisters and brothers in the faith! It would, however, have meant social revolution for the early, powerless Christians to announce a full frontal assault on the institution of slavery. This was a social revolution the church could not contemplate for two reasons: first, slave revolts being the most feared threat in a world where 20 to 23 percent of the population consisted of slaves, Christianity would have been exterminated instantly as a seditious threat to the order of the world; second, the fledgling church was being nurtured and grown through households, and to overthrow the constitution of the household by attacking its fundamental order would have resulted in the crash of its own support network. That considerations of the group's reputation were on the minds of the early Christian leaders is made evident from the Pastoral Epistles. Slaves are to honor their masters "so that the name of God and the teaching may not be blasphemed [i.e., slandered]" (1 Tim 6:1). Similarly, the pastor gives instructions to older women that they are to teach the younger women in the church "to love their husbands, to love their children, to be self-controlled, chaste, good managers of the household, kind, being submissive to their husbands"—in short, all the things Plutarch or Xenophon would have wished for from a wife—"so that the word of God may not be discredited" (Tit 2:3-5; see chapter two).

We should also note carefully amidst the many concessions the early church leaders made, however, the tremendous qualifications they placed on the slave-master relationship, just as they had on the wife-husband relationship. In addition to the clear statements that before God (and in Christ) there is no distinction between slave and free, and to Paul's bold prefacing of instructions to slaves and masters with that all-encompassing admonition to "be subject to one another out of reverence for Christ," the canon includes the very important letter to Philemon, a Christian slave owner. The slave Onesimus had left Philemon's house and sought out Paul, whom he knew to have a lot of influence with his master. While with Paul, he came to the faith. Now Paul sends Onesimus back (with the letter) with the hope that Philemon will release his slave to join Paul and be of help to him in prison. In the letter he includes these words: "Perhaps this is the reason he was separated from you for a while, so that you might have him back forever, no longer as a slave but more than a slave, a beloved brother—especially to me but how much more to you, both in the flesh and in the Lord" (Philem 15-16). For Christian master and Christian slave, Paul leaves no doubt that the relationship of "brother" was the fundamental one, and "slave-master" the secondary, indeed incidental one. A master could no longer treat his slave in way that would be unsuitable for one sibling to treat another.

These texts say less than liberationists would wish, but they also say far more than the supporters of hierarchies (like patriarchy) would wish—if we truly read them rather than use them as legitimation for power structures. The way in which the New Testament speaks to the institution of slavery, making so much room for a pattern of relationship that, ultimately and rightly, the church rejected as contrary to God's purposes for humanity in creation and redemption, should caution us strongly against taking its words about the role of women in the home and in the church as God's whole word on the subject. We otherwise would stand in danger of mistaking concession for command, expedience for excellence. The larger principles of mutual submission, of seeking to serve rather than to rule, of seeing others in the Spirit rather than according to the flesh are, like leaven in bread, slowly helping us to rise above the best level we could attain on our own (namely, the ethics of the pre-Christian, Greco-Roman and Jewish cultures). God cannot accomplish his whole purpose at once, for his church and the society around it cannot so quickly leave behind the "futile ways inherited from [their] ancestors" and attain the "freedom of the glory of the children of God" (1 Pet 1:18; Rom 8:21). The church has come to recognize and been bold enough to affirm that "there is no longer Jew or Greek," and eventually that "there is no longer slave or free," and in this generation is coming to understand that "there is no longer male and female" (Gal 3:28), but that all these distinctions based on the flesh and on this temporary ordering of the world are not ultimate.

Conclusion

The early Christian leaders found the recognition that God had created a new family in Christ to provide a powerful resource for the transformation of the individual believer and the formation of vital and nurturing communities of believers. The concept of having been born into a new household and a new heritage, and having been set apart from a fleshly, worldly heritage and destiny provides a powerful image for engaging in a close examination of our desires, our prejudices, our assumptions about what makes a person worthwhile, and the goals we have set for ourselves in life. It invites us to explore what the imperishable seed of the Word says about the heritage into which we have been born, and the way of life and relationship we are called to live out, and thus also to discover what "futile ways inherited from [our] ancestors" persist in our own lives and pollute our relationships and our ambitions.

The teaching of the New Testament about what it means for Christians to relate to one another as family could have a remarkable effect on the depth and fruitfulness of what we call "community." For this to happen, however, we need to answer for ourselves a basic question about whom we will regard as our family. Will we persist in thinking of blood relations as our real family and the church of God as "nice people" with whom we are happy to associate casually but who are, nevertheless, outsiders to the real family when push comes to shove? The church has an enormous opportunity, as it is instructed by its Scriptures, to realize the depth of mutual commitment, help, encouragement and healing that would come from choosing to live as a real family, related by blood—the blood of the Lamb. This begins as we speak to one another as family and make our fellow Christians feel that they can talk about any aspect of their lives freely with us as family. It continues as we respond to one another's needs as we would to a natural sister, brother, child or parent, making no distinction between the level of care we owe to a Christian sibling and the level owed natural kin. We have a tremendous opportunity before us to honor Christ by saying his blood is more important than our own in determining who shall be our family.

Our churches will be better equipped to serve as vessels of God's love and favor as we adopt and help one another in the church keep before their eyes the "ethos of kin" that Jesus, Paul and the other New Testament voices instruct Christians to take up toward one another. Many Christians are less than kin and less than kind to one another. Violations of the spirit of unity and of the command to put the interests of the other ahead of a person's own interests need to be addressed gently but forthrightly in the context of the vision the New Testament gives us of what the church could be for the believers and for the world in need of Christ. Such a vision can be a powerful motivator to individuals, who long at a deeper level to give themselves to a greater cause than themselves, and can turn the manifestations of strife, rivalry and partisanship in the church into opportunities to commit to be sisters and brothers in fact and not just in religious platitudes. For all the pain that the family of God has caused one another, there is a remedy at hand: humility, forgiveness, restoration.

The early Christians' sense of the breadth of their new family challenges modern Christians, who tend too often to think of *the* church as their own little corner of it (that is, the local church they attend, and occasionally the larger denomination of which they may be a part), to investigate the welfare of our family in places outside the local congregation. How can we find ways to live out our kinship with our sisters and brothers in other churches and other denominations? This is a way to test our willingness to place a shared love of God and Christ (and indeed, a shared experience of being loved by God and Christ) ahead of the denominational differences about which we can become so puffed up. What about our family of faith abroad? Where are the needs that beset them? How can we make our brotherhood in Christ real to them by the sharing of goods, by persistence in prayer, by emotional support and presence, and the like?

One very important area in which our growth in this kinship ethic can make a difference is in the faith of our children and youth. In the baptismal service of many denominations (chiefly those that baptize infants and small children), the congregation responds to the newly baptized by promising to do all in their power to assist the baptized in their growth in the faith. In baptism, all the children of a church become our children. It is always a grievous thing when pastors have to call time and time again for Sunday school teachers and youth group leaders—better an empty choir loft than a lack of investment on the part of mature Christians in the lives and the training of the youth in the "instruction and discipline of the Lord."[29] Our children's roots in the faith will be all the deeper, and their equipment to engage adult life as Christians all the more complete, if many adults take a keen interest in them, making opportunities to talk with them about God, about living a life that honors God, about the ways in which one can sink deep roots in God's love. Perhaps now more than ever, youth need solid Christian voices—and loyal Christian ears as well, to listen to the struggles of youth in a way that will always point them back to Jesus.

Recovery of the family of faith would be a timely response to one important facet of the postmodern paradigm, namely, the importance of relationship as a means of discovering truth. Studies of Generation X have shown relationship to be the way of reaching those born into a postmodern worldview, the way to show the reality of our faith. A church can no longer afford to be mainly a group of people who agree on propositional truths (i.e., doctrines)—all the more, as we have seen, because this trend has become a significant source of disunity and rivalry rather than cooperation and partnership—but must become a group of people committed to one another in love, loyalty and mutual support. This is no new evangelization strategy, no trendy tool, but the heart of life together in Christian community as the early Christian leaders and our Lord himself envisioned and prescribed it.

---

[29]I say this as a choir director and organist, by the way.

Seven

PURITY & POLLUTION
Structuring the World
Before a Holy God

T hroughout the Old and New Testaments, the reader will encounter words like *holy, clean, pure, undefiled, unblemished, sanctified, saints, unholy, unclean, impure, defiled, common* and the like. Perhaps some of the least popular portions of Scripture include the lengthy discussions of how purity is lost and how it is to be regained. We cannot hope, however, to understand the early church's radical reconfiguring of the Jewish purity system unless we first understand that system. Moreover, unless we can gain some sympathetic understanding concerning why purity, as even Leviticus conceives of it, would be worthwhile or important to people, the Jewish opponents of the Jesus movement and of the early church will continue to appear incomprehensible, shallow and legalistic. Perhaps the greatest loss, however, would be our inability to appreciate the new contours of purity and pollution that continue to be forces guiding, shaping and providing boundaries for the early Christians, for whom these concepts were vital elements for understanding the world in which they lived.

There are a number of factors that make purity and pollution, and the meaningfulness of making distinctions between the pure and defiled, difficult for twentieth-century people to comprehend. First, Christians have largely been instructed to see "ritual law" first as passé—something fulfilled in Christ and no longer of any meaning or importance except as it illumines the work of Jesus—and as something external, legalistic and antithetical to true religion. This perspective is the end result of the work, in the first instance, of Christian theologians and, in the second instance, of Christian polemics (beginning with Jesus' own) against early Judaism, the parent religion, in the first century and after. Our own theological location, therefore, makes an insider's understanding of purity codes and pollution taboos a long reach.

Second, Protestant Christianity has to a large extent deregulated access to God—the holy is not so powerful and dangerous as to require that only professionals have direct relations with it, but the way to God stands open for all. This has been compounded by the general effects of the Enlightenment in the Western world, which has rigorously insisted on rationalism in our understanding of the forces at work in the world and so has no room for taboos and purification rites. Few, I suspect, have the awesome appreciation of the holiness of God's presence that one finds in Isaiah's confession before the One whose train filled the temple (Is 6:1-8), or in Peter's earnest plea that Jesus, the holy One, should leave the presence of the sinful fisherman (Lk 5:8). While we may dress well for church, we do not, as a rule, take special care to avoid certain pollutions before entering the place of God's special presence (e.g., intercourse or corpse pollution). Our entrance into sacred spaces is not hedged in by a standard of purity to be attained before entering the presence of the holy One, and we frankly regard any culture that still has such regulations as primitive.

Those seeking a culturally sensitive and finely tuned reading of the New Testament, however, will need to step behind millennia of ideology to recover the internal meaningfulness of the observance of purity regulations if they are to attain an understanding of the radical rewriting of purity codes by Jesus and the early church. We will have to work especially hard in this regard, all the more as the concepts of purity and pollution were vitally meaningful to the writers of the New Testament, charged with notions of sacred power and danger. While Jesus and his disciples reviewed their inherited lines of purity and definitions of what constitutes pollution, pondering how many had been transcended in the cross and resurrection, they were also deeply engaged in creatively redrawing those lines and reframing those definitions for life in the new people God was calling out and bringing together in Jesus. These concepts were still essential for the creation and maintenance of group boundaries, ethos and identity as the "holy people," the "saints" or "holy ones."

Purity codes are a way of talking about what is proper for a certain place and a certain time (however one's society fills in the content). Pollution is a label attached to whatever is out of place with regard to the society's view of an orderly and safe world. Purity has to do with drawing the lines that give definition to the world around us, distinguishing, for example, what belongs to an individual from what belongs to others, and then defending these lines from being crossed by unwelcome forces. We will feel that the Jewish and Greco-Roman worlds with their aversions toward defilement and regulations for purity are less completely foreign if we come to understand that while we would never use the words ourselves, we still interact with our world in ways deeply reminiscent of purity codes and fear of pollution. As we look into our own lives and ask what sorts of lines we hold dear, or consider what boundaries we are heavily invested in keeping solid, or ponder what sorts of things or persons we respond to as being out of place, we discover that we carry about within us a purity code that is every bit as complex as that articulated in Leviticus. The underlying rationales we project onto our codes are completely different, of course, from the ones we encounter in the first century, but the dynamics are strikingly similar and merit some consideration as a point of entry into that cultural context.

Mary Douglas, a pioneering anthropologist, gives us a place to start our reflections by comparing pollution with our concept of "dirt."[1] Soil outside the house is proper and the way things ought to be. A clump of dirt in the middle of a living room would be considered out of place and would prompt a series of acts designed to remove the dirt from where it ought not to be.[2] Our reaction to seeing a pile of mud in the middle of our houses may even be emotional, but it is based on the gut-level con-

---

[1]Mary Douglas, *Purity and Danger* (London: Routledge & Kegan Paul, 1966), p. 35.

[2]Why do we not leave the soil in the middle of the living room? Why do we spend so much energy cleaning our houses, whether removing layers of dust, vacuuming crumbs or wiping smudges off windows? It is not sufficient to say that we do this because "that's the way we're supposed to do things," although the fact that so many of us could not consider doing otherwise is instructive of how deeply ingrained these codes are. I can only speculate, but I think it has something to do with our desire to create a space that is free from the undomesticated forces of nature, particularly the forces of decay that soil represents rather directly. People in the Western world abhor the idea of living in homes with mud floors, I suspect, not because it would be uncomfortable but because it would not allow for the distinction between uncontrollable nature and controllable culture.

viction that a boundary has been crossed that ought not to have been. To continue with this train of thought, we might observe how many people enact a brief ritual as they enter interior space from the outside, namely wiping off their shoes or even removing them. We may even follow different customs in our homes—for some, wiping off the shoes is sufficient, but for others the removal of the shoes is required to keep the inside space pure.

Watching how people handle their food is an especially fruitful way to discover their purity codes and the places where defilement threatens to creep into their lives. Food spread out over the kitchen counter (while one is preparing dinner, for example) is clean and in its proper place. Food might even be able to enter the living room if it is properly contained. If the food, however, were spread out over the staircase, we would see it as "unclean" and polluting—we would cleanse the stairs and probably dispose of the food as "defiled" as well. Eating out poses many threats to a person's purity, hence the proliferation of hand sanitizers, the care taken not to eat what falls onto the bare table or the floor, and the inspection of the silverware for particles of food left from the last meal.

We may briefly consider our aversions to the bodily discharges and other biological byproducts of our fellow humans. We may change our gait specifically to avoid stepping in a drop of spit on the sidewalk—not because the spit is likely to pass on some disease to us but merely because it is out of place and does not belong even on the soles of our shoes. We take great care not to contact urine or feces (even our own) and regard the blood or semen of another person as an automatic pollution.[3] But some people take even greater pains to avoid physical contact with any surface on which another human being may have left some "pollutant," handling doorknobs with a tissue, taking pains not to touch a public toilet and the like. The main reasons, I suspect, for most of our food and bodily fluid codes would be couched in medical terminology. Defilement for us has become largely microbial.

These codes, however, also have a significant social component even if the underlying rationale is medical. A person who is fastidious about antimicrobial precautions would probably not feel comfortable eating at

---

[3]A notable difference between our notions of pollution and the ancient Israelite notions is that, for us, only the substance is polluting whereas, for the Jew, the person with the discharge would also be unclean and capable of communicating uncleanness.

the home of someone who is much less cautious about such things, and so social boundaries between people would be formed on the basis of adherence to or nonadherence to certain standards of purity.

In our world, this does not only apply to things like food and dirt. It also applies to times and seasons. We too separate family time from work time, vacation time from time on the job, weekends from weekdays. We offer extra inducements to people to violate the purity of time, paying double on holidays or time-and-a-half after the workday is properly finished. We may be reluctant to call someone at home about a business matter, or perturbed when someone calls us about the same during family time. There is a sense of pollution or violation of that time set apart for family.

We also have purity codes involving people. People of different races or classes often view one another as off limits with regard to dating and marriage. "Mixed" couples face a tremendous amount of prejudice because of a widely held perception that an important boundary is being crossed, even though no satisfactory rationale for maintaining that boundary can be given. An extreme case would involve the homeless in our society. Living in and around Atlanta and New York, I witnessed many homeless people, and I witnessed the interactions of domiciled people with the homeless. Simply put, most people avoided interaction with them at all costs. Rarely would a person even look at a homeless person, let alone talk to one or eat with one. The homeless are people who have lost their place in society—they now have no "proper" place and so are regarded as virtually unclean. Living in the public places, they are out of place and their presence is regarded by many as "defiling" the public spaces. One's first reaction to a homeless person may be to ponder the lack of rigor with regard to hygiene, to speculate about the diseases the person may be carrying, and therefore to have a strong aversion to giving one the right hand of fellowship or the kiss of peace.

It is likely that many will not uniformly see their own codes reflected in the above discussion, but I hope that it will stimulate you to reflect on the lines you defend, the pollutions against which you guard yourself, and the "purification rituals" you pursue where pollution is incurred. This will help cross the cultural chasm between us and the writers of the New Testament (to say nothing of the compilers of the Torah) as well as allow us to see what lines Jesus might challenge us to cross in order to fulfill the royal law of love. I ceased to despise the Pharisees' lack of compassion long ago (or, rather, I came to see how much I had in common with them), when I was confronted with my own purity codes and the separateness from other classes of people I was conditioned from birth to observe!

Defining Holiness, Purity and Pollution

So far I have described purity and pollution more or less metaphorically for an era in which the terms themselves have lost most of their power and affect. Arriving at definitions is more difficult, since the terms refer largely to the irrational powers inherent in things that humans have intuited and regulated but not rationally defended and organized. Mary Douglas has probably done more than any other researcher to explain the meaning and significance of purity and pollution within human cultures, working mainly as an anthropologist observing living tribes but also crossing over into detailed studies of Leviticus. She begins by looking at the notion of "dirt," which is simply "matter out of place."[4] For something to be even considered dirt in the first place, there must be some system in place that lays out the natural order of things that is being violated by this dirt.[5] Societies of human beings create such a system and then continue to interpret their experiences and world through it as a result of "reflection in the relation of order to disorder, being to non-being, form to formlessness, life to death." In effect, every removal of dirt affirms the meaningfulness of the system, since an individual is acting out and thus reinforcing for himself or herself the conviction that there is a proper place for the substance in question and an improper place for that substance where it becomes "pollution"—and the dirt is now being removed from the improper place. Purity, then, is fundamentally concerned with the ordering of the world and making sense of one's everyday experiences in light of that order, which is usually conceived of as being a divine ordering of the cosmos (and thus "the way things are and have to be"). It tells us "what and who belong when and where,"[6] and thus enables us to know when order is being maintained and when something is out of place.

A closely related concept (indeed, the concept that governs and neces-

---

[4]Douglas, *Purity and Danger*, p. 35.
[5]Ibid., p. 41.
[6]Jerome H. Neyrey, "The Idea of Purity in Mark's Gospel," *Semeia* 35 (1986): 93.

sitates considerations of purity and pollution in ancient Israel at least) is that of holiness. This concept is especially difficult to define since by its very nature it is removed from the sphere of the ordinary, the describable, the definable. The "holy" is set apart from the everyday. It is that which is whole, complete and perfect[7] and therefore stands out as something "other" and awe-inspiring. One recognizes the sacred or holy by the sense of its being charged with power either for blessing or destruction. Friedrich Hauck distinguishes two aspects of the conceptualization of what we might call the "sacred" or "holy," whether in primitive cultures, in Greek culture or, we might add, in Jewish culture.[8] Many events connected with the life process (like birth, death and sexual intercourse) are thought to be "filled with power" (taboo). This power, however, is dangerous and makes the one who participates in, or contacts those who participate in, such events dangerous as well. Purification rites are necessary to dispel this power and contain the danger. On another level, however, the holy is thought to be "friendly and benevolent," such that contact and interaction with the divine is desirable. If propitious, it can send creative power into the processes of society and cultivation so that families and crops reproduce in safety.

It is this combination of potential danger and potential blessing—shared by Jew and Gentile in the ancient world![9]—that gives rise to the conviction that the holy can only be approached with care on the part of the members of the society.[10] "To be able to enter into dealings with deity, human beings must set themselves in a fitting, higher state. They must accept purifications to remove or wash away what is unclean," namely, that which "conflicts with the deity."[11] Both in the Greco-Roman world and to a much more rigorous extent in the Jewish world, there is

---

[7]Douglas, *Purity and Danger*, p. 54.
[8]Friedrich Hauck and Rudolf Meyer, "*Katharos*, etc.," TDNT 3.413-31, pp. 414-15.
[9]I emphasize this now since there is a marked tendency to ignore the importance of purity codes and pollution taboos in the Greco-Roman world and to focus solely on Jewish purity maps. New Testament authors were able, however, to connect with both Jewish Christians and Gentile Christians rather directly as they spoke of purity codes and invoked pollution taboos.
[10]The Persian king Artazerxes, for example, orders that the rituals in the restored temple in Jerusalem are to be performed as meticulously as God ordained them so as to avoid divine wrath coming on the "kingdom of the king." Even a pagan king could thus fear the holiness of a shrine to what he would have considered a local, tribal divinity for fear of the dangers of sacrilege pollution (1 Esd 8:21).
[11]Hauck and Meyer, "*Katharos*, etc.," p. 415.

the conviction that the person who would be close to God must be pure
and whole like God. Defilement and unwholeness separated people from
contact with the pure and whole God.[12] Thus the blemished and
deformed persons are barred from access to the sanctuary, since it would
affront holiness to be presented with unwholeness. The blemished or
deformed animal is likewise barred from sacrifice, since such unwholeness would provoke rather than please the holy deity. Most sources of
defilement or pollution, moreover, stem from some condition that betrays
the unwholeness of a person or creature (skin diseases, bodily discharges,
corpses), and it is essential to contain and eliminate pollution before
entering the presence of the divine.

Thus we can begin to understand why defilement and pollution
should be viewed as negative, undesirable and something to be avoided
or, if incurred, quickly remedied. Pollution is dangerous in the presence
of a holy God. It disqualifies the person from entering that presence and
fellowship and, should he or she be foolish enough to stand before the
holy God in an unclean state, threatens obliteration. It entails the loss of
privilege (or absence of privilege) and hence is a dishonorable condition.
Defilement means that a line inscribed in God's ordering of the cosmos
has been transgressed, and such disruption of God's order contains
within it the potential for provoking unseen power that may react in a
hostile and destructive way.

Cultures like ancient Israel, then, draw extensive lines of purity, of
clean and unclean, in an attempt to create a model of God's cosmic order
and to help an individual locate his or her place in that order so that the
person may know when pollution has been contracted and what needs to
be done to dispel it, so that access to the holy God and his benefits will
remain open. These lines, and concern with remaining pure or returning
to a state of purity with regard to these lines, serve central social functions

---

[12]Frederick W. Danker cites Plato *Laws* 4.716C-D: "God, it must be granted, is the measure of
all things, and certainly, as everyone would affirm, in a sense far higher than is true of any
human being. Whoever, then, would be the friend of such a Being must certainly strive in
every way to be like him. . . . The bad person is impure *(akáthartos)* in his very being,
whereas the good person is pure *(katharos)*; and it is not right for either God or a good person to receive gifts from one who is polluted" (*Benefactor: Epigraphic Study of a Graeco-
Roman and New Testament Semantic Field* [St. Louis: Clayton, 1982], pp. 355-56). Taking
purity language already in a strictly ethical direction, Plato expresses the conviction that
the one who would be close to God must be pure and whole like God, and that defilement
and unwholeness separates one from contact with the pure and whole God.

for the maintenance of a culture. Purity issues undergird morality and the ethos of a group, identify the boundaries of the group, protect the social group from erosion from without the group, and create internal lines within the group, giving structure and hierarchy to the group. These social effects must never be lost to view, even while pondering the theological or ideological rationales for the regulations.

Purity and Pollution in the Greco-Roman World and Literary Sources

Although largely regulated by what we might call rational law, Greek culture was also pervaded with pollution taboos. Through these taboos the society identified conditions that were especially dangerous in light of the sacral energy they produced and the attention of spiritual entities they attracted. Birth, death, sexual activity, murder, sacrilege and madness are all notable examples of polluting conditions or events.[13] A number of these conditions are not indicative of moral failure, such as giving birth, dying, incurring a debilitating mental condition and participating in the perpetuation of the human race. The attention given to murder, as well as to other generally taboo acts like incest and parricide, as pollution shows how pollution beliefs reinforced ethics at some important junctures. In such cases the pollution was considered sufficiently serious as to merit the attention of the avenging gods. The danger of pollution is especially pronounced here, since it was presumed that unseen forces would work to bring about the demise of the murderer or violator of some other ethical taboo. The Greeks did not regard this vengeance as individualistic either—an unpunished murderer could lead to divine anger being focused on an entire city.[14] If transgression of some moral norm did not provoke public outrage, invoking the danger of pollution for the whole community could rally interest in correcting the wrong or punishing the

---

[13]Robert C. T. Parker, "Pollution, the Greek Concept of," in *The Oxford Companion to Classical Civilization*, ed. Simon Hornblower and Antony Spawforth (Oxford: Oxford University Press, 1998), p. 553. Friedrich Hauck ("*miainō*, etc.," *TDNT* 4.644-47, p. 645) gathers references to pregnancy, childbirth, menstruation, corpses, tombs and, for the Pythagoreans, eating of animals (because the meat is dead flesh) as pollutants in various sectors of the Greco-Roman world.

[14]Parker, "Pollution," p. 554. Parker gives as an example a question posed to an oracle at Dodona: "Is it because of a mortal's pollution that we are suffering the storm?" (SEG 19.427), as well as a reference to the classical Greek orator Antiphon: "According to Antiphon's *Tetralogies*, for instance, murder pollution threatens the victim's kin until they seek vengeance or prosecute, the jurors until they convict. Thus the threat of pollution encourages action to put right the disorder."

wrongdoer, as well as deterring wrongdoing in the first place.[15]

The dynamics of murder pollution and its purification drive what is perhaps the most famous Greek tragedy, Sophocles' *Oedipus the King*.[16] The city of Thebes is suffering plague because it has been polluted by the presence of a murderer who has gone unpunished (*Oed.* 95-101). Expelling the polluting presence either by execution or exile will cleanse the city and end the plague. The opening scenes of the drama thus attest to the use of purity and pollution language to uphold justice and morality, as well as to the great danger to the common good (and the individual good, since the defiled one must be eliminated) inherent in pollution. King Oedipus makes it his own mission to "drive pollution from the land" (*Oed.* 136), and, of course, the prophet Teiresias must reveal to him: "You are the land's pollution" (*Oed.* 353). As the drama unfolds, Teiresias' words are proven true, leading to Oedipus' self-blinding. He laments that he was allowed to survive infancy, to become "a child of impurity" (*Oed.* 1360). Finally, Creon tells him to go inside the palace, away from the public view, if not out of "shame before the face of men" than at least out of "reverence" for the Sun: "Do not show unveiled to him pollution that neither land nor holy rain nor light of day can welcome" (*Oed.* 1423-29).

From here, the terminology can be applied as a sanction promoting or prohibiting a wide variety of behaviors, as in the sequel drama *Oedipus at Colonus* (280-84). Oedipus labels the citizens' intent to cast him out after promising him hospitality "unholy," a "blot" or "stain" on their city's reputation if they carry it out. Greek and Latin ethical philosophers take up the language of pollution to dissuade people from vice, as when Epictetus urges his students not to defile the indwelling deity "with unclean thoughts and filthy actions" (*Diss.* 2.8.13).[17]

In addition to a wide range of pollution taboos covering both natural and ethical phenomena, the Greek society also observed distinctions between sacred space and common space, the former being highly

---

[15]Douglas, *Purity and Danger*, p. 133. Murder as a pollution that threatens those who allow a murderer to escape justice is also prominent in Plato's *Euthyphro* 4B-C: "It is ridiculous, Socrates, for you to think that it makes any difference whether the victim is a stranger or a relative. . . . The pollution is the same if you knowingly keep company with such a man [i.e., the killer] and do not cleanse yourself and him by bringing him to justice" (Plato, *The Trial and Death of Socrates*, trans. G. M. A. Grube [Indianapolis: Hackett, 1975]).

[16]Quotations are taken from Sophocles, *Oedipus* and *Oedipus at Colonus* (David Greene and Richmond Lattimore, eds., *Sophocles I* [New York: Pocket Books, 1967]).

[17]Reference given in Friedrich Hauck, "*molunō, molusmos*," *TDNT* 4.736-37.

restricted because the designated space was held to be the special ground of a particular deity, the latter being ordinary space accessible to mortals. While the map of sacred space promoted by the canonical traditions of Judaism centered on a single sacred site, namely, the temple in Jerusalem, Greek and Roman purity maps had sanctuaries and holy places throughout the land, much as the Canaanite religion to which Israel so frequently reverted throughout its history had "high places."[18] Nevertheless, both cultures understood the danger of encroachment, that is, unauthorized people trespassing into sacred spaces. Once again, this kind of transgression of a taboo placed not only the offender but also the surrounding area under the threat of divine vengeance unless reparations were successfully made.

Again the second play in the Oedipus trilogy provides an excellent example. At a pause in his endless wandering (now as a blinded beggar), Oedipus sits down to rest in a sacred grove. When a stranger encounters him, his first words are: "First move from where you sit; the place is holy; It is forbidden to walk upon that ground. . . . It is not to be touched, no one may live upon it; Most dreadful are its divinities, most feared" (*Col.* 36-40). The Chorus of citizens of Colonus arrives, censures Oedipus for profaning the sacred grove, and then explains the elaborate rite of expiation for the profanation of the sacred grove, making amends to the Eumenides with ritual libations and prayers (*Col.* 466-490).

Entrance to sacred shrines required that the visitor obey the purification requirements specific to the shrine. Without a centralized cult, these tended to vary considerably. Giving birth, sexual intercourse and contact with a corpse rendered a person impure. Persons with pollution of such kinds might be instructed to wait a full day or two before entering the sacred precincts, and all might be required to perform certain ritual washings of their hands, feet or whole bodies.[19] Some shrines might even pre-

---

[18]Which was a persistent problem throughout the period of Israel's monarchy—local sacred sites die hard!

[19]Parker, "Pollution," p. 553. Everett Ferguson gives an example of such an inscription at the temple of Athena in Pergamum: "Whoever wishes to visit the temple of the goddess . . . must refrain from intercourse with his wife (or husband) that day, from intercourse with another than his wife (or husband) for the preceding two days, and must complete the required lustrations. The same prohibition applies to contact with the dead and with the delivery of a woman in childbirth" (*Backgrounds of Early Christianity* [Grand Rapids, Mich.: Eerdmans, 1993], pp. 174-75).

scribe clothing and the way hair was to be worn.[20] Not all such purity requirements were external. A law in Lindos stipulated moral purity for those who would enter a temple: "It is of primary importance that those who enter be pure and sound in hands and mind and have no guilt on their conscience."[21] Those who functioned as priests—that is, the mediators between gods and people—had more intense rules governing the purity they were to maintain for their service in sacred places.

Greeks and Romans had fully developed sacrificial systems. Individuals might bring an animal to a deity's temple for sacrifice, perhaps to show gratitude for a favor received, perhaps as an inducement to the divinity to grant a petition that would be uttered during the sacrifice.[22] There were also public sacrifices performed on behalf of the whole city and even the province, which were frequently occasions of civic celebration and public feasting. The sacrifice began with the participants purifying their hands while hair was cut from the animal and burnt on an altar. At this point the officiant would offer a prayer, specifying the favor that was requested or expressing the cause of the sacrificial act (e.g., thanksgiving). The animal was then killed and its entrails examined (the condition of which revealed whether or not it was accepted). Finally, the meat was divided. The gods' portion was burnt (and thus transferred to the divine realm), the priests received a portion (which they might sell in the market), and the worshipers shared the rest either in a banquet at the temple or at home.[23]

Sacrifice in Rome and her colonies followed a similar practice. The Roman rites appear particularly to have affirmed the gods' superiority to

---

[20]According to Ferguson a woman's hair might be required to be worn loose and a man's head to be uncovered (*Backgrounds*, p. 175).

[21]From an inscription (SEG 983.4-7) cited in Danker, *Benefactor*, p. 356. One might compare this with the emphasis in the letter to the Hebrews on the importance of cleansing the "conscience" (the same noun is used) as a prerequisite for entering God's presence.

[22]Robert C. T. Parker, "Sacrifice, Greek," in *The Oxford Companion to Classical Civilization*, Simon Hornblower and Antony Spawforth (Oxford: Oxford University Press, 1998), p. 628; see also Ferguson, *Backgrounds*, p. 179. This last aspect is emphasized in Plato *Euthyphr.* 14C-E, where Socrates sums up Euthyphro's view of piety thus: "To sacrifice is to make a gift to the gods, whereas to pray is to beg from the gods? . . . It would follow from this view that piety would be a knowledge of how to give to, and beg from, the gods, . . . a sort of trading skill between gods and men."

[23]Parker, "Sacrifice," p. 628. He refers the interested reader to the lengthy description of a sacrifice in Homer *Od.* 3.430-63. As one of the foundational texts for Greek religion and culture, this passage might be expected to reflect the practice followed in Greek rites.

human beings in a number of ways. First, the gods' portion was consumed first (by fire) before any mortal took a share in the animal. Second, the portions reserved for the gods, as well as the offering of incense and pure wine with the meat, spoke to the gods' privilege above mortals.[24]

This cursory introduction to the presence of pollution taboos, purification rites, designation of sacred spaces and exposure to the dynamics of sacrifices suffices to assure us that the Gentile understood the significance of purity codes and the dangers of pollution vis-à-vis the holy. While the New Testament authors are predominantly dealing with the reworking of Jewish purity codes, we can be sure that the significance and impact of their discussions would not be lost on Gentile Christians. Both Jew and Gentile are being educated into a new set of purity maps and pollution taboos as they are socialized into the Christian culture, but for both, "holy," "pure" and "defiled" will be deeply meaningful ways of organizing their experience and defining what is suitable for the Christian body. We turn now to those specific purity maps that provide the immediate background for Jesus' ministry and the early Christian movement.

Purity and Pollution, the Holy and Profane in the Jewish World

God specifically ordered Aaron to "distinguish between the holy and the common, and between the unclean and the clean," and to teach the people how to do the same so as to observe God's commandments regarding holiness and purity (Lev 10:10). This verse introduces us to the two main pairs of terms used within Israel to construct its purity maps. Each pair has a neutral term and a marked term. *Common* (or *profane*) is a neutral term, referring to the ordinary spaces and things of the world that are accessible to human beings. *Holy* is the corresponding marked term, referring to special spaces or things that have been "set apart" from the ordinary (the common) as belonging in some special way to God. *Clean* is a neutral term, referring generally to a person or thing in its normal state. "That which is clean may be thought of as that which is in its proper place within the boundaries established by God in creation, and whose own external boundaries are whole and intact."[25] A person who

---

[24]John Scheid, "Sacrifice, Roman," in *The Oxford Companion to Classical Civilization,* ed. Simon Hornblower and Antony Spawforth, (Oxford: Oxford University Press, 1998), p. 631.

[25]Richard P. Nelson, *Raising Up a Faithful Priest: Community and Priesthood in Biblical Theology* (Louisville: Westminster John Knox, 1993), p. 21.

was "whole," who suffered no discharges or erosion of the skin surfaces, was "clean." An animal that fit within the proper categories for its living environment was "clean." *Unclean* is the corresponding marked term, denoting that something has crossed the line from the normal state into a dangerous state of pollution.[26] Breaches of boundaries rendered something unclean, as when a person had a discharge or a torn surface (leprosy, for example), or when an animal combined characteristics thought to be proper to different environments (like lobsters, who lived in the sea but walked on legs). One would use a category from each pair to describe any single object or person. The typical lay Israelite would be "clean" and "common" most of the time. If he or she incurred defilement, he or she would become "unclean" and "common." The tithes collected for the priests were "clean" and "holy," while food sold in the market was (supposed to be) "clean" and "common." The food tithes were thus to be eaten only by the holy priests in a state of "cleanness," and if the common lay Israelite ate of them, he or she would "profane" what was holy and risk divine wrath.[27] A graveyard was "unclean" and "common," while the temple precincts were "clean" and "holy."

The one combination that would be especially problematic is "unclean" and "holy." Under special circumstances the same substance could be both (for example, the ashes of the red heifer in Num 19). It is more common to see these two marked terms as being incompatible and, in fact, a dangerous combination.[28] We find throughout Torah, and literature reflecting an interest in Torah observance, a strong commitment to the sanctification of the holy, that is, the preservation of the holy from being profaned and used as common, or from being brought into contact with the impure (the "unclean"). In this way, the source of holiness, God, would continue to show favor toward Israel and would not be provoked either to withdraw from the people or consume them.

We should pause at this point to emphasize that for the Jew at the turn

---

[26]David P. Wright and Robert Hodgson Jr., "Holiness," in *ABD*, ed. David N. Freedman (New York: Doubleday, 1992), pp. 246-47.

[27]See, for example, the apocryphal book of Judith. Judith, the Jewish heroine of the story, tells Holofernes, the general of Nebuchadnezzar and the archvillain of the story, that God is going to hand the Jews besieged in Bethulia over to the general on account of their eating of the tithes in their desperation. The sacrilege pollution will result in punishment (Jdt 11:12-13).

[28]Nelson, *Raising Up*, p. 33; Jacob Milgrom, *Leviticus I-XVI*, AB (New York: Doubleday, 1991), p. 732.

of the era, there was no distinction between moral and ritual law. Idolatry, sexual perversity and failure to keep the dietary laws (*kashrut* regulations) were all pollutions for which the land would vomit forth its inhabitants. The separation of moral law from cultic law was a Christian innovation developed to negotiate the fact that Christians claimed the Old Testament to be authoritative, yet regarded a large portion of its legislation—the cultic law—to be irrelevant. For non-Christian Jews, however, it was all equally "law of God," and purity and pollution concerns thus ran throughout the whole law, enforcing both ritual and ethical cleanness, the requirement for living in the presence of a holy God.

It was a core conviction of Israelite and early Jewish religion that the one holy God lived in the midst of his special people—the people he had selected from all the nations of the earth to be a "special possession" (Deut 4:20; 7:6, my translation). The presence of the holy One in their midst gave access to great benefits: the availability of divine power for the protection of the people, the increase of the produce, the preservation of peace and the security of the nation (see Lev 26:3-12). These benefits would be enjoyed as long as the people collectively did their part to respect the holiness God requires of those who serve him and the sacred places where that service occurs, and as they maintained the purity required of those who dwell in the land, especially when they approached the temple (but even when they remained far away). "The LORD has rewarded me according to my righteousness; according to the cleanness of my hands he recompensed me" (Ps 18:20, my translation; see 18:21-24). Observing the divine regulations for purity led to the expectation, and in this psalm the celebration, of God's favor.

Corresponding to the potential benefit of the power of the holy in the midst of the people is the potential danger of the holy should the people not respect the holiness of God. Sacrilege and profanation of holy things were expected to bring disaster for the perpetrators and possibly even their race. Confronting the holy with the unclean "generated an incompatible and dangerous combination."[29] Just as Leviticus 25:3-12 detailed the benefits that would accrue to Israel as she observed God's purity regulations, so Leviticus 26:14-33 detailed at greater length the disasters that would overtake Israel if the people refused to observe God's commandments. Indeed, the Israelites were told that the former inhabitants

---

[29]Nelson, *Raising Up*, p. 33.

of the Holy Land were being expelled and destroyed specifically because of their uncleanness (Lev 18:24-25, 27; 20:22-23). God's holy land was defiled by their practices and so "vomited them out."

The familiar story of Isaiah's prophetic commissioning in Isaiah 6:1-8 is a stunning example first of the awesomeness of the experience of the holy and then of the vital and overwhelming sense of danger and dread that overtakes the unclean one who enters the presence of the holy God: "Woe is me! I am lost, for I am a man of unclean lips, and I live among a people of unclean lips; yet my eyes have seen the King, the LORD of hosts" (Is 6:5). Isaiah has crossed too far into the presence of holiness, given his state of uncleanness, notably conceived here in terms of ethical pollution (false speech). Rather than be consumed by God's holiness, Isaiah is cleansed from his pollution by God's seraph. The unclean people in the midst of whom he lives will not, however, heed Isaiah's message and be cleansed by repentance, with the result that God will drive them out of his holy land, even as Leviticus had admonished.

The Purity Maps of Torah and Early Judaism

Having some sense now of the power of the holy, and the importance of distinguishing between what is clean and unclean so as not to provoke the holy with the latter, we are in a position to consider the purity maps of Israel by which holy and common, clean and unclean, were identified and negotiated. Since pollution happens when a boundary is crossed that should not be crossed, it is essential to know where the lines and gradients are so that one can avoid them or, having crossed them, know how to return to a state of cleanness. These maps involve persons, places, times, foods and the physical body of the individual. One essential aspect of these maps to watch out for is their mutual reinforcements or correlations. Once these are understood, the purity codes of Torah cease to be a jumble of random and incomprehensible rules and become an orderly system by which Israel's distinctive identity in the midst of the nations is modeled and preserved.

Maps of people. Israelites are distinguished from non-Israelites in terms of purity. The former are "a holy people and blameless race" (Wis 10:15), set apart by the holy God to be his special possession among the nations. The Gentiles, as a rule, practiced abominations, as did the Canaanites, whom the holy land "vomited out" on account of their defilement and abominations (Lev 18:24-30), and so are themselves off the purity map altogether as long as they practice idolatry and the other polluting practices that God hates. There is thus an important, boldface line drawn around Israel, circumscribing it from association with the practitioners of abomination.[30] The rite of circumcision—a religious rather than a medical procedure in Israel—comes to inscribe on the body of the male Jew this distinctiveness from the Gentiles. Gentiles are not excluded from the people of God, but they must enter it not only by putting away their idols but also by accepting circumcision (as does Achior the Ammonite in Jdt 14:10).

Within Israel there were many gradations of holiness—an internal hierarchy based on access to the holy God in his holy temple. At the top of this hierarchy stood the high priest, then the priests in general and, third, the Levites (the descendants of Levi who had been set apart to care for the tabernacle, to provide music for services and the like). The priests, and especially the high priest, had to observe especially stringent rules of purity on account of their greater and frequent access to the holy things of God's temple and the holy places where God dwelt in a special way (see Lev 21:1-15). As people who were constantly moving between the realm of the holy and the profane, between God and humankind, they had to maintain a state of cleanness (or purity) in order to fulfill their duties. Along with the privilege of being, in effect, the elite of Israel on account of brokering access to the divine, came the added risks and responsibilities (seen, e.g., in the deaths of Nadab and Abihu, two of Aaron's sons).[31]

The lay Israelites were "holy to the Lord" as part of the people of God's special possession, to be sure, but they were not as holy as the priests, who had been set apart within the holy people for special service and

---

[30]The attention given to, and actions taken against, intermarriage between Jews and Gentiles is one facet of the importance of maintaining the boundary between Israel and the nations. The book of Ezra and literature associated with it (Neh and 1 Esd) censure the marriage of Israelites to non-Israelite wives as a violation of the Deuteronomic pollution taboo against intermarriage with the natives of Canaan who had polluted the holy land. The mass divorces (and disowning of the children of such unions) undertaken as part of Ezra's reforms is thus a purifying of the people and a reinforcement of the Jew-Gentile boundary (1 Esd 8:68-70, 82-85, 92-95; 9:7-9, 36; see also Ezra and chapter five of this book). This boundary was reinforced every time Ezra was read.

[31]It is noteworthy, however, that priests did not regard themselves as contaminated by contact with a nonpriest in and of itself, as long as the nonpriest was not carrying some pollution (e.g., from a seminal emission or contact with a corpse). "There are classes of defilement, but no class of persons are more defiling than others" (Mary Douglas, "Atonement in Leviticus," *JSQ* 1 [1993-1994]: 112).

access to God. The lay Israelite male's access to the holy places was thus limited to the courtyard beyond the holy places, which they would enter in a "clean" state. The priests did not bar their access to God but rather facilitated their safe interacting with the beneficent and yet dangerous center of holiness. Israelite women were unclean one quarter of their adult lives on account of menstruation (seven days of uncleanness each month), with the result that their access to the holy places was even more limited. Finally, those whose Israelite lineage could not be verified, and those (males) whose reproductive organs were damaged, were in the outer margins of Israel's purity map.[32] Those "born of an illicit union" (Deut 23:2) and their descendents to the tenth generation were barred from the congregation.

There is thus a deeply engraved map of persons with regard to holiness. Gentiles tend to be removed from the map entirely, and the boundary between Jew and Gentile is especially important to maintain so that the holiness of the Jewish race remains intact. There are also lines of holiness gradients within Israel, mirrored in the architecture of the temple itself. Greater status and privilege attended those closer to the top (or perhaps center) of this holiness map, with a carefully drawn margin at the periphery for those whose genealogical "wholeness" (hence holiness) was in question.

Maps of spaces. At the center of the Jewish map of the world stood Jerusalem, God's holy mountain, at the center of which stood the temple, a copy of the "holy tent" in the "holy heavens" (Wis 9:8-10). The temple was the place where the sphere of human action intersected with the sphere of God's realm: the holy places were a sort of overlapping area where these two spheres coexisted and thus where transactions (such as sacrifices) between the two spheres became possible. The temple's heart was the holy of holies, the place on earth where God (who was known to inhabit the cosmos and not be limited to a stone building) was accessible in a special and immediate way. Only the high priest would enter this room, and that only once a year on the Day of Atonement. The chamber leading to the holy of holies was called the holy place, in which priests could perform ministrations at the altar of incense or sprinkle the blood of sacrifices as necessary. Also within the priests' purview was the outside altar, the place where sacrifices occurred. Outside the priests' court-

---

[32]Neyrey, "Idea of Purity," pp. 95-96.

yard would be found the courtyard of Israelite men, the courtyard of Israelite women, and finally, at the outside, the court of the Gentiles, where foreigners could worship the God of Israel.

The holiness of the temple as sacred space, and hence the sense of power and danger that emanated from it, is difficult for twenty-first century people to imagine. Unauthorized entrance of the holy places was fully expected, however, to bring death to the encroacher—even to the non-priest who threatened to treat the holy places as accessible to himself or herself. The stories of Gentile governors or kings who attempted to enter the holy places but were repulsed and chastened by the unseen hand of God are vivid expressions of this belief (see 2 Macc 3; 5:15-20; 9:1-28; 3 Macc 1:8—2:24; 4 Macc 3:20—4:14).

The city that housed the temple, Jerusalem, was also considered holy. Indeed, the Qumran sect believed that special rules of purity needed to be observed by the inhabitants of the city on account of the presence of the temple in it (such as abstinence from sexual intercourse while in the city). The land in which the temple sat, that is, the land in which God had chosen to dwell in a special way, was also holy. This was attested in Leviticus 18 and 20—God did not cast all Gentile sinners out of all lands but only out of the land he had set apart as holy. The lands outside of Israel (that is, Gentile lands) would be considered common. A person was not defiled simply by being away from Palestine, but the lands of the Gentiles were not the lands of God's holiness. They were, moreover, full of abominable practices, so that one had to be especially on guard against involvement in the pollution of the inhabitants of the lands (such as idolatry). Keeping boundary lines visible and intact in the Diaspora was especially important, since the Jews had to maintain obedience to God's law and observance of purity regulations in an environment that was rife with opportunities for pollution.

Maps of time. The sabbath, or seventh day of the week, was set apart as a holy day. It was not to be profaned (treated as common or ordinary) by working on that day, that is, by bringing the activity of the other six days into the sacred time of the seventh day. The severe penalties for profaning the sabbath (nothing short of death; see Ex 31:12-17) shows the importance of this sacred time as a marker of the social identity of the Jewish people. Indeed, it was one of the marks of the Jew that outsiders knew about, together with circumcision and avoidance of pork, hence a mark that clearly functioned to "set apart" the people of Israel from the nations around them. In a world without weekends, the sabbath was truly distinctive. Of the two rationales given in Torah for keeping the sabbath holy, the first is by far the most prominent. This rationale grounds sabbath observance in God's own activity. God worked for six days to create the universe and then rested on the seventh day, thus setting it apart (making it holy). Keeping the sabbath is a sort of witness to the world that this one God created all things. It is also an essential element of Israel's falling in line with God's order and rhythms to rest on the seventh day (Gen 2:1-3; Ex 20:8-11; 31:15, 17).[33]

Israel observed other sacred days, like Passover, the week-long Festival of Booths, the Day of Atonement and Rosh ha-Shanah, but the sabbath was by far the most important sacred time, the most visible sign of the Jew's distinctiveness, and therefore, not surprisingly, a frequent point of contention between Jews (like Jesus and the Pharisees).

Dietary regulations. One of the better known aspects of Jewish purity codes and pollution taboos are the food laws of Torah. Food is something that a Jew would have to encounter daily; moreover, it was also one of the more important reminders of his or her distinctiveness and "set-apartness" for God that was built into the purity system of Torah.

Animal blood was a holy substance and was strictly forbidden to the Israelite, even to the priest (Lev 17:10-14; Deut 12:16). Since it was held to contain the "life" of the animal, which God has put into the animal, it belonged to God alone. It was appropriate only for use in sacrificial rituals and never for ingestion—it was simply too holy, a substance within God's province. The Jews regarded this prohibition as binding on all humanity, with the result that the Gentiles' lack of concern to drain the blood from their meat was regarded as one of the abominations committed by them (and not merely a neutral choice).

Jewish meat was limited to land mammals that both ruminated (chewed the cud) and had a split hoof (rather than a paw, like the weasel, or a single hoof, like the horse). It was essential that the animal should have both features, as is shown by the special attention in Leviticus 11 to the marginal class of animals—those that chew the cud but do not part

---

[33]Deuteronomy adds a second motive: remembering God's gracious deliverance of Israel from slavery in Egypt, from a time in which there was no rest (Deut 5:12-15). This motive appears primarily to reinforce, however, the command to extend sabbath rest to the slaves and resident aliens—to show mercy even as God had shown Israel mercy.

the hoof (the camel, rock badger and rabbit) and those that part the hoof but do not chew the cud (the pig). Their seafood was limited to fish with both fins and scales (so that eel and shellfish were unclean). Birds could be eaten as long as they were not birds of prey (that is, feeding on other animals or carcasses). Insects were unclean, save for the locust and grasshopper family.

How a creature is equipped to move in its environment is an important marker or clean and unclean (Lev 11:3, 9, 12, 20-21), but so is its diet. Whatever feeds on other animals, ingesting their blood or preying on their carcasses (Lev 11:13-19), is unclean for Israel, which is also to avoid blood and the eating of what has "died on its own" (Deut 14:21).[34] Just as the diet of human beings at the creation of the world was to be vegetarian, so the proper creatures to eat (now that meat is allowed after Noah) still follow, by and large, a vegetarian diet. The logic of this system is not to be found in modern medical analysis of the diet but in the meaningfulness assigned to the dietary regulations by the Torah itself (see discussion of Lev 20:22-26 below).

One other aspect of foods bears mention, namely the assigning of specific portions of sacrifices to God, to priests and, in the case of "well-being sacrifices," to laypersons. God's portion was too holy for any human to ingest; the priests' portions were too holy for the laypeople to ingest (Lev 22:10). Finally, only the clean have access to these portions at all. A priest who has contracted some uncleanness may not eat of the sacred portions lest he be "cut off" (Lev 22:1-9); no lay person who has contracted uncleanness may eat of the leftover portions of the "well-being offering" under the same penalty of divine destruction (Lev 7:19-21). While distinguishing between clean and unclean animals is common to all Israelites as a sign of Israel's separation from the nations, there is another dimension to food (seen especially in tithes, reserved for priests alone, and well-being offerings, divided between God, priests and worshipers) that reinforces the social structures within the group.

The dietary laws reinforced Jewish identity and group boundaries also in some very practical ways. The fact that Jews studiously avoided certain foods was well-known to the Gentiles in whose midst they lived, particularly their avoidance of pork. The Jews' cuisine, therefore, becomes

---

[34]See Baruch Levine, *Leviticus*, JPS Torah Commentary (Philadelphia: Jewish Publication Society, 1989), pp. 247-48.

another essential point at which the lines between insider (Jew) and out-sider (Gentile) are drawn. Jews had to be sure that the source of their food was clean—that is, that an animal had been killed in the proper way, so as to drain all the blood rather than leave it to settle in the meat, and killed without any connection with the polluting idols of the world around them.[35] This would not have been so great a concern in Judea, but would have occupied the Jews' attention in the Diaspora. The result of these concerns is that Jews tended to develop their own markets for food and gather their communities around these markets, showing how remarkably effective dietary restrictions can be for reinforcing social grouping.[36]

Maps of the body. Mary Douglas's extensive study of modern tribal cultures, as well as ancient Israelite culture, leads her to the insight that "the body is a model which can stand for any bounded system."[37] Many purity codes display a strong interest in the wholeness of the surfaces of the human body, which in turn reflects the interest in the wholeness of the boundaries of the social body (the firm, fixed definition of who belongs to the group and who does not). Concern over what enters and exits a body also correlates with the larger concern over what enters and exits the social body and the desire for regulating that flow. Given this analysis, it comes as no surprise then that so much discussion of pollution with regard to the human body focuses on surfaces (clothing and the skin), on fluids that cross through the gates of the body, and on bodies that have crossed the boundary between life and death.[38]

Many cultures regard death as a moment at which the numinous can

---

[35]For this reason, Jews in the Diaspora also tended to avoid using oil or wine processed by Gentiles (see Ed P. Sanders, *Judaism: Practice and Belief 63 B.C.E.—66 C.E.* [Philadelphia: Trinity Press, 1992], p. 216; Josephus *J.W.* 2.591; *Life* 74).

[36]A number of potential pollutions are prominent topics notably avoided by Judith in the tale bearing her name. Judith takes clean food and her own dishes for her stay in the Gentile camp (Jdt 10:51), refusing to eat Holofernes' food or use his tableware lest she give offense to God (Jdt 12:1-2). Furthermore, she performs ritual washings every night in running water so as to be cleansed before eating in her tent (Jdt 12:7-9). On her return to Bethulia, she denies having been polluted by the Gentile (sexual relations with Gentiles being regarded throughout this work as polluting; Jdt 13:16, see also Jdt 9:2, 4)

[37]Douglas, *Purity and Danger*, p. 115.

[38]Neyrey, "Idea of Purity," pp. 102-3. This interpretation is in no way contradictory to that given by Milgrom (see below), wherein bodily pollutions are related to the experience or symbolism of death. The life and death of the culture is indeed at stake in the construction of the purity regulations, not only in regard to the body but also diet. Observance of the rules will mean a strong sense of group and a strong commitment to maintain the group's

break into regular life, hence an occasion for pollution. This was also the case in Israel. Touching a corpse, being in the same room as a corpse, even overshadowing a corpse as it passed by outside in a funeral procession were considered defiling. This was one of the more "serious" physical pollutions, since it took seven days to dispel the pollution rather than one day (which was more usual for bodily pollutions). Priests were not to contract this pollution for any but their closest kin. The one who had contracted this pollution was to be sprinkled on the third and seventh day with a special mixture of the ashes of a red heifer and water, prepared by and kept in stock by the priests (Num 19 provides the details for the preparation of this purification agent and its use).[39]

The rotting appearance of the skin associated with a variety of disorders lumped together under the heading of "leprosy" is another potent source of uncleanness. This condition is closely connected with death, as seen in Aaron's response to God's striking Miriam with leprosy: "Do not let her be like one stillborn, whose flesh is half consumed when it comes out of its mother's womb" (Num 12:12). Leviticus 13 contains lengthy guidelines for diagnosing "leprosy," all of which focus on the erosion of the surface and the loss of integrity to the body's outer boundary. The result is a state of uncleanness and communicable defilement, with the result that the leper is excluded from the general population as long as the outbreak lasts (Lev 14:45-46).[40]

While sweating, crying, urinating, defecating, even bleeding from a cut were not regarded as polluting, those discharges related to the sexual apertures and reproductive processes were. Menstruation and inadvertant intercourse with a woman during her period resulted in seven days of being unclean; irregular discharges for both male and female resulted in

---

ethos and identity as distinctive rather than allow too much permeability with regard to the surrounding cultures that threaten to assimilate the group.

[39]In the apocryphal book bearing his name, Tobit piously buries the corpses of the executed Jews. Aware that he has contracted corpse pollution, he washes himself after moving the body and sleeps outside his home (Tob 2:9). This story shows how Diaspora Jews still observed pollution and purity rules as far as possible, even though they were not near or planning to approach the temple. The ashes of the red heifer were not available to Tobit, so he improvises purification rituals as best he can to observe the line between clean and unclean.

[40]Numbers 5:2-4 prescribes exclusion for the leper, the person suffering a polluting discharge and the person who has contracted corpse defilement.

uncleanness as long as the discharge lasted.[41] Nocturnal emissions and sexual intercourse rendered the man or couple unclean until the next sunset (see Lev 15:1-30 for detailed regulations). Usually an immersion in a special bath (called a *mikvah*, a deep cistern hewn out of bedrock and thus not "pollutable") was part of the purification process. Childbirth was a more serious source of pollution (Lev 12:2-5), probably because of the large discharge of blood and tissue loss that accompanies even this life-giving event (Lev 12:7). This lasted forty days if the child was male, eighty days if the newborn was female.

In addition to substances that passed out of the sexual orifices, pollution could come through what passed into the mouth. Here the dietary regulations concerning what is abominable to eat (like blood) and what is clean or unclean for the Jew come into play. Eating unclean food is a different class of pollution from suffering a discharge or touching someone who has a discharge—Leviticus specifies what is to be done *when* discharge pollution occurs but does not envision the possibility of purifications after eating pork. The Torah commands the Jew neither to eat nor touch unclean meats (i.e., touch the carcasses of the unclean animals). It provides purification rites for those who do in fact touch the carcasses (Lev 11:24-38) but not for those who eat of the unclean or abominable animals.

Pollution could attack the Israelite through his or her food from a number of indirect sources as well. Unclean "swarming" creatures like lizards and rodents would defile clay plates and jars (which would have to be broken) as well as utensils made of wood, cloth or skins (which would have to be immersed). The liquid contents of such vessels would also pass on contamination if used (Lev 11:29-35). One also had to take care about the pollution of food stored in the house: open containers of liquids and wet foods and seeds were liable to contract pollution (e.g., Lev 11:37-38), whether from corpse contamination or the carcasses of swarming creatures. Israelites would be especially careful to protect the foods that were set apart for the priests in Jerusalem from such contamination, so as not to send pollution to the temple and defile its personnel!

Negotiating with the holy and coping with pollution through ritual. Not all boundaries within the system are intended never to be crossed, and a

---

[41]One cannot help but recall the woman with a hemorrhage lasting twelve years, whose cleanness could not be restored by any medical technician (Mk 5:25-26).

complex system of rituals was developed in order to allow, for example, the polluted person to be integrated back into a state of cleanness (or purity), or for ordinary objects and persons to pass into the realm of the holy.[42] Almost all rituals are concerned with status, whether they are status-elevation rituals (like the ordination of Aaron and his sons, and then the ordination of priests for active service ever after), status-reversal rituals (like the purification of the leper, the woman after childbirth or the sanctuary from accumulated pollutions) and status-maintenance rituals (which involve the reinforcing of the status quo, e.g., the daily burnt offerings given to honor God as an ongoing sign of Israel's covenant loyalty and submission).

The ritual process, which shows a remarkable consistency across diverse cultures and across centuries, involves three phases. In the first, the person or persons undergoing the rite are separated from the population in some symbolic or physical way. They enter, then, a second phase of liminality—an in-between state in which they neither belong to their former status nor have yet entered into their new status. At the end of this marginal period comes the entrance of the person or persons into their new condition, marked usually by some "rite of aggregation." [43] The liminal state between separation from old and aggregation to new state has been of special interest to anthropologists observing tribal rituals. In this state a future king might be begrimed, insulted and abused by his future subjects; a group of adolescents might be camped together, cordoned off with pollution taboos and subjected to what we could only describe as severe hazing.[44] This in-between period is thus often radically different—

---

[42]For example, Aaron and his sons moved from the realm of the common to the holy by the application of holy anointing oil and the rite of ordination. Tithes and offerings pass from the sphere of the common to the holy by being set apart from the bulk of the produce and transferred to the priests. Spoils of war can be consecrated by being set apart and placed under the ban (herem), being transferred to God by destruction. There were proper rites for removing something from the sphere of the sacred to the sphere of the profane—redemption of the firstborn by means of money, for example. There were ritual provisions for all these legitimate moves across the boundaries; other moves were illegitimate, resulting in death (e.g., profaning the sabbath, eating holy food in an unclean state). See the fine discussion in Wright and Hodgson, "Holiness," p. 245.

[43]This is developed at great length by Victor Turner, The Ritual Process (Ithaca, N.Y.: Cornell University Press, 1969); see also Milgrom, Leviticus I-XVI, pp. 566-69.

[44]We are not entirely without such rites of passage even in the Western world. Adolescents frequently are separated from their communities of origin and encamped with their "peers" for four years at college, after which they are gathered back into the real world

even inverted—from what the people undergoing the ritual experienced before and after the rite. The liminal period is a time for breaking down and distancing oneself from the state that one had previously and for preparing for the state into which one was about to enter.

Jewish rites show a remarkable reserve in regards to the liminal period. The high priest is not buffeted before his installation, for example. Priests and ex-lepers are, however, isolated for seven days "in humility and sacrality" as they move from one state (nonpriests, unclean leper) to another (priest, whole person).[45] The three-stage ritual process is observable in many rites both within the Judaism of the Second Temple period and within early Christianity. The process itself could become a framework for understanding a person's whole life experience, as it does in the letter to the Hebrews (see chapter eight of this book).

Most pollutions had a specific purification rite prescribed in Torah. Simple pollutions could be dispelled with the passing of a single day and frequently the immersing of the body in a bath. This might include laundering affected clothing. Corpse impurity was removed by sprinkling the person affected on the third and seventh day with a special mixture of the ashes of a red heifer and water, prepared by and kept in stock by the priests. More serious pollutions (and sins, especially intentional sins) would pollute the very holy places, even from far away. The holy places were a sort of mirror of the condition of the people, compared by Jacob Milgrom to the picture of Dorian

---

in a new status (adults) with new rights and responsibilities. People called out by God for ministry but not yet ordained may be subjected to three or so years of hard training in seminary.

[45]Nelson, *Raising Up*, p. 58. See Exodus 29 for the rite of ordination of the Aaronic priests (the rite of separation being the purification with water and the endowing of special vestments together with the marking of the priests' right ears, thumbs and toes with blood from the first sacrifices, the liminal period involving the seven days of sacrifices and eating together of the holy food from the offering. The rite of aggregation is not prescribed but effected as the newly ordained priest enters on his service at the close of the seven days. The rite for the cleansing of the leper is found in Leviticus 14:1-32 and is strikingly parallel to the ordination of the priest. Here the three steps of the ritual process are fully prescribed. The ex-leper is separated from his former state of being a leper by the ritual involving the two birds (Lev 14:1-8a); the liminal state is represented by his living inside the camp but outside his tent for seven days, concluding with the complete razing of the hair from his body (Lev 14:8b-9); the rite of aggregation is accomplished on the eighth day with the sacrifice of two male lambs, the ex-leper being marked on his right ear, thumb and big toe with blood and oil from the sacrificial offerings. After those sacrifices are completed, the ex-leper is once more at home in the camp.

Gray.[46] As the people were polluted, or worse, defiled themselves, the pollutions also showed up on the surfaces of the holy places. Individual accidental transgressions polluted the altar, and the blood of the purification offerings brought by Israelites for such transgressions was dashed upon that structure to remove the threat of the pollution (Lev 4:27-31).[47] Communal accidental transgressions polluted the altar and the holy place, both of which were sprinkled or received the blood from the purification offering that was made "when the sin . . . [became] known" (Lev 4:13-21). Intentional (avoidable and cognizant) transgressions polluted the holy of holies. These pollutions were removed on the Day of Atonement, with blood being sprinkled inside the inner curtain, in the holy place and at the altar (Lev 16:1-20). It is debated whether the blood that "makes atonement" should be understood as cleansing or washing away the pollution,[48] or as repairing the "covering" of God's holiness that had been eroded by the pollution (and if eroded all the way through by successive years of pollution would cause God's holiness to "break out" against the people and consume them).[49] Either way, the removal of pollution from the presence of a holy God was essential if God was to continue to live in the midst of Israel without either withdrawing (thus making his favors unavailable) or consuming the people. The second half of the Day of Atonement rites then focus on the purification of people from their sins, as they confessed, repented and laid them symbolically upon the head of the second goat—this one used not as a source of blood for cleansing the holy places but as a vehicle for removing the pollution from the people out to the desert, the realm of the demon Azazel (Lev 16:20-28).

"Ethical" holiness and pollution. Many pollution taboos found in Torah enforce certain codes of social behavior. We must remind ourselves, however, that the pious Jew observed no distinction between moral law and

---

[46]See Milgrom, *Leviticus I-XVI,* pp. 49, 253-61; *Numbers,* JPS Torah Commentary (Philadelphia: Jewish Publication Society, 1989), pp. 444-47. The reference is to a story by Oscar Wilde, in which a man retains his youthful appearance while his likeness in a demonic oil portrait within his house ages with time, reflecting the decay of his soul.

[47]This category would include the more serious physical pollutions as, for example, after a woman underwent childbirth or a leper was pronounced cleansed of the affliction. This offering was not made to purify the human being but to remove the pollution that came on the altar by a form of sympathetic defilement.

[48]The more typical understanding, as given in Milgrom, *Numbers,* p. 444.

[49]Mary Douglas ("Atonement," pp. 116-18, 123-30) offers an eloquent defense of this latter reading. See especially p. 123: "Major transgression has ruptured . . . the protective covering of God's righteousness," which is repaired by atonement.

cultic law. The fact that both eating unclean food and committing incest brought about pollution shows the essential integration of the Torah as a single code. Leviticus could speak at length about enacting holiness through the avoidance of defiling foods (Lev 11), but holiness is also enacted through the pursuit of fairness, honesty and justice in all dealings with other people (Lev 19). Distinguishing between virtue and vice, justice and injustice, was every bit as important as distinguishing between clean and unclean foods, and we ought not to forget that the second greatest commandment is found in the middle of the holiness code: "You shall love your neighbor as yourself" (Lev 19:18). The system of sacrifices also shows the essential unity of what we now call the moral law and the ritual law. The sin offering, which is better called a "purification offering,"[50] was offered both for certain moral offenses and for the pollutions incurred without any moral failure (like childbirth). Both were equally deviations from the norm requiring purgation of the pollution.[51] Both ethical transgressions like fraud with regard to business and capital, and the unnoticed contraction of ritual uncleanness from contact with an unclean person or animal, required a kind of "guilt offering" (Lev 5:2-7; 6:2-7).

Several kinds of behavior are severely sanctioned against, there being no remedy prescribed for the pollution, save the death of the one who has incurred the defilement. Murder is a pollution of this kind, and if the murderer cannot be found and executed, an elaborate ritual is prescribed for the transfer of the pollution from the populated areas to the wilderness (Deut 21:1-9). Certain kinds of sexual intercourse are labeled "abominations," that is, acts wholly polluting and off the purity scale entirely. Such are incest, adultery, rape of a married woman who cries out or who is in the fields, bestiality and homosexuality. Again, only the death of the guilty suffices to expunge the pollution of the land by such acts. Finally, idolatry is a pollution that requires the death of the polluter. The land had formerly been "polluted," especially by the idols and the sexual aberrations of the Canaanites, and was not to be thus polluted again, lest the land vomit out the new inhabitants as it had the former ones.

---

[50]See Milgrom, *Leviticus I-XVI*, p. 253; Sanders, *Judaism*, p. 108.

[51]Thus Sanders, *Judaism*, p. 108. For a precise and detailed discussion of the Jewish sacrificial system, impossible to attempt here on account of space limitations and focus, please see Sanders, *Judaism*, pp. 103-18, 251-57; Milgrom, *Leviticus I-XVI*, pp. 253-65, 440-57.

Psalm 51 provides an excellent example of the conceptualization of ethical sin within the framework of purity laws and pollution taboos. The prayer is linked to David's act of adultery (and conspiracy to bring about the death of Uriah), and moral sin, like the pollution attached to irregular discharges, sticks to one until it is washed away or cleansed (Ps 51:2, 7). The alternatives are either that God will put a clean heart in the sinner or will cast the unclean one from his holy presence and withdraw his Holy Spirit (Ps 51:10-11). It is a purification that is entirely God's to grant, however, unlike the ritual ablutions for most pollutions that an individual can perform on himself or herself. There is no "purification offering" prescribed for adultery, and so David offers the only sacrifice he can—"a broken spirit; a broken and contrite heart" (Ps 51:17). The seriousness of such a sin in terms of the normal purification required (death) makes God's forgiveness and cleansing of the sinner all the more generous, surprising and, above all, not to be taken for granted. Torah has much to teach us about the abhorrent nature of sins against God's prescribed order for human society. Only as we come to appreciate the revulsion of sin (and feel revulsion ourselves) will Scripture have done its work building the all-important barrier between our desires and forbidden things, as well as teaching us to value sufficiently the mercies of God that have been shown to us.

The Meaningfulness of Purity Regulations and Pollution Taboos in Judaism

Rather than seek out modern rationalizations for the purity laws of Judaism, such as considering their repercussions for health and hygiene, we should seek out the insider's rationale for following this rather intense code. The Torah itself provides important passages communicating to the law-observant Jew the meaningfulness of the regulations he or she follows.

The central rationale for observing purity regulations and controlling and containing pollution is given in Lev 11:44-45 and 19:2: "Be holy, for I am holy. . . . You shall be holy, for I am holy." The holy God chose Israel and associated himself with Israel in terms of honor, putting his own holy name on the people and providing his presence, dwelling in the midst of Israel in a special way. This association with the holy One requires that the people be holy as well. Contact with this deity demands maintaining that degree of purity and, indeed, sanctity, that allows for that contact to be beneficial and not destructive.[52] By keeping God's commandments—not just the ten, but the whole covenant!—the Israelites avoided the profanation of the "holy name" that was over them and upon them (Lev 22:31-33), and so avoided the ruinous path of exchanging God's favor for God's wrath. Just as the holy is "different from the profane or the ordinary," that is, "is the 'other,'" so the people commanded to be holy to their God will be different from the peoples around them.[53] Holiness and distinctiveness go hand in hand in Torah and in Judaism, and the pursuit of holiness must be worked out in the practicalities of everyday life, such as in making "a distinction between the unclean and the clean, and between the living creature that may be eaten and the living creature that may not be eaten" (Lev 11:47), and refusing to "defile yourselves with any swarming creature that moves upon the earth" (Lev 11:43, my translation).

God's selection of Israel for himself and for a special destiny of life in God's holy land is the ultimate reason for observing distinctions between clean and unclean and holy and common. This comes to eloquent expression in Leviticus 20:22-26:

> You shall keep all my statutes and all my ordinances, and observe them, so that the land to which I bring you to settle in may not vomit you out. You shall not follow the practices of the nation that I am driving out before you. Because they did all these things, I abhorred them. But I have said to you: You shall inherit their land, and I will give it to you to possess, a land flowing with milk and honey. I am the LORD your God; I have separated you from the peoples. You shall therefore make a distinction between the clean animal and the unclean, and between the unclean bird and the clean; you shall not bring abomination on yourselves by animal or by bird or by anything with which the ground teems, which I have set apart for you to hold unclean. You shall be holy to me; for I the LORD am holy, and I have separated you from the other peoples to be mine.[54]

---

[52]Even at war the holy God moved with the armies of Israel, with the result that the war camp had to be a place of holiness, even as the camp of the Israelites around the tabernacle, with care being taken to defecate only outside the camp (and bury the dung) and to immerse oneself and leave the camp after nocturnal emissions until the pollution dissipates: "Because the LORD your God travels along with your camp, to save you and to hand over your enemies to you, therefore your camp must be holy, so that he may not see anything indecent among you and turn away from you" (Deut 23:14).

[53]Levine, *Leviticus*, p. 256.

[54]Deuteronomy also incorporates this rationale between a prohibition of Canaanite mourn-

Prior to this passage, Leviticus 18:24-30 had already explicitly made the connection between observing purity, containing and controlling pollution, and possessing the land. The former inhabitants "defiled themselves" by their sexual practices and their idolatries (the whole of Lev 18), and so "the land vomited out its inhabitants." If the Israelites do as the nations around them do, and as the Canaanites had done, they will suffer the same: "the land will vomit you out for defiling it, as it vomited out the nation that was before you" (Lev 18:28). Sexual abominations, idolatrous rites, unauthorized rituals, ingestion of what is abominable and the amassing of pollutions without their timely purgation do not merely bar one from access to the temple but threaten the very security of the nation in its land.

The present passage, however, goes beyond issues of national security, as it were, to national identity. The food laws are singled out by the text as an especially important set of symbols for the social body. The Jews' continual observance in their diet of what foods are clean as opposed to unclean for them (but fine for Gentiles to eat) is a reminder that they are not part of that larger group but have been set apart by God even as they set apart clean food from the unclean food. They are "confronted daily at the dinner table" by the fact of having been called to be separate from the nations.[55] There is a symbolic correlation between living beings and foods: to all the nations belong all foods; Israel is distinct from the nations just as the clean foods are distinguished from the unclean foods; the animals proper for God (i.e., for sacrifice) are an even narrower subset of these clean foods, and all blood strictly belongs to God.[56] The care about ingestion will be extended to care about with whom one ingests food (see discussion of Jub and Acts 10 below).

---

ing practices (cutting the forelocks and lacerating the skin, Deut 14:1) and a recapitulation of the dietary laws of Leviticus (Deut 14:3-21): "For you are a people holy to the LORD your God; it is you the LORD has chosen out of all the peoples on earth to be his people, his treasured possession" (Deut 14:2). Holiness is, again, directly concerned with the wholeness of the body and the guarding of the bodily orifices (here, the mouth). See also Exodus 22:31, which connects the special connection between Israel and the holy God with the observance of dietary laws: "You shall be people consecrated to me; therefore you shall not eat any meat that is mangled by beasts in the field; you shall throw it to the dogs." It is instructive to compare this with the command in Deuteronomy 14:21 to abstain from eating what has died on its own but permitting the sale of such meat to the non-Jews in the community.

[55]Milgrom, *Leviticus I-XVI*, p. 730.

[56]David P. Wright and Hans Hübner, "Unclean and Clean [OT]," in *ABD*, ed. David N. Freedman (New York: Doubleday, 1992), p. 740; Milgrom, *Leviticus I-XVI*, pp. 721-22.

A Hellenistic Jewish writing from the mid-first century A.D., 4 Maccabees promotes strict adherence to Torah's regulations in the midst of an unsupportive, Greek dominant culture by praising an aged priest, seven brothers and the mother of the seven who die under brutal torture under Antiochus IV rather then ingest a mouthful of pork. In his homily the author presents a most dramatic expression of the correlation between distinguishing between the clean and unclean in terms of food and the maintenance of Jewish identity and boundaries in the midst of the Hellenistic dominant culture. In fact, all the characters in the drama seem to recognize this correlation themselves. The goal of Antiochus is explicitly to destroy the distinction between Jew and Greek (the former in favor of the latter), and the symbol for his attempt to force Greek culture and identity upon the inhabitants of Jerusalem is, in this episode, the ingestion of pork. The martyrs will not accept the food any more than they will accept the loss of their distinctive religious and social identity, and their refusal to obey the king with regard to the former actually preserves the latter as the story unfolds—their courage for their ancestral law emboldens widespread resistance and eventually victory.

The purity code articulated in Torah thus creates a distinctive social ethos and identity for Israel, by which it may distinguish itself, and keep itself distinct from, its neighbors: "You shall not do as they do in the land of Egypt, where you lived, and you shall not do as they do in the land of Canaan, to which I am bringing you. You shall not follow their statutes. My ordinances you shall observe and my statutes you shall keep, following them: . . . by doing so one shall live: I am the LORD" (Lev 18:3-5). Keeping the purity laws meant keeping their privileged place in the shadow of God's holiness, their identity as a holy people and their hold on the holy land.

A second way in which observing these ordinances would be meaningful would be the way in which they allowed the community of Israel to move in step with, or mirror, the divine order. This mirroring emerges already from Leviticus 20:22-26, as Israel is enjoined to make distinctions between clean and unclean, even as God separates Israel from other nations. As God separates the realities of the world into the categories of clean and unclean, Israel falls in line with God's order as it continues to do the same. This is also prominent in the command to observe the sabbath: as the Jew rests from work on that day, he or she is put in touch with the divine realm where God also rests (Ex 31:12-17). By observing the holiness of times and the distinction between clean and unclean, law-observant Israel becomes a living reflection of the character of the holy God in the midst of the world, a holy island of order in the midst of the Gentiles' aberrations.

An especially prominent way in which the Torah continued to be meaningful in the Hellenistic and Roman periods (what we might call the inter-testamental period) is through a moral interpretation of all of its precepts, especially of the dietary laws. The *Letter of Aristeas* contains, in addition to a legendary account of the translation of the Torah from Hebrew into Greek, a lengthy explanation of the dietary laws of Israel. The dietary peculiarities, which are incomprehensible to Gentiles, encode moral instructions that should be recognized by all as respectable. Animals that chew the cud and part the hoof represent the importance of meditating on virtue and discerning between right and wrong (*Let. Aris.* 150), while forbidden animals represent various vices associated popularly with the animal in question (like sexual looseness with the weasel or violence with the birds of prey; *Let. Aris.* 144-48): "All that is said of food, then, and of unclean creeping things and of animals is directed toward justice and just intercourse among men" (*Let. Aris.* 169). While the *Letter of Aristeas* represents something approaching an allegorical interpretation of the dietary laws, other Jews interpret their value in terms of the exercise they gave to the moral faculty, teaching self-restraint. Obedience to Torah means that, "when we crave seafood and fowl and animals and all sorts of foods that are forbidden to us by the law, we abstain because of domination by reason," the result of which is growth in the virtue of self-control and mastery of the passions and desires (4 Macc 1:31-35). In an environment that increasingly valued religion as a means to advancement in virtue (and that despised irrational religious practices), such avenues of interpretation allowed Torah's prescriptions to continue to be meaningful for Jews and thus be readily embraced and defended.[57]

Finally, one additional modern theory about the meaning of these purity codes merits attention.[58] Jacob Milgrom has suggested with regard

---

[57]The late-first-century Christian author of the *Epistle of Barnabas* also uses this moralizing approach to the dietary laws. Unlike his earlier Jewish counterparts, however, the real meaning of the laws is observable apart from the literal practice of the laws—something that not even Philo, the most imaginative Jewish allegorizer of Torah, would ever consider.

[58]The views of Mary Douglas are not hereby excluded—it rather happens that her understanding of the meaningfulness of these regulations (as means by which the external boundaries and internal lines of the group are created and reinforced) has explicit attestation in Leviticus.

to the pollutions caused by the human body that death and decay are the common denominators. The pollution taboos of Leviticus and Numbers, as he correctly observes, tend to focus on "death, blood, semen, and skin disease." Since blood and semen are essential to life and the reproduction of life, the loss of these substances is a symbol of death. With regard to the postpartum mother, which might seem out of place in this list, the emergence of new life should not obscure the irregular flow of blood that follows in the weeks after birth, not to mention the voluminous loss of blood and tissue during the event itself. The leper's disease is explicitly compared to becoming a corpse as Aaron prays for Miriam "let her not be as one stillborn" (Num 12:12, my translation) and has the same level of pollution contagion.[59] The daily regulations concerning bodily purity, then, may well function as material symbols for the command to choose life and not death, that is, to keep the whole covenant with God.

Concern for Purity in Early Judaism

To what degree were Jews concerned to avoid pollution and maintain purity? Were there occasions of heightened interest in these regulations? Interest in purity was high, of course, in connection with the temple. The temple staff (mainly the priests but also the Levites as a whole) had to protect themselves from pollutions that would be fine for laypeople while they were away from the temple. Priests were strictly forbidden to contact corpse impurity for any but their closest relations (hence the response of the priest to the man who had fallen prey to bandits on the road from Jericho to Jerusalem; see Lev 21:1-6) and had special strictures on whom they might marry (Lev 21:7-9). Purity for priests, and performing the rites in precisely the prescribed way, was a matter of life and death (the deaths of Nadab and Abihu, two of Aaron's sons, stood in Scripture as a perpetual warning).

Contact with the holy God and the places sanctified by God's presence and for God's service required cleanness, however, on the part of all who would enter. At the initial encounter between Israel and their God in Exodus 19:10-15, the people were solemnly instructed to purify themselves by immersions, laundering of clothing and abstinence from intercourse. Ever after, we find that approaching the temple, the abode of God, was a time for special observation of increased purity and purifications. A Jew might plan

---

[59]See Milgrom, *Numbers*, p. 346; *Leviticus I-XVI*, pp. 45-47.

to enter Jerusalem a week or so before a festival to undergo purification from corpse contamination, if he or she had not done so already, and would abstain from intercourse the night before a festival day began (which began, we must recall, at sunset the following day). The people are to be separated "from their uncleanness, so that they do not die in their uncleanness by defiling my tabernacle that is in their midst" (Lev 15:31). Strong taboos attached to the conjunction of contracting uncleanness and then eating some of the meat of an offering (the well-being offering being shared between God, the priest and the worshipers who brought the animal; see Lev 7:19-21). Anytime an Israelite visited the temple, then, great care would be taken to approach safely—in a state of cleanness.[60]

We must remember, however, that the multiplication of pollution in the land (quite apart from entering the temple precincts) was itself a dangerous thing, since it resulted in the expulsion of the Canaanites and would threaten the same for Israel. This did not mean that an individual would need always and obsessively to avoid pollution, since the Torah regards many kinds of pollution as natural and unavoidable.[61] A person would need only to be aware of how and when he or she contracted it so that he or she could observe the proper purifications in connection with the pollution (usually just an immersion and the passing of time—"he shall be unclean until evening").[62] Such impurities would include child-

---

[60]Sanders, building his case on a comment by Josephus that specifically connects purification rites with the sacrifices to be performed in the temple (Josephus *Ag. Ap.* 2.198), regards visits to the temple as the main occasion for being concerned about recovering a state of cleanness (*Judaism*, p. 71).

[61]Wright and Hübner provide a helpful discussion of permitted versus prohibited impurity, to which I am indebted here ("Unclean and Clean [OT]," pp. 729-41, especially pp. 730-35).

[62]In this regard, many portraits of the Pharisees and other observant Jews may be overdrawn. Neyrey writes, for example, that "according to Jewish religion and culture, Jesus would be expected to be a defensive person [with regard to avoiding pollution] and avoid all contact with uncleanness" ("Idea of Purity," p. 105). Being an observant Jew, however, did not mean avoiding all uncleanness but rather knowing when he or she has incurred pollution so as to attend to its purification at once. An observant Jew took special care around the avoidance of unclean food, sexuality and idolatry, even going so far as choosing table companions carefully and buying oil and wine from people of like scrupulousness (since these were wet foods and products, and thus more liable to pollution), but he or she did not "avoid all uncleanness." Pharisees did not avoid funerals to avoid corpse defilement but grieved with the grieving. Tobit is praised for incurring uncleanness to bury the executed Jews in Nineveh. Similarly, they did not avoid intercourse and the pollution that came from emitting semen—but they did immerse themselves afterward and took care not to pollute anything that was headed for the priests as part of their tithe.

birth, the pollutions acquired from contact with a corpse, an irregular or menstrual discharge, contact with a person with such a discharge, sexual intercourse, contact with certain unclean animals, contraction of a skin condition that would qualify as leprosy, as well as the pollutions acquired by certain priests who prepared the ashes of the red heifer (for removing corpse defilement) or who took the carcasses of atonement offerings outside the camp for burning. A Jew need not be fearful of such pollution coming between himself or herself and God (although, of course, pollutions like leprosy would be feared on account of their dreadful social consequences), as long as he or she observed the purifications commanded in Torah (usually ablutions and the passage of time, sometimes accompanied by a purification offering to cleanse the defilement of the holy places by the pollution, even if it occurred far from the temple). The pollution would be removed and the person restored to a clean state, and no danger would accrue. Neglecting or delaying the purifications, however, would be dangerous. This would be to hold impurity in the land that is holy to the Lord and among the people holy to the Lord—it would also be a source of contagious pollution in many cases, thus multiplying itself.

To be avoided by all Jews, however, were the prohibited pollutions. These included the intentional (or neglectful) delay of purifications for permitted pollution, since such delay constituted a willful transgression and polluted the holy places (see Lev 17:15-16; Num 19:12), corpse pollution for priests (save for the priest's closest of relatives), sexual pollutions (incest, intercourse with a menstruating woman, bestiality and homosexuality; Lev 18:6-30; 20:10-21), defilement by association with idols and idol worship (e.g., Lev 20:2-5), murder (see Num 35:33-34), neglect of circumcision (Gen 17:14)[63] and defilement of the sacred (e.g., entering the temple while unclean or breaking the sabbath).

One important variable in observance of purity laws became an occasion for some degrees of segregation within Israel. The majority of the people were not, it appears, concerned with "secondary pollution," that is, the pollution caused by touching something touched by a person or thing that was in a state of uncleanness. Pharisees, on the other hand, were concerned about this level of contamination, with the result that the stricter Jews were wary about how close their association should be with less strict Jews.

---

[63]Thanks to Milgrom for his insight in classifying this among those transgressions that lead to one's being cut off by God from the holy people (*Numbers*, p. 406).

Pharisees would trade with less observant Jews, trusting them to tithe and preserve the purity of the priests' portions, but would not eat with them, for example. Essenes (including the men who inhabited the Qumran settlement) were the most strict about the avoidance of pollution and the safeguarding of their priestly purity (since the Qumran covenanters, at least, regarded themselves as the true priests, whose role in the temple would be restored when God intervened at the end of time).[64] They went to the extremes of segregation from the rest of the holy people of God. Purity regulations designed to bind Israel together in solidarity in the midst of the nations thus also contained the seeds for sectarianism within Israel.

In conclusion we should observe that purity (and returning to a state of purity after some contamination) tended to be regarded as a positive good in and of itself as an expression of a person's set-apartness by God and for God, an enacting of his or her status as a member of God's holy people. Jews accepted, by and large, their commission to "advance the holy into the realm of the common and to diminish the impure and thereby enlarge the realm of the pure."[65] Observance of purity regulations was an expression of piety valued by Jews not only when approaching the temple, and not even only while occupying the Holy Land, which could not tolerate an excess of pollution, but even in the Diaspora.[66] The observant Jew was interested in maintaining purity in connection with having "clean hands and pure hearts" (Ps 24:4), that is to say, purity of thought and deed in addition to purity of diet and body. Far from being merely an external set of rules, these ordinances were an outward reflection of central religious convictions, including obedience to God's desire that Jews should be holy to him as he was holy, indeed that they should be a living reflection of God's holiness in the midst of an unclean world.

---

[64]For a detailed analysis of Essene purity codes and observances, see Sanders, *Judaism*, pp. 352-60.
[65]Milgrom, *Leviticus I-XVI*, p. 732.
[66]See Sanders, *Judaism*, pp. 218, 229-30.

Eight

PURITY &
THE NEW TESTAMENT

W*e have seen that both the Greco-Roman and Jewish cultures were con*cerned with purity and pollution, particularly in relation to approaching the divine and remaining in a place of favor with the divine. The presence of God meant potential blessing and potential danger. Great care was taken, therefore, to enter God's presence or, increasingly among Jews, live out one's life in God's presence, in a clean state so as not to bring defilement before the face of a holy God. What was clean or pure reflected God's own order (the boundaries and differentiations established in creation) and God's activity (e.g., resting on the seventh day and making a distinction between Israel and the nations). Purity codes and the desire to avoid defilement upheld strong social boundaries both within Israel and between Israel and the Gentile nations, allowing Jewish culture to retain its distinctive identity in the midst of a dominant, Gentile world. Above all, we must remember that Jewish observance of purity codes was not a matter of externalistic religion but was regarded by the practitioners as a meaningful component of living out the covenant God gave to Israel that also included a strong ethical dimension—the pious Jew knew that "a clean heart" was as critical as "clean hands."

Rewriting Israel's Purity Maps

Beginning with the ministry of Jesus, we find the Christian movement interacting creatively and innovatively with the purity maps of Israel. The Gospels contain a multitude of instances where Jesus "crosses the line" intentionally with regard to the maps of persons, foods, times and space, for which he is frequently challenged and offers explanations or defense. For the Christian reader of these Gospels, God's authorization of Jesus (at the baptism and transfiguration) and his vindication of Jesus (at the resurrection) give Jesus the authority to redefine the sacred purity regulations of Judaism, even to rewrite the very maps laid out in Torah itself. "Far from separating Himself from what is unclean [as the Pharisees might regard Jesus], God repeatedly draws near to Jesus,"[1] indeed, explicitly associates Jesus with himself in the closest of ways, for example as God's "beloved Son" in whom God "is well pleased" (see Mk 1:11). Moreover, the second word of God in the Synoptic Gospels is specifically to listen to Jesus (see Mk 9:7), hence give heed to his authoritative revisions of the maps of clean and unclean.

The second part of the New Testament reveals that a great deal of development still lay ahead for the early church as it worked out the implications of Jesus' death and resurrection, and even more the pouring out of God's Holy Spirit on Jewish and Gentile Christian alike, for the purity regulations laid out in Torah. Two broad principles emerge from this process, guiding Christians in their decisions about the ongoing application of Torah's ordinances. First, since the "dividing wall of hostility" that separated ethnic Jews from Gentiles had been broken down by God in Christ, all replications of that boundary were also abolished. Thus the dietary laws, that were seen in Leviticus specifically to model the separation of the people of God from Gentiles, the mark of circumcision and the concern with physical pollution all were seen to be no longer binding in light of God's new acts of salvation. Indeed, to return to the observation of those boundary-making regulations would be to build up again what God had broken down. Second, the death of Jesus and his ascension into the heavenly realms was interpreted as a priestly sacrifice that decisively made for peace between God and the Christians. The sacrificial cult in all of its facets, therefore, was seen to have been replaced by the cross (in terms of purification offerings, guilt offerings and atonement offer-

---

[1]Jerome H. Neyrey, "The Idea of Purity in Mark's Gospel," *Semeia* 35 (1986): 114.

ings; see Heb 9:1—10:18) and by the believers' acts of praise, witness and service (as a sort of thanksgiving offering; see Heb 13:15-16).

The early church did not, however, reject the concepts of purity, defilement and holiness. Such language continued to be a significant aspect of Christian teaching and ideology, and to function in ways familiar from the discussion of purity regulations in Israel. First, these concepts were used extensively to articulate an ethic for the Christian community—to set off certain behaviors as polluting and therefore unsuitable and dangerous for the sanctified people of God, and to promote a condition of communal wholeness and abstinence from destructive vices as the purity proper for the saints. Second, and in closely connected ways, purity and pollution language strongly reinforced the boundaries between the new community of Christians (both Jew and Gentile) and the non-Christian world (both Jew and Gentile).

Pure and defiling foods. Mark 7 and the parallel account in Matthew 15 preserve an exchange between Jesus and the Pharisees that focuses on issues of defilement through the mouth. The Pharisees, it would appear, had developed a prescription for rinsing the hands before eating as a guard against polluting themselves. When they observe Jesus' disciples eating without following this rite, they challenge Jesus (Mt 15:2), who in their view has not taught his disciples an adequate way of preserving purity. This sets the scene for Jesus' radical reinterpretation and redrawing of purity and pollution lines, now entirely in an ethical direction: "It is not what goes into the mouth that defiles a person, but it is what comes out of the mouth that defiles" (Mt 15:11). Jesus explains this radical statement privately to his disciples: whatever enters the mouth passes through the system and leaves, but what comes out of the mouth comes from the heart of a person. In Matthew's form of the saying, it is speech that can defile, if that speech is the embodiment of evil intentions, murder, adultery, false witness, slander and other vices (Mt 15:19). It is speech that suggests sins, that destroys reputations, that pollutes relationships, and this is the defilement to be concerned about.

Mark's version of this episode is even more radical.[2] Matthew is con-

---

[2]No attempt will be made here to adjudicate which is more authentic, that is, whether Matthew has made Jesus more conservative or Mark has made Jesus more radical. It is, after all, the word of Scripture and not a reconstruction of the "historical Jesus" behind the Scripture that guides the church.

tent to leave the debate poised against the hand-rinsing purification (Mt 15:20), but Mark's Jesus overturns the dietary regulations as a whole. Jesus' rebuttal to the Pharisees is now: "There is nothing outside a person that by going in can defile, but the things that come out are what defile" (Mk 7:15). The focus is removed from the mouth (and thus from speech alone) to the distinction between the inner person and the world outside the person. It is vice or sin that defiles a person, whether spoken, enacted or merely thought or desired. Moreover, Mark interjects an interpretation into Jesus' discussion of why what enters the mouth cannot defile (since it passes through the stomach and then on out): "Thus he declared all foods clean" (Mk 7:19). Since true defilement comes from inside a person (from ethical vice), all regulations about pollution from unclean food become pointless distractions. Included in this position would be a denial of the principle that eating with those who are unclean may defile as well, a principle that now can legitimate the mixed body of Jews and Gentiles and justify their table fellowship.

The thesis that personal ethics rather than external rites are the key to being clean in God's sight reappears in Jesus' denunciation of the scribes and Pharisees:

> You clean the outside of the cup and of the plate, but inside they are full of greed and self-indulgence. You blind Pharisee! First clean the inside of the cup, so that the outside also may become clean. Woe to you, scribes and Pharisees, hypocrites! For you are like whitewashed tombs, which on the outside look beautiful, but inside they are full of the bones of the dead and of all kinds of filth. So you also on the outside look righteous to others, but inside you are full of hypocrisy and lawlessness. (Mt 23:25-28)

The cup and plate also function as images for the Pharisees themselves, who strictly observe purification rituals for the body but, Jesus suggests, are polluted inwardly by greed and slavery to the passions. Jesus censures them for not pursuing the cleansing that alone makes the others meaningful. Now it is Luke's parallel saying that appears more radical than Matthew's version: Jesus tells the scribes to "give for alms those things that are within" (that is, to reverse the practice of robbery and greed), after which "everything will be clean for you" (Lk 11:37-41). Once again the emerging principle is that ridding oneself of ethical vice is a necessary cleansing and indeed the only observance of clean and unclean that God requires.

Pauline Christianity moved in the direction taken by Mark and Luke. Paul declares that "nothing is unclean in itself" (Rom 14:14), but thinking makes it so. Here we enter into Paul's commitment to limit the freedom found in Christ out of sensitivity for those who have not yet had their symbolic world opened up that far. Even though "everything is indeed clean," it becomes evil for the person who eats and makes a sister or brother stumble.[3] There continued to be streams within the church that "demand[ed] abstinence from [certain] foods" (1 Tim 4:3), but the dominant voices within the church came to agree that all foods "God created to be received with thanksgiving by those who believe and know the truth. For everything created by God is good, and nothing is to be rejected, provided it is received with thanksgiving; for it is sanctified by God's word and by prayer" (1 Tim 4:3-5; see also Col 2:20-23). Within this general abolition of dietary regulations, however, we find the promotion of a few strategic pollution taboos attached to meat offered to idols and to blood (see the apostolic decree in Acts 15:20-21, 28-29). The first of these ensured that a strong boundary would be maintained between the monotheistic Christian group and the idolatrous world, and the second maintained a universal prohibition of Torah—not one that sought to separate ethnic Jews from Gentiles.

Rewriting maps of holy and defiling people. The interest in revising dietary laws corresponds directly with the revision of maps of people that was taking place within the Christian movement (since food regulations and the ethnic isolation of Israel were explicitly linked by Lev 20:22-26). Once again the movement toward the abolition of the Jewish purity maps of people took its bearings from Jesus' own activity.

Jesus' healings of the diseased and encounters with "sinners" are immersed in issues of purity rules and pollution taboos, in which we see Jesus consistently showing a willingness to cross the lines in order to bring the unclean ones back to a state of cleanness and integration into the community. Jesus enacts a conceptualization of holiness as mercy, love and compassion. Such a position is very much in keeping with the prophetic tradition of Israel that he quotes so frequently. For example, when Pharisees, who seek to preserve purity through defensive strategies

---

[3]Please see chapter six and the issue of insisting on our freedom to do what is right in our eyes versus acting with sensitivity to the way this will affect those sisters and brothers who witness it.

(abstaining from contact with the unclean or potentially unclean), challenge his eating with sinners and thus inviting pollution, he quotes Hosea 6:6: "I desire mercy and not sacrifice" (my translation; see also Mt 9:10-13). The holiness God seeks, according to Jesus' understanding, entails reaching out in love and compassion, restoring the unclean and the defiled and the sinner to wholeness. The command to "be holy, for I am holy" (Lev 11:45) is fulfilled not in the protection of purity ("separate yourselves from uncleanness," see Lev 15:31), but in the action of extending wholeness to the unclean ("be merciful, just as your Father is merciful," Lk 6:36).

Early in his ministry Jesus encounters a leper (Mt 8:2-4; Mk 1:40-45). The leper is perpetually unclean, but Jesus nevertheless touches him and makes him clean. Jesus is not defiled by this touch but rather extends cleansing by this touch. Remarkably, Jesus stays at the house of "Simon the leper" in Bethany (which in Hebrew means "house of affliction," quite probably a leper colony) in connection with his last visit to Jerusalem, an open and flagrant flouting of purity laws since whoever stays under a roof with a leper, as with a corpse, contracts defilement. A hemorrhaging woman, unclean from an irregular flow of blood (Lev 15:19-30), pushes her way through a crowd (thus polluting them) and touches Jesus (taking the risk of polluting him, in fact) and is healed. Power goes out from Jesus rather than pollution going into or onto Jesus (Mt 9:20-22). Jesus is not reluctant to touch a corpse, and his touch restores life to the body of Jairus' daughter (Mt 9:23-26) and the son of the widow in Nain (Lk 7:11-17).

Perhaps one of the more dramatic healings is the exorcism of the demon-possessed man (or in Mt 8:28-34, men) in the Gerasenes (Mk 5:1-20). Demon possession is a state of impurity since one is inhabited by an unclean spirit (Mt 12:43; Mk 5:8; Lk 6:18). This may be related to the tendency among Greeks to view the insane as polluted. The man possessed by Legion, moreover, was living in the tombs—unclean places from which he would have been contracting corpse defilement continuously. Jesus restores this man also, bringing him from the unclean margins of society back to his home, "in his right mind," clothed (he had apparently also been naked, which was also "unclean" outside of one's home). The Gospels thus present Jesus encountering a stream of ritually impure and potentially polluting people, but in the encounter their contagion does not defile Jesus; rather his holiness purges their pollutions, renders them clean[4] and integrates them again into the mainstream of Jewish society where they can reclaim their birthright, as it were, among the people of God.

A critical extension of the principle that God's holiness in Jesus was cleansing and sanctifying the unclean is the early church's discovery that Gentiles could be brought into the people of God without first taking on the marks of the ethnic Jew. While not the first text in which these issues are worked out, Acts 10:1—11:18 nevertheless presents the early church's breakthrough in terms of the distinction between Jew and Gentile as a distinction between clean and unclean. We also find the correlation between food and people made explicit here. The episode begins with Peter's vision of a nonkosher picnic. A sheet is let down from heaven, filled with both clean and unclean animals. Peter is told to "kill and eat," but he refuses, saying that he has "never eaten anything that is profane [common] or unclean." The heavenly voice answers, "What God has made clean, you must not call profane" (Acts 10:9-16). The vision is repeated three times in his sleep for emphasis and to render unmistakable the divine source of the vision.[5]

---

[4]Neyrey, "Idea of Purity," pp. 111, 124.

[5]Colin House offers a challenging interpretation of this vision. According to House, we must pay close attention to Peter's claim never to have eaten anything "common or unclean" ("Defilement by Association: Some Insights from the Usage of *Koinos/Koinoō* in Acts 10 and 11," *AUSS* 21 [1983]: 143-53). The first of these terms refers to the clean animals in the sheet that had been rendered "common" by their association with the unclean animals on the same table. God's response merely addresses the common food and not the unclean animals, which apparently God never expected Peter to eat in the first place. "He was never directed to consume the 'unclean' creature, but rather immediately to desist from describing as 'common' the creatures that God had declared 'cleansed' " (p. 148). The question at issue in this vision is thus, as House reads it, not "whether Gentiles were to be accepted into the church" but rather "how *he*, Peter, could associate with Gentiles and not be defiled" (p. 149). He contends that the cross did not remove the distinction between clean and unclean but only the "wall of separation" that kept the clean from mingling freely with the unclean. The decisive evidence for this is that the divine voice says, "What God has cleansed, you must not call common" rather than "you must not call unclean." While I commend House's interest in precision and his willingness to challenge long-held readings of this passage, a number of factors suggest to me that his reading will not replace the interpretation that sees here the removal of the category of "unclean" for the Gentiles (as in Hans Hübner, "Unclean and Clean [NT]," *ABD*, p. 742). First, *koinos* is not rigidly distinguished from *akathartos*, as House would maintain. Mark 7 uses "common"where it should properly read "unclean" (Friedrich Hauck, "*Koinos*, etc.," *TDNT*, p. 797). In Peter's own interpretation of the vision in Acts 10:28, he shows that he understands the two words to be synonymous, for he recalls that God instructed him that he "should not call anyone profane or unclean." Decisive, moreover, is the sequel to this vision in which God

Peter understands intuitively the correlation between a vision about foods and the new maps that are being drawn concerning people. In Acts 10:28, Peter applies the principle to fellowship with Cornelius and to the acceptability now of entering Cornelius' house, since "God does not show partiality" (Acts 10:34, my translation): "You yourselves know that it is unlawful for a Jew to associate with or to visit a Gentile; but God has shown me that I should not call anyone profane or unclean. So when I was sent for, I came without objection."[6] In Acts 10:44-47, God reveals that he has in fact cleansed the Gentile members of the household since God is willing to pour out his Holy Spirit upon them (just as God had done for the circumcised believers up to that point in the narrative). Peter therefore orders them to be baptized on the spot, employing a truncated greater to lesser argument: since God has

---

pours out the Holy Spirit on the Gentiles, a fact that is taken as proof positive of the Gentiles' acceptance into the holy people of God "as they are" without any further requirements that would mark their transition from the unclean nations to the holy people (like circumcision). "God has cleansed" the Gentiles in the Cornelius episode, for only if this is the case would their contact with the holy be possible (and not destructive to them). Therefore, I would not place so much weight on the "disjunctive conjunction" ē ("or") in "common or unclean"; the two words were synonymous in common parlance (which reflects, by the way, a departure from the proper use of the term as the neutral state that contrasts with holy), and the "unclean" had been cleansed by God "by faith" (see Peter's commentary on this vision and episode in Acts 15:8-9) for the reception of the Holy Spirit.

[6]Dwellings of Gentiles and table fellowship with Gentiles were treated as polluting. The chief priests avoided entering the praetorium in Jerusalem so that they could eat the Passover (Jn 18:28; priests could not eat their sacral portions in a state of defilement; Lev 22:1-16). Here in Acts 10:28-29 and 11:3 the same kind of pollution taboo regarding Gentile dwellings is evidenced. The Mishnah contains an extensive discussion of clean and unclean dwellings (the tractate called *Oholoth,* or "Dwellings"), in which one finds the maxim "the dwellings of Gentiles are unclean" (18.7). The reason for this judgment appears to be, in the context of that paragraph, the fear of corpse defilement, since Gentiles were thought to dispose of abortions down their drains or bury them (and stillbirths) in their homes. Corpse pollution lasted for seven days rather than one day, and those temple attendants who went to the Roman garrison to get the high priest's vestments for Passover did so more than seven days in advance of the festival (Raymond E. Brown, *The Gospel According to John (xiii-xxi),* AB [New York: Doubleday, 1970], p. 846). The Mishnah dates in its present form from A.D. 200, so it is important to seek out evidence from earlier texts that would suggest that the rules and rationales therein had already been developed by the time of the first century. In this case we do have an expression in the Qumran *Temple Scroll* showing Jewish disgust for the practice of Gentiles burying their dead "even in their houses" (48.11). Another extremely important text in this regard is Jubilees, an interpretative paraphrase of Genesis 1 through Exodus 14 that was considered inspired and authoritative at Qumran and read more widely as edifying literature: "Separate yourselves from the nations, and *eat not with them.* And do not according to their works, and become not their associate. For all their works are unclean, and all their ways are a pollution and an abomination and uncleanness" (Jub 22:16, emphasis mine).

already poured out the Holy Spirit, what would be the reason to deny the lesser rite of baptism? Since God has shown his acceptance of the household, why should the mortal believers deny them acceptance "as they are"?

Peter is criticized upon his return to Jerusalem for his violation of a pollution taboo, crossing an essential boundary separating the holy (Jewish) people of God from the nations by eating with Cornelius and his household (Acts 11:2-3). Peter recounts the whole story then from vision to outpouring of the Holy Spirit (Acts 11:4-17) as justification for his course of action. He makes it clear that the acceptance of the Gentiles was God's action, so that he needed simply to fall in line with what God was doing (this being, we will recall, one internal rationale for purity regulations). The result is acceptance of the principle now that "God has given even to the Gentiles the repentance that leads to life" (Acts 11:18). When Pharisees who had joined the Christian movement later attempt to uphold the old purity maps and boundaries for the new community, insisting that Gentile Christians "be circumcised and ordered to keep the law of Moses" (Acts 15:5), Peter refers again to the story of Cornelius as an incontrovertible proof to the contrary: "God . . . testified to them by giving them the Holy Spirit, just as he did to us; and in cleansing their hearts by faith he has *made no distinction* between them and us" (Acts 15:8-9). God had himself decisively reversed the policy of Leviticus that had enjoined the Israelites to "make a distinction" between clean and unclean, between themselves and people of other races.[7]

The Galatian controversy centers on the question of the Jewish purity map of persons. Paul's narrative of his encounter with James, Peter and John (Gal 2:6-10) shows that there was widespread agreement that there should be a mission to the uncircumcised to be led by Paul and Barna-

---

[7]Acts 15:20 concludes the debate by creating a new set of pollution taboos for the Gentile Christians based on universal purity laws (that is, those that were not meant to distinguish Jew from Gentile, but that all were supposed to follow)—abstinence from food sacrificed to idols, from blood, from meat from strangled animals and from fornication. Chilton rightly notes that this is a decisive intensification of Paul's policy (indeed, "a reversal of Paul's position"), since now a minimum set of Torah-based regulations are required of Gentiles as a condition of free table fellowship and mingling with Jewish believers (although it maintains the stance that the "dividing wall" between the races themselves was no longer a valid expression of God's will). See Bruce Chilton, "Purity and Impurity," in *Dictionary of the Later New Testament and Its Developments*, ed. Ralph P. Martin and Peter H. Davids (Downers Grove, Ill.: InterVarsity Press, 1997), p. 994. See also Hans Hübner, "Unclean and Clean (NT)," in *ABD*, ed. David N. Freedman (New York: Doubleday, 1992), p. 744.

bas, and a mission to the circumcised to be led by Peter (Gal 2:7-10). At that point, "even Titus, who was with me, was not compelled to be circumcised, though he was a Greek" (Gal 2:3), probably because the issue of Jewish and Gentile Christian mingling at the table had not yet presented itself as an issue. This became the issue later at Antioch and was raised by "certain people" who "came from James" (Gal 2:12). Peter and even Barnabas, who had formerly eaten with the Gentile Christians (thus crossing a significant boundary line from the Jewish point of view), were shamed into keeping themselves separate with regard to foods and eating by these more strict Jewish Christians (Gal 2:12-13).

In Paul's understanding, honoring the old purity lines between Jew and Gentile in such ways meant "not acting consistently with the truth of the gospel" (Gal 2:14), which claims that both ethnic Jews and "Gentile sinners" are made right in God's sight on the same basis, namely through trust in Jesus and not through the regulations of Torah (the "works of the Law" like circumcision, dietary laws and sabbath observance). This strikes at the heart of the rationale for keeping the purity regulations of Torah with regard to persons, foods and times, namely that by so doing one was in fact justified, that is, brought in line with what God was doing (e.g., in patterns of work and rest, in distinguishing between clean and unclean, in being separate and "other"). This will be stated even more forcefully in Ephesians 2:11-20, as Jesus "has made both groups into one and has broken down the dividing wall, that is, the hostility between us. He has abolished the law with its commandments and ordinances, that he might create in himself one new humanity in place of the two, thus making peace, and might reconcile both groups to God" (Eph 2:14-16). The "dividing wall" was precisely what the purity regulations of Torah sought to erect (see Lev 20:24-26), and God's creative purposes for one humanity worshiping the one God required the abolition of that law as a whole.

The positive proof for Paul, as it was for the author of Acts in the Cornelius episode, is the giving of the Holy Spirit to the Gentile Christians (Gal 3:2-5). Once again God's decision to impart what was holy and intimately attached to God's own holiness (the Spirit) to these Gentiles required that they had already been made clean or pure in God's sight. This purification had already taken place apart from carving into their bodies the sign of circumcision, the mark that placed them within the "clean" as the Jewish maps of people defined it. The Galatian Christians, now confronted with a Jewish-Christian missionary movement, the goal of which was to circumcise the Gentile Christians and bring them into the people of God as Torah defined it (see Gal 6:12), were thus urged to "stand firm" rather than "submit to a yoke of slavery" (Gal 5:1). The old maps of being pure in God's sight and of falling in line with God's order had been breached in the cross of Jesus.[8] Henceforth "there is no longer Jew or Greek, there is no longer slave or free, there is no longer male and female; for all of you are one in Christ Jesus" (Gal 3:28). In some of his most radical statements, Paul claims that "in Christ Jesus neither circumcision nor uncircumcision counts for anything," but only "faith working through love" and "a new creation" formed by following the Spirit (Gal 5:11; 6:15, my translation).[9]

Purity and time. The central question raised in New Testament texts concerning the observance of sacred versus ordinary time concerns keeping the sabbath and profaning the sabbath. Jesus enters into debate about what profanes or sanctifies the sabbath on two points. The first involves human comfort and hardship. A group of Pharisees censure his disciples who, feeling hungry, have profaned the sabbath by gathering grain from a field. Jesus retorts with two unrelated arguments. First, he claims, in effect, that he and his disciples have embarked upon a holy mission for God, as had David and his soldiers at the time when they ate the priests' portions of bread, and so are set apart from the regular restrictions. Moreover, as the priests carried out their ordinary work of offering sacrifices in the temple even on the sabbath day (Num 28:9-10), so Jesus' presence, which is "greater than the temple," sanctifies the work done by the disciples (Mt 12:3-6). To this is added an appeal to the principle of mercy (Hos 6:6 is repeated at Mt 12:7), which Mark reflects in his preservation of the saying that "the sabbath was made for humankind, and not humankind for the sabbath" (Mk 2:27). The shared implication of these two sayings is

---

[8]See Philippians 3:2-6 for Paul's own location of himself in terms of the old maps of purity and his rejection of these maps in favor of the new possibility for righteousness to be found in Christ. There too he claims that "true circumcision" is the spiritual circumcision practiced by the Christian as he or she worships in the Spirit and seeks conformity with the death of Jesus (Phil 3:7-11)—anything else is just "mutilation of the flesh."

[9]The reader may now work through Romans, particularly chapters 1 through 3, with an eye to the challenges Paul poses to the traditional Jewish purity maps of persons. Pay special attention to the topic of God's impartiality, the redefinition of what kind of circumcision matters in God's sight and the invocation of God's oneness as a rationale for the oneness of humanity under God.

that the sabbath is not being sanctified if it means hardship for human beings—it is to be a day of joy and rest, and if that means preparing a meal rather than feeling pangs of hunger, so be it.

The second debate is much more prominent in the Gospels, being shared by all four, and asks whether or not healing is a lawful work on the sabbath. Several different Jewish voices challenge the appropriateness of performing a work of healing on this day (the Pharisees at Mt 12:10, 14; the synagogue leader at Lk 13:14). There are six days for work, after all, and a person can be healed on any of those days without having to violate the sabbath (Lk 13:14). Jesus rejects this position, however, framing an argument from the lesser to the greater to show the absurdity of the opponents' position. Both the Pharisees and the synagogue leaders would agree that providing one's animals with basic care and helping them out of distress was acceptable on the sabbath; how much more, then, should it be acceptable to help the more valuable creatures (the daughters and sons of Abraham [Lk 13:16]) out of their distress on that day! Again we see the importance of compassion as a guiding value here, even though it is not explicitly named. For Jesus, the doing of good is always timely, while the withholding of good is an evil work that defiles the sabbath (Lk 6:9; the failure to do the good is to do harm).

The debate in John 5:10-11, 17-18 (surrounding another sabbath day healing) adds an important dimension to this discussion, asking in effect, "What does it mean to be in line with God's rhythms with regard to time?" The sabbath, we recall, is a reflection of God's own rhythm of work and rest in the first week of creation. Sabbath observance became thus a way of moving with God through the cycles of life, a falling into line with the divine order. Jesus brings a new dimension to this, claiming that God is still working, even on the sabbath, to bring healing to the cripple (and later to the blind man; see Jn 9:3-4, 16 on the "works of God"), and so Jesus claims that he is truly moving in synch with God's rhythms. Acts of compassion are never out of season, and time is hallowed not by abstaining from such acts but by their performance. In this episode, however, Jesus goes further than healing on the sabbath—he orders the man to "take up his mat and walk," that is, to carry a burden on the sabbath (forbidden in Neh 13:15-21 and Jer 17:19-27). The man is, of course, himself challenged on this point, and his only defense is that the "man who made me well" said to do it. A person able to perform such cures cannot be a "sinner" in God's sight (see Jn 9:16, 24-25, 31-33) but instead righteous. It follows that his teaching must also be in keeping with God's standards rather than unlawful in any way. Even if following Jesus means contravening Jewish purity maps, the disciple can thus be assured that obeying Jesus is what sets one in order with God's rhythms.[10]

Reconfiguring sacred space. The early Christians radically changed the Jewish maps of sacred space, largely depicting the replacement of the Jerusalem temple as sacred space with new configurations of sacred space located in the individual believer, the community of Christians and the presently unseen realm of God. Once again this innovation has its roots in Jesus' ministry. Jesus clearly assumes the holiness of the Jerusalem temple (see Mt 23:16-21). In fact, in his view the priestly aristocracy has insufficiently recognized its sanctity. His high view of the holiness of the temple leads him to drive the moneychangers and merchants from the court of the Gentiles, thus from the sacred precincts where such business dealings are out of place. Calling this act a cleansing of the temple is somewhat misleading: Judas Maccabaeus and his brothers had cleansed the temple in 164 B.C. from the defilements perpetrated during the Hellenization of Jerusalem so that it could be restored as a sacred center for the worship of God. Jesus gives no evidence of such an expectation or purpose. It is instead a prophetic indictment of the temple and particularly of the temple authorities for sanctioning the profanation of holy space (Mt 21:12-13) and thus hindering God's purposes for that space that will be fulfilled now not in that space but in the new community of the disciples, who will be sent to bring all the nations to the worship of the one God (Mt 28:19-20).

Jesus' overturning of the tables is a symbolic announcement of the temple's desacralization on account of the priests' abuses. Mark's account of the episode makes this all the more clear through the placement of the indictment of the temple within (rather than before, as in Mt 21) the story of the cursing of the fig tree. Just as Jesus came to inspect the fig tree, whose leaves gave the sign of being fruitful, at a time when one would

---

[10]Discussions of the sabbath do not figure prominently in the rest of the New Testament, save in Romans 14:5-6; Galatians 4:10 (possibly); and Colossians 2:16. In the latter two, sabbath observance for Gentile Christians is opposed along with all the regulations that represent the separation of Jew and Gentile effected by works of Torah. In Romans 14:5-6 it is allowed, presumably for the Jewish Christian, and is said to be of equal value in God's sight as not observing the sabbath, as long as whatever position one takes is taken to honor God and is not allowed to become a source of division and derision within the church.

not expect such an inspection ("for it was not the season for figs," Mk
11:13), so Jesus came to the bustling temple to inspect its fruits. Finding
none on the tree, he cursed it and after a short while it withered away.
Finding none in the temple, he effectively curses it in his indictment and
will shortly after predict its destruction (Mk 13:1-2). After a few decades
the temple was destroyed and the Jews' sacred space obliterated.[11] The
rending of the curtain in the temple's holy place may be read more accurately as the desacralization of the space at the death of Jesus in preparation for its destruction, rather than in the more popular and benign
reading of this sign as the signal that the way into God's presence is now
open to all. Access to the holy of holies per se is not broadened; rather,
access to God is thereafter to be sought in places other than the heart of
Judaism.

In John's Gospel, Jesus is even more explicit about the reconfiguration
of sacred space. Jesus sets aside limited locales of sacred space (the fixed
centers both of Jerusalem and Mount Gerizim, the sacred site for Samari-
tans) in favor of sacred space that opens up wherever people worship
God "in spirit and truth" (Jn 4:21-23). Moreover, at the indictment of the
Jerusalem temple (which now opens rather than closes Jesus' public ministry), Jesus announces a new sacred space that replaces the Jerusalem
temple (Jn 2:19-22; cf. Mk 14:58). This is none other than Jesus' body, cru-
cified and raised from the dead.[12]

Stephen's speech in Acts 7 also constructs "holy space" apart from the
temple. Holy space is wherever God is and not vice versa. The encounter
of Moses with God at the burning bush shows this: space becomes holy
because God is there (Acts 7:33). Stephen invokes the principle that God
does not live in houses made by human hands (Acts 7:48; see Acts 17:24),
a principle that appears as early as Solomon's prayer at the dedication of
the first temple (1 Kings 8:27-29). In the context of Acts 1—6, which has
underscored the presence and activity of God's Holy Spirit in the midst of
the community gathered around the apostles, this speech advances the

---

[11]Luke looks back upon these prophecies from the vantage point of post-A.D. 70 and thus
recasts many of the murkier sayings from Mark's "apocalyptic discourse" (Mk 13) in such
a way as connects them with the destruction of Jerusalem and the temple by Roman
legions in A.D. 70, when Jerusalem was surrounded by armies and the temple trampled by
the Gentiles (Lk 21:20-24), profaned and destroyed.

[12]Ephesians 2:20-22 and 1 Peter 2:5-9 share the conviction that connection with Jesus means
connection with sacred space, with the result that the Christian community, joined as it is
to Jesus, becomes the new temple. See below.

position that sacred space is to be found where Christians gather, where God's Holy Spirit manifests itself in power and in the virtuous conduct of the adherents.[13]

Just as the indwelling of the Holy Spirit was decisive in the revision of the Jewish maps of people (those maps that had placed Gentiles outside God's people), so it also became decisive for the remapping of sacred space. According to Paul even the Christian's body is now sacred space, the dwelling of the Holy Spirit. Therefore, one who harms the Christian (or a fellow Christian, for that matter) contracts sacrilege pollution and comes under God's ban (1 Cor 3:16-17)! What Acts suggests, several other authors make explicit: the Christian community—the people who are joined to Jesus, in whom the sacred breaks forth—constitutes the new sacred space where God dwells. In Ephesians 2:20-22, Gentile and Jewish Christian are joined together "with Christ Jesus himself as the corner-stone," in whom "the whole structure is joined together and grows into a holy temple in the Lord; in whom you also are built together spiritually into a dwelling place for God," an image also invoked in 1 Peter 2:5-9, extending it to include the offering of "spiritual sacrifices acceptable to God through Jesus Christ" by this "holy priesthood."[14]

While some authors would re-create sacred space in the realm beyond the visible, as does the author of Hebrews (for whom the true tabernacle is the divine realm that Jesus entered at his exaltation; Heb 4:14; 9:11-12), the community of those who had been sanctified to enter those heavenly places became the center of sacred space. As a holy temple and spiritual abode for God, however, pollution must be kept from this new community since it is entirely inappropriate and dangerous to bring defilement into the presence of the holy. This becomes an important impetus to ethical behavior, which is itself defined in terms of

---

[13]The response to Stephen is, of course, a response to sacrilege. The sacrilege pollution is purged by throwing Stephen outside the city ("outside the camp" being the place for polluted things) and killing him (much like Achan had been killed under the ban). Jesus had also been accused of incurring sacrilege pollution (Mk 14:58), which no doubt contributed to his arrest, as Paul will be accused of profaning the Jerusalem temple by bringing a Gentile into it along with him (Acts 21:27-29; 24:6, 17-18). As vigorously as Christians reconfigured sacred space, so vigorously did non-Christian Jews defend their sacred space!

[14]Note here an aspect of the Christian map of persons: the believers are now the "priests," those closest to the center of holiness. This is especially poignant since Gentile Christians (those who would be placed on the farthest periphery in Jewish maps) were by far the larger part of the audience of 1 Peter.

what is pure and defiling for the believer.

Purity, pollution and ethics. The Christian culture did not abandon the central command of Torah to be holy as God is holy (Lev 11:44-45; 19:2). Imitation of God's character and deeds remains a core value within Christian culture:

> Like obedient children, do not be conformed to the desires that you formerly had in ignorance. Instead, as he who called you is holy, be holy yourselves in all your conduct; for it is written, "You shall be holy, for I am holy." (1 Pet 1:14-16)

> Beloved, we are God's children now; what we will be has not yet been revealed. What we do know is this: when he is revealed, we will be like him, for we will see him as he is. And all who have this hope in him purify themselves, just as he is pure. (1 Jn 3:2-3)[15]

This process of purifying oneself to become, in the end, pure or holy as God is pure or holy is now wholly redesigned with very little recourse to the kinds of regulation one finds in the Torah with regard to diet, bodily substances or blemishes, and the like. Holiness and purity both still require boundaries to be drawn and maintained between the surrounding culture and the Christian group, but this is explicitly due to the inconsistency of the values of the two groups and therefore is not replicated so intensely at the level of the individual body or the diet. Instead the early Christian leaders focus mainly on the ethical streams of purity and pollution found in the Old Testament and develop this as the core of a new purity code in which separation from vice[16] and not separation from Gentiles in and of themselves is the main principle. The revulsion and aversion felt toward the unclean and polluted is now invoked in the service of defining and arousing commitment to the moral ethos of the group.

Just as Paul established the Christian's body itself as sacred space, the dwelling of the Holy Spirit (1 Cor 3:16-17), so he draws out certain ethical consequences of this idea. Prostitution and fornication are now singularly inappropriate for the Christian, since such acts profane the Holy Spirit and the body of Christ, joining that which is holy dangerously to that

---

[15]See also Jesus' formulations of sayings after the pattern of Leviticus 19:2 in Matthew 5:48 and Luke 6:36.

[16]This principle was observed already at work in Matthew 15 and Mark 7. The ability of Paul to use the terms *impurity* and *unrighteousness* (or some specific vice) as synonyms shows the virtual identification of purity codes with ethical conduct in the early church (see Rom 6:19; 2 Cor 6:6; Gal 5:19; Phil 4:8; 1 Tim 4:12; 5:2).

which is profane, even defiled (1 Cor 6:15-19). The threat of sacrilege pollution undergirds the sexual ethos of the group. Giving free reign to sexual passion is very frequently sanctioned against as impurity throughout the New Testament (see Eph 4:19; 5:3-5; 1 Tim 5:2; Jude 7-8). A particularly instructive example is 1 Thessalonians 4:3-7:

> For this is the will of God, your sanctification: that you abstain from fornication; that each one of you know how to control your own body in holiness and honor, not with lustful passion, like the Gentiles who do not know God; that no one wrong or exploit a brother or sister in this matter, because the Lord is an avenger in all these things, just as we have already told you beforehand and solemnly warned you. For God did not call us to impurity but in holiness.

The process of being set apart for God (made holy) is now an ethical rather than a ritual one. Here it occurs as a person separates himself or herself from sexual looseness and from domination by the sexual drives. In particular, solidarity within the group is reinforced as adultery or other illicit sexual activity within the group—a disruptive and destructive force within a church indeed!—is singled out as especially revolting in God's sight and contrary to the holiness in which God called the Thessalonian Christians.[17]

Disruptions within the social body are also discouraged as defilements. As part of the process of seeking to heal the rift between himself and the Corinthian believers, Paul invokes first God's promises of dwelling with the people if they "touch not the unclean thing" in light of which purification is called for: "Since we have these promises, beloved, let us cleanse ourselves from every defilement of body and of spirit, making holiness perfect in the fear of God" (2 Cor 6:14—7:1).[18] The defilement

---

[17]The claim that such sexual looseness (= impurity) characterizes the Gentiles, by which Paul (who is addressing Christian Gentiles) means non-Christian Gentiles, also serves to remind the audience of the boundaries and differences that separate them from their pagan neighbors. This topic is taken up in the following section, but it is helpful to note that at many points the ethical use of purity language is inseparable from the boundary-forming use of the same.

[18]On the literary integrity of this epistle, please see David A. deSilva, "Measuring Penultimate Against Ultimate Reality: An Investigation of the Integrity and Argumentation of 2 Corinthians," *JSNT* 52 (1993): 41-70; deSilva, "Recasting the Moment of Decision: 2 Corinthians 6:14—7:1 in Its Literary Context," *AUSS* 31 (1993): 3-16; deSilva, *The Credentials of an Apostle: Paul's Gospel in 2 Corinthians 1 Through 7* (N. Richland Hills, Tex.: BIBAL Press, 1998), chap. one.

Paul has in mind is primarily the tear in the social body of the church that has alienated him from some significant part of the congregation as well as caused ongoing friction within the church.[19] In Philippians 2:14-15, murmuring and arguing are what blemish the Christians. As they abstain from such pollution of their harmony and solidarity, they become "blameless and innocent, children of God without blemish." Finally, proper care for the social body can be promoted by means of purity concerns, as in James 1:27: "Religion that is pure and undefiled before God, the Father, is this: to care for orphans and widows in their distress, and to keep oneself unstained by the world."

It may be no accident that several prominent classes of sin censured as defiling in the New Testament correspond closely with sources of defilement in Leviticus. First, the two codes share an emphasis on extramarital sexual intercourse as abomination (prohibited impurity) in God's sight. Second, both focus on disruptions of the body as a source of defilement. Where in Leviticus this pertained to the physical body, however, in the New Testament it pertains to disruptions in relationships within the church as body of Christ. Finally, participation in activities too closely associated with idolatry defiles (whether in regard to the actual meat offered to an idol or to seeking peace with and prosperity by means of an idolatrous regime).[20] Like Leviticus, however, the New Testament uses pollution taboos to erect a fence between the Christian community and a wide array of unethical behavior. Every bit as polluting as sexual sin is guile, insincerity and self-serving motives and agenda—as Paul affirms that he has behaved toward his Corinthian friends "in holiness" (2 Cor 1:12) insofar as he has been free of such interpersonal evils, he labels them as defilements from which believers are to keep separate. Additionally, we may recall that Jesus especially highlighted attachment to money as a source of defilement (Mt 23:25; Lk 11:39-41).[21]

---

[19]The defilements are filled out in greater detail in the vice lists of 2 Corinthians 12:20-21, which include both sins of the body and sins of relationship. See also 2 Timothy 2:21-23, where "all who cleanse themselves" of the quarrels and wranglings that injure the unity of the body (in addition to cleansing themselves from "youthful passions") are set apart for an honorable place in God's house.

[20]This last topic will be treated more fully in the following section.

[21]All of these might, however, be subsumed as bodily disruptions with regard to the church body. Whenever we put our own agenda ahead of the good of the body or our attachments to and desires for wealth ahead of the work of God and the care for the needy, we contribute to the erosion of the body of Christ.

Pursuing purity and avoiding defilement, as these are defined within the Christian culture, are motivated in the first instance by the eschatological facets of the Christian worldview. In light of the coming judgement by the holy God, it will be of great advantage to be found "pure and blameless" in "the day of Christ" (1 Cor 1:8; Phil 1:10; 1 Thess 5:23). The danger of encountering the Holy One in a state of pollution is invoked for the sake of rousing commitment to abstain from vices and associations held to defile the believer. "Leading lives of holiness and godliness," which are taken by the author of 2 Peter to be synonymous, is the only prudent way of life in light of the coming conflagration of the visible world, since it is only those "without spot or blemish" that will be admitted to the new creation "where righteousness is at home" (2 Pet 3:11-14).

The majority of these texts confirm the observation of the German scholar Otto Procksch that "the reference to holiness is always to the static morality of innocence rather than ethical action."[22] That is to say, holiness, ethically and cultically speaking, is the *absence* of defilement or blemish (separation from what displeases or provokes the holy God). It would generally fall to words such as *righteousness* to capture the active aspects of Christian ethics, the positive pursuit of good works, acts of love and service, and the like. It is precisely in this essential flavor of withdrawal from what is polluting and unpleasant in God's sight that holiness and purity language was also able to have such a powerful social-engineering impact. Withdrawal from the "unclean thing" also means withdrawal from those public spaces and those social interactions surrounding the unclean thing (like idolatrous rituals) and thus could be employed by early Christian leaders to enforce the boundaries and distinctiveness of the Christian community with regard to the surrounding culture.

Holiness, pollution and group boundaries. The early church leaders continued to use purity codes and pollution taboos to set the Christian group apart from its Greco-Roman and non-Christian Jewish environments. Like the parent body, Judaism, these leaders accomplished the goal of reinforcing the boundaries and identity of the social body of the church *in part* by means of calling for the careful guarding of the purity of the physical body of the individual Christian. A member's attention to keeping the physical boundaries intact and impermeable in a number of areas

---

[22]Otto Procksch and Karl G. Kuhn, *"Hagios, etc,"* TDNT 1.88-115, p. 109.

safeguards the boundaries of the group, keeping them distinct and visible, and keeps its social ethos intact by stressing the distinctiveness of its values.

Thus there continue to be regulations concerning sex and marriage with the Christian movement, as there had been in Israel and continued to be among Jews. There is to be no new intermarriage between the Christian community and the nonbelieving world (1 Cor 7:39); there is to be no fornication, which is taken to characterize the "Gentile" (i.e., the non-Christian Gentile) world.[23] Distinctiveness of sexual conduct and marital practice (which were elements of the Torah's purity regulations) continue to reinforce the social boundary around the Christian group.

Food laws, although radically fewer than those prescribed by Torah, also appear, largely in connection with meat from animals that had been sacrificed to idols. The question of whether or not to ingest such meat was deeply connected with the group's basic conviction that its members needed to keep themselves entirely separate from the idolatrous worship that surrounded them in the Greco-Roman world. Rejection of idolatry was at the core of the church's social ethos (see 1 Thess 1:9-10). Paul agreed that the food must never be eaten at an idol's temple itself—there was no justification for such a defilement as sitting at the table of demons (1 Cor 10:14-21)—but held that the food in and of itself was not defiling, unless the eater or the eater's companions could not detach the meat from the idol. The apostolic decree found in Acts 15 reflects a more conservative solution, forbidding meat that had been sacrificed to an idol regardless of where one might eat it (Acts 15:29). Whichever position prevailed in a given locale, Christians still observed pollution taboos with regard to foods as a means of reinforcing the distinctive identity and ethos of the group. Both sets of rules for the individual body show not only the theoretical connection between the human body and the social body but also the very practical way in which such regulations for the individual body do in fact protect and underscore the boundaries of the social body.

Purity and pollution language also reinforced group boundaries at the ideological level, and this is by far the more frequent strategy found

---

[23]For a rich discussion of this aspect of Paul's instructions in 1 Corinthians, see Jerome H. Neyrey, "Body Language in 1 Corinthians: The Use of Anthropological Models for Understanding Paul and His Opponents," *Semeia* 35 (1986): 138-42. The connection between Paul's discussions of eating (whether the Lord's Supper or meats that had been sacrificed to idols) and group boundaries is further explored in pp. 142-48 of the same essay.

within the New Testament. The church's rejection of Jewish purity regulations serves as a strategy by which the church defines and sustains its own distinctive identity[24] with regard to the parent body, as comes to expression quite pointedly in Titus 1:13-15, where dietary regulations and other external observances of purity and pollution taboos are rejected as "Jewish myths" and "commandments of those who reject the truth" (Tit 1:14). Receiving the gospel is what makes one pure, and those who do not believe can never attain purity: "To the pure all things are pure, but to the corrupt and unbelieving nothing is pure. Their very minds and consciences are corrupted" (Tit 1:15).

More frequently, one finds this realm of language being used to maintain the Christians' separateness from non-Christian Gentiles. First, the very choice of the term *saints*—the "holy ones" or "those who have been made holy"—reflects an application of purity language directly to group identity, an application that immediately suggests a contrast between the Christian group and the unbelieving population, who remain profane and alienated from the holy God. The Christians have, in the first instance, been "set apart" from their former lives: "Fornicators, idolaters, adulterers, male prostitutes, sodomites, thieves, the greedy, drunkards, revilers, robbers—none of these will inherit the kingdom of God. And this is what some of you used to be. But you were *washed*, you were *sanctified*" (1 Cor 6:9-11, my emphasis). This purification sets them apart from their pagan past. The conceptual boundary between holy and unclean now reinforces the believers' awareness of the inappropriateness of returning to that lifestyle and even promotes their commitment to preserve the purity of the new life intact (see also Eph 4:19).

Being holy, the Christians must also observe the boundary between themselves and those who still embrace the lifestyle of their unsanctified past. Paul draws these lines most forcefully in 2 Corinthians 6:14—7:1:

> Do not be mismatched with unbelievers. For what partnership is there between righteousness and lawlessness? Or what fellowship is there between light and darkness? What agreement does Christ have with Beliar? Or what does a believer share with an unbeliever? What agreement has the temple of God with idols? For we are the temple of the living God; as God said, "I will live in them and walk among them, and I will be their God, and they shall be my people. Therefore come out from them, and be separate

---

[24]Neyrey, "Idea of Purity," p. 122.

from them, says the Lord, and touch nothing unclean; then I will welcome you, and I will be your father, and you shall be my sons and daughters, says the Lord Almighty."

The staccato questions, like rain wearing a pit into rock, drive home the incompatibility of the holy (the "temple of God," which is the church) with the defiled realm of Satan, idolatry and disregard for God's law. The consequence must be for the Christians to be wary of the influences of, and partnership with, the unclean world from which they must keep themselves separate (thereby not to become polluted) so as to remain a suitable dwelling for the holy God in their midst. The emphasis on separation here, it should be added, never replaces the missionary emphasis of Pauline Christianity, indeed of most forms of Christianity attested in the New Testament. The boundaries of the group are always permeable to those who would enter by receiving God's favor extended in Jesus, but the boundaries must remain high and impermeable to the influences of the world and those who persist in opposition to the gospel.

Gentiles can in fact still be used as a term to denote outsiders, now specifically non-Christians. This is all the more striking given the fact that the Christian addressees of these texts are usually Gentile Christians (whose place in the people of God *as* Gentiles Paul vehemently fought for). Nevertheless, they are being led to regard themselves as "other" than the Gentiles around them, who have not yet attached themselves to the church and remain hostile to the ethos they have embraced. When the term appears in 1 Thessalonians 4:3-7 or 1 Peter 4:1-4, it is used to identify a lifestyle in which the Christians can no longer join and to separate them from their former associates (see also 1 Cor 10:20; 1 Pet 2:12).

James uses purity and pollution language "to undergird an ethic of holy non-conformity,"[25] that is, to orient believers toward rejecting the intrusion of the values of the dominant, non-Christian culture (like showing partiality to the rich and treating the poor dishonorably—although in keeping with their status in the eyes of the world) as pollution of their community and toward preserving wholehearted and integrated commitment to the codes of conduct laid out by Jesus and developed by his disciples. It is thus a mark of "pure and undefiled" religion to "keep oneself unstained [i.e., undefiled] by the world" (Jas 1:27). The Christian is

---

[25]John H. Elliott, "The Epistle of James in Rhetorical and Social-Scientific Perspective: Holiness-Wholeness and Patterns of Replication," *BTB* 23 (1993): 71-81.

reminded that the surrounding, non-Christian culture, referred to in a broad sweep as "the world," is not a neutral or friendly environment but one that is actively hostile to the holiness of the group and thus to its standing in God's favor, in close association with the holy One. The believer is thus oriented away from emulating the values of the world or entering into partnerships with the world and summoned back toward the center of holiness ("Draw near to God, and he will draw near to you"). The believer is called to put away all such interests in and attachments to the world as threaten the wholeness/holiness of one's heart: "Cleanse your hands, you sinners, and purify your hearts, you double-minded" (Jas 4:8).

New Testament authors can use the language of pollution not only to reinforce separation between the Christians and the host society and its values but also to drive a wedge between congregations and questionable Christian teachers, as displayed in 2 Peter. In this letter "Christian" teachers of whom the author strongly disapproves are labeled "blots and blemishes," that is, defilements on the body of Christ (2 Pet 2:13). They are censured for having once "escaped the defilements of the world [a reminder of the purity cordon separating the people of God from the unbelieving, disobedient world] through the knowledge of our Lord and Savior Jesus Christ" only to turn back to a life of vice, greed and sexual looseness (2 Pet 2:20-21).

The person who succumbs to some new defilement of the world is not, however, merely to be cast out of the holy community. Rather, the call is always to seek to restore such people. Jude 23 expresses this in a carefully nuanced way: on the one hand, the Christians are called to rally around their wayward sisters and brothers to reclaim them, but on the other hand, they are cautioned to fear the pollution itself and not embrace that which defiles as they attempt to restore the sisters and brothers: "Save others by snatching them out of the fire; and have mercy on still others with fear, hating even the tunic defiled by their bodies *(ton apo tēs sarkos espilōmenon)*." This is a timely warning (perhaps unfortunately tucked away in the infrequently read letter of Jude) for the struggles of many North American and Western European Christians, who fall too far to one side or the other of this balanced approach. On the one hand, some are too quick to cast out the sinner along with the sin; on the other hand, some are more than willing to embrace the defilement in an effort to obey the command to love the defiled one.

John makes extensive use of purity language in Revelation, much of which serves the purpose of reinforcing the boundary between the Christian group and the dominant culture at a time when the boundary threatens to become porous on account of the preaching of the Nicolaitans and local prophets like "Jezebel" (Rev 2:6, 14-15, 20), in whose eyes participation in dinners involving idolatry is not a betrayal of their Christian calling. In John's interpretation of the cosmos there is a potent, defiling force that has spread its uncleanness across the known world. This is the "Great Whore," which is at once demythologized as "the great city that rules over the kings of the earth," namely, imperial Rome.[26]

The visionary persona of Rome is described as "holding in her hand a golden cup full of abominations and the impurities of her fornication; and on her forehead was written a name, a mystery: 'Babylon the great, mother of whores and of earth's abominations.' And I saw that the woman was drunk with the blood of the saints and the blood of the witnesses to Jesus" (Rev 17:4-6). John has created an image suggestive of pollution and the communication of pollution with every phrase. Rome is the source of abomination, passing the contagion thereof by means of illicit unions with those in power across the inhabited world. Association with Roman power (and profit therefrom, Rev 18:3) is thus labeled the equivalent of the pollution acquired through sexual abomination. She herself is "drunk" with "blood," and if ingesting the blood of animals is forbidden (the substance belonging to God alone), how much more should this be true of the blood of God's holy ones? Hence Rome has incurred mortally serious sacrilege pollution (together with the assurance of God's destruction of the polluted city; Rev 19:2). Moreover, she has prepared a polluting drink, revoltingly identified as the "impurities of her fornication" (hence biological pollutants), which the "nations" and the "inhabitants of the earth" do in fact drink (Rev 17:2; 18:3). As John looks out on his world, he sees the provinces befuddled into accepting the ideology of Rome and its "rule of peace and law," interpreting this as their willing participation in the defilement that she spreads over the earth.

---

[26]This would be the most natural connection for John's audiences to make. For them, Rome was *the* world power, a single, self-glorified city ruling the *orbis terrarum*, the circle of lands around the Mediterranean that constituted the inhabited world. For them also the realities of a cult of the rulers of this empire were everywhere to be seen in their cities, hence a readily available connection. See Charles H. Talbert, *The Apocalypse* (Louisville: Westminster John Knox, 1997); A. Y. Collins, *Crisis and Catharsis* (Philadelphia: Westminster Press, 1984); David A. deSilva, "The Image of the Beast and the Christians in Asia Minor," *TJ* (n.s.) 12 (1991): 185-206.

Moreover, the beast that has elevated Rome has immersed itself in the pollution of sacrilege against God, God's holy ones and God's abode: "On its heads were blasphemous names. . . . The beast was given a mouth uttering haughty and blasphemous words, and it was allowed to exercise authority for forty-two months. It opened its mouth to utter blasphemies against God, blaspheming his name and his dwelling, that is, those who dwell in heaven" (Rev 13:1, 5; see 17:3). Again, this is a most potent defilement requiring cleansing, inviting divine wrath.

God's purgation of his world of these defiled and defiling creatures is assured throughout Revelation (see Rev 14:8; 18:2; 19:2). It is imperative, therefore, not to participate in the defilement and so escape the coming judgment (Rev 18:4). If partnership with Rome (and the idolatrous, dominant culture more generally) is the source of defilement—a dangerous condition given the imminent pouring out of God's wrath—separation from close association with that culture and its idols (including not only the traditional Greco-Roman pantheon but also the emperors and Roma herself) is the way to maintain purity. This is expressed frequently through discussion of clothing. Those few whom Jesus commends in Sardis "have not soiled their clothes" and so will "walk with me, dressed in white," a privilege that will be extended to all who conquer (Rev 3:4-5). Before the throne stands a multitude "robed in white," who have "washed their robes and made them white in the blood of the Lamb" (Rev 7:9, 14), that is, purified themselves from the sins of the idolatrous culture and attached themselves to the Lamb in holiness. Clean robes—participation in the cleansing that Jesus' blood provides and perseverance in the separation from the idolatrous culture—are essential for entering the holy city, New Jerusalem, for this is the wardrobe of heaven's inhabitants (see Rev 19:7, 14).

Failure to keep oneself pure means exclusion from the real presence of God: "Blessed are those who wash their robes, so that they will have the right to the tree of life and may enter the city by the gates. Outside are the dogs and sorcerers and fornicators and murderers and idolaters, and everyone who loves and practices falsehood" (Rev 22:14-15). The New Jerusalem is all holy space, with no special temple for the location and limitation of God's presence: "I saw no temple in the city, for its temple is the Lord God the Almighty and the Lamb" (Rev 21:22). The whole vast city is holy of holies, and nothing unclean can enter any place of the city: "Nothing unclean will enter it, nor anyone who practices abomination or falsehood, but only those who are written in the Lamb's book of life" (Rev 21:27).

Rituals: Boundary Crossing in the Early Church

Particularly in the Gospels and Acts (insofar as the events take place within the geographical bounds of Palestine) one finds references to the observance of Jewish rites connected with purification. Thus John and Jesus are circumcised "on the eighth day" after their births, marking the boys as members of the holy people of God and distinguishing them from the Gentiles (Lk 1:59; 2:21), a rite also performed on Timothy, the adult child of a Jewish mother and Greek father (who had not had the boy circumcised as a child; Acts 16:3). Mary and Joseph bring the necessary purification offering after childbirth (notably the offering allowed for the poor among the people; Lk 2:22-24). Jesus commands the leper whom he has healed to make the necessary purification offerings at the temple and follow the procedure mapped out in Leviticus 14 (Mk 1:44). The miracle at Cana involves six large water pots (made of stone, which does not contract pollution) used for observing rites of purification (Jn 2:6). John remarks on the crowds of pilgrims beginning to assemble in Jerusalem a week before the Passover so as to observe the necessary purifications (probably for corpse pollution) and to be certain of being "clean" so as to celebrate the Passover at the appointed time (Jn 11:55). Finally, we find even Paul observing rites of purification for himself and sponsoring four others who have taken a vow, so as to show that he walks in an orderly, Torah-observant manner (Acts 21:21-26).

Within a short span of time, however, the early Christians left these rites behind in favor of a new framework of ritual actions by which the believers were able to pass from the sphere of the unclean to that of the clean, from a profane state to a holy state of being consecrated to God. These rituals served important social and ideological functions for the early church, and their power for shaping Christian identity and fostering strong commitment to the distinctive ethos of the church need not be lost in our Christian communities.

Baptism. John's baptism resembles a purificatory washing to remove the pollution of sin, to restore a condition of cleanness so that one can encounter God. It is voluntarily undertaken by the Judeans who wish to be prepared in light of the declaration that the holy God is coming: purification from sin is pursued by those fleeing the wrath to come (see

Mt 3:1-12). The early church retains the form of this rite but greatly develops its meaning. Baptism becomes the rite of passage par excellence for the Christian movement. It is the ritual by which a person enters the holy people of God (that is, leaves the realms of the profane and the polluted), replacing the Jewish entrance ritual of circumcision:[27]

> In him also you were circumcised with a spiritual circumcision, by putting off the body of the flesh in the circumcision of Christ; when you were buried with him in baptism, you were also raised with him through faith in the power of God, who raised him from the dead. And when you were dead in trespasses and the uncircumcision of your flesh, God made you alive together with him, when he forgave us all our trespasses. (Col 2:11-13)

Paul's interpretation of the significance of baptism corresponds closely with the ritual process as defined by anthropologists like Victor Turner.[28] Entering the water is a rite of separation, as the initiate dies to his or her past life, associations and social group. Paul frequently uses the language of death to interpret the significance of the immersion:

> How can we who died to sin go on living in it? Do you not know that all of us who have been baptized into Christ Jesus were baptized into his death? Therefore we have been buried with him by baptism into death. . . . Our old self was crucified with him so that the body of sin might be destroyed, and we might no longer be enslaved to sin. . . . So you also must consider yourselves dead to sin and alive to God in Christ Jesus. (Rom 6:2-4, 6, 11)

The baptized are purified of that part of their past they no longer wish to own, as the plunge into the water enacts symbolically the initiates' renunciation of former allegiances, affiliations and relations.[29] Whatever status or identity they had before the rite, the waters of baptism wash it away (see 1 Cor 6:9-11). But the ritual provides not only a way for the initiates to "die to their old life" but also to be "reborn to the new."[30] Rising from the water corresponds to the rite of aggregation. As they emerge from the waters, they are joined to a new community, the "sanctified,"

---

[27]There is also a ritual of excommunication, referred to far less frequently but rather notably in Matthew 18:15-18 and 1 Corinthians 5:1-5. The person who insists on persisting in sin, bringing its pollution into the holy community, is to be cast out from the congregation.

[28]See Victor Turner, *The Ritual Process* (Ithaca, N.Y.: Cornell University Press, 1969), chaps. 3-4.

[29]Ruth M. Kanter, *Commitment and Community: Communes and Utopias in Sociological Perspective* (Cambridge, Mass.: Harvard University Press, 1972), p. 73.

[30]Mary Douglas, *Purity and Danger* (London: Routledge & Kegan Paul, 1966), p. 96.

who are "washed with pure water" (Heb 10:22). They leave behind their old way of life and are freed by their symbolic death to embark on a new way of life:

> We have been buried with him by baptism into death, so that, just as Christ was raised from the dead by the glory of the Father, so we too might walk in newness of life. . . . For whoever has died is freed from sin. . . . So you also must consider yourselves dead to sin and alive to God in Christ Jesus. . . . No longer present your members to sin as instruments of wickedness, but present yourselves to God as those who have been brought from death to life, and present your members to God as instruments of righteousness. (Rom 6:4, 7, 11, 13)

In Turner's model the rite of passage is a transition from one status in society to a new status in society. It is at this point that baptism presents an important difference, for this rite is a transition from one society to another society. Baptism leaves the Christians marginal with regard to the unbelieving society, with no real place in that society any more, and assimilates them to a new community. This transition is reinforced with all manner of purity and pollution language,[31] encouraging the continued detachment from the old, polluted, defiled way of life that stood in imminent danger of experiencing God's wrath (holiness breaking out against the unclean and the abomination). The Christian is to respond to his or her experience of having been cleansed by continuing to walk and grow in the virtues for which God called him or her apart (see 2 Pet 1:9). The rite, still common to all Christians, affords rich opportunities for believers to reflect on the separation that baptism has effected in them and the new life for which it has cleansed and freed them. It matters little in what way a believer has experienced baptism (whether by sprinkling, pouring or immersion, whether as an infant, adolescent or adult)—the ritual act is there, and the images painted by Paul await to strengthen the believer for the journey out from the way of life into which we are born naturally into the way of life for which we have been born spiritually.

Jesus' death as sacrificial act within a ritual process. As is well-known, the

---

[31]For example, Romans 6:19 describes the Christians as having moved from a state of impurity and being "slaves to impurity" to a state of slavery "to righteousness for sanctification."

crucifixion was viewed within the Christian movement not merely as a noble death but as a sacrificial offering. This interpretation extends back into the pre-crucifixion sayings of Jesus himself (Mk 10:45; 14:22-25). In John's Gospel, Jesus declares in his "high priestly prayer" that he "sanctifies himself"—that is, transfers himself to the realm of the holy as a sacrificial offering made over to God—in order to sanctify the disciples and consecrate them to God (Jn 17:19). The reader of the New Testament will frequently find brief references through the epistles to Jesus' death as an "atoning sacrifice" that cleanses the believer from the pollution of sin (1 Jn 1:7—2:2; see also Rom 3:25). The believers are said to be "sprinkled with his blood" (1 Pet 1:2) and, more fully, ransomed "with the precious blood of Christ, like that of a lamb without defect or blemish" (1 Pet 1:19). The quality of the offering assures its acceptability in God's sight. The immense cost also requires faithful response on the part of the Christian, the ongoing preservation of that distinctiveness and cleanness for which Jesus' blood was poured out.[32] One of the more concentrated occurrences of purity and ritual language in connection with Jesus' death is found in Ephesians 5:25-27: "Christ loved the church and gave himself up for her, in order to make her holy by cleansing her with the washing of water by the word,[33] so as to present the church to himself in splendor, without a spot or wrinkle or anything of the kind—yes, so that she may be holy and without blemish." The combination of Jesus' death, the rite of baptism and the reception of the word moves the believers from a state of defilement and blemish to a state of cleanness and wholeness, thus rendering them suitable for presentation to the holy One.

The text that plunges deeper into the language of cult and ritual with regard to leading out the significance of Jesus' death is the epistle (or, per-

---

[32]See Hebrews 10:27-29 for an example of the kind of warning that could be developed against "profaning the blood by which the believers had been sanctified." In this case, "profanation" would happen as the believer returned to the bosom of the unbelieving society, rejecting that consecration (that separation) for which Jesus' blood has been spilled. The unique value of this one sacrifice could thus become an important tool for motivating perseverance in commitment to the group and its way of life.

[33]John's Gospel also speaks of the disciples being cleansed by the word Jesus has spoken (Jn 15:3). Keeping that word makes the disciple a suitable abode for the Father and the Son (hence a holy sanctuary; Jn 14:23). Jesus' prayer in John 17 is closely related to John 15:3, in that Jesus prays that God will "make holy" the disciples "in the truth," which is God's "word" (Jn 17:17).

haps better, the sermon) to the Hebrews.[34] The author engages in a thorough critique of the old cult on the basis of its inability to broaden access to God. Since the people were perpetually kept at a distance from God, the author reasons, the whole Levitical system of sacrifices must have been ineffective with regard to purifying the whole person. If purification were ever decisive, the sacrifices would stop (having done their work; Heb 10:1-4) and access to the holy of holies would not still be limited to one person (Heb 9:6-10). Jesus' journey to the cross and to the heavens, thus his ministry from crucifixion to ascension to exaltation, is interpreted by the author of Hebrews as a single, decisive ritual movement that removes the sins separating humankind from God's presence and full, bold access to God's favor. Elements from the purification offerings, the red heifer ritual, the covenant inauguration ritual and the Day of Atonement rites are reconfigured to describe the procedures and significance of this new and better rite.

Jesus' execution on the cross is transformed into the sacrifice of a willing victim on behalf of the believers. Just as the bodies of purification offerings are burned outside the camp, so "Jesus also suffered outside the city gate in order to sanctify the people by his own blood" (Heb 13:11-12). He leaves human society (the camp), bearing abuse, disgrace and hostility. He goes outside the camp to a place characterized by both liminality and sacrality. To the eyes of the unbeliever, Jesus dies a shameful death in a place of uncleanness, outside the lines of society; in the eyes of God, Jesus' journey outside the margins of the camp is a ritual act of sacred power, his death becoming a purification offering, his blood serving to cleanse the conscience of the worshipers who wish to approach God (Heb 9:13-14). The Christians are thus rendered fit for access to God in ways that the Israelites never enjoyed.

The ritual movement does not stop at Calvary, however. After his death Jesus passes through the visible heavens (still a part of the material creation destined for "shaking"; Heb 4:14; 12:26-27) in order to arrive in "heaven itself," that is, the unshakable realm of God's throne (Heb 9:24).

---

[34]For a detailed analysis of the purity and ritual language of Hebrews, please see David A. deSilva, *Perseverance in Gratitude: A Socio-Rhetorical Commentary on the Epistle "to the Hebrews"* (Grand Rapids, Mich.: Eerdmans, 2000), especially on Hebrews 7:11—10:25.

This is the heavenly sanctuary, of which the earthly temple is but a shadowy copy (Heb 8:2, 5; 9:24).[35] Jesus thus enacts in the true tabernacle the atonement ritual that had for millennia been enacted in the earthly copy, cleansing now the invisible holy places (Heb 9:23) from the pollution of the sins of the people that had accumulated there (as in the earthly copy). The blood of Jesus thus removes the pollution of sin both from the conscience of the worshiper and the presence of God, such that no defiling obstacle remains between God and human being. It is thus first a purification offering, a heavenly Day of Atonement.[36] The worshiper may now approach the throne of favor (Heb 4:14-16; 10:19-22) assured that the holiness of God will not consume him or her. As the last movement in this ritual, Jesus sits at God's right hand (Heb 10:11-14). Unlike the Levitical priests who continually stood to perform their service, there is no more need for Jesus to stand at the heavenly altar; his priestly work is complete (although he still intercedes for believers from that advantageous position; Heb 7:25).

The death of Jesus is not only a purification offering that the hearers have appropriated by the water of baptism (Heb 10:22) but also a consecration offering, akin to the offering of the ram that made Aaron a priest (a text that also combines a ritual setting with the language of perfection; see Ex 29 in the Septuagint).[37] The Christians have already enjoyed a level of access to God in the worship of the community, and no doubt the private prayer of the individual believer, that reflects their consecration and their perfection in the inner person, the conscience. In this state

---

[35]The author thus removes sacred space from the physical structures of Jerusalem to the heavenly realm, following a well-established tradition in Hellenistic Judaism (see Wis 9:8; T. Levi 2-5).

[36]Such a radically new sacrifice, not prescribed anywhere in Torah, must have some legitimation. After all, the divine prescribes the sacrifice; it is not for the human to invent. Starting from the conviction that Jesus' death was in fact the decisive purification for sins, the author finds in Psalm 40 the necessary lever by which to topple the Levitical sacrificial system. The psalms are equally the "word of God" and in fact represent a later word than Torah. The psalmist (in the Septuagint version) says: "Sacrifices and offerings you have not desired, but a body you have prepared for me; in burnt offerings and sin offerings you have taken no pleasure. Then I said, 'See, God, I have come to do your will, O God' " (Ps 40:6-8 LXX; Heb 10:5-7). The author of Hebrews interprets the passage by placing the words on the lips of Jesus himself, finding here both God's rejection of animal sacrifices (Heb 10:8) and God's institution and authorization of a new kind of sacrifice (Heb 10:9-10).

[37]Revelation 1:5 and 5:9-10 also envision the believing community's consecration to priesthood as the effect of Jesus' death, taking on for the church the calling of Israel to be a priestly kingdom for God (Ex 19:6).

they "continually offer a sacrifice of praise to God, that is, the fruit of lips
that confess [acknowledge] his name" as well as the offerings of doing
good and sharing, "for such sacrifices are pleasing to God" (Heb 13:15-
16).

Their consecration, however, is not for this world alone. Here we find
the author of Hebrews employing ritual language as a means of creating
an ideology of the Christian life that will tend to sustain commitment to
the group and to maintain its distinctive social identity and ethos. The
author capitalizes on the fact that Jesus is not merely priest but "forerunner on our behalf" (Heb 6:19-20). The believers have been enabled to cross
boundaries hitherto impassable for any human being. They have been
sanctified to such a degree by Jesus' blood that they may enter the holy
places of the true sanctuary to which not even a high priest had access
before (Heb 10:18-22). In their present state they are in the midst of a great
ritual process devised by God for their elevation to great privilege and
honor.

With Jesus as forerunner, the believers are called to "run with perse-
verence" (Heb 12:1) the course that Jesus ran. This route has already
taken them outside the camp. The Christians have been separated
from their former "normal" identity as Jews or pagans, having suffered the loss of property and reputation and other such things as bind
them to their former status in that society. Out of gratitude to Jesus for
his own journey outside the camp on their behalf, the Christians are
called to persevere in their journey, to sacrifice the sense of at-home-
ness and belonging in human society and enter a place of liminality.
They find themselves thus living between the home they left behind
and the kingdom they are in the process of receiving (Heb 12:28; 13:11-
14). This liminal state involves both "humiliation and ordeal, but also . . .
sacrality and power."[38] It is a state of bearing Christ's reproach (Heb
13:13), of persevering in the endurance of society's hostility and shaming techniques, but it is also the place wherein God's presence is
known, a state of holiness in which the believer can "approach the
throne of grace with boldness" (Heb 4:14) and enjoy "the altar" from

---

[38]Richard P. Nelson, *Raising Up a Faithful Priest: Community and Priesthood in Biblical Theology*
(Louisville: Westminster John Knox, 1993), p. 58. Nelson's discussion is profitably influ-
enced by Turner (*Ritual Process*, pp. 94-147), who discusses the paradoxical qualities of the
liminal period of rituals (subjection to humiliation and loss of status but at the same time
charged with awareness of the sacred and its power) at length.

which the Levitical priests themselves have no right to eat (Heb 13:10).[39]

Within the liminal state they have been brought together into a community[40] marked by cooperation, sharing and equality, within which they are rendered sacred for intimate access to God and being fitted for their new, glorious, normal state, which they shall enter at the eschatological shaking of the material realm. The rest of the believer's life is therefore to be lived out in this liminal state, in the margins between status in this world and the next. The author urges the addressees to continue to persevere in the margins, for the margins of society are pregnant with promise as the threshold over which they, like Jesus, will pass into the unshakable realm, the full presence of God. Like Abraham, Moses, the martyrs and marginalized, Jesus and even their departed leaders, the hearers are called to embrace the liminal status they currently have in this world, seeking not to return to their former "normal" state but pressing on to arrive at their perfected state (following their forerunner and pioneer),[41] namely, their entrance into the abiding realm where their honor as God's children will be fully manifested at their aggregation into the city of God.

The author of the epistle to the Hebrews thus weaves into his response to the needs of his readers a well-developed sermon on the power of the rites of purification and consecration performed on the believer in Jesus' death as the preparation for the ultimate passage into the heavenly holy places. The Christian is invited to see the time between coming to faith (baptism) and death (or parousia) as the liminal period between separation from the old social groups and entrance

---

[39]William L. Lane, *Hebrews 1-8* (Waco, Tex.: Word, 1991), pp. 543-44; Victor C. Pfitzner, *Hebrews* (Nashville: Abingdon, 1998), p. 199; J. W. Thompson, *The Beginnings of Christian Philosophy: The Epistle to the Hebrews,* CBQMS 13 (Washington, D.C.: Catholic Biblical Association, 1982), p. 147.

[40]The formation of intimate relationships between those who are undergoing a rite of passage together is a prominent feature of the liminal state in the rituals studied by Turner (*Ritual Process,* pp. 94-147).

[41]On the meaning of "perfection" here, please see "A Closer Look: Perfection in Hebrews," in deSilva, *Perseverance in Gratitude,* pp. 194-204. Briefly, all the occurrences of "perfection" terminology in Hebrews have in common the sense of crossing a boundary and arriving at one's final state, a state in conformity with God's design for the person (whether this be maturity as opposed to childhood, consecration to priesthood as opposed to remaining profane, or arriving at the heavenly realm as opposed to remaining part of the material realm destined for removal and destruction).

into the fullness of the new state of being. The author's contrasts between the ineffective Levitical priesthood and Jesus' effective mediation also sustain the group's boundaries with regard to the parent body, Judaism. The emphasis on the purification of the believers and on the necessity of remaining in the liminal state, consecrated and awaiting entrance into the heavenly tabernacle, also sustains the group's boundaries vis-à-vis the unbelieving society—a boundary that had begun to erode (Heb 10:25) on account of the pressures of their Greco-Roman neighbors. Pondering the larger picture of this ritual process was intended to equip believers to endure deprivation in this world for the sake of their loyalty to Jesus and witness to God's standards, knowing that being pushed to the margins of this world means being led to the threshold of their eternal inheritance.

Conclusion

The New Testament authors model for us that there are reasons and times to cross purity lines and reasons and times to build these lines. Recall the analysis of some possible purity lines to be drawn in twentieth-century North America or Western Europe. Many of these lines are socioeconomic. There is a marked tendency for human beings to marry, make friends, even select a church home on the basis of belonging to a common social and economic class (hence falling together within the same lines in the purity map). There is also a marked tendency for human beings to avoid contact with those of a noticeably different socioeconomic standing, seen in the extreme case by the widespread aversion toward the homeless. Many lines are based on ethnicity, and again these lines have a strong impact on dating and marriage, on the formation of friendships and again on the constituency of a given congregation. There are also strong "medical" lines, by means of which people may separate themselves from those who are less attentive to hygiene or cleanliness based on the possibility of disease (the extreme case being those suffering from AIDS, who are regarded as polluted and polluting). As we ponder our own location on these maps and compare this with a survey of our meaningful social interactions during the past month, we will probably discover that the lines drawn between people in our society (its purity map, although the term is not used) very effectively shape our interactions and, to a large extent, determine our social groupings.

The problem with this, of course, is that we allow our own cultural purity maps[42] to separate us, on the one hand, from our sisters and brothers in Christ (we value our cultural maps more than the work of Jesus, bringing into one group many people-groups and nations and languages and tribes), and on the other hand, from those to whom we could go as ambassadors for God. The examples of Jesus and Paul challenge us to set aside these lines of classification that perpetuate dividing walls of hostility and mistrust and apathy in favor of honoring the boundaries that God has drawn—which include no lines separating believer from believer, whether they be of different race, class or medical status!

As Jesus demonstrated, the lines separating believers from unbelievers always remain permeable for mission, for reaching out in love to bring some measure of relief or restoration, as well as for conversion and entrance into the church. When a church fails to make a visitor welcome (or worse, tries to make someone feel unwelcome) on account of a difference in race, attire and the like, then Jesus' designs have been defeated in favor of the world's classification lines. The result is that we find *ourselves* on the outside again, living at home in the world's maps rather than enacting Jesus' program. To follow Jesus we will need to transgress with uncomfortable frequency those purity maps instilled in us from birth and reinforced at every turn by our society. If we never cross those lines, we can be sure that we are not keeping pace with the Master!

We cannot compromise our mission to extend God's love and healing to the world around us. At the same time, we cannot compromise our commission to be a distinctive people "holy to the Lord." From what are we to remain separate? The authors of the New Testament writings provide rather clear and detailed instruction on this point, and we need only to pay attention to the lines they draw.

One set of clearly defined lines seeks to keep us separate from our own continued involvement in the sins, lies and vanities of the unbelieving world, and specifically of the nation in which we live and into which we have been socialized. Just as the addressees of Revelation had to beware of drinking in the pollution of the self-promoting Roman ideology, so each Christian today faces the same struggle vis-à-

---

[42]More properly, the purity maps from the culture and society we have left behind and to which we ought to have died in our baptism.

vis the self-promoting, self-justifying, self-glorifying ideologies of the nation in which he or she may find himself or herself. Believers must remain separate from the lines a nation draws to mark its external boundaries (as well as the internal lines, as we have already observed). In America, for example, Christians need to remind themselves repeatedly that the church and her concerns do not stop at the U.S. borders, but rather they should hold in their hearts the global Christian family as their first nation, their first allegiance. In addition, Christians must remain separate from the sins, the idolatries (in effect) and the ungodly agenda promoted in the society around them. Once again to consider America (since this is the arena with which I am familiar), one facet of the current, popular ideology promotes consumerism and feeds greed and self-indulgence. It is a society that knows only the words *mine* and *more,* and rarely *enough.* It would be easy to drink in this mentality, to participate in this idolatry and to allow this agenda to direct one's life. The call to "come out and be separate, and touch not the unclean thing," however, demands that we "cleanse ourselves" from every "defilement of body and of spirit" (2 Cor 6:14—7:1), from everything that erodes the integrity—the wholeness—of our commitment to do God's will and to embody God's values.

A second prominent line urges us to abstain from polluting the church, keeping the holy congregation without blemish. Christians are put on their guard against defiling the body of believers with their own persistence in one sin or another, or with bringing the lies of the world into the church, thus defiling its vision, hindering its mission and muting its witness. Since disruption of the (social) body is a source of defilement, it is also incumbent on each believer to abstaining from the murmuring, the grumbling, the wrangling and the power plays that pollute a congregation.

Our study of purity and pollution has left us, then, with the task of discovering and properly handling the boundaries God has drawn between his holy people and the unbelieving world. The boundary must remain clear and fixed with regard to perceptions of people, values and agenda that derive from the society around us rather than from the Spirit of God. The boundary must remain porous with regard to outreach and admission of converts into God's holiness. We are challenged to resist the temptation to collapse God-made boundaries and replicate society-made boundaries within the Christian community and within our individual lives. Rather, we are pushed toward recovering the sacred liminality, the threshold existence outside society's lines and awaiting God's kingdom. In these margins we are free to invent the quality of community that God desires for all his daughters and sons.

Conclusion

The analysis in this book of four prominent aspects of the cultural environment of the first-century world has uncovered a number of penetrating insights for examining our own level of acculturation to the non-Christian (or at least, not distinctively Christian) society around us. It also has equipped us with proven tools and models for breaking free as a community of believers from the values, lines and agenda that that society has inscribed into our minds and hearts. The more multifaceted our reading of the New Testament becomes, the more we can perceive of its challenge to us *and* the more we discover of the resources its writers provide for the ongoing nurturing of a distinctive Christian culture.

The early Christian leaders understood that the believers would need to measure their own worth and seek honor in terms of the values taught by Jesus and the Spirit, and must no longer be bound to the approval of unbelievers or the values of the unbelieving society that they had internalized before their conversion. We too are thus invited to examine how we measure ourselves and others as well. Do we continue to promote in ourselves and those around us the values and standards set by the surrounding culture, or do we seek God's approval and point our neighbors to God's values as the source of abiding self-worth? Leaders are especially charged with directing congregations toward functioning as that alternative "court of reputation" that grants esteem to one another on the basis of our worth in Christ and celebrates those who advance in discipleship (rather than rise along worldly ladders).

Because of the prominence of patronage and benefaction in the ancient world and the widespread awareness of the obligations owed to generous people, the early Christian had a powerful resource for achieving integrity of faith and life that would greatly benefit us today to recover. That resource is the central and centering focus on gratitude. As we allow ourselves to grasp the value of the gifts God has bestowed upon us and will yet bestow on us, we come to understand that the whole of our life needs to be brought together in a coherent, single-hearted response of gratitude to God. The way we spend our time, use the resources of which we are but stewards and choose our activities are all to reflect gratitude and enact gratitude. This God-centered and God-honoring focus leads us to select only those pursuits that honor God, to seek opportunities through word and deed to bear witness to God's generosity and to show obedience to God's commands and loyalty to Jesus—even and especially when this takes us into uncomfortable areas.

Immersing ourselves in the context that gives meaning to the use of the words *brother* and *sister* leads to the insight that the shapers of the Christian movement intended for its members to adopt toward one another the ethos of family (in its best sense). We are thereby challenged to extend the intimacy, mutual commitment and mutual support of natural family to the family related by the blood of Jesus. We are urged to enact the values that defined the best of families in the ancient world—shunning competition in favor of cooperation, sharing resources freely as any have need, showing forbearance and forgiveness, and pursuing harmony. This family must always include not only our local congregation nor even our own denomination, but the whole family of God in every corner. The prayer of Jesus, "that they may all be one," must find fulfillment in our hearts and bearing toward one another (organizational structures being quite beside the point).

Finally, our investigation of the ways in which Jesus and the early church crossed long-honored lines of demarcation and separation, and formed new boundaries designed to preserve the ethos and distinctiveness of the church, leads us to deep self-examination of the boundaries that have been drawn in our society to separate us from too close an association with people of other races, classes, nations and backgrounds. God is bringing together a people from every side of these lines of classification, and it falls to us to set aside the lines learned from our society and our particular upbringing so as not to divide what God joins together. This new community from every race, class, nation and background, however, is still called to holiness—a holiness that we honor and preserve as we cleanse ourselves from the defilements of sin and our churches from the defilements of divisions.

These four facets of the New Testament message, taught to congregations and spread through the lives of believers like leaven, hold great promise for revitalizing communities of faith that have lost their distinctive, godly flavor in the midst of their society. Just as first-century Christian leaders were able to use them to sustain loyalty to Jesus and to the way of the Spirit, so Christian leaders today will find them powerful strategies for motivating single-hearted commitment to the Master who calls us to reflect his holiness in the world, to pursue only the honor that lasts eternally, and to support one another along the journey as the closest of kin. And perhaps not surprisingly, "grace" still stands at the center of this Christian ideology as we are challenged to give of ourselves to Jesus as he has given himself to us—and not to grow slack in our service until we have matched love for love.

Bibliography

Chapters One & Two: Honor

Adkins, Arthur W. *Merit and Responsibility: A Study in Greek Values.* Oxford: Clarendon, 1960.

Aristotle. *Nicomachean Ethics* 3, 8.

deSilva, David A. *Despising Shame: Honor Discourse and Community Maintenance in the Epistle to the Hebrews.* SBLDS 152. Atlanta: Scholars Press, 1995.

———. *The Hope of Glory: Honor Discourse and New Testament Interpretation.* Collegeville, Minn.: Liturgical Press, 1999.

———. "The Noble Contest: Honor, Shame, and the Rhetorical Strategy of 4 Maccabees." *JSP* 13 (1995): 31-57.

———. "The Wisdom of Ben Sira: Honor, Shame, and the Maintenance of the Values of a Minority Culture." *CBQ* 58 (1996): 433-55.

Dodds, Eric R. *The Greeks and the Irrational.* Berkeley: University of California Press, 1966.

Elliott, John H. "Disgraced Yet Graced. The Gospel According to 1 Peter in the Key of Honor and Shame." *BTB* 24 (1994): 166-78.

Jewett, Robert. *Saint Paul Returns to the Movies: Triumph over Shame.* Louisville: Westminster John Knox, 1998.

Karen, Robert. "Shame." *The Atlantic Monthly*, February 1992, pp. 40-70.

Malina, Bruce J. and Jerome H. Neyrey. "Conflict in Luke-Acts: Labeling and Deviance Theory." In *The Social World of Luke-Acts: Models for Interpretation*, pp. 97-124. Edited by Jerome H. Neyrey. Peabody, Mass.: Hendrickson, 1991.

———. "Honor and Shame in Luke-Acts: Pivotal Values of the Mediterranean World." In *The Social World of Luke-Acts: Models for Interpretation*, pp. 25-66. Edited by Jerome H. Neyrey. Peabody, Mass.: Hendrickson, 1991.

Moxnes, Halvor. "Honor and Shame." *BTB* 23 (1993): 167-76.

———. "Honor, Shame, and the Outside World in Paul's Letter to the Romans." In *The Social World of Formative Christianity and Judaism*, pp. 207-18. Edited by Jacob Neusner, Peder Borgen, E. S. Frerichs and Richard Horsley. Philadelphia: Fortress, 1988.

———. "Honour and Righteousness in Romans." *JSNT* 32 (1988): 61-77.

Neyrey, Jerome H. "Despising the Shame of the Cross." *Semeia* 68 (1996): 113-37.

———. "Loss of Wealth, Loss of Family and Loss of Honour: The Cultural Context of the Original Makarisms in Q." In *Modelling Early Christianity: Social-Scientific Studies of the New Testament in Its Context*, pp. 139-58. Edited by Philip F. Esler. London: Routledge, 1995.

———. *2 Peter, Jude*. AB. New York: Doubleday, 1993.

Pitt-Rivers, Julian. "Honour and Social Status." In *Honour and Shame: The Values of Mediterranean Society*, pp. 21-77. Edited by John G. Peristiany. London: Weidenfeld and Nicolson, 1965.

Williams, Bernard. *Shame and Necessity*. Berkeley: University of California Press, 1993.

Chapters Three & Four: Patronage

Aristotle. *Nicomachean Ethics* 8.

Boissevain, Jeremy. *Friends of Friends: Networks, Manipulators and Coalitions*. New York: St. Martin's, 1974.

Chow, John K. *Patronage and Power: A Study of Social Networks in Corinth*. JSNTSup 75. Sheffield: Sheffield Academic Press, 1992.

Cicero. "On Duties."

———. "On Friendship."

Danker, Frederick W. *Benefactor: Epigraphic Study of a Graeco-Roman and New Testament Semantic Field*. St. Louis, Mo.: Clayton, 1982.

Davis, John. *The People of the Mediterranean: An Essay in Comparative Social*

Anthropology. London: Routledge & Kegan Paul, 1977.

deSilva, David A. "Exchanging Favor for Wrath: Apostasy in Hebrews and Patron-Client Relations." *JBL* 115 (1996): 91-116.

Dio Chrysostom. *Oration* 31. (To the Rhodian Assembly)

Edwards, Ruth B. "Χάριν ἀντὶ χάριτος (John 1.16): Grace and the Law in the Johannine Prologue." *JSNT* 32 (1988): 3-15.

Elliott, John H. "Patronage and Clientism in Early Christian Society." *Forum* 3 (1987): 39-48.

Hals, Ronald M. *Grace and Faith in the Old Testament.* Minneapolis: Fortress, 1980.

Lacey, Douglas R. de. "Jesus and Mediator." *JSNT* 29 (1987): 101-21.

Levick, Barbara. *The Government of the Roman Empire: A Sourcebook,* pp. 137-51. London: Croom Helm, 1985.

Lull, David J. "The Servant-Benefactor as a Model of Greatness (Luke 22:24-30)." *NovT* 28 (1986): 289-305.

Moxnes, Halvor. "Patron-Client Relations and the New Community in Luke-Acts." In *The Social World of Luke Acts,* pp. 241-68. Edited by J. H. Neyrey. Peabody, Mass.: Hendrickson, 1991.

Osiek, Carolyn, and David Balch. *Families in the New Testament World.* Louisville: Westminster John Knox, 1997.

Peristiany, John G., and Julian Pitt-Rivers. *Honor and Grace in Anthropology.* Cambridge: Cambridge University Press, 1992.

Pliny the Younger. *Letters* 10.

Saller, Richard P. *Personal Patronage Under the Early Empire.* Cambridge: Cambridge University Press, 1982.

Seneca. *On Benefits (De Beneficiis).*

Ste. Croix, Geoffrey E. M. de. "Suffragium: From Vote to Patronage." *British Journal of Sociology* 5 (1954): 33-48.

Stambaugh, John E., and David L. Balch. *The New Testament in Its Social Environment.* LEC 2. Philadelphia: Westminster Press, 1986.

Stoops, Robert F., Jr. "Patronage in the *Acts of Peter.*" *Semeia* 38 (1986): 91-100.

Wallace-Hadrill, Andrew, ed. *Patronage in Ancient Society.* London: Routledge, 1989.

Winter, Bruce W. *Seek the Welfare of the City: Christians as Benefactors and Citizens.* Grand Rapids, Mich.: Eerdmans, 1994.

Chapters Five & Six: Kinship

Aristotle. *Nicomachean Ethics* 8, 9.

Balch, David. *Let Wives Be Submissive: The Domestic Code in 1 Peter.* SBLMS 26. Missoula, Mont.: Scholars Press, 1981.

Barton, Stephen C. *Discipleship and Family Ties in Mark and Matthew.* Cambridge: Cambridge University Press, 1994.

Bell, Albert A., Jr. *Exploring the New Testament World.* Nashville: Thomas Nelson, 1998.

Bossman, David M. "Paul's Fictive Kinship Movement." *BTB* 26 (1996): 163-71.

deSilva, David A. *4 Maccabees.* Guides to Apocrypha and Pseudepigrapha. Sheffield: Sheffield Academic Press, 1998.

Dudry, Russ. "'Submit Yourselves to One Another': A Socio-Historical Look at the Household Code of Ephesians 5:15—6:9." *RQ* 41 (1999): 27-44.

Duling, Dennis C. "Matthew 18:15-17: Conflict, Confrontation, and Conflict Resolution in a 'Fictive Kin' Association." *BTB* 29 (1999): 4-22.

Elliott, John H. *A Home for the Homeless: A Sociological Exegesis of I Peter, Its Situation and Strategy.* Philadelphia: Fortress, 1981.

Ferguson, Everett C. *Backgrounds of Early Christianity.* 2d ed. Grand Rapids, Mich.: Eerdmans, 1993.

Finley, Moses I. *The Ancient Economy.* Berkeley and Los Angeles: University of California Press, 1973.

Foxhall, Lin, and Keith R. Bradley. "Household." In *The Oxford Companion to Classical Civilization,* pp. 354, 359. Edited by Simon Hornblower and Antony Spawforth. Oxford: Oxford University Press, 1998.

Hanson, Kenneth C. "*BTB* Reader's Guide: Kinship." *BTB* 24 (1994): 183-94.

———. "The Herodians and Mediterranean Kinship. Part I: Genealogy and Descent." *BTB* 19 (1989): 75-84.

———. "The Herodians and Mediterranean Kinship. Part II: Marriage and Divorce." *BTB* 19 (1989): 142-51.

Jameson, Michael H. "Houses, Greek." In *The Oxford Companion to Classical Civilization,* pp. 359-60. Edited by Simon Hornblower and Antony Spawforth. Oxford: Oxford University Press, 1998.

Joubert, Stephan J. "Managing the Household: Paul as *Paterfamilias* of the Christian Household Group in Corinth." *Modelling Early Christianity: Social-Scientific Studies of the New Testament in its Context,* pp. 213-23. Edited by Philip F. Esler. London: Routledge, 1995.

Malina, Bruce J. *The New Testament World: Insights from Cultural Anthropology,* pp. 117-48. Rev. ed. Louisville: Westminster John Knox,

1993.

Moxnes, Halvor, ed. *Constructing Early Christian Families: Family as Social Reality and Metaphor.* London: Routledge, 1997.

Neyrey, Jerome H. "Loss of Wealth, Loss of Family and Loss of Honour: The Cultural Context of the Original Makarisms in Q." In *Modelling Early Christianity: Social-Scientific Studies of the New Testament in Its Context*, pp. 139-58. Edited by Philip F. Esler. London: Routledge, 1995.

Osiek, Carolyn, and David L. Balch. *Families in the New Testament World: Households and House Churches.* Louisville: Westminster John Knox, 1997.

Plutarch. "Advice on Marriage."

———. "On Affection for Offspring."

———. "On Fraternal Affection."

Purcell, Nicolas. "Houses, Italian." In *The Oxford Companion to Classical Civilization*, pp. 360-62. Edited by Simon Hornblower and Antony Spawforth. Oxford: Oxford University Press, 1998.

Scott, Bernard B. *Hear Then the Parable.* Minneapolis: Fortress, 1989.

Stambaugh, John E., and David L. Balch. *The New Testament in Its Social Environment.* Philadelphia: Westminster Press, 1987.

Wright, Christopher J. H. "Family." *ABD*, pp. 761-69. Edited by David N. Freedman. New York: Doubleday, 1992.

Xenophon. *Oeconomicus.*

Chapters Seven & Eight: Purity

Booth, Roger P. *Jesus and the Laws of Purity: Tradition History and Legal History in Mark 7.* JSNTSup 13. Sheffield: JSOT Press, 1986.

Buchanan, George W. "The Role of Purity in the Structure of the Essene Sect." *RevQ* 4 (1963): 397-406.

Douglas, Mary. "Atonement in Leviticus." *JSQ* 1 (1993-1994): 109-30.

———. *Purity and Danger.* London: Routledge & Kegan Paul, 1966.

Elliott, John H. "The Epistle of James in Rhetorical and Social Scientific Perspective: Holiness-Wholeness and Patterns of Replication." *BTB* 23 (1993): 71-81.

Grant, Richard M. "Dietary Laws Among Pythagoreans, Jews, and Christians." *HTR* 73 (1980): 299-310.

Harrington, Hannah K. *The Impurity Systems of Qumran and the Rabbis.* SBLDS 143. Atlanta: Scholars Press, 1993.

House, Colin. "Defilement by Association." *AUSS* 21 (1983): 143-53.

Houston, Walter. *Purity and Monotheism: Clean and Unclean Animals in Biblical Law.* JSOTSup 140. Sheffield: Sheffield Academic Press, 1993.

Isenberg, S. K., and D. E. Owen. "Bodies Natural and Contrived: The Work of Mary Douglas." *RelSRev* 3 (1977): 1-16.

Levine, Baruch A. *Leviticus.* JPS Torah Commentary. Philadelphia: Jewish Publication Society, 1989.

Milgrom, Jacob. *Leviticus I-XVI.* AB. New York: Doubleday, 1991.

Nelson, Richard P. *Raising Up a Faithful Priest: Community and Priesthood in a Biblical Theology.* Louisville: Westminster John Knox, 1993.

Neusner, Jacob. "The Idea of Purity in Ancient Judaism." *JAAR* 43 (1975): 15-26.

Neyrey, Jerome H. "Body Language in 1 Corinthians: The Use of Anthropological Models for Understanding Paul and His Opponents." *Semeia* 35 (1986): 129-70

———. "The Idea of Purity in Mark's Gospel." *Semeia* 35 (1986): 91-128.

———. *Paul, In Other Words.* Louisville: Westminster John Knox, 1990.

———, ed. "The Symbolic Universe of Luke-Acts: 'They Turn the World Upside Down.'" In *The Social World of Luke-Acts: Models for Interpretation,* pp. 271-304. Peabody, Mass.: Hendrickson, 1991.

North, John A. "Priests (Greek and Roman)." In *The Oxford Companion to Classical Civilization,* pp. 570-71. Edited by Simon Hornblower and Antony Spawforth. Oxford: Oxford University Press, 1998.

Parker, Robert C. T. "Pollution, the Greek Concept of." In *The Oxford Companion to Classical Civilization,* pp. 553-54. Edited by Simon Hornblower and Antony Spawforth. Oxford: Oxford University Press, 1998.

———. "Sacrifice, Greek." In *The Oxford Companion to Classical Civilization,* pp. 628-69. Edited by Simon Hornblower and Antony Spawforth. Oxford: Oxford University Press, 1998.

Pilch, John J. "Biblical Leprosy and Body Symbolism." *BTB* 11 (1981): 108-13.

Scheid, John. "Sacrifice, Roman." In *The Oxford Companion to Classical Civilization,* pp. 629-31. Edited by Simon Hornblower and Antony Spawforth. Oxford: Oxford University Press, 1998.

Wright, David P., and Robert Hodgson Jr., "Holiness." *ABD,* pp. 237-54. Edited by David N. Freedman. New York: Doubleday, 1992.

Wright, David P., and Hans Hübner. "Unclean and Clean." *ABD,* pp. 729-45. Edited by David N. Freedman. New York: Doubleday, 1992.

Index of Subjects

Index of Scripture Texts

330

Index of Other Ancient Literature